MW01633235

CupCayla

AND THE BIG FROSTING MESS

WRITTEN AND ILLUSTRATED BY KEITH MURPHY

Dedicated to my mom, Laurie
and my children Ethan, Peyton
and Ayla-Mae

I love you AEU 

CUPCAYLA AND THE BIG FROSTING MESS

For information contact:
Keith Murphy at cupcayla@yahoo.com

Written and illustrated by Keith Murphy
ISBN: 978-0-578-29558-9 (paperback)
Library of Congress Catalog-in-Publication Data is available

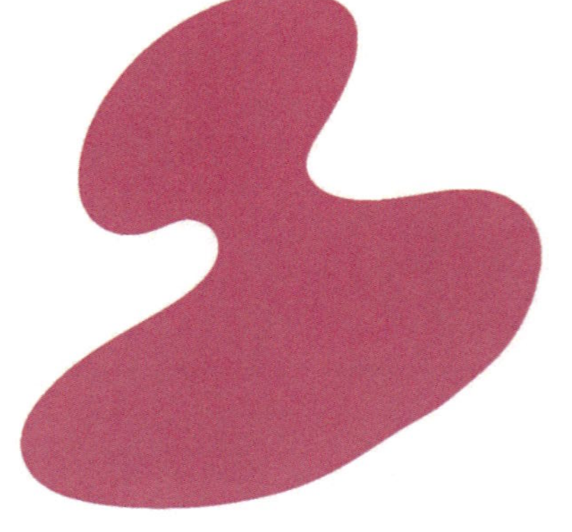

Did You Know?

- that a baby lion is called a cub. Lions live in family groups called a pride, headed by one or two dominant males. They spend most of the day sleeping and they hunt together at night. Male lions are generally big enough to protect the pride from other male lions and hyenas, but female lions have difficulty doing so on their own so the pride works together to protect the family. Each pride has an area of land that it considers its own territory and will chase away any strange lion walking across its land.

- that in Africa the wild vegetation is often called 'the bush' or 'the bushveld'.

- that vervet monkeys live in family groups called troops of between 15 to 80, with a very defined hierarchy. Sentries warn the troop if a predator such as a leopard or an eagle is approaching by coughing or barking.

- that leopards are very good tree climbers and drag their kills up a tree to hide them from lions and hyenas.

- that elephants do not like lions.

- that warthogs have very sharp tusks and kneel down to dig for tasty roots in the ground.

- that the cheetah is the fastest animal over short-distances, reaching speeds of 56 miles per hour over open veld.

- that a kudu is a very big type of antelope that can jump over very tall fences or bushes.

- that crocodiles drag their prey underwater to drown them.

- that hyenas have very strong jaws. They are scavengers and will steal whatever food scraps they can find. They will often try to steal lion kills.

- that wildebeest, zebra and impala will often graze together so that they can alert each other if a predator, such as a lion or leopard, is around.

- that a giraffe can defend itself from a lion by giving it a fierce kick.

Patsy Smith Roberts' first visit to Africa in the early 1990s ignited a passion for the continent as well as for wildlife photography. A self-taught photographer, she exhibits and sells her work at wildlife shows across the USA. Patsy lives on St. Simons Island, Georgia.

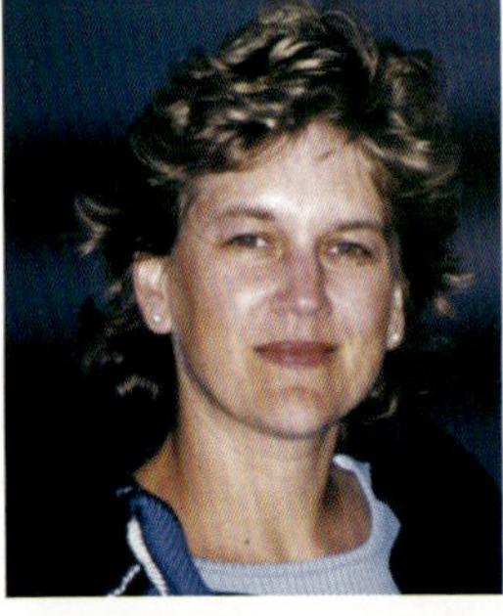

Gillian Cullinan is a freelance magazine writer who met Patsy while on an assignment in Botswana's Savuti region, an area famous for its lions. Gillian lives with her husband and two sons in Cape Town, South Africa.

These photographs were taken in the country of Botswana in Gametrackers and Abercrombie & Kent camps.

1, 2 , 3...
GRRRRRRRRRR...
ROARRRRRRR...

And side by side, they practiced their roars
as the sun sank on another day in the African bush.

Later his dad took him aside...

"Rory, I'm proud of you.
You were really brave calling me
even though you were scared."

Rory felt so proud. Small as he was,
he had become an important member of the pride.

"You've got the courage to be
a great hunter like your mother
and
one day you'll be able
to protect the pride like me."

"Daaaaaaaad,"
shouted Rory, "Hyeeeeeena."

His Dad flashed past him
into the
snapping,
snarling
fight.

As they neared the pride, she sniffed...
"I know that smell –
it's a hyena
looking for scraps."

Rory's heart raced as his mother
leapt forward to chase it away.
Rory was so terrified
he couldn't move.

But then he took a deep breath and rushed through the grass...

And she gave Rory a kiss...
"Now let's get back to the others."

And a crocodile can lie as still as a log...

but all that means is that everybody
is good at different things
and you will be able to roar
when the time is right."

A kudu can leap over tall bushes...

Just because a cheetah
is faster than a
tortoise doesn't mean
it wins every race.

Just be yourself...
everyone is special
in his own way.

Just because an
elephant is bigger
than a warthog,
doesn't make it
more important.

"Rory, you have a big spirit but you are still a little cub," she said gently. "There are many dangers in the bush... you can't go wandering about by yourself."

Rory hung his head.

"You don't need to roar to get our attention. Making a lot of noise isn't going to make you any more special.

We love you just the way you are.

Just at that moment, Rory's mother came bounding through the grass with a growl...

"GRRRRRRRR"

The leopard turned tail and slunk away.

Rory stalked off in a huff to sit under a tree. Looking up, he saw a leopard staring down at him.

"I'm practicing my roar," Rory answered hesitantly – knowing this was one of the animals his parents had warned him about...

"Wait right there," said the leopard. "I'll come right down so I can listen to you."

Next he tried a louder growl...

"Grrrrr..."

on a herd of zebras who whinnied,
"You don't scare us."

Finally he roared his best roar...

"Grrrrr..."

at a troop of
vervet monkeys
in the treetops
who laughed and
dropped sticks on
his head.

So Rory decided to practice his roar.

From way up high he heard,
"What's a little cub like you doing
out and about by yourself?"

Rory looked up... up... up...
It was a giraffe.

"No one takes any notice of me
so I'm practicing my roar," said Rory.

The giraffe fluttered her sweeping eyelashes
and said, "Well, you can practice a roar on me
and I'll tell you what I think."

So Rory got ready...
"One, two, three... **Grrrrrrr**."

"Well, kid you've got potential,
but it doesn't set my heart racing
quite yet," she said gently.

"Just keep practicing."

"Mum, can you teach me how to hunt... show me how to catch a warthog?"

She was already half asleep. "Later Rory."

"When I can roar just like my dad, then everybody will notice me."

"Dad," shouted Rory.

"Tell me where you've been and what you saw."

But Rory's dad was thirsty, tired and wanted a nap...

"Not now, Rory."

with loud purrs and a ruffle of his mane.

Rory's mum went to meet him...

ROARRRR...
ROOAARRRRRRR...
Rory's dad was home.

But Rory, the littlest cub, was excited.

ROAR...

The wildebeest splashed through the water to get away.

ROAR...

The ground shook,
birds flew from the trees.

ROAR...

The impala at the waterhole looked up, ready to run.

One quiet morning in Africa, there was a great ROAR...

All the lionesses and cubs
in the pride stopped to listen.

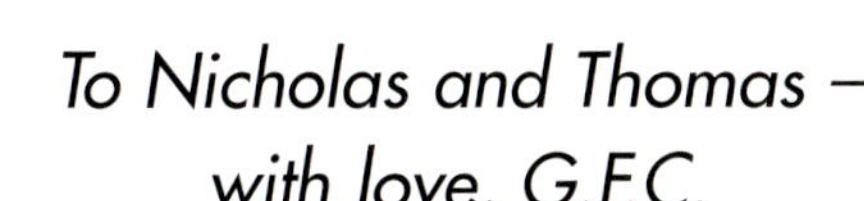

To Nicholas and Thomas –
with love, G.F.C.

For the little cub that lives in the hearts of children and adults.
May he always fill you with courage, curiosity and countless pleasures –
P.S.R.

Published by:

Savuti Muti Publishing
P.O. Box 22096
St. Simons Island, Georgia 31522
www.patsysmithroberts.com

Printed in China.
ISBN 978-0-939801-09-1

Production Date: 12/27/2013
Plant & Location: Printed by Everbest Printing (Guangzhou, China), Co. Ltd
Job / Batch #: 30117-0

Fifth Printing

Acknowledgements

Whatever it was that drew me to Africa that first time is still a mystery. It opened a world of beauty and tranquility that I never knew existed. When I found Botswana on my second trip, I had the feeling that I was finally home.

My friend Peter Nelson led me to Gametrackers, a safari company owned by Orient Express Hotels, years ago. The staffs in the camps are so dear to me and have made it easy for a woman traveling alone. The guides are tireless in their efforts to make sure I get the best possible photographs. I send them all a great big thank you and lots of love.

A special thank you to my friend Sandy Fowler who always manages to find a spare tent for me.

The government of Botswana is to be commended for the fine job it has done with its conservation program that has allowed me to photograph these magnificent animals in their natural habitat. I always know what a privilege it is to see them.

A thank you to Becky Parker for all her hard work on design and also to Gill for making my photographs come to life with her words.

And, last but not least, for friends who have encouraged me and for those who have begged me to stop — thank you without reservation!

Patsy Smith Roberts

A huge thank you to my husband, Matthew, for his continual support and encouragement, and to Patsy for initiating this project.

Gillian Cullinan

Rory

The Adventures of a Lion Cub

For- Charles My Africa- to You! Best Wishes, Patsy S. Roberts

2014

Text by Gillian Cullinan

Photography by Patsy Smith Roberts

Published by Savuti Muti Publishing

Kindergarten Phonics & Read

with Spelling, Handwriting, and Language Skills

Teacher's Manual *(Part 1)*
Lessons 1 to 90

Visit **McRuffy.com** for helpful resources to teach this curriculum!

Teacher's Manual *(Part 1)*
ISBN 978159269-3528

McRuffy Press Kindergarten Phonics & Reading Curriculum
ISBN 978159269-1906

Written and illustrated by
Brian Davis M. A. Ed.

Graphic Design by
Sherylynn Davis

McRuffy Press, LLC
P.O. Box 212
Raymore, MO 64083

816-331-7831

sales@mcruffy.com

www.McRuffy.com

Pup and Cat Games

Play games on the back of the workbook

The Pup and Cat Games can be played many ways:

For all games, choose if you are playing as a pup or a cat. Players do not have to choose different animals. Write the word down to remember which you are. Players complete a task in order to move on the board. Roll a die, spin a spinner, or draw a number to move on the board. Use game pieces or small objects to mark your space.

Play as a pup: If you are a pup and you land on a pup space, roll again and move **forward**. If you are a pup and land on a cat space roll again and move **backward**. Your turn ends after your second roll even if you are on a pup space.

Play as a cat: If you are a cat and you land on a cat space, you roll again and move **forward**. If you are a act and land on a pup space roll again and move **backward**. Your turn ends after your second roll even if you are on a cat space.

The first player to reach the end of the path is the winner. Although all players can finish the round with a chance to tie, so remember who took a turn first.

Games (tasks to complete before moving on the board)

Read the word game: Read a word from a card in order to move.

Write the word game 1: See a word from a card and then write it in order to move. Your rule may be you can see the card as you write it, or your rule could be that you cannot see the word as you write.

Write the word game 2: Hear a word from a card and then write it.

Rhyming games: See or hear a word and say or write a rhyming word.

Beginning letter games: See or hear a word and say or write a word with the same beginning letter.

Vowel sound game 1: See or hear a word and say or write a word with the same vowel sound.

Vowel sound game 2: See or hear a word and change the vowel sound. Say or write the word.

Spelling game: Hear a word and spell it.

What does it mean game: See or hear a word and tell what it means.

Sentence Game: See or hear a word and use it in a sentence.

McRuffy Kindergarten SE Phonics & Reading

This curriculum has been designed to teach children the basics of reading. The main emphases of the program are decoding words (phonics), reading (giving meaning to printed material), spelling and writing (encoding) and handwriting. Another goal of the program is to give parents and teachers a complete and easy method to follow. Successful learning begins with successful teaching.

Children are natural learners. Compare an infant to an average five year old child. The differences are remarkable. The five year old has learned to walk, talk, has started to gain understanding of right and wrong, and has gained social skills. The challenge of teaching is to take those learning skills and guide them in a more formal way.

It is important to understand what the child is bringing to the formal learning situation. For reading, the child has already developed a vocabulary. This involves being able to discriminate between sounds. The child can tell the difference between the words cat and dog when the child hears them.

The child is able to manipulate words to express meaning. If a child is hungry he or she will choose words that are adequate to convey that message: "Can I have a cookie?" The child understands that words communicate ideas.

What the child may not have is an understanding of printed language. It is important for parents to read to children even before the children begin reading. This models the idea that thoughts can be communicated by a written language. It is the child's first personal encounter with reading.

Multi-sensory Learning

People learn by receiving information in some form. Our five senses are the highways for input. Reading is learned using a combination of our senses. Sight, hearing, and touch are employed in the process of learning to read.

This curriculum primarily uses visual, auditory, and kinesthetic methods of teaching. Information is presented visually by using flashcards, reading sentences, etc. Examples of auditory methods include saying words or sounds and hearing words or sounds. Handwriting kinesthetically reinforces the learning.

A fourth group of methods is called tactile learning. Using the sense of touch may help some students. Tracing letters cut from sandpaper is frequently used as a way to teach children the forms of different letters. Tactile methods are not in the lesson plans, but a list of ideas that can be used in many of the lessons is include in the reference section.

Readiness

The first step is for children to develop phonemic awareness. This is an intuitive understanding that words can be related by the way they sound. Teaching children rhymes is one way to develop this awareness in children. When children start to learn phonics, they are actually learning a new concept. The child learns that there are little pieces or building blocks of words called sounds. These sounds are represented by letters.

Before children can begin reading they have to reach a certain level of maturity or readiness. Children progress to this point at various rates. Generally, a child is ready somewhere between the ages of four and six. This is not a question of ability, it is a question of growth. If the child shows an interest in reading begin by introducing a few letters sounds.

If you decide your child is ready, it's important to set reasonable expectations. The child is not likely to learn each letter sound the first time. Lessons introduce sounds. It will take practice for the child to learn the sounds. Remember, the child has a whole school career ahead of him or her.

Secondly, children grow and learn in spurts. Some children just seem to struggle along. They don't seem to be grasping what you're teaching. Children should be challenged but not pushed beyond their limits.

Stay with the program. Tell yourself you are a good teacher. There will come a day when things will just click and the child will learn more easily. Sometimes it takes a child awhile to simply grasp the concept of reading.

The program contains a lot of review and some drilling. The first unit (45 lessons) uses only eight letters and four sight words. The child won't get too far behind if you continue to introduce more letter sounds. If it gets to the point that you're too uncomfortable going on, stop and just work on learning those sounds and words that can be formed with those letters.

Incorporating the Preschool-TK Program

The Preschool-TK (Transitional Kindergarten) program is designed to focus on skills leading up to Lesson 1 of this curriculum. It is not a prerequisite to begin this program, but for some students it may be a more natural place to start. Also, many Preschool-TK lessons could be done in conjunction with this program. Activities from the Preschool-TK program could be occasionally added to the daily lessons in this curriculum, especially lessons after the main concepts have been taught in the week. Any lessons except perhaps the Alphabet section on the Preschool-TK program would not be out of sequence for any part of this curriculum, since they are complimentary skills that would only enhance lessons.

If students don't display a readiness to learn phonics, such as not being able to identify letters, you can also delay the start of lesson 1 of this curriculum or if students are struggling with the lessons you may stop and work on the Phonemic Awareness and The Alphabet sections of the P-K4 program.

If delaying the start of this program to do Preschool-TK only, later lessons could be combined to assure all K concepts are taught before continuing to the First Grade program within a 180 day school year. Use just the key parts of the weekly lessons and then move on. Key parts would likely include the lesson of that introduces the concept, the reading books (and questions about the books), choice of some workbook pages including the weekly assessment to determine if more time needs to be spent on the concept.

Suggested places to accelerate the curriculum include:

Lessons 26-45: words *the, is, in, on*. If combined into one week, the course would be shortened by 3 weeks.

Lessons 71-85: l, f, k, red, green, blue. If combined it would shorten the course by 2 weeks.

Lessons 91-100: x, w, v. If combined it would shorten the course by 1 week.

The Use of Drilling

We feel that with this curriculum, reliance on drilling should be minimized. Drilling, particularly drilling flashcards can be used in this curriculum and flashcards are included. Repetition helps the child retain the information that was learned.

But, drilling words in isolation should not be overused. Having students read the words in context of our stories will more quickly build a strong reading vocabulary, especially if students are given opportunities to reread the stories. This will build fluency and word knowledge.

You may encounter two problems with drilling. Children may become bored and drilling may take too much time. To fight boredom, drilling methods can be varied. Games are a good way to drill. Children enjoy playing. A list of game ideas is in the reference section.

Part of the daily routine is to drill flashcards of words already learned. When the child is first learning to read, it may take quite awhile to sound out ten words. Even after the child can read the cards more quickly, there may be 70 or 80 flash cards to review. This can be solved by simply reducing the number of cards each day. If you do this, cycle through the cards instead of using the same five or ten cards over and over.

In this curriculum drilling is used in one particular instance to introduce a skill. Daily routines are detailed in the reference section. Step e is to review the five short vowel sounds. The child will use only the short a sound (except for the words in, is, and on) in the first unit.

Nevertheless, the child should say all five short vowel sounds daily. This will help build a solid foundation for using those sounds later on. Vowel sounds can be difficult to discriminate. This helps the child to clarify the differences before having to hear them in words. The same is done for the long vowel sounds beginning in unit 3.

Learning Sequence

If you look at the sequence of the introduction of letter sounds, you will notice it is not in alphabetical order. Unit one is built around the short a sound. Consonants were chosen by looking at how many two and three letter short *a* words could be formed with them. In other words, utility was the deciding factor.

The curriculum at times includes words that may not be in the child's vocabulary. This has been done to help expand the child's vocabulary. Take time to explain unusual words like *vole*, to the child. Look up definitions in a dictionary with the child.

Although the curriculum's daily routine teaches letter recognition, the main emphasis should be on letter sounds, not letter names. Also, because small letters (lower case) are used more frequently, emphasize them more than the capital letters.

Handwriting

The curriculum offers optional handwriting books in a variety of styles. Handwriting assignments are also given in the lesson plans. These can be completed on standard handwriting paper. The handwriting book offers tracing exercises and expanded handwriting opportunities. It also gives students examples of how words should be written.

The handwriting program has two purposes. Traditionally, handwriting lessons were focused on developing penmanship. This involves developing fine motor skills and hand-eye coordination skills.

This also requires knowledge about how letters are formed. Handwriting skill may be developmentally related, it is somewhat dependent upon the maturity of the child. Therefore, rather than having a set standard for acceptable handwriting, look for improvement. Is the child progressing?

Handwriting in this curriculum also reinforces the phonics concepts and reading skills. Children learn words better when they have the opportunity to write words. You can add excitement to your instruction by allowing students to write with different writing utensils and different writing surfaces.

Notes on the special edition:

There many exciting changes in the special edition. Workbooks have been revised. The most obvious change is the use of color. Some activities have been revised, particularly in the later lessons.

We hope that you and your child enjoy using this curriculum. More importantly, we hope it is a fruitful learning experience. Your questions and comments are appreciated. Please feel free to contact us at:

McRuffy Press
P. O. Box 212
Raymore, MO 64083

sales@mcruffy.com

www.mcruffy.com

Reference Section

Program Contents

1. Teacher's manual
2. Copy Masters
3. Cardstock items
4. Workbooks 1 and 2
5. Pre-Readers (10)
6. Reading books (20)

Organization of the Teacher's Manual

The teacher's manual consists of:

1. Introduction
2. Reference section
3. Lesson plans

Lesson Plan Key

Lesson Objectives briefly state the concepts that are covered in the lesson. They answer the question: "What should the child be learning?" The objectives are numbered. The numbers correspond to the numbers in the teaching section.

The ***Preparation*** section lists any materials needed as well as any advance preparation needed to teach the lesson.

The ***Teaching*** section explains how to teach the lesson. Again, the numbers correspond with the numbers under lesson objectives. Some lessons are scripted. They have words in bold print that can be read directly to the students. It does not have to be followed exactly. Modify it if you would feel the child would understand better if things were said in a different way. You may have to elaborate more and check for understanding more.

Type Style Key

Notice the print type in the teaching section:

- Instructions to the teacher are in regular print.
- Statements that can be read to the student (the script) are in **bold print**.
- Blends or letters that are to be pronounced phonetically are *italicized.*
- Words that are the student's answers or responses are in parenthesis ( ).
- Long vowels to be pronounced phonetically are *italicized* and capitalized.

Lesson Plan Information Boxes

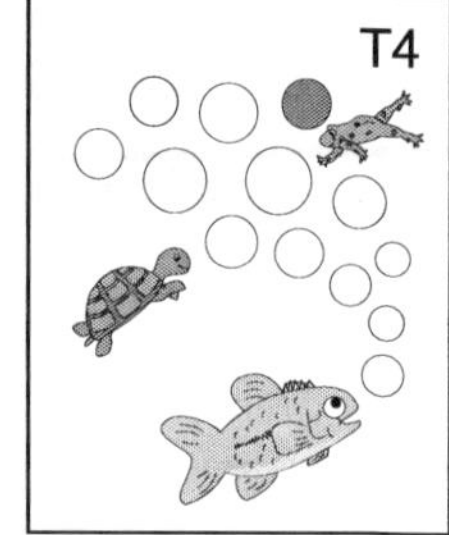

A representation of the workbook pages is included in the lesson plan. The letter T and number indicate the part of the Teaching section the worksheet is assigned.

Handwriting guides show the formation of the letters when new ones are introduced. Two styles are displayed.

Handwriting Guide
Traditional or **Modern**

Bb Bb

The Games box indicates when games can be played. The games may be played on the lesson or any subsequent lesson. Some games have different parts that might emphasize the current skill. Those parts are indicated after the name of the game.

Games:

Ruff's Lunch - Slider Strip 14
Reading Baseball - Long E
Wiggle Worm 6

Organization of Workbooks

The entire curriculum is broken into four units. These roughly correspond to quarters. Workbook One contains the first two units. Workbook Two contains units 3 and 4 workbook pages.

- Unit 1 (lessons 1 to 45)
- Unit 2 (lessons 46 to 90)
- Unit 3 (lessons 91 to 135)
- Unit 4 (lessons 136 to 175)

Use of flashcards and word-changing drills:

Flashcards can be used for drilling purposes. Flashcards may also be used in place of other cards in any of the folder games (Make-it, Play-it Games) to target words that students need to practice.

An alternative to flashcard drills is word changing drills. Simply write a word on an erasable surface such as a chalkboard or dry erase board. Change one letter at a time and have the students read the new word.

For example write the word cat (students read the word). Erase the c and write b. Students read the word bat. Erase the t and write g. Students read the word bag. Erase the a and write an i. Students read the word big.

This provides a method to thoroughly review concepts and words very quickly in a way that emphasizes common phonetic structure of various words.

Special notes:

Lessons 22 to 45 teach few phonics concepts. This allows struggling students to catch up and it allows for previously learned concepts to be reinforced in the context of reading.

Game Ideas

Games

Games are included in the deluxe package. Following is a list of other game ideas.

Other games

1. "I spy" Give a clue such as: "I spy something that begins with t" and have the child guess what is in the room that you are referring to. You can do it for beginning sounds, ending sounds, blends, vowels, etc.

2. Memory game: Use index cards. Put one word on each card (five to ten words) then make an identical set. Turn the cards upside down and mix them up. The child turns up two cards at a time trying to match them. The child has to read the word to keep the match. The child can play you or him or herself by seeing how few turns it takes to match the cards.

3. Listening game: Have the child listen to a sentence or story. Have them clap each time they hear a specific sound. For example, have them listen for the b sound.

4. Hide and seek: Hide flashcards around the room. The child has to find and read the words.

5. Use the game boards and playing pieces from other games. Have the child move for each flashcard read correctly.

6. Informal learning. Have the child pick out words or letter sounds around them. While traveling, look at road signs, in stores look at packaging.

7. Find the word: Set flash cards face up and ask the child to find the word that:

   begins with (pick a letter), ends with, etc.

8. Change a letter. Using a chalkboard, writing in sand, or something that is easily changed, have the child change one word to another, like bat to cat.

9. Use a chalkboard in place of flashcards while drilling. Ask the child to spell words or dictate sentences.

10. Make picture flashcards by cutting out photographs in magazines and pasting them on index cards. Have the child match the pictures to their beginning or ending letter. The child can also match vowel sounds or words.

Ideas for Tactile and Kinesthetic Learning

1. Write words or letters in sand
2. Use finger paints to write letters
3. Form letters and words out of clay
4. Draw letters on pieces of cloth and trace them with a finger, use cloth with different textures
5. Draw large letters on a cement surface using chalk, walk on top of the lines drawn
6. Use various writing instruments like markers, colored pencils, and paints
7. Trace letters on wooden alphabet blocks with fingers
8. Cut out letters from construction paper
9. Cut out letters from newspapers, magazines, cereal boxes, etc.
10. Use yarn and safety needles to form letters
11. Glue unusual items like macaroni, rice, or beans onto paper to shape into letters
12. Cut letters out of cookie dough, bake and eat
13. Trace words or letters in the air or in water
14. Arrange small objects like pennies into letter shapes
15. Carve letters into potatoes and use paint or ink to make potato prints
16. Use a flannel board and flannel board letters
17. Have the child feel his or her throat as he or she makes a new letter sound

Daily Routines

Unit 1 Daily Routine

a) Review the alphabet. Using flashcards, have the child point to each letter and say its name. (If the child hasn't learned to identify the letters, you may want to say them with the child.)

b) Review letter sounds. Point to the letters the child has learned. Have the child pronounce each sound.

c) Review the terms upper-case and lower-case letters, or point to letters and ask if they are upper-case or lower-case. You may also refer to upper-case letters as capital letters.

d) Review the terms vowel and consonant: follow the same procedure as above.

e) Say the five vowels. Have the child say the five short vowel sounds. Use the short vowel chart.

f) The child should write their name on the handwriting paper during the handwriting part of the lesson.

g) Use the flashcards or word changing drills to review wordsthe child has already learned.

h) Do a Phonemic Awareness Skills warm-up excerices. (See the pages in the Phonemic Awareness section in the Resource Pack)

i) Vocabulary discussion: review any current words and choose some past vocabulary words. Use the Word Lists section in this teacher's manual for reference. Post important vocabulary words in the classroom. Ask for simple definitions. Some lessons introduce words with definitions. These words can be added to vocabulary lists. The definitions do not need to be the exact definitions taught. Instead, look for a clear understanding of the meaning. Have students use the words in sentences. You may also make up sentences to help clarify meaning.

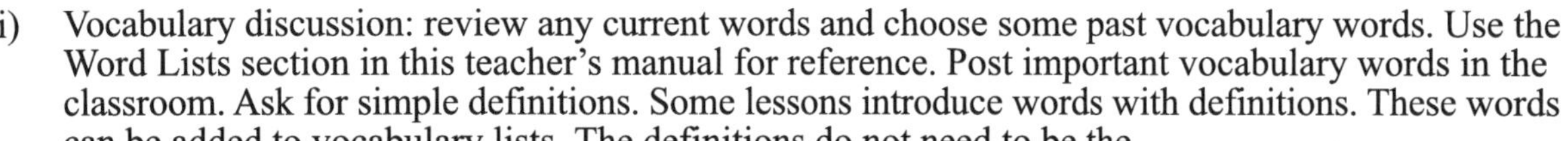

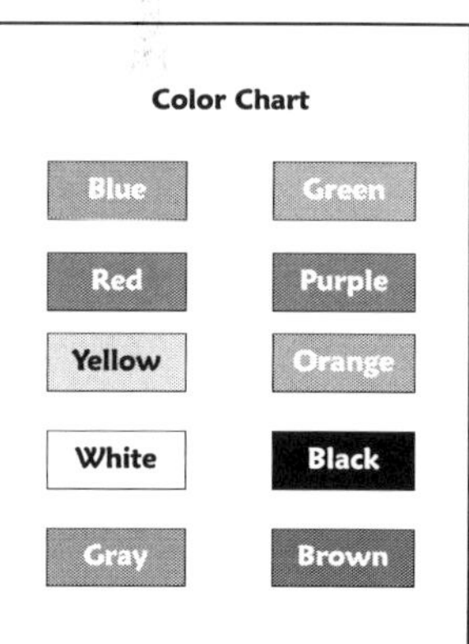

Unit 2 Daily Routine

Follow unit 1 routine. If there are some things you feel the child has definitely mastered, you may want to review them only once or twice a week.

Drill color names. Use a color chart. Ask questions like:

What color ends with w?
What does the word red begin with?
What color has two e's in it?
What color is spelled b-l-u-e?

Units 3 and 4

Continue daily routines and drill long vowel sounds using the long vowel chart.

Story Creating

Several ideas are included in the lesson plans for story creating. Ideas for stories are based on the reading material. This develops a frame of reference and structure for the story. The term story creating is basically creative writing, but not limited to writing. In the classroom story creating can be approached several ways.

Students may dictate stories to students. This may be helpful for students early in the year who have very little written vocabulary.

Students may tell the story with pictures and whatever inventive spelling they can manage. This should be followed up with an opportunity for students to tell their stories. Look for students' ability to tell a story.

Students write the story with inventive spelling. Different educators have opposite opinions about using inventive spelling. Some feel that it reinforces poor spelling habits. Others see it as a stage in student writing ability and students will gradually adapt standard spelling. In either case, inventive spelling can give the teacher feedback as to the progress of the child. Even if words aren't spelled correctly do they reflect an understanding of phonics? It may also let you know what words might be added to a spelling list.

After students begin reading books, story ideas are presented once a week. You may attempt to try every story creating suggestion or just some.

You may decide to employ more of the writing process (writing, editing, rewriting, etc.) or just let students create.

Stories can be created individually, teams, or as a whole class. Students should have the opportunity to share their stories for others.

Story page and book page copy masters are in the copy master section. These can be reproduced to provide students a form for creating stories. The story page provides a box for illustration and a few lines for writing. This may be the entire story for young students. The book pages can be copied and folded to make a book. These can be printed two sided and several sheets may be stapled together to create a book.

Creative Drama and Puppet Cut-outs

Students may interact with the reading books in a very creative way. Once a week, (every five lessons) students are given the opportunity to act out the book. This can be done as a skit or a puppet theater. The puppet cut-outs may be used in this activity. They may be colored glued to craft sticks. The puppets are surrounded by a dashed cut-out line. The purpose is to allow students to be creative and demonstrate an understanding of the story.

Although activities are given for each book, you may chose not to have students act out every story. You may also vary the level of development of the plays. In some plays you may want the students to create props, costumes, scenery, etc. Other times, you may want students to pantomime. You may want to even film some of the plays or perform them for other classes or family members.

Pronouncing Sounds

When teaching letter sounds, it is important that the child learns the sounds as isolated from other sounds as possible. For example, the b sound is not bu. If we tried to blend b and at to make bat and we pronounced b as bu, bat would sound more like bu-at. It makes it harder to blend.

This happens mostly with the following letters: b, d, g, m, n. The best way to pronounce them is by thinking of their sounds at the end of the word. Examples: tub, had, tag, Tom, fan.

With some letters it is helpful to put a vowel sound before the consonant. The l sound can be pronounced ul and the r sound can be pronounced er.

In this program, only the ending sound of x will be learned (ks).

Some consonants have more than one sound.

- c has the k and s sounds
- s has the s and z sounds
- g has the g and j sounds

The hard c as in cat will be denoted by an italicized c or k (*c k*). C as in circus will by denoted by an italicized s *(s)*. Likewise s will be denoted by an italicized s or z. G will be denoted by an italicized g or j, depending on the sound.

Phonics Terminology

Blend: Verb-to combine distinct sounds into a single speech unit. Noun- a speech sound created by combining two distinct sounds.

Consonant: a sound produced by partial or complete obstruction of the air stream.

Compound word*: a word composed of two or more words.

Diacritical mark*: a mark added to a letter to indicate a distinct sound.

Digraph: a pair of letters that represent a distinct speech sound.

Diphthong*: a speech sound that begins as one vowel sound and moves to another within the same syllable.

Phoneme: the smallest unit of speech sound.

Phonetic awareness: awareness that words are composed of individual speech sounds.

Phonological awareness: awareness that words are related by sounds.

Rime and Onset: A rime is a word ending. The onset is the first letter, digraph, or blend. For example the rime –at can have the onsets such as c, th, spl to make the words cat, that, splat.

Voiced sound: a sound uttered with vibration of the vocal chords.

Vowel: a speech sound created by free flowing air through the larynx.

*These concepts not taught in this Kindergarten curriculum.

Scope and Sequence

Scope refers to the scope of concepts the curriculum teaches. It answers the question: "What will the child know as a result of learning what this curriculum has taught?" Sequence refers to the order in which concepts are taught.

Unit 1

1 Short a
2 b
3 blends
6 c as in cat
8 t
12 p
14 n
18 s
21 h
22 the word a
23 sentences
26 the
31 is
36 in
41 on

Unit 2

46 short i
51 m
54 questions
56 r
58 g
61 d
66 short o
71 l
76 f
78 red, green, blue
81 k
82 ck ending
83 yellow, orange, black
86 short u
88 brown, pink, purple

Unit 3

91 x as an ending sound
93 white, violet
96 w
97 v
101 short e
106 y and z
111 long a
112 s & j sounds of c and g
116 j
121 long i
126 sh
131 long o

Unit 4

136 qu
137 go, so, no
141 long u
146 st blend
151 long e
156 mp
161 oa
166 ay
171 gr

Reading Books

The curriculum uses two sets of books. The first set is called First Step Readers, also referred to as pre-readers. These books are very short (about four sentences on four pages). They are intended to give the child a very early opportunity to read books somewhat independently. Each pre-reader has a word list on the back cover that can be reviewed before reading (the lesson it begins on is also listed):

First Step Readers

Lesson	Book	Lesson	Book
26	*Sat*	51	*Map & Ham*
31	*A Can*	56	*The Ram*
36	*The Hat*	61	*The Big Pig*
41	*Nan*	66	*Hot Dog*
46	*Cat In A Bin*	71	*Lill*

Included in the curriculum are twenty reading books. Use of the reading books is detailed after lesson 75. The books will follow this order:

Reading Books

Lesson	Book	Lesson	Book
76	*Cat Nap*	126	*Sam and the Shark*
81	*Sam and Kit*	131	*Rose the Mole*
86	*Pup in Mud*	136	*Quack and Quill*
91	*Mop, Mop, Mop*	141	*The Mule Ride*
96	*Vic's Van*	146	*Kate's Nest*
101	*Red and Bess*	151	*Can a Deer Steer?*
106	*Fuzz the Yak*	156	*Ruff Camps*
111	*The Ape and Cake*	161	*Goat and Toad*
116	*Jane's Jet*	166	*Kay and the Ray Gun*
121	*Ruff's Cab*	171	*Greg's Grape Ride*

Coloring sheets for each book are located in the resource pack. Coloring sheets may be reproduced. These are included as an extra activity for students who like to color or need the practice. Each sheet has two blank sets of lines under the pictures. Students may make up and write their own captions, copy a sentence from the book, or leave it blank.

Word List

The following word list is provided in case you would like to create other sentences for your child to read. They are listed by the lesson that introduces them.

Lesson

7 cab

8 at, bat, cat, tab

13 cap, pat, tap

14 ban, can, nab, nap, pan, tan

19 bass, pass, sap, sat

21 has, hat

26 the

31 is

36 in

41 on

46 bib, bin, bit, hip, his, hiss, hit, nip, pin, pit, sin, sip, sis, sit, tin, tip

51 ham, him, man, map, mass, mat, miss, mitt, Pam, Sam, Tim

56 ram, ran, rap, rat, rib, rim, rip

58 bag, big, gag, gap, gas, hag, pig, rag, rig, sag, tag

61 dip, bid, hid, did, rid, dig, Dan, bad, had, pad, sad, dad, dam, mad, dim

66 Bob, boss, cop, cob, cot, not, top, toss, sob, pot, hot, hop, cod, Tom, Todd, sod, mob, mom, mop, moss, nod, pod, pop, rod, rob, rot, Ron, Ross, dot dog, Don, bog, cog, hog, God, Todd, got

71 lab, lad, lag, lap, lass, lid, lip, lob, log, lop, loss, lot, ball, call, hall, mall, tall, doll, Bill, dill, ill, hill, mill, pill

76 fad, fall, fan, fat, fib, fig, fin, fit, fog, fill, if, off

78 red, green, blue

81 kid, Kim, kiss, kit, kill

82 back, pack, rack, sack, tack, lack, pick, sick, tick lick, kick, dock, mock, sock, rock, tock, lock

83 yellow, orange, black

86 buck, bud, bug, bull, bum, bun, bus, but, cub, cud, cuff, cup, cut, duck, dud, dug, dull, full, fun, fuss, gum, gun, Gus, hub, hug, lug, mud, mug, mutt, nut, pug, pull, pun, putt, puck, pup, rub, rug, run, rut, sub, sud, suck, sup, tub, tug, tuck

88 brown, pink, purple

91 ax, lax, tax, fix, mix, six, box, fox, ox

93 white, violet

96 wag, wig, win, wit, won, van, vat, wax, will, wall, was

Word List page 2

Lesson

101 bed, beg, Ben, bet, Bess, Deb, deck, den, fed, hen, keg, Ken, led, leg, less, let, men, mess, met, net, neck, peg, pen, pep, pet, peck, red, egg, set, Ted, ten, vet, web, wed, wet, Ed, well

106 yell, yes, yet, yak, yack, yam, yip, zig, zip, zag, zap, razz, fizz, buzz, fuzz

111 Abe, age, ape, ate, babe, bake, base, cage, cake, came, cane, cape, case, cave, date, Dale, Dave, fade, fame, face, Gabe, gage, game, gape, gate, gave, gaze hale, hate, Kate, lame, lane, lace, late, made, mace, mate, name, Nate, pace, page, pave, rage, race, rake, raze, sage, same, save, take, tale, tame, tape, vase, wade, wake, wave, wage

116 jab, jag, jam, jig, Jim, job, jog, jot, Jack, Jud, jug, jet, Jed, Jeff, Jess Jade, Jane, jazz, Jake, jut

121 bike, bite, dike, dime, dine, dive, file, fine, fire, five, hide, hike, hive, kite, hire, life, lime, line, live, mice, Mike, mile, mine, nine, nice, pike, pile, pine, pipe, ride, ripe, side, site, tide, tile, time, tire, wide, wife, wipe, wire, vile, vine, vice, vise, size, rise, rice, wise

126 ash, bash, cash, dash, dish, fish, gash, gush, hash, hush, Josh, lash, mash, mesh, mush, rash, rush, sash, shack, shad, shade, shake, shale, shall, shame, shape, share, shave, shed, shell, shin, shine, ship, shock, shod, shop, shot, shuck, shun, shut, wish

131 bode, bone, code, cone, cope, core, cove, dome, dote, dove, doze, hole, home, hone, hope, hose, joke,lobe, lode, lone, lope, lore, mode, mole, mope, more, node, nose, note, poke, pole, pope, pore, pose, robe, rode, role, rope, rose, rote, rove, sole, tote, tome, tone, vole, vote, woke, yoke, zone, shone, shore, wore

136 quack, quake, quell, quick, quip, quit, quite, quill, quite, quiz, quoll, quote

137 go, so, no

141 use, cube, cute, tube, Jude, rude, huge, Duke, Luke, mule, rule, fume, dune, June, tune, cure, pure, fuse, lute, mute, ruse

146 stab, stack, stag, Stan, stash, stage, stake, stall, stare, state, stem, step, stick, still, stock, stop, stoke, stone, store, stove, stub, stuck, stuff, stun, cast, fast, last, past, vast, best, nest, pest, rest, test, vest, west, mist, cost, bust, dust, fist, gust, just, list, lost, must, rust, haste, baste, paste, taste, waste

151 bee, beep, beef, beet, deed, deem, deep, deer, eel, fee, feed, feel, feet, geek, heed, heel, jeep, jeer, keel, keen, keep, lee, leek, leer, meek, meet, need, peek, peel, peep, peer, queen, reed, reef, reek, reel, see, seed, seek, seem, seen, seep, steed, steel, steep, steer, tee, teem, teen, veer, wee, weed, week, weep, sheet, sheen, sheep, sheer, be, he, me, she, we

156 camp, damp, lamp, ramp, stamp, tamp, temp, limp, comp, pomp, romp, stomp, bump, dump, hump, jump, lump, pump, rump, sump, stump

161 boar, boat, boast, coal, coat, coast, coax, foal, foam, goal, goat, hoax, load, loaf, moan, moat, oak, oar, oat, road, roam, roar, roast, soak, soap, soar, toad, toast

166 bay, day, Fay, hay, jay, Kay, lay, may, nay, pay, ray, say, stay, way

171 grab, gram, grass, grace, grade, grape, graze, gray, grate, green, grid, grill, grim, grin, grip, gripe, grit, groan, grove, grub, gruff, grump, Greg

Spelling List

Spelling list include five words each week. Teacher may also want to add their own words to the lists. In the copy master section is a form that can be copied for test taking. Lesson plans also include activities that use the spelling words.

Lesson

31	the, is, cat, hat, sat
36	in, can, has, bass, nab
41	bat, pan, on, pass, tab
46	bin, his, hip, hit, tip
51	ham, map, him, miss, man
56	rat, ram, rib, ran, rip
61	dig, dim, dad, hid, bad
66	dog, got, mop, toss, nod
71	ball, doll, hill, lap, lid
76	fan, fall, fog, fill, off
82	kiss, kid, back, sick, rock
86	bus, duck, pup, hug, fun
91	fix, mix, six, box, fox
97	van, vat, wig, wax, won
101	bed, hen, well, get, neck
106	yes, yell, zip, fizz, buzz
111	bake, face, cage, made, late
116	jam, jab, jug, jet, Jane
121	mice, dime, nine, kite, bike
126	ship, fish, shape, shine, shell
131	nose, joke, rope, home, bone
136	quack, quake, quick, quit, quill
141	use, cute, tube, rule, cure
146	taste, stick, stone, stop, nest
151	she, deer, queen, feel, steep
156	camp, stomp, bump, limp, jump
161	boat, toast, soap, road, goal
166	day, pay, stay, way, may
171	green, grape, grass, grin, grace

Resource Packet Items

Resource Packet items are in the plastic bag. They include:

- Vowel Charts
- Character Cut-outs
- Flashcards
- Copy Masters
- Color Games
- Game cards (bagged in a smaller bag)
- Slider Word Drills
- Vocabulary Development and Assessment

Slider Word Drills

Sliders are changing word manipulatives. Sliders use a strip of paper that slide in the holder to complete a series of words.

Student copies can be found in the resource pack. An additional reproducible copy is included in the copy master section so teachers can demonstrate how to assemble the materials or to reproduce materials to fix students mistakes. Each slider is printed on a sheet. Easy assembly instructions can be found on the slider sheets.

The use of sliders can be extended beyond the lesson. Students can find the words to answer questions. Following are question formats that emphasize different reading skills.

Phonics questions:

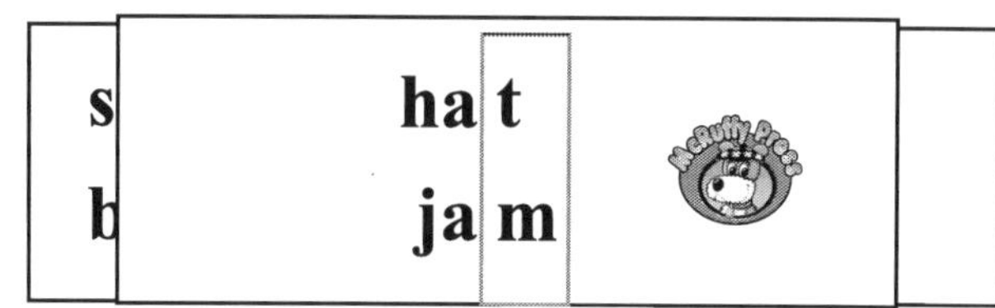

Find the word that begins with _______.

Find the word that ends with ______.

Find the word that rhymes with _______.

Semantic Questions (Vocabulary)

Find the word that means __________.

Find the word that is a kind of ________.

Find the word that is something you _________.

Syntax Questions (sentence structure)

Find the word that completes this sentence: (Say a sentence that can be completed by one of the words on the slider)

Listen to this sentence. What word is on the slider?

Copy Masters

The following materials may be photocopied for your personal or single classroom use. They may not be copied in whole or in part for resale or redistribution. These can be found in the Resource Pack.

1. Assessment Recording Form: This is a recording sheet for the results of the assessments and the unit tests.
2. Ruff's Pre-Writing Sheet: Unassigned sheets for practice of basic strokes used in letter formation.
3. Blank handwriting paper: This has been provided as an alternative to handwriting tablets.
4. Sliders
5. Arrow chart: Instructions for the use of this chart are given in Lesson 11.
6. Story Pages and Book page copy masters: These can be copied for story creating activities.
7. Spelling copy masters: This sheet can be copied and cut apart for students to use on spelling tests.
8. Story coloring pages are included for each book as a bonus activity.

Vocabulary Development

Vocabulary growth occurs when students encounter new words in phonics and reading activates (including stories read to students). See the Resource Pack for Vocabulary Development sheets.

1. Explain and use the terms *definition* and *define*. "When I say tell me the *definition* of the word *dog*. I am asking you to describe the meaning of the word *dog*. Everyone may not use the same exact words to describe the word dog, but a good definition would help other people understand what is meant. Another way to ask about the meaning of the word would be to say, "define the word *dog*." You might say something like, "*A dog is a furry animal that barks and is often a pet*."""
2. See the Daily Routine: Post a list of helpful new vocabulary words and pick words to review daily.
3. Have students write the word and make an illustration to help remember the definition.
4. Ask students to define well known words as practice for creating definitions for unknown words. For example, ask students to define the word *cat*.
5. Use reading activities to increase vocabulary development. Use frequently occurring prefixes and affixes and root words as clues. Unlock is the opposite of lock. Helpless is a combination of help and less, meaning not being able to help themselves.
6. Look for additional meanings to words that are already familiar. For example a duck is a bird and also an action. You can *wave* your hand and a boat can make a *wave* on a lake. A *can* holds things and you *can* do things.
7. Relate words to their opposites as new words are learned: sit, stand, hot, cold, back, front. The word lists on the back of reading books could be used for this activity.
8. Sort objects or pictures into groups. For example from a group of pictures of dogs and other animals, sort the dogs into a group. Discuss why those pictures were chosen. How are the dogs different from the other animals? How are all the dogs alike? Sort other groups such as foods, shapes, colors.
9. Have students distinguish shades of meaning. For example something might be described as big or tall. But a big object might not always be tall, like a big puddle of water. Hop and jump can describe the same action or slightly different with hopping keeping both legs together and jumping as more in stride.
10. Have students break multi-syllable words into parts by clapping and counting syllables. These may be words encountered while listening to stories being read to students.

Phonemic Awareness and Auditory Discrimination

Some students may not be at a stage of development to understand the basics of phonics. Before students can be successful at decoding, they must begin to develop phonemic awareness. This is a general understanding that words can be related by sounds. Sat and cat sound alike, although sat is an action and a cat is an animal. Following are exercises that help develop phonemic awareness. These are provided to help those students that are still developing this understanding.

In general: If students have difficulty with these exercises, have them echo (repeat after) other children or the teacher. Children at an early stage of phonemic awareness are most familiar with hearing words in bigger "chunks". Exercises that emphasize bigger parts of words would be the beginning point. This would include rhyming and alliteration exercises (same beginning sounds, like tongue twisters), same or different exercises, and using pictures. More difficult tasks include the auditory discrimination and auditory blending exercises particularly when they involve blending or hearing each individual sound.

The initial sounds in words that are the most distinct are: /f/, /m/, /r/, /s/. Early exercises should emphasize words that begin with these sounds.

Working with children in groups: Students can respond to exercise by saying the answer either as a group or a called upon individual. If one individual answers, you may have the group echo the answer. For example bat, sat, cat. Which word begins with /s/? One student answers /sat/. The rest of the class echoes /sat/, /s/, or /s-at/

Questions that have a choice of two answers can also be responded to by clapping, stand, sitting down, or raising hands. An example would be, do you hear /s/ in /sat/? Students may also make response cards, which are just 2 pieces of paper marked with two different answers. A happy face can mean yes. A sad face can mean no. Students hold up their answers and the teacher can make a quick visual check.

Teachers may also ask for written responses even if students don't have writing skills. Make a numbered response sheet with a box for each number. Students will color the box red if the answer is no and green if the answer is yes. You may use the happy and sad faces instead of coloring, since students would more readily remember the code. In that case, number the page and draw circles instead of boxes.

Rhyming exercises: 1. What rhymes with *bat*? 2. Complete a rhyming sentence pair.
3. Read nursery rhymes, poems, jingles and pick out words that rhyme (either the student or teacher depending on the level) 4. Read nursery rhymes. Have students fill in the last word in the rhyme.
5. Have students think of other words that might rhyme with the words in the nursery rhyme.
6. Have students make up new rhymes.

Alliteration 1. For example read the *The B Book* by Stan and Jan Berenstain (Berenstain Bears) to children. Talk about the words in the book and how they are alike. There are other books in this series that feature similar alliteration. What are other words that could have been in *The B Book*? 2. Teach tongue twisters. 3. Have students make up new tongue twisters.

Same or Different? Say two words. Ask students if they are the same or different. Examples: cat-cat (same), bat-cat (different), ham-hand (different), bubble-buckle (different), hat-hit (different). The easiest exercise would only deal with same or different beginning sounds. Next, would be exercises that changed ending sounds, then changing beginning or ending, changing vowel sounds and other medial sounds. Students can respond by raising one hand on different and both hands for same pairs, or saying same or different, or make response cards – one with two happy faces for same. One with a happy and a sad face for different (or other pictures that are the same or different).

Phonemic Awareness and Auditory Discrimination

The Odd Word: Which begins with a different sound? Dog, boy, dim. Ending sounds and vowel sounds can also be stressed. (ending sounds: red, hat, fit vowel sounds: cat, ran, big).

Use Pictures: 1. Group pictures by beginning sounds, vowel sounds, or ending sounds. 2. Find pictures in magazines and make a poster 3. Group pictures that rhyme (cat, hat, bat) 4. Draw pictures that begin with the same sounds. 5. Make a picture letter book (ABC book)

Is the sound in the beginning, middle, or end (use advanced and learned words)? For example where is the *b* sound in these words? Bat, rabbit, cub. Hearing medial sounds (any sound that is not at the beginning or end) is most difficult. Hearing beginning sounds is the easiest skill. This exercise would be done after students have had some success hearing letters in each position of a word.

What other words begin (or end) with the *b* sound?

Say a key word or sound. Say a list of words. Students respond by raising their hands on words that begin (or end) with the same sound. Do the same for word families: find the words that end with *at, fad, hat, man, sat.*

Find the letter that makes the *b* sound in the following words. (Use a list of advanced words or learned words.)

Read a story. Have the student listen for the sound and respond (clapping, response cards, etc).

Phoneme deletion exercises:	Say "stop". Now say it without the *s*.
Phoneme addition exercises:	Say "top". Now add *s* to the beginning. Say 'top". Now add *s* to the end.

Word family drills (auditory-visual): Write *at* on the board. 1. Say different beginning sounds and students say the words. For example: *b* The student response would be *bat* 2. Say *bat.* The students will tell you the beginning sound and letter name.

Count the sounds. How many sounds do you hear in *bat*? (3) How many times do you hear the *b* sound in bubble, bumblebee, bathtub?

Auditory blending: 1. Say two words that make a compound word (pause between words). Students repeat them as one compound word. (foot ball, football) 2. Say two syllables. Have students blend into a word: tur (pause) tle. Turtle. 3. Say sounds slowly to model blending and gradually speed up or emphasize beginning or ending blending: Model visually and auditorially. c-a-t ca-t c-at Blending initial consonant with the ending (c-at) is the easiest skill. Ca-t would be next. C-a-t is the most difficult.

Segmenting words (opposite of auditory blending)

Onset and Rime:	Say cat students respond by saying c-at
Compound words:	Say football. Students respond with foot (pause) ball.
Syllables: Say turtle.	Students respond by saying tur-tle.
Affixes (prefixes and suffixes):	Say walking: walk-ing Say preschool: pre-school

Listening to Literature

Choose additional material to read to students each week. Use a variety of material, including fiction (literature) and non-fiction (informational) books, poetry, and other material. Read at least one book per week.

Include the following activities when applicable:

1. Emphasize the cover of the book at the title page. Look at the cover. If the back cover has printing, read it to the child. Show students the cover and ask "what do you think this book is about?" Read the title. Read the name of the author and illustrator, using the terms *author* and *illustrator*. Define the role of the author (writes the words) and illustrator (draws the pictures). If there are other works by the same author or illustrator, you may mention those books. One the title page you may note when the book was written.

2. Compare to other books that have been read to students. For example you might have read a fictional story about a cat. Read a non-fiction book about cats. Ask questions such as: "How is this book different from the story of the cat?" "How are they alike?" "What things did you learn about cats?" Include questions that encourage comparisons and opinions: "Which book did you like the best? Why?" You may also compare books by the same author or illustrator.

3. Compare characters and experiences in the book to familiar stories or characters within the same story. For example: "What did the third little pig do differently from the first two pigs?"

4. Encourage questions about unfamiliar vocabulary: "Were there any words in the story you are not sure what they mean?" "What do you think the word *feline* means?" If there are words you think the students may not know, you may discuss them before reading or wait and have students try to determine the meaning from the context.

5. Have students retell the story or parts of the story in their own words.

6. Discuss illustrations or photographs in the book. Show a picture and ask students to describe what is happening in the picture in a fiction book. In a non-fiction book ask what information can be learned from the picture. Such as a book about the sense of smell. "What things would smell good on this page? What other things might smell like that?"

7 In information text, have students identify the main topic of the text and key details. "What did the author want us to know about cats?" (How to take care of them.) "What are some of the things the author told about taking care of cats?"

8. Ask questions about the key details. "What re some things you can feed kittens? How often should they be fed?"

9. Ask questions about two ideas, events, or individuals in the text. "How are grown cats different from kittens?"

10. Identify how the author supports ideas in the text. "Why does the author think cats make good pets?"

11. Compare two different texts on the same topic. For example, read a book and an article from the Internet on the same topic. "How are they alike?" "What things did both tell you?" "What was something the (book or article) told you that the other one didn't?"

12. Incorporate the reading activities with writing activities. See the next page for additional details.

13. Emphasize basic story structure. "Where was the boy when the story began?" What did he do next?" What happened at the end of the story?"

14. Find and discuss unfamiliar vocabulary in the stories before reading to students. Discuss and give a simple definition the words before reading. When reading, stop the story and point out the words. Review the words after the story and have students restate the definition in their own words.

Kindergarten Writing

Students at the kindergarten level can participate in writing activities. Try to include at least one writing activity a week. "Writing" can be broadly defined at this level as any expression of an idea put on paper. At the earliest stages this may simply be drawing a picture. As skills develop, writing may include a few words, and even a few simple sentences.

Another early writing activity is dictation. The student tells the story to the teacher and the teacher writes the words. In a classroom setting, this can be a group activity. Teachers and students can also work collaboratively by having the child write whatever words they can. Teachers can help write any words by telling the students the letters or writing the letters for the student.

Have students share their writing. Encourage others to ask questions and give suggestions to improve the writing.

1. Incorporate reading with writing activities. Use kindergarten writing to state an opinion about a topic or a book.
2. Have students create their own informational text. For example create a book of the five senses.
3. Write a story about an event. For example the students can write about a recent field trip.
4. Use computer programs to produce writing when possible. For example, help students find illustration or photographs online. Students may type words on paper, print and add their own drawings, copy and paste digitally, or cut-out pictures with scissors.
5. Create a few research projects such as how to take care of a kitten, or the sense of sight. Have children find books in the library, or even help them search on the internet. In a classroom setting, students may work in groups on a writing project.
6. Pose a question to research, such as *Do rabbits make good pets?*
7. Start with a basic sentence and add to it. Have students dictate the words while the teacher writes in a dry erase board in a classroom or a piece of paper in a homeschool setting. For example: The dog ran. Ask: *What color is the dog?* Students may choose brown. Write the sentence: The brown dog ran. *Where was the dog running?* Students may answer *to a tree.* Write the sentence: The brown dog ran to a tree.

Assessment Item Analysis

An assessment item analysis is a list of concepts that each test item focuses on. The student takes an assessment every five lessons (one week). To better assist you in focusing instruction on the particular needs of your child, compare the test results to the item analysis of the test. A letter from the following key is placed above or next to each item on the test to tell you which is the correct answer, and why another answer was most likely chosen.

The key is:

e Incorrect ending sound

b Incorrect beginning sound

v Incorrect vowel sound

r Reversing the order of letters (such as tab or bat) or reversing the actual letters such as b and d

i Incorrect concept, idea, or word meaning

s spelling

c Correct answer

You may wish to modify instruction for the child's need if a consistent pattern of wrong answers is noticed.

If your child consistently misses the items that test ending sounds, (for example) instruction can be altered to emphasize endings of words.

Lesson 5

1.	r ab	c ba
2.	c b	b a
3.	c ab	r ba
4.	i b	c a
5.	c a	b b

Lesson 10

1.	r at	c ta
2.	b ca	c ba
3.	b t	c c
4.	c ab	r ba
5.	b b	c t

Lesson 15

1	c p r b	2	c bat r tab
3	c ab r ba	4	b cat c pat
5	r pat c tap	6	b t c c
7	b na c ta	8	c an r na
9	e cab c cat	10	e tap c tab

Lesson 20

1	b n c s	2	c c b s
3	c sat e sap	4	c nap e nab
5	c ban e bat	6	e cap c cat
7	b pass c bass	8	c sap b tap
9	b can c pan	10	b cab c nab

Lesson 25

1	e hat c has	2	b cat c sat
3	e bat c bass	4	b pat c hat
5	e sat c sap	6	b ban c can
7	c tab e tap	8	b pass c has
9	e nab c nap	10	c tan b pan

Lesson 30

1	c The i Tan	2	e cap c cab
3	e bass c ban	4	b hat c bat
5	b can c tan	6	c the i tab
7	c sat b pat	8	c an b at
9	c nab r ban	10	e tan c tap

Lesson 35

1	e	cab
	c	cat
2	c	is
	i	has
3	c	as
	b	is
4	r	nap
	c	pan
5	c	bass
	b	pass
6	i	the
	c	hat
7	b	tan
	c	ban
8	e	i
	c	is
9	i	is
	c	the
10	c	sap
	r	pass

Lesson 40

1	b	an
	c	in
2	e	sap
	c	sat
3	b	can
	c	pan
4	c	has
	e	hat
5	e	in
	c	is
6	c	nab
	e	nap
7	c	the
	i	tab
8	e	cat
	c	cab
9	b	tap
	c	pat
10	b	is
	c	as

Lesson 50

1	c	bit
	v	bat
2	c	sit
	v	sat
3	c	tap
	v	tip
4	v	has
	c	his
5	c	sip
	v	sap
6	c	pat
	v	pit
7	c	nip
	v	nap
8	c	ban
	v	bin
9	c	pin
	v	pan
10	v	tin
	c	tan

Lesson 55

1	e	man
	c	mat
2	c	Tim
	e	Tin
3	c	Sam
	b	Pam
4	c	hit
	v	hat
5	c	map
	b	nap
6	v	sip
	c	sap
7	c	him
	v	ham
8	e	tan
	c	tab
9	c	mitt
	e	miss
10	e	Pan
	c	Pam

Lesson 60

#		
1	c	ram
	v	rim
2	v	bag
	c	big
3	c	gab
	r	bag
4	c	tag
	e	tab
5	c	rip
	v	rap
6	b	big
	c	pig
7	r	sag
	c	gas
8	c	rag
	e	rat
9	c	rib
	b	bib
10	c	ran
	b	man

Lesson 65

#		
1	c	did
	v	dad
2	r	dig
	c	big
3	r	rid
	c	rib
4	c	Dan
	e	Dam
5	c	dig
	b	pig
6	e	dim
	c	dip
7	v	bid
	c	bad
8	c	sad
	b	pad
9	c	pad
	b	dad
10	v	had
	c	hid

Lesson 70

#		
1	c	boss
	v	bass
2	v	Dan
	c	Don
3	v	hit
	c	hot
4	v	tip
	c	top
5	v	dig
	c	dog
6	c	cab
	v	cob
7	c	mop
	v	map
8	v	rid
	c	rod
9	c	rot
	v	rat
10	v	Tom
	c	Tim

Lesson 75

#		
1	c	lad
	v	lid
2	b	hill
	c	mill
3	c	lop
	v	lip
4	v	lit
	c	lot
5	c	lass
	v	loss
6	c	dill
	v	doll
7	v	lab
	c	lob
8	v	log
	c	lag
9	c	bill
	r	dill
10	v	lap
	c	lip

Lesson 80

#		
1	b	had
	c	fad
2	v	fan
	c	fin
3	c	red
	i	rod
4	c	fog
	v	fig
5	c	fat
	v	fit
6	i	big
	c	blue
7	c	fill
	b	bill
8	c	green
	i	red
9	c	got
	i	green
10	v	if
	c	off

Lesson 85

#		
1	b	back
	c	pack
2	v	lack
	c	lock
3	s	kat
	c	cat
4	c	yellow
	i	yes
5	i	off
	c	orange
6	c	kiss
	s	ciss
7	s	rok
	c	rock
8	c	tick
	v	tock
9	c	sack
	v	sick
10	c	black
	i	blue

Lesson 95

1.	v fox	c fix	v fax
2.	i pink	c purple	i white
3.	e sick	e sit	c six
4.	b fax	b max	c lax
5.	v ax	c ox	v ix
6.	c tax	e tack	e taps
7.	v six	c sax	v sox
8.	i yellow	c white	i orange
9.	b fix	c mix	b six
10.	c box	b fox	b ox

Lesson 100

1.	v wig	v wog	c wag
2.	c won	v win	v wun
3.	v vot	c vat	v vit
4.	b bit	b hit	c wit
5.	c van	b ban	b pan
6.	b pig	c wig	b big
7.	b max	b tax	c wax
8.	c win	e wig	e wit
9.	b tan	b van	c man
10.	c fax	v fox	v fix

Lesson 105

1.	e Bed	c Ben	e Beg
2.	b fed	b bed	c wed
3.	v pot	v pat	c pet
4.	b mess	c less	b Bess
5.	c men	b ten	b pen
6.	c leg	v log	v lag
7.	b egg	c peg	b keg
8.	v Tod	v Tad	c Ted
9.	v tan	c tin	v ten
10.	c let	v lit	v lot

Lesson 110

1.	c less	b yes	b mess
2.	c zig	b pig	b big
3.	v yip	c yap	v yep
4.	c buzz	b fuzz	b cuzz
5.	b pet	b set	c yet
6.	v zap	c zip	v zop
7.	b ram	c yam	b ham
8.	v zig	c zag	v zug
9.	v bizz	c buzz	v bazz
10.	e zip	c zig	e zid

Lesson 115

1.	e	age	e	ape	c	ace
2.	c	cape	b	tape	b	gape
3.	c	wage	b	page	b	sage
4.	c	sale	e	same	e	sake
5.	c	Same	v	Sam	e	Sane
6.	e	race	c	rake	v	rack
7.	v	can	c	cane	e	came
8.	c	wade	e	wake	e	wave
9.	b	faze	c	gaze	i	haze
10.	c	made	e	mare	e	male

Lesson 120

1.	b	set	c	jet	b	let
2.	b	cob	b	mob	c	job
3.	c	age	s	aje	e	ace
4.	e	Jame	e	Jade	c	Jane
5.	b	ham	c	jam	b	ram
6.	c	Jeb	r	Jed	e	Jet
7.	v	jig	c	jog	v	jug
8.	v	Jam	c	Jim	v	Jem
9.	v	job	c	jab	v	jub
10.	c	Jack	v, e	Jane	e	Jake

Lesson 125

1.	v	bit	c	bite	v	bat
2.	b	Bike	b	Mike	c	Hike
3.	e	side	e	site	c	size
4.	c	line	e	lime	e	life
5.	b	file	b	mile	c	tile
6.	b	nine	c	mine	b	fine
7.	b	ripe	b	wipe	c	pipe
8.	c	time	b	mime	b	dime
9.	b	hive	c	five	b	live
10.	e	pike	e	pine	c	pile

Lesson 130

1.	c	shop	v	ship	v	shap
2.	b	fish	b	wish	c	dish
3.	c	shake	e	shame	e	shave
4.	v	mash	v	mesh	c	mush
5.	b	rod	b	cod	c	shod
6.	c	shot	e	shop	e	shock
7.	e, v	Jack	c	Josh	e, v	Jake
8.	c	shack	v	shuck	v	shock
9.	b	lash	b	rash	c	sash
10.	e	shush	e	shut	c	shun

Lesson 140

1.	r	p	c	q	r	b
2.	c	go	b	so	b	no
3.	c	quack	s	quak	v	quake
4.	e	quip	c	quit	e	quill
5.	c	no	e	not	e	non
6.	b	lick	b	pick	c	quick
7.	c	quote	v	quite	v	quate
8.	s	qiz	s	quis	c	quiz
9.	c	quite	b	kite	s	kwite
10.	b	make	c	quake	b	lake

Lesson 145

1.	c	pure	b	qure	b	cure
2.	v	male	c	mule	v	mole
3.	v	rile	v	role	c	rule
4.	s	huje	c	huge	v	hug
5.	e	muse	e	mute	c	mule
6.	b	tune	b	dune	c	June
7.	c	cube	b	tube	b, e	Jude
8.	b	fuse	c	use	b	ruse
9.	v	Lake	c	Luke	v	Like
10.	v	fuzz	v, e	fuss	c	fuse

Lesson 150

1.	c	stake	e	state	e	stage
2.	b	shack	v, e	stake	c	stack
3.	c	stick	v	stack	v	stock
4.	c	step	e	stem	e	stet
5.	v	must	c	mist	v	mast
6.	v	stag	s	staje	c	stage
7.	c	best	b	nest	b	pest
8.	b	dust	c	rust	b	gust
9.	b	fast	b	last	c	vast
10.	c	paste	b	taste	b	baste

Lesson 155

1.	e	beef	e	bee	c	beet
2.	c	sheep	b	steep	b	seep
3.	v	deer	c	veer	b	steer
4.	b	meek	c	week	b	peek
5.	r	beep	c	deep	r	peep
6.	c	Need	v	Ned	s	Nede
7.	e	seed	e	seep	c	seek
8.	v	red	s	rede	c	reed
9.	s	fede	c	feed	v	fed
10.	b	deem	c	seem	b	teem

Lesson 160

1.	c	camp	e	cap	e	came
2.	v,e	dumb	c	damp	v	domp
3.	b	samp	b	shamp	c	stamp
4.	c	romp	v	ramp	v	rump
5.	c	lamp	v	lump	v	limp
6.	c	bump	r	dump	r	pump
7.	v	stamp	v	stump	c	stomp
8.	c	jump	b	hump	b	lump
9.	e	ran	e	ram	c	ramp
10.	c	hump	e	hum	e, v	hume

Lesson 165

1.	c	oak	e	oat	e	oar
2.	b	boat	b	coat	c	goat
3.	c	roar	b	soar	b	boar
4.	b	coast	b	roast	c	toast
5.	e	boar	e	boast	c	boat
6.	b	foal	c	goal	b	coax
7.	v	hox	c	hoax	b	coax
8.	b	toad	c	road	b	load
9.	b	oak	v	sock	c	soak
10.	b, e	foam	b, e	roam	c	moan

Lesson 170

1.	c	stay	e	state	s	sta
2.	b	nay	c	may	b	ray
3.	b	bay	r	pay	c	day
4.	b	Kay	b	Jay	c	Fay
5.	e	lace	c	lay	e	late
6.	c	ray	e	race	e	rage
7.	e	pace	e	page	c	pay
8.	e, v	sam	e	same	c	say
9.	e	hate	e, v	hat	c	hay
10.	c	way	e	wage	e	wave

Lesson 1

Lesson Objectives

1. Students will identify the letters a through e.
2. Students will learn the terminology capital and small letters.
3. Students will distinguish between capital and small letters.
4. Students will say the short a sound.
5. Students will write the letters A a.

Preparation

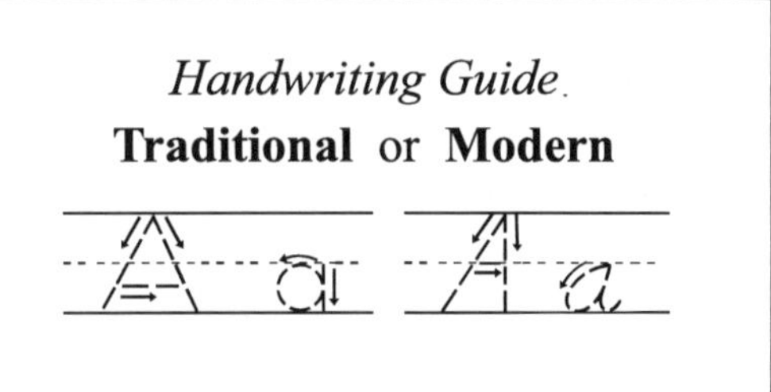

* Cut apart alphabet flashcards.
* Workbook page, blue crayon
* Prepare handwriting paper.[1]
  Print the student's name on the top line.
  Skip a line, print an A on the next line,
  print a on the next line, print Aa on the next.

Teaching

1. Use the flashcards (a through e) to drill the names of the letters.

2. Put capital letters in a row, put corresponding small letters underneath. Introduce terms. Say: **The big letters are capital letters, say "capital letters".**

3. **Point to the capital** (choose various letters)**. We'll call the other letters small letters. Point to the small** (choose various letters). Mix up the cards and ask the student to pick up various small and capital letters.

4. Pick up the letter a. Ask: **What is the name of this letter?** (Answer: a) **The name of this letter is a. Letters not only have names they also have sounds. One of the sounds this letter has is the short a sound.**

   Short a makes the *a* sound like the beginning sound of apple. (Emphasize the a.) **Say *a*** (student makes the sound). **Say short a goes *a*.** Turn to lesson 1 in the workbook. Have the student color all the bubbles with the letter that makes the *a* sound blue. Color the other bubbles red.

   T4

5. **Now we will write the letter a**[1] (see handwriting guide).
   The students should write their names underneath where it is printed, then copy the letters at the beginning of each row 3 times using correct spacing (one or two fingers). Ask the students to read the paper.

[1] If you purchased a McRuffy Press Kindergarten SE Handwriting book, use the corresponding page as the handwriting practice and disregard the instructions to prepare handwriting paper found in the Teacher's Manual. The handwriting workbook provides additional handwriting activities.

Lesson 2

Lesson Objectives

1. Students will identify the letters f through j.
2. Students will review short a sound.
3. Students will learn the b sound.
4. Students will write the letter b.

Preparation

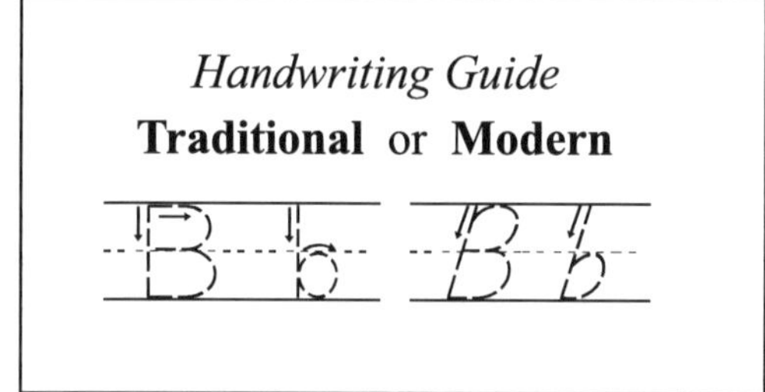

* Cut apart alphabet flashcards.
* Prepare handwriting paper.[1]
  Line 1 2 3 4 5
  name, blank, b, B, Bb
* Workbook page, brown and red crayon

Teaching

1. Use flashcards (f through j) to drill names of letters. Review the terms capital and small letters.

2. Use the a, A, b, B flashcards, and have the student say the names and sounds of the letters. Mix up the cards. Say: **Point to a letter that makes the *a* sound.** (Repeat a few times.)

3. **Today we will learn a new letter sound. It is the sound of this letter.** Point to the b flashcard. **Do you know what letter this is?** (b) **B makes the *b* sound. Say *b*.** *(b)* **Can you think of things that begin with the *b* sound?**

   Have the student say words that begin with b. Turn to lesson 2 in the workbook. Have the student color the bears that have the letter that makes the *b* sound brown and the *a* sound red.

4. Practice writing the letter b.[1]

[1] If you purchased a McRuffy Press Kindergarten SE Handwriting book, use the corresponding page as the handwriting practice and disregard the instructions to prepare handwriting paper found in the Teacher's Manual. The handwriting workbook provides additional handwriting activities.

Lesson 3

Lesson Objectives

1. Students will identify letters k through o.
2. Students will review a and b sounds.
3. Students will blend b and a sounds.
4. Students will write blends.

Preparation

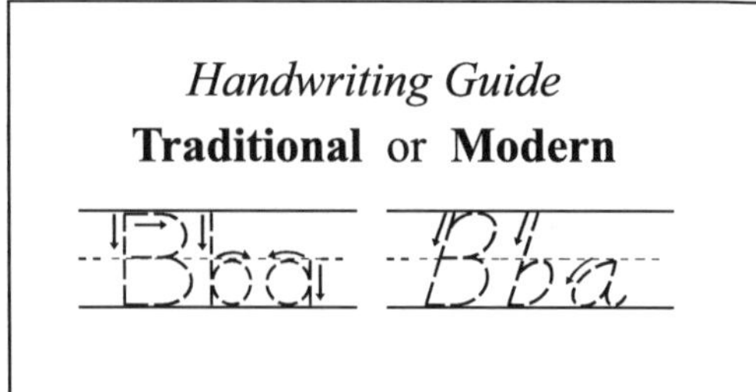

* Cut apart alphabet flashcards.
* Prepare handwriting paper.[1]
  Line 1 2 3 4 5
  name, blank, ba, ab, Ba
* Workbook page

Teaching

1. Use flashcards (k through o) to drill names of letters. Review the terms capital and small letters.

2. Use the a, A, b, B flashcards and have the student say the names and sounds of the letters. Mix up the cards. Say **Point to a letter that makes the *a* sound.**

3. **Raise your left hand. Today we will put the b and a sounds together. When we do this, we start with the letter on the left, make its sound, then add the next sound. Look at these two letters.** Show the student b and a. Put them next to each other to make the blend *ba.*

   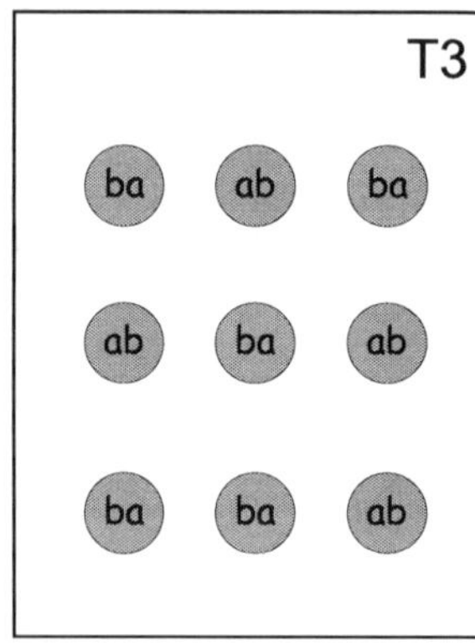

   Ask: **What sound does the b make?** (*b*) **What sound does the letter a make?** (*a*) **When we put sounds together, we say we blend them. Say blend.** (*blend*) **Now we will blend the letters b and a. Remember to start with the letter on the left. Say *b-a, ba.***

   Repeat for the blend ab. Use the workbook page for Lesson 3 to have the student practice blends. You may ask students to cover certain blends with small object such as pennies, bingo chips, or counters. For example: Cover all the ba blends. Or, cover the ab blends on the second row.

4. **Now let's look at the handwriting paper. What is the first blend you see under your name?** (*ba*) **What is the next blend?** (*ab*) **What is the last blend?** (*ba*)

   Now have the students write their name and each blend three times.[1] When they have finished, have them read the paper.

[1] If you purchased a McRuffy Press Kindergarten SE Handwriting book, use the corresponding page as the handwriting practice and disregard the instructions to prepare handwriting paper found in the Teacher's Manual. The handwriting workbook provides additional handwriting activities.

Lesson 4

Lesson Objectives

1. Students will identify the letters p through t.
2. Students will learn the terminology vowel and consonant.
3. Students will review blends.
4. Students will write blends.

Preparation

* Cut apart alphabet flashcards.
* Workbook page
* Prepare handwriting paper.[1]
  Line 1 2 3 4 5
  name, blank, Ab, ba, ab

Handwriting Guide
Traditional or **Modern**

Aab Aab

Teaching

1. Use flashcards (p through t) to drill names of the letters. Have the student identify capital and small letters.

2. **There are two kinds of letters. One kind of letter is a vowel. The other kind of letter is called a consonant. Say vowel.** (vowel) **Say consonant.** (consonant) **So far you have learned two letter sounds, *a* and *b*.**

   The letter a is a vowel. There are only five vowels in the alphabet. They are a, e, i, o, and u. All the other letters are consonants. The letter b is a consonant. Use the a and b flashcards. **Which letter is a vowel? Which letter is a consonant?**

3. Review blends using the workbook page. Have students practice reading the row of blends at the top of the page. Circle the pictures that begin with the blend *ba*.

   Pictures: duck, bat, alligator, bag, giraffe, bath tub.

4. **You will write two sounds together again today. What do we call two sounds put together?** (blend) **Does the first (second, third) blend begin with a vowel or consonant?**

   Have the students write their names and then write each blend 3 times.[1] When they have finished, have them read the paper.

[1] If you purchased a McRuffy Press Kindergarten SE Handwriting book, use the corresponding page as the handwriting practice and disregard the instructions to prepare handwriting paper found in the Teacher's Manual. The handwriting workbook provides additional handwriting activities.

Lesson 5

Lesson Objectives

1. Students will review the letters a through t.
2. Students will review the terms vowel, consonant, capitals, small letters.
3. Students will take an assessment of a, b and blends.
4. Students will write blends.

Preparation

* Workbook page
* Prepare handwriting paper.[1]
  Line 1 2 3 4 5
  name, blank, Ba, ba, ab

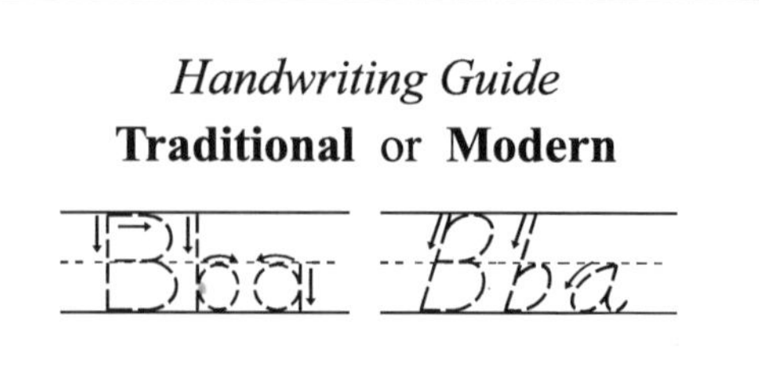

Teaching

1. Use flashcards (a through t) to review letters.

2. Have the student pick out the flashcards that are vowels. Use the vowel chart and match the flashcards to the chart. **What are all the other letters called?** (consonants) Ask various questions like: Pick up a capital letter. Is it a vowel or a consonant?

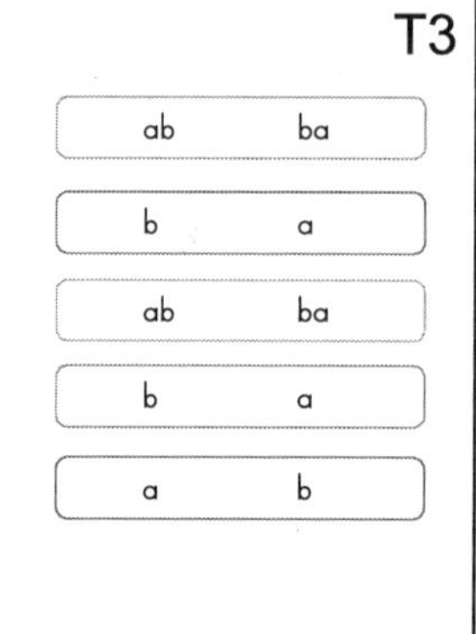

3. **Now let's see what you've learned the last few days. Look at your workbook. Look at the first box. See the number one beside it.**

   Give the student the following directions:
   1. **Circle the blend *ba.***
   2. **Circle the *b* sound.**
   3. **Circle *ab.***
   4. **Circle the vowel.**
   5. **Circle *a.***

4. **You will write two sounds together again today. What do we call two sounds put together?** (blend) **Does the first (second, third) blend begin with a vowel or consonant?**

   Have the students write their name and then write each blend 3 times.[1] When they have finished, have them read the paper.

[1] If you purchased a McRuffy Press Kindergarten SE Handwriting book, use the corresponding page as the handwriting practice and disregard the instructions to prepare handwriting paper found in the Teacher's Manual. The handwriting workbook provides additional handwriting activities.

Lesson 6

Lesson Objectives

1. Students will identify the letters u through z.
2. Students will learn the *c* sound and the blend *ca.*
3. Students will practice listening skills.
4. Students will write the letter c and blends.

Preparation

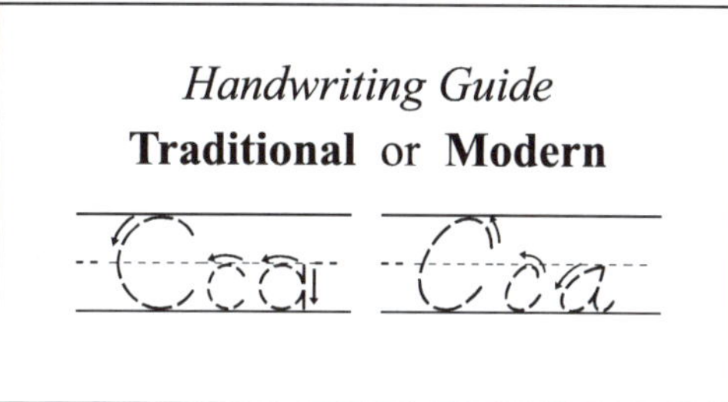

* Cut apart alphabet flashcards.
* Prepare a handwriting paper.
  Line 1 2 3 4 5
  name, blank, C, c, ca
* Workbook page, crayons

Teaching

1. Use the flashcards (u through z) to drill the names of the letters.

2. Write the letters a and b. Review their sounds. Review the blends ab and ba. Then say, **Today you are going to learn a new letter sound.** Write the letter c. **What letter is this?** (c) **The letter c has two sounds. It sometimes makes the s sound, *s* , but the sound we are going to use for now is the k sound. Say *k.*** *(k)* **Now blend c and a. Say *ca.*** *(ka* or *ca)*

3. **Let's practice what you've learned. Look at your workbook page. What shapes do you see on this page?** (circles and squares) **Some of the shapes have single letters. Some of the shapes have blends. I will give you directions for coloring the shapes. Listen carefully.**

   1. **Color the circle that has the *ba* sound blue.**
   2. **Color the square that has the *k* sound red.**
   3. **Color the square that has the *b* sound brown.**
   4. **Color the circle that has the *ka* sound green.**
   5. **Color the circle that has the *a* sound yellow.**
   6. **Color the square that has the *ba* sound purple.**
   7. **Color the square that has the *ka* sound orange.**
   8. **Color the circle that has the *ab* sound black.**

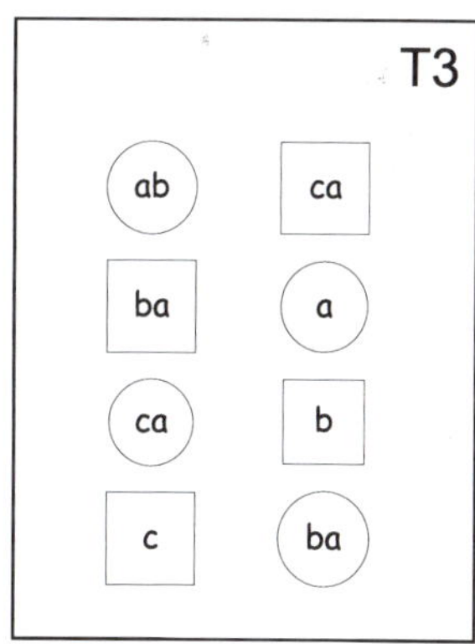

4. Have the students practice writing the letters and blends.

Games:

The Fish Pond - letter recognition
Go Bananas - letter recognition

This box identifies when you may start playing a game. Games are found in the Resource Pack.

The games can be played any lesson after this one. Some folders have more than one way to play. The appropriate concept is identified (letter recognition in this case).

Lesson 7

Lesson Objectives

1. Students will begin the daily routine.
2. Students will review c, b, and a.
3. Students will identify pictures that begin with the *k* sound.
4. Students will write the letter c and blends.

Preparation

* Use flashcards to review the alphabet
* Workbook page
* Prepare a handwriting paper
  Line 1 2 3 4 5
  name, blank, Cc, ca, Ca

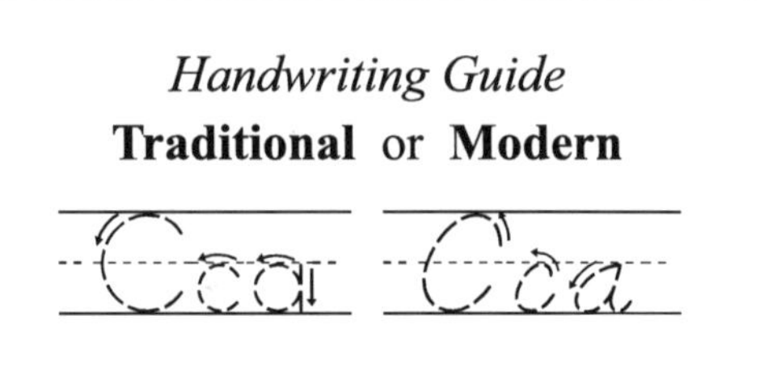

Teaching

1. See teaching the daily routine in the reference section.

2. Write the letters a, b, and c. Ask students if they can hear one of these sounds at the beginning of each of these words: **bat** (b), **call** (c), **add** (a)

   The word call rhymes with tall. They both end with the *all* sound. Can you make another word that rhymes with *all* and begins with *b*? (ball)

   The word bat rhymes with hat. They both end with *at*. Can you think of another word that rhymes with bat and begins with *c*? (cat)

   The work add rhymes with sad. Sad has the *ad* sound at the end of it. Can you make another word that rhymes with add by putting a b at the beginning? (bad)

3. Students should practice reading the row of blends at the top of the workbook page.

   Next, students will write a c under the pictures that begin with the *c* sound and a b under the pictures that begin with the *b* sound. The pictures are (row 1) balloon, cat, camera (row 2) can, bear, candle.

4. Have the students practice writing the letters and blends.

Lesson 8

Lesson Objectives

1. Students will review the letters of the alphabet.
2. Students will learn the t sound.
3. Students will write the letter t and blends.

Preparation

* Workbook page
* Prepare a handwriting paper.
Line 1 2 3 4 5
name, blank, Tt, at, ta

Handwriting Guide
Traditional or **Modern**

Teaching

1. Use the flashcards to review the letters of the alphabet.

2. Write the letters a, b and t. Point to b. **What letter is this?** (b*)* **Is b a consonant or a vowel?** (consonant) Point to the a. **What letter is this?** (a) **Is "a" a vowel or a consonant?** (vowel) **Remember when we put two sounds together we call it a blend. Try to blend b and a. Say *ba.*** *(ba)*

   Today you will learn a new letter sound. What letter is this? Point to the t. (*t*) **T makes the *t* sound. Now let's add the t sound to the end of the blend *ba.* Say *ba--t.*** *(ba--t)*

   Repeat the procedure for the words tab and at.

   Can you think of words that rhyme with *at*? Raise your hand every time I say a word that ends with the a-t sound, *at*: (sat, bad, ham, pat, rat, tab, cat)

   Use page 8 of the workbook to practice reading blends the two lines of blends. Next, students will circle the pictures that begin with t. You may tell students the names of the pictures: train, apple, tree, butterfly, rabbit.

3. Write the letters and blends using the handwriting paper. Have the student read the paper after it is completed.

Lesson 9

Lesson Objectives

1. Students will review the *t* sound.
2. Students will review the terms, consonant and vowel.
3. Students will create a story.
4. Students will write the blend ta and the letter t.

Preparation

* Workbook page, blue and red crayons
* Prepare a handwriting paper for the blend ta, Ta, and letters Tt.

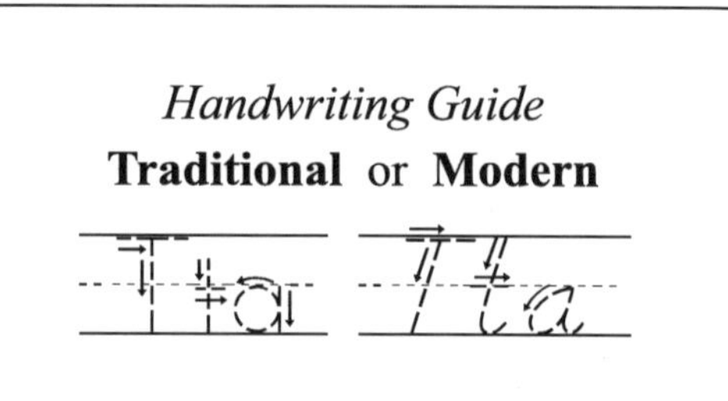

Teaching

1. Write the letters a and t. Point to t. **What letter is this?** (t) **Is t a consonant or a vowel?** (consonant) Point to the a. **What letter is this?** (a) **Is "a" a vowel or a consonant?** (vowel)

   Remember when we put two sounds together we call it a blend. Try to blend t and a. Say *ta.* *(ta)* Repeat the procedure for the blend *at.*

2. Use the workbook to practice identifying vowels and consonants. Color the balloons with vowels on them red. Color the balloons with consonants on them blue.

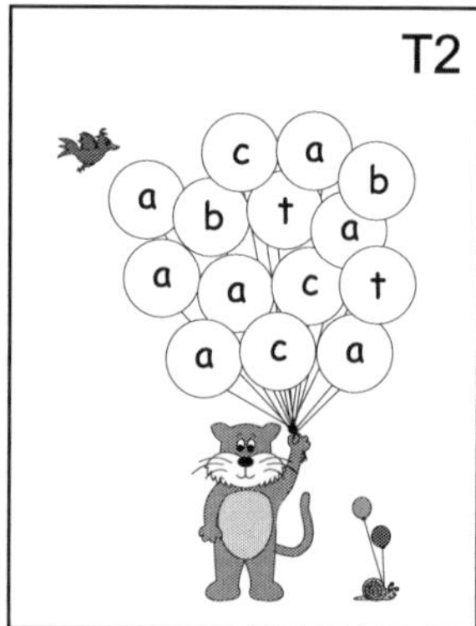

3. Say the following words to students: **Terry, terrified, tiger**. Ask students what sound these begin with (*t*). Have students think of other words that begin with t. Make a list for the students.

   Say: **Today we will make up a story that uses a lot of t words. The story will be called, Terry the Terrified Tiger. What does terrified mean?** (scared, afraid) **What do you think the tiger will be afraid of?**

   You may do the story one of two ways. Have the students create their own stories drawing pictures (no words). You may also decide to have students dictate the story to you, either individually or as a group. You may want to start with the following: **Once upon a time, there was a tiger named Terry. He was terrified of the dark.**

   The plot could be Terry getting over his fear. He may have help, like that of a tiny toad. Maybe there could be a tattletale in the story that tells the other animals that Terry is terrified.

   If the story is written as a group, have students draw pictures to illustrate the story.

4. Write the blends *ta, Ta* , and the letters Tt.

Lesson 10

Lesson Objectives

1. Students will take the Lesson 10 assessment.
2. Students will review any concepts missed on the assessment.
3. Students will review the story from Lesson 9.

Preparation

* Assessment 10 (in the workbook)
* Assessment progress chart for recording assessment score (in the Resource Pack)
* Story or stories from Lesson 9

Teaching

1. Give the student the assessment. The student should print their name on the lines at the top of the page. **Look at the boxes. Find the box that has the number one by it. Find ta** (give correction if necessary). **Good, now take your pencil and circle *ta*.**

   Look at the box underneath it. This box has the number 2 by it.
   Find the blend *ba*. Circle it.

   3. Circle *c*

   4. Circle *ab*

   5. Circle *t*

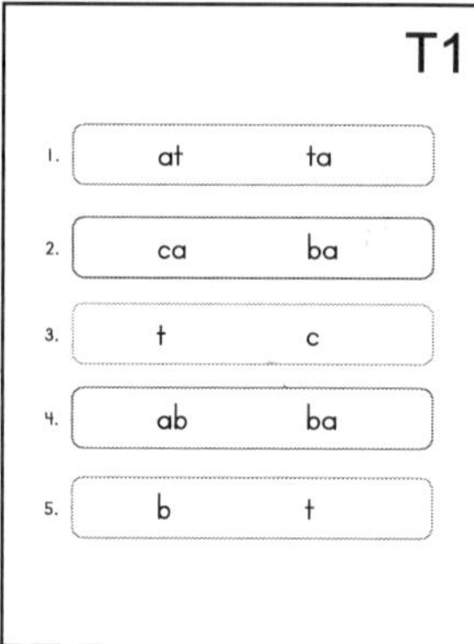

2. Review any items that were missed on the assessment.

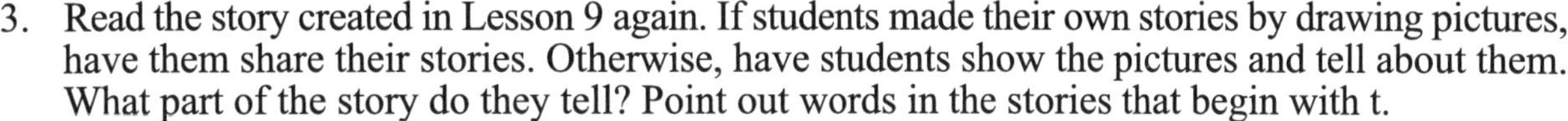

3. Read the story created in Lesson 9 again. If students made their own stories by drawing pictures, have them share their stories. Otherwise, have students show the pictures and tell about them. What part of the story do they tell? Point out words in the stories that begin with t.

Lesson 11

Lesson Objectives

1. Students will follow left to right progression.
2. Students will form words.
3. Students will learn the meanings of the words tab and cab.
4. Students will write words.

Preparation

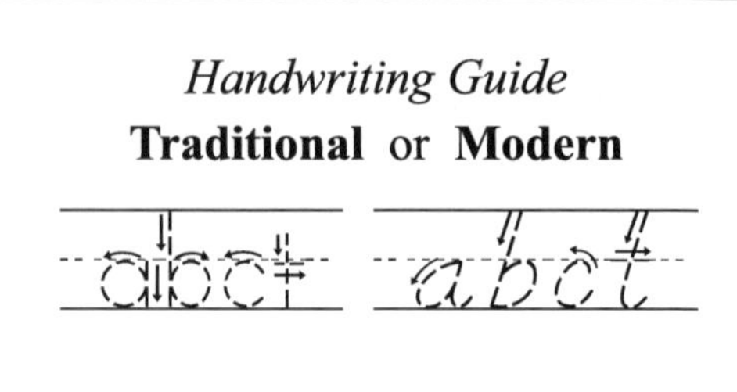

* Workbook page
* Left-Right Arrow Chart (found in the Resource Pack)
* Optional: soda can (opened or unopened), toy truck or tractor with a cab or a toy taxi cab (see part 3)
* Handwriting paper with the words cat, tab, and cab

Teaching

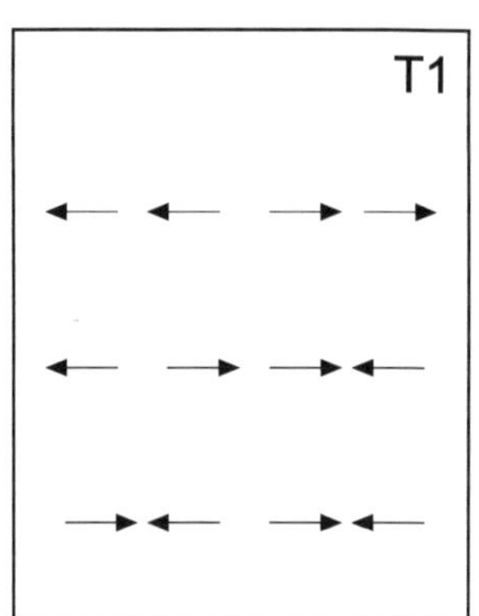

1. It is important that students know to read from left to right. Younger students may not make a clear distinction between the two. If a student needs practice on this skill, use the Left-Right Arrow Chart. Put the chart on a wall. Have the student stand a few feet back.

   Point to the first arrow. Have the student move both arms in the direction of the arrow while calling out left or right. Do the first row the same way. Have the student try the next two rows without your help.

2. **Today you are going to put three letters together. Look at the page for lesson 11 in your workbook. Look at the big letters at the top of the page. What letters do you see?** (c a t) **Look at the numbers and the arrow under the letters.**

   When you read words, you start at the left and read to the right. You read in the direction of the arrow. Say each of the sounds quickly and listen for the word it makes. Help the student sound out the words on the practice page.

T2

c a t
1 2 3

t a b
1 2 3

c a b
1 2 3

3. Write the words cat, tab, and cab. Ask students to tell what the word cat means. Next ask: **Do you know what a tab is?** (It is a small flap that makes things easier to handle.) You may use the can and point out the tab. Ask: **How does it make the can easier to use?** (You can lift the tab to open the can.) Add these words to a vocabulary list and review throughout the week.

   What is a cab? (It is something people can ride in.) **The part of a truck you ride in is called the cab.** (You may use toys to demonstrate this.) **Another kind of cab is a taxi cab. If someone needs to go someplace and they don't have a car, they may call a taxi cab. A person will come in a car and take someone where they need to go. The person that rides has to pay the taxi cab driver.**

4. Have the student write the words cat, tab, and cab.

Lesson 12

Lesson Objectives

1. Learn the *p* sound
2. Review beginning sounds
3. Write the letter p and the blend pa

Preparation

* Workbook page
* Prepare handwriting paper with the blend pa and the letters P and p.

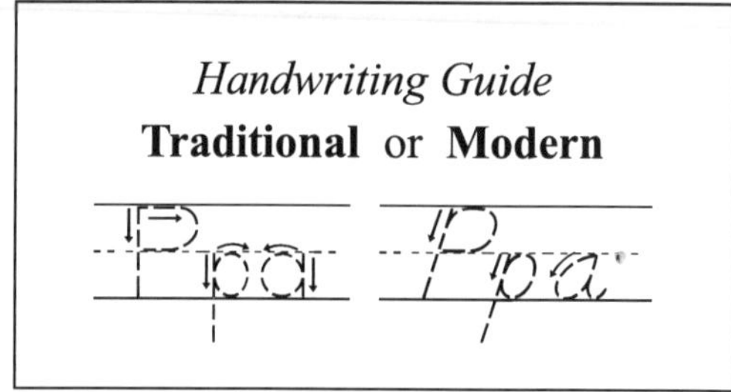

Teaching

1. **Today you are going to learn a new letter sound.** Write the letter p. **Point to the letter p. The letter p makes the *p* sound. Say the p sound.** *(p)* **Think of things that begin with the *p* sound.**

   Have the student say words that begin with p. **Now let's blend p and a.** Write the letter a after the p and have the student read the blend.

   Say the following words. Have students raise their hands if they hear the *pa* blend:

   Pacifier, bat, pan, pass, pot, patch

2. Have the student say words that begin with the consonant sounds that they have learned (b, c, and t). Next have the student do the workbook page. Practice reading the row of blends. Write the beginning sound of each picture.

   Next, have children use blank paper or the back of the worksheet. Have students draw pictures (one each) of things that begin with the *b, c, p,* and *t* sounds.

3. Write the letters and blend.

Lesson 13

Lesson Objectives

1. Make words using the letter p.
2. Listen for ending sounds.
3. Review vocabulary.
4. Handwriting pat, tap, cap

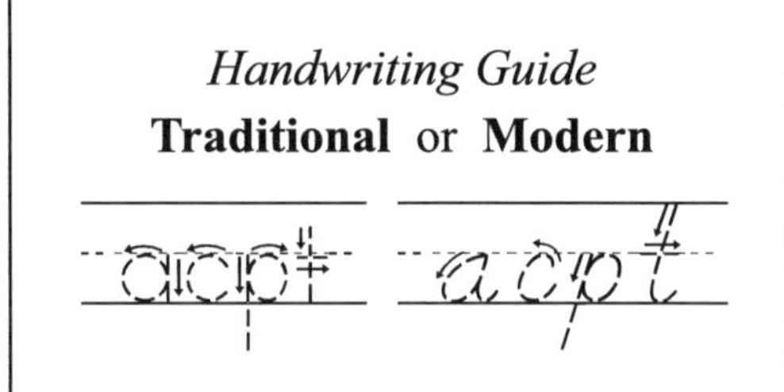

Preparation

* Workbook page
* Prepare handwriting sheet.

Teaching

1. Form the words bat, cat, pat, tap, and cap. Put the letters a-t together. Switch the beginning letters b, c, and p. Have students read the words (bat, cat, pat). Put the letters a-p together. Switch the beginning letters c and t.Have the students read the words (cap and tap).

   Say the following words. Have the students raise their hands if they hear the *ap* blend:

   Nab, happy, sap, cat, apple, mat, map, tab, tap

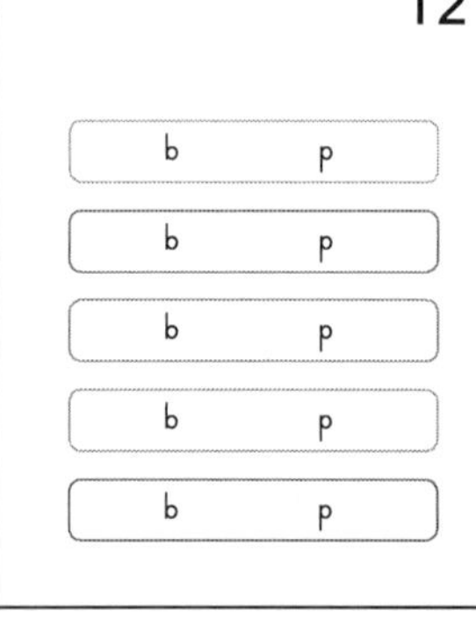

2. Write some of the words from step 1. Ask the student what is the ending sound of each word. Next put the letters b and p together. **These letters look a lot alike. They also sound a little alike, but when you say *b* you use your voice. When you say *p* you don't use your voice.**

   Have the student feel his or her throat as the student makes the sounds. Next have the student do the workbook page. **Find the number one. What letters are in the box?** *(b* and *p)* **In box one, circle the letter that makes the *p* sound.**

   In the next boxes listen for the ending sound of the words I say. The words will end with either b or p. In box 2, circle the sound you hear at the end of the word cap.

   In box _____, circle the sound you hear at the end of the word:

   3. tab
   4. tap
   5. cab

3. Review the vocabulary words: cab and tab (See Lesson 11 Teaching part 3). Add the word: tap: to hit lightly. Have students model tapping.

4. Have the student write the words pat, tap, and cap. The student should read the paper when finished.

Lesson 14

Lesson Objectives

1. Students will learn the sound of the letter n.
2. Students will create a story.
3. Students will write the words nab, nap, and can.

Handwriting Guide
Traditional or **Modern**

Preparation

* Workbook page, yellow and blue crayons
* Handwriting paper

Teaching

1. **Today you are going to learn a new letter sound.** Write the letter n. **Which letter is the new letter?** (n) **Point to the letter n. Can you guess what sound n makes? The letter n makes the *n* sound. Say the n sound.** *(n)* **Think of things that begin with the *n* sound.** Have the student say words that begin with n. **Now let's blend n and a.** Write the blend na and have the student read the blend. Repeat for a and n.

   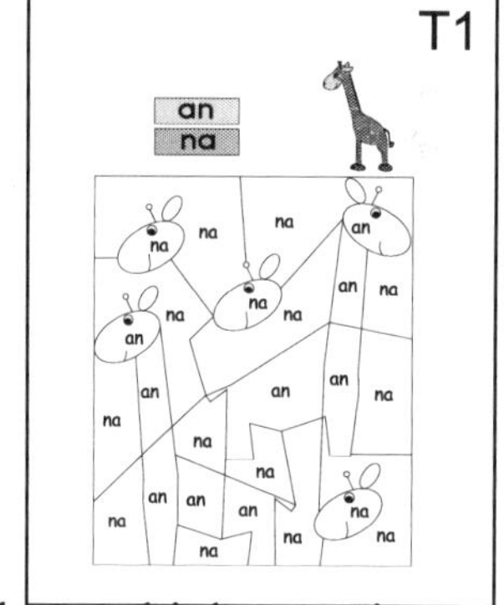

   Let's make some words with the letter n. Write the word nab. Have students attempt to read it. Ask: **What does the word nab mean?** Students may not know. Demonstrate nabbing by grabbing some object. Show the students the object. **I just nabbed this. What is another way to say what I did?** (grabbed, took, snatched, etc.) **When you nab something you are grabbing it. Pretend to nab something.** Students can act out nabbing something. You may ask students what they nabbed. (I nabbed a ________.)

   Students should know the meaning of nap. Highlight that the word can has multiple meanings. Write the words. Have students read them. **The word *can* has two meanings. It is a container. You put things in a can. It also means *able to do something*. I can swim. What does nap mean?** (to sleep) **It can be something you do. You will nap for an hour. It is also what we call sleeping for a short time. I will take a nap.**

   Have the student do the workbook page. Color the spaces with the *an* blend yellow. Color the spaces with the *na* blend blue.

   Add the words *can* and *nab* to the vocabulary list and review tap, tab, and cab.

2. **Nan nabbed nine nickels. What do you think she did with them? She could only spend the nickels on things that had an n in them. What could she buy? We will write a story telling what Nan bought with nine nickels.** Don't worry about the true cost of things. Nan may have found a really good garage sale. Buy up to nine things or some things could cost two or three nickels if you run short of ideas. Have students try to think of things with the n sound in them. If you run short of ideas some suggestions are: candy, cans of anything, banana, panda, fan, chicken, kitten, banjo, crayon, nuts, necklace, nest, noodle.

3. Have the student write the words nab, nap, and can.

Lesson 15

Lesson Objectives

1. Students will take an assessment.
2. Students will review any concepts missed on the assessment.
3. Students will tell stories.
4. Students will learn the words tan, pan, and ban.
5. Students will write the words tan, pan, and ban.

Preparation

* Lesson 15 assessment
* Handwriting paper with the words tan, pan, ban

Handwriting Guide

Traditional or **Modern**

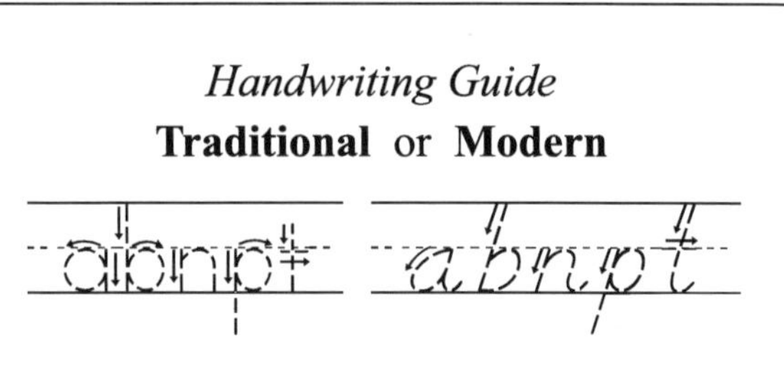

Teaching

1. The layout of this assessment is different. Now ten items are on the assessment. Help the student to follow the correct order using the numbers.

   Key: **1.** ***p*** **2. bat 3. ab 4. pat 5. tap**

   6. ***c*** **7. ta 8. an 9. cat 10. tab**

2. Review any answers missed on the assessment.

3. Have students tell about the stories they made in Lesson 14. If the story was completed with the teacher, read the story again. Talk about the things that have an n sound in them.

4. Write the rime *an*. Write the letters b, c, n, N, p, and t. **What letter would you put at the beginning of *an* to make a word that finishes this sentence; Lift the tab to open the _______.** (c-can)

   What letter would you put at the beginning of *an* to make a word that means something you cook with? (p-pan) **What letter makes *an* a word that means light brown?** If students don't know introduce it and add to the vocabulary list. (t-tan) **What letter would make *an* into a girl's name?** (N-Nan). **Why do we use the capital N?** (It is someone's name.)

   If I put b at the beginning of *an*, what word do I make? (ban) **What is a ban? It's a law or rule that is made to solve some problem. There is a ban on littering. What problem might this solve?**

   There is a ban on yelling in a library. What problem might this solve? Lots of places ban smoking. What problem might this solve? If you could ban something, what would you ban? (I would ban _________.) **Why?**

5. Have the student write the words tan, pan, and ban. The student should read it when finished.

Lesson 16

Lesson Objectives

1. Students will review beginning and ending blends.
2. Students will write words ending with n.

Preparation

* Lesson 16 Slider (in resource pack)
* Scissors, glue
* Copy master of the workbook page for Lesson 16 (see copy master section)
* Handwriting paper with the words an, ban, can, tan

Handwriting Guide
Traditional or **Modern**

abcnt abcnt

Note: there is no workbook page for lesson 16.

Teaching

1. Students will make the slider (printed on cardstock). A slider is a changing word drill. A copy master is provided to help you demonstrate the assembly of the slider. You may want to reproduce this first, in case students need a second copy. Students should cut along the dotted lines. Next, fold on the gray lines. The pictures of apples are to give students a reference point for applying glue. Put glue on the apples and stick it to the back of flap 1.

   Insert slide into holder. It should move freely. If not, trim from the top of the slide. As the slide is moved, it should complete a word that ends with *an*. Once completed, ask the students the following:

   Make your slider show the word that is:

   the first part of the word bandage (ban)
   something you cook with (pan)
   a light brown color (tan)
   a girl's name (Nan)
   something that holds beans, soup, or pop in the store. (can)

2. Have students write the words an, ban, can, tan..
   The student should read it when finished.

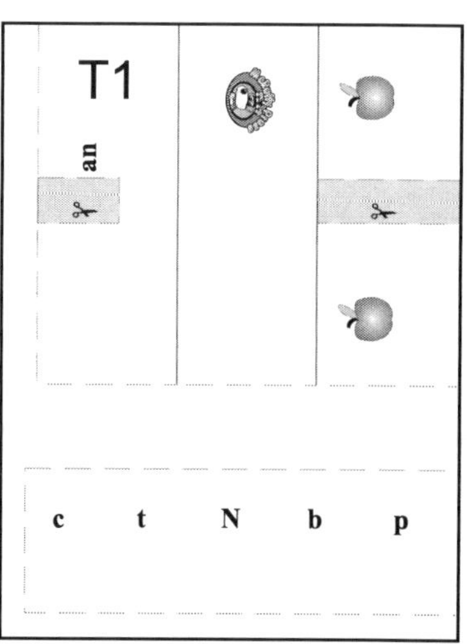

Lesson 17

Lesson Objectives

1. Students will learn the meanings of the words cap and tap.
2. Students will review blends.
3. Students will write words containing the letter P.

Preparation

* Workbook page, scissors
* Have the student pick three words to write.

Teaching

1. Write the word cap. **What is this word?** (cap) **What is a cap?** (It's something you wear on your head. It's like a hat.) **Pretend you are putting on a cap.** (Students should act out putting on a cap.) **What kind of cap did you put on? What does it look like? Where would you wear it?**

   Erase the c and replace it with t. **What is this word? (tap)** On a desk, table, or other surface do the following actions: slap your hand on table, knock on the table, and tap on the table. **Which time did I tap?** (third) Demonstrate a tap again or repeat all three if students weren't sure of the answer. **How was the tap different?** (It was softer.) **If I strike something softly it is a tap. Show me how to tap.**

2. Use the workbook page. Have the student cut out the boxes. Next, the student should sort the blends and the letter a in one stack face down. Put the consonants in another stack. Use the boxes to play a game. Have the student take a box from each stack and form a word (or blend if the letter a is drawn).

   If the student can read the word he or she gets a point. Keep playing (reshuffling the cards when necessary) until the student gets10 points.

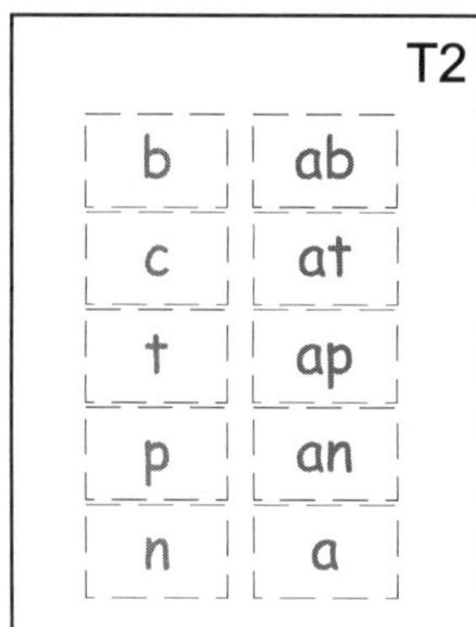

   A second game could be played with several variations. Ask students to make words based on meanings.

   1. Give a definition, like something you cook with (pan).
   2. Complete the sentence, A _____ says meow. (cat)
   3. Have students make a word that goes with your actions – such as tapping on a table (tap).
   4. Have students put together onset consonants with rimes and act them out, such as: **Put c and ap together. Act it out.** (Students would pretend putting on a cap.)

3. Have the student choose three words from the game to write.

Lesson 18

Lesson Objectives

1. Students will learn the s sound.
2. Students will learn words that begin with s.
3. Students will write the letter s.

Handwriting Guide
Traditional or **Modern**

Ss Ss

Preparation

* Paper, scissors
* Workbook page
* Handwriting paper with the letters s and S

Teaching

1. **Today you are going to learn a new letter sound.** Write the letter s. **Point to the letter s. The letter s makes the *s* sound. Say the s sound.** (*s*) **Think of things that begin with the *s* sound.** Have the student say words that begin with s. **Now let's blend s and a.**

   Have students take a piece of paper and fold it into fourths. Cut the fourths apart. Students will only need three of the pieces. Have students write the number 1 on a fourth, the number 2 on a fourth, and the number 3 on a fourth. **Listen to these words. They all have the s sound. If the s sound is at the beginning of the word, hold up the paper with the 1 on it. If the s sound is in the middle, hold up the paper with the 2 on it. If the s sound is at the end of the word, hold up the card with the 3 on it.**

   Snake (1), **bus** (3), **mister** (2), **compass** (3), **silly** (1), **lesson** (2), **sunny** (1), **messy** (2), **kindness** (3)

   On the workbook page, have the student practice reading the row of blends at the top of the page. Have the student write the beginning sounds of the pictures. The pictures are:
   Row 1, bat, snail, saw. Row 2, snake, star, pan

2. Write the words cap and bat. Have students read the words. **Look at the word cap. What if we replaced the c with s? What is the new word?** (sap) **Where does sap come from?** (Trees, it is the sticky stuff inside trees.) **Have you ever eaten sap? What do you put on pancakes?** (syrup) **Syrup is made from the sap of maple trees. It wouldn't taste very good right from the tree, but after it's cooked it tastes much better.**

   What word do we make when we replace the b in bat with s? (sat) **Stand up and act out the word sat.**

3. S is a difficult letter to write. Let the student practice writing S and s several times.

Lesson 19

Lesson Objectives

1. Students will use s as an ending sound.
2. Students will create a story.
3. Students will write words using the letter s.

Handwriting Guide
Traditional or **Modern**

Ss Ss

Preparation

* Workbook page
* Handwriting paper

Teaching

1. Write the word bass. **How many s's do you see in this word?** (two) **Are they at the beginning or end of the word?** (end) **Some words that have an s sound at the end are spelled with two s's.**

   What is a bass? I'll give you a hint. Raise your hand when you think you know. It swims. It lives in water. People catch them with hooks. (a fish) Have students act like a bass.

   Can you change the word bass into pass? Change the b to p. Ask students what it means to pass something. Have students act out the word pass. **You can pass a football or you can pass the potatoes. How are the two different kinds of passing different?** (fast-slow, throwing-handing, etc.)

   T1

   ap
   at
   ba
   pa
   s s s s s s

   Have the student complete the words on the workbook page by cutting and pasting the letter s. Draw lines to match the words to the correct pictures. Ask how the pictures match the words. **What does a tree have to do with sap?** (Sap comes from trees.) **Why does the chair match the word sat?** (It's something people may have sat on.) **Why does a fish match the word bass?** (A bass is a kind of fish.) **Why does a football match the word pass?** (You can pass a football.)

2. Silly Sam the Singing Snake. **Once upon a time there was a snake named Sam. He loved to sing. His singing wasn't very good because he hissed so much. Sam was very good at making the s sound, so he started singing songs about things with the s sound in them. We will create a story about the things Silly Sam the singing snake sang about. Remember, they must have the s sound in them. What are some things Sam can sing about?** Ideas: sunshine, swing sets, slithering, supper, bass, snails, snow, socks. Students can draw pictures and even make up songs that Silly Sam may have sung about. Students may use familiar tunes for the melody.

3. Have the student write the words pass, bass, and sat.

Lesson 20

Lesson Objectives

1. Students will take the Lesson 20 assessment.
2. Students will review missed concepts.
3. Students will review stories from Lesson 19.
4. Students will write the words sap, sat, pass.

Preparation

* Lesson 20 assessment
* Stories from lesson 19.
* Handwriting paper

Handwriting Guide
Traditional or **Modern**

Teaching

1. Have students circle the correct letter or word in each box on the assessment page:

   Key: **1.** ***s*** **2.** ***c*** **3. sat 4. nap 5. ban**
   6. cat 7. bass 8. sap 9. pan 10. nab

2. Review any missed concepts on the assessment.
3. Have students share stories from Lesson 19.
4. Have the students write the words sap, sat, pass.

Lesson 21

Lesson Objectives

1. Students will learn the sound of the letter h.
2. Students will match words and pictures.
3. Students will write the letters h and H, and the words has and hat.
4. Students will review words.

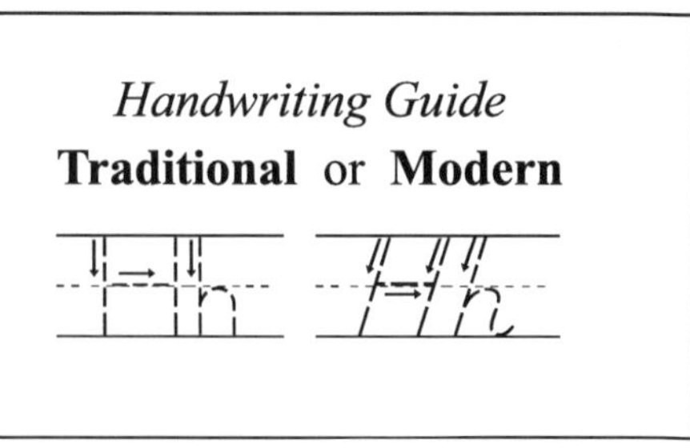

Preparation

* Workbook page
* Slider lesson 21 (It will be used in Lesson 22, also.)
* Scissors, glue

Teaching

1. **Today you are going to learn a new letter sound.** Write the letter h. **Point to the letter h. The letter h makes the *h* sound. Say the h sound.** (*h*) **Think of things that begin with the *h* sound.**

   Have the student say words that begin with h. **Now let's blend h and a.** Write the blend ha and have the student read the blend. Write the words, has and hat.

   What sound does the word has end with? (s or z) **In this word the s makes a little different sound. It sounds a little bit like the z sound. Sometimes if a word ends with an s sound, the s actually makes kind of a z sound.**

   Does the s sound at the end of the word pass make an s or a z sound? (s)
   How do you spell pass? (p-a-s-s)
   How many s's are at the end of the word *has*? (1)
   The s sound in the word *has* is only spelled with one s.

   Write the letters hap. **Read these letters. Can you think of a word that begins with hap?** (happy, happen, happiness, etc.)

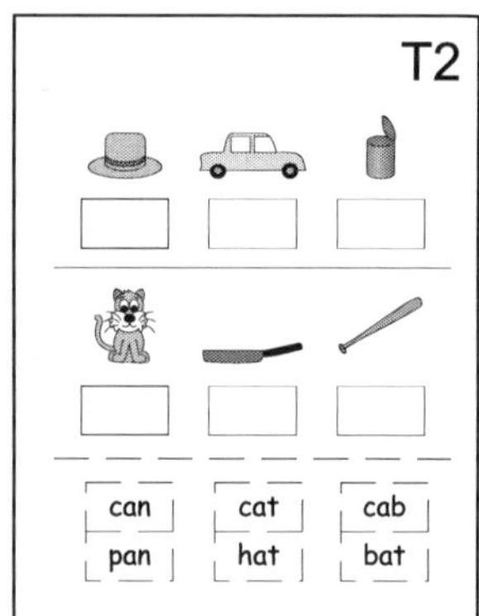

2. Use the workbook page. The student will cut and paste the correct word to the picture.

3. Have the students write the words and letters Hh, has, and hat.

4. Use the slider to review words. The copy master section of the Resource Pack has a copy master that can be reproduced. Students have a copy in the flash card pack. Ask students to make different words by sliding the ending and beginning consonant strips. Ask students which are real words and which are nonsense words.

   You may put questions in a problem-solving format.
   Make a word that rhymes with man. (can, ban, tan, pan)

   Ask students to find words based on meaning. For example, make a word that is something you wear on your head. (cap or hat) Have students question other students about words on the slider.

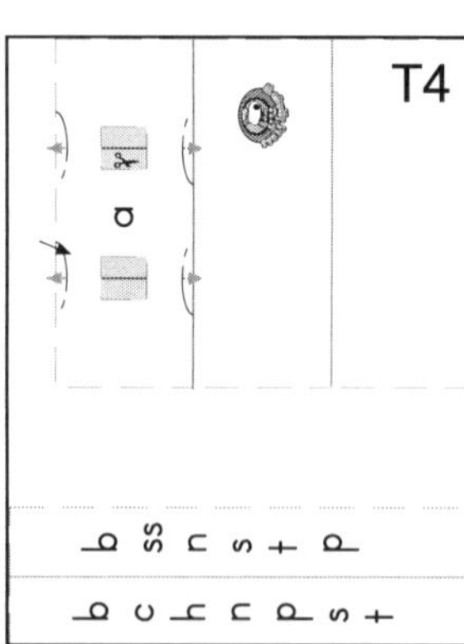

Lesson 22

Lesson Objectives

1. Students will learn a as a word.
2. Students will review words.
3. Students will write using correct spacing.

Preparation

* Workbook page
* Paper and pencil (or chalkboard)
* Slider from lesson 21
* Handwriting sheet
  Line 1. name 3. a pan 5. a cab

Handwriting Guide
Traditional or **Modern**

abcnp abcnp

Teaching

1. Write the letter a on the paper. **What letter is this?** (a) **We've used the letter a to make words. Today we'll learn a new word that uses the letter a. This word has only one letter in it. What letter is it?** (a) **That's right.**

   The letter a is a word. We sometimes use the word a before the names of things, like a car, or a horse. Look at the workbook page. On the page are names of three things that have the word a before them. Read the words and cut and glue the correct picture next to them.

   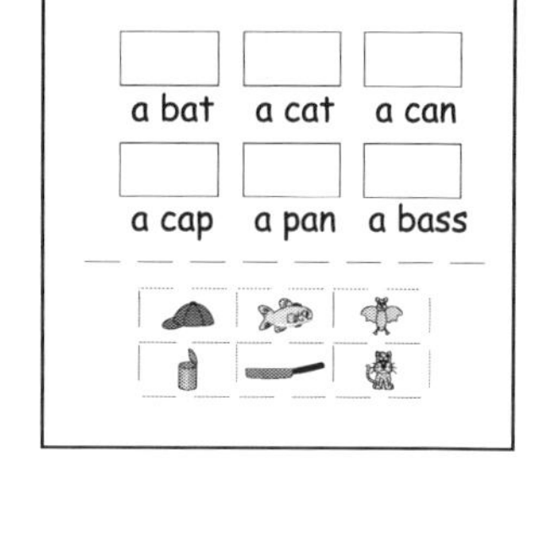

   Have students read the line of blends at the top of the page.

2. Students will use the slider to play a game. The teacher makes a word and shows it to one student. The student has to get the other students to guess the word. The student may act the word out, tell what it means, or use an incomplete sentence. For example: cat. The student can act like a cat, or say "It's an animal that is a pet.", or The (blank-the student can say blank or cover their mouth in place of the blank) purred loudly.

   The other students guess by making the word on the dial-a-words. In a homeschool setting the game can be played the same way with the teacher and the student taking turns guessing or giving clues.

3. **Look at the handwriting paper. How many words do you see on this paper?** (5) (counting the student's name) **Read the words.** (Give the student time to read them.)

   Look at the words a pan. Notice the space between a and pan. When we write words next to each other we leave a space. It helps us to see where one word ends and the next word begins. Make sure you leave a space about finger wide when you write the words.

Games:

The Fish Pond - Spelling
Go Bananas - Spelling
Ruff's Lunch - Slider Strip 1

Lesson 23

Lesson Objectives

1. Students will be introduce to sentences.
2. Students will write a sentence.

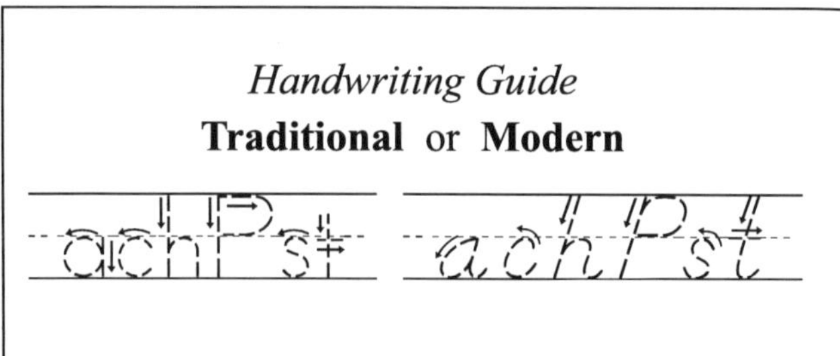

Preparation

* Workbook page
* Handwriting sheet with the sentence: Pat has a cat.

Teaching

1. **We can put words together to make sentences.** Write the sentence: Pat has a cat. **Can you read this sentence?** Have the students read the sentence.

   Point to the letter a. **What letter is this?** (a) **Remember sometimes the letter a is used as a word in a sentence. Now look at this sentence. Does the word Pat begin with a capital P or a small p?** (Capital P)

   Sentences always begin with a capital letter. Now look at the end of the sentence. What do you see? dot, circle, etc. **We put a mark after the last word in a sentence to show that the sentence has ended. A dot like this is called a period.**

   Replace the word cat with a blank: **Pat has a ________.** Ask students what other words they know that can replace cat. (hat, cap, bat, can, bass, pan)

   Have the students read the sentences on the workbook page. The students should cut out and glue the pictures above the words that match them.

2. Have the students write and read the sentence: Pat has a cat.

Lesson 24

Lesson Objectives

1. Students will read sentences.
2. Students will illustrate a sentence.
3. Students will write a sentence.

Preparation

* Workbook page
* Handwriting paper sentence:
  A cat has a hat.

Handwriting Guide
Traditional or **Modern**

Aachst Aachst

Teaching

1. Write the sentence: Nan can pass Pa___. **Read this sentence. A letter is missing. What letter should fill in the blank, b or t?** (t) Write the sentence: A __at is tan. **What's the missing letter, b or t?** (b)

   Have students do the same thing on the workbook page. Students will choose one of the two letters to complete the word. Circle the correct letter and write it on the blank. Number one is an example. Have students trace the n and the circle. If students need additional help, tell students what the unfinished word should be.

   1. pan, 2. cat, 3. hat, 4. sat, 5. cap, 6. tab.

T1, T2

1. Pat can tap a pa n .	(n) t
2. A ca__ has a bass.	p t
3. Pat has a tan __at.	h s
4. A cat __at.	b s
5. Nan has a __ap.	s c
6. A can has a ta__.	b c

2. Have students draw a picture for one or more of the sentences from the workbook page.

3. Review the term sentence and period. Have the student point out the capital letter at the beginning and the period at the end. Remind the student to use correct spacing between words.

   Have the students write the sentence: A cat has a hat.

Lesson 25

Lesson Objectives

1. Students will take an assessment.
2. Students will review missed concepts.
3. Students will create sentences.
4. Students will write the sentence:
   Pat can tap a hat.

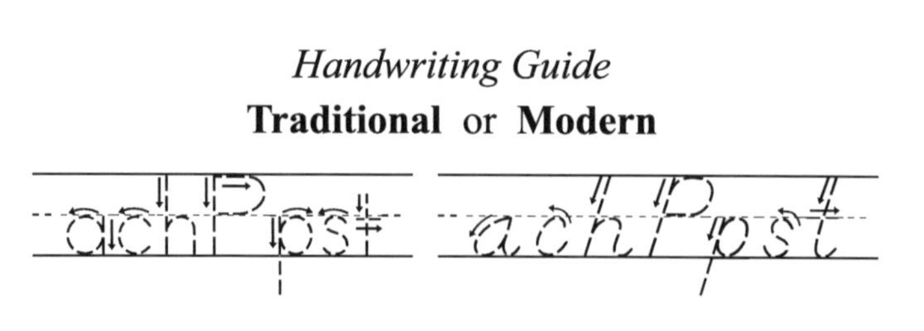

Preparation

* Lesson 25 assessment
* Handwriting paper

Teaching

1. Students will circle the correct word on the assessment page.

   1. has 2. sat 3. bass 4. hat 5. sap

   6. can 7. tab 8. has 9. nap 10. tan

2. Review any missed concepts on the assessment.

3. Students will write their own sentence and draw a picture to illustrate it. Remind students to begin the sentence with a capital letter and end it with a period. If necessary give students a beginning:

   Nan can ______, Pat has __________, A cat can________

4. Write the sentence: Pat can tap a hat.

Notes:

Handwriting Guides will now only be included in weeks that new letters are introduced.

Beginning with Lesson 26 a new First Step Reader is introduced every 5 lessons until Lesson 76 when the 20 longer books begin.

Have the students read the word list on the back of the First Step Reader before reading the story inside. The books should be reread and the word list reviewed each day as a part of the lesson until a new reader begins. Rereading builds reading fluency as well as a larger reading vocabulary.

Lesson 26

Lesson Objectives

1. Students will learn the word **the**.
2. Students will write the word **the** in a sentence.
3. Students will read the First Step Reader *Sat*.

Preparation

* Workbook page, crayons
* Handwriting paper with the sentence: The cat sat.

Handwriting Guide
Traditional or **Modern**

the the

Teaching

1. Write the word *the*. **What are the consonants in this word?** (t and h) **What is the vowel?** (e) **This is a word I will not have you sound out. The word is the. Say the.** (the) **Remember, t-h-e spells the.**

   T and h together make one sound that is different than the sound they make in the words we've learned so far. Th makes a *th* sound in *the*. That's why we'll just remember the word instead of sounding it out. We use the word *the* like we use the word a.

   ***The* comes before a word that is a thing, like the hat, or the doll.**

   Look at the workbook page. Underline the word *the* each time you see it in the sentence. Now read the sentence. Draw a picture to go with it.

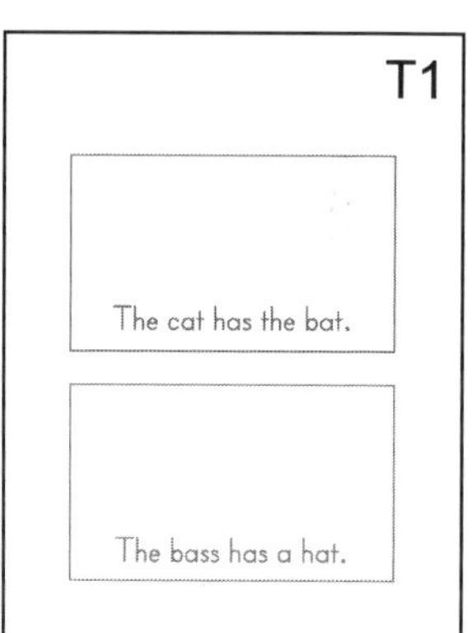

2. Use the handwriting paper to write and read the sentence: The cat sat.

3. **Has an animal ever frightened you? An animal frightens someone in the book. We'll read the story to find out what this animal is.** Have the students read the First Step Reader *Sat*. Read the word list on the back before beginning the story.

Pat sat. The cat sat. The bat sat. The bass sat.

Lesson 27

Lesson Objectives

1. Students will complete sentences.
2. Students will write a sentence.
3. Students will read the First Step Reader *Sat*.
4. Students will act out the story.

Preparation

* Workbook page
* Handwriting paper with the sentence: The cat can bat.

Teaching

1. Show the student the sentence on the handwriting paper. Review the term sentence and period. Have the student point out the capital letter at the beginning and the period at the end. Point out the spacing between words.

   Look at the workbook page. Look at the sentences under the box. How are the sentences alike? (They all begin with the same words. They all have blank lines.) **Let's read the words in the colored box.** bat, hat, pan, cab, can, cat. **You will make up four sentences by writing a word from the colored box on the blanks in each sentence. Choose a different word for each sentence.**

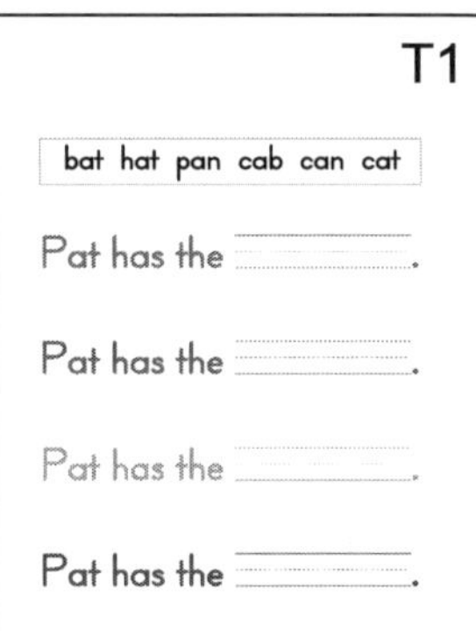

2. Write and read the sentence: The cat can bat.

3. Have the student read the word list and the First Step Reader *Sat*.

   Ask the questions:

   Who sat on the chair first? (Pat)

   What sat on the chair next? (the cat)

   What sat on the chair last? (the bass)

4. Have students act out the story *Sat*. Different children could play the roles of the animals and Pat. Students can also make props, such as the bat, fish, the water, and the cat. Different children could carry each prop. In a homeschool setting, a child could act out the story as a puppet show.

Lesson 28

Lesson Objectives

1. Students will review sentences.
2. Students will write a sentence.
3. Students will read the First Step Reader *Sat*.
4. Students will answer questions about the story.

Preparation

* Workbook page
* Handwriting sheet with the sentence: Pat can pass the pan.

Teaching

1. Have the student read the sentences on the workbook page. Have the student circle the word *the*. Ask: **What does each sentence begins with?** (capital letter) **What does each sentence end with?** (a period)

   Ask the student questions such as:

   How many words end with the *t* sound? (6)
   How many words end with the *n* sound? (5)
   What words begin with the *h* sound? (has, hat)
   How many times is the word *the* used? (6)
   Read the sentence that uses the word *the* twice.
   What words are animals? (cat, bat)
   Who had a hat? (Pat)
   What color was the can? (tan)
   What did the bat do? (nap)
   What does nap mean? (to sleep)

T1

The the

1. The cat sat.
2. The bat can nap.
3. Pat has the hat.
4. Nan has the tan can.
5. The cab can pass the cat.

2. Have the student write and read the sentence: Pat can pass the pan.

3. Have the student read the word list and the First Step Reader *Sat*.

4. Ask the following questions:

   What scared Pat? (a bat)
   What would you do if you saw a bat? (Answers vary.)
   What fell in the water? (a chair)
   Could this story really happen? (Answers vary. Have students give a reason for their answers.)
   Do you like this story? Why or why not?
   What do you think happened next? What might sit in the chair next if the fish is frightened?

   You may have students draw pictures of what they think happened next. The students may also try to write a sentence to go with the picture.

Lesson 29

Lesson Objectives

1. Students will identify words that rhyme.
2. Students will write a sentence.
3. Students will read the First Step Reader *Sat.*
4. Students will answer questions about the words in the book *Sat*.

Preparation

* Any nursery rhyme that the students are familiar with
* Workbook page
* Handwriting paper with the sentence: A cat has the hat.

Teaching

1. **Today we will learn about words that rhyme. If two words have the same ending blend they rhyme. The words man and pan rhyme. They both end with the ending blend *an.***

   I will say pairs of words. Clap your hands if they rhyme. Stomp your feet if they don't.

   tack- sack (hands), big-bit (feet), log-frog (hands),
   ship-hip (hands), lamb-comb (feet), sad-lad (hands)

   Why don't big and bit rhyme?
   (They have different ending sounds.)
   Why don't lamb and comb rhyme?
   (They have different vowel sounds.)

   Read the nursery rhyme and have the student listen for words that rhyme. Have the student match the rhymes on the workbook page for Lesson 29.

T1	
tab	bass
sap	hat
can	cab
pass	nap
bat	tan

2. Have the student read the sentence. Point out the words that rhyme. Have the student write the sentence: A cat has a hat.

3. Have the student read the word list and the First Step Reader *Sat*.

4. As the student looks at the word list on the back of the reader, ask these questions:

   What words begin with capital letters? (Pat, The)
   What word has the most letters? (bass)
   What words rhyme with hat? (bat, cat, Pat, sat)
   What vowels do you see in the words?
   Don't include the words *word list.* (a, e)
   What word is an animal that flies? (bat)
   What word is something you could have used a chair to do? (sat)
   What word is an animal that has paws? (cat)

<u>**Sat**</u> word list:

bass
bat
cat
Pat
sat
The

Lesson 30

Lesson Objectives

1. Students will take the assessment.
2. Students will review missed concepts.
3. Students will write the sentence: The bass can nap.
4. Students will read and retell the story *Sat*.

Preparation

* Lesson 30 assessment
* Handwriting paper

Teaching

1. Students will circle the correct word on the assessment page.

   1. The 2. cab 3. ban 4. bat 5. tan

   6. the 7. sat 8. an 9. nab 10. tap

2. Review any missed concepts on the assessment.

3. Write the sentence: The bass can nap.

4. Have the student read the word list and the First Step Reader *Sat*.

   Have the students tell the story in their own words.

   Example: Pat sat in a chair watching a fish. A cat jumped on his lap. A bat frightened Pat and the cat, so they ran away. The bat sat on the chair. The chair fell in the water. After the chair fell in the water, a bass sat on it.

Lesson 31

Lesson Objectives

1. Students will learn the word is.
2. Students will use the word **is** in a sentence.
3. Students will spell five words.
4. Students will read the First Step Reader *A Can*.

Preparation

* Workbook page, red and blue crayons
* Handwriting sheet with the sentence: Sap is tan.

Teaching

1. Write the word has. **Say this word. What sound does the s make in has?** *(z)* **S usually makes the *s* sound, but many times it will make *z* sound, like the letter z. This happens sometimes when a word ends with one s.**

   Write the word *is*. **Can you make the short i sound?** *(i)* **Today we are going to learn a word that begins with the *i* sound. Look at this paper. What two letters are in this word?** (i and s) **The s is at the end of the word. What sound do you think it will make?** *(z)* **Say *z*.** *(z)* **Now put the *i* sound together with the *z* sound. Say them with me i-z. Good, you've learned to read a new word: is.** Have the student do the worksheet to distinguish the word *is* from other words. Color all the circles with the word *is* red. Color the other circles blue.

2. **Look at the handwriting paper. Point to the word *is*. Let's read the sentence together. Sap is tan. Now you can write the sentence. Remember to begin it with a capital S and put a period after the last word.**

3. A weekly spelling list will begin with this lesson. Students will be asked to spell five words in the beginning. This week's list: the, is, cat, hat, sat. Give the students a list. Students should number down a piece of paper from 1 to 5.

   On line 1, write the word is. You just learned the word so if you don't know how to spell it I'll help you this time. Tell the students i-s if they need the help. **I am going to say some more words. If you don't know how to spell them, raise your hand. I will help you today. On line 2, write the word the...the. On line 3, write cat...cat. On line 4, write hat...hat. On line 5, write sat...sat.**

   Check the student's papers to make sure the words are spelled correctly. Students will use this list to learn the words.

4. Before reading the story, ask the students the question. **Do you remember what a tab is?** It's a small flap that makes things easier to handle. See if you can find the tab in this story. Have the student read the word list and the First Step Reader *A Can*.

A Can word list:
a
can
cat
has
pass
tab
tap
The
the

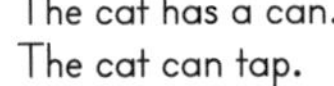

The cat has a can. The cat can tap.

The cat can pass the can.

The can has a tab.

Lesson 32

Lesson Objectives

1. Students will review sentence structure.
2. Students will write a sentence.
3. Students will read the First Step Reader *A Can*.
4. Students will review spelling words.

Preparation

* Workbook page
* Handwriting paper with the sentence: Pat is a cat.

Teaching

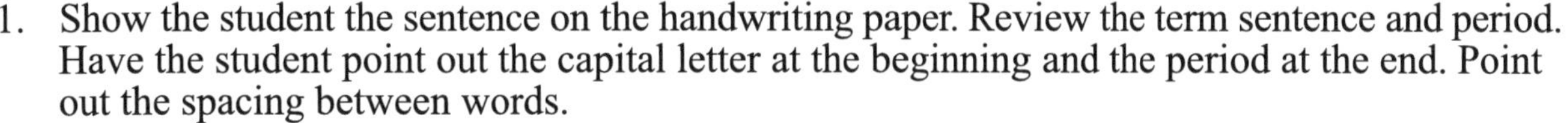

1. Show the student the sentence on the handwriting paper. Review the term sentence and period. Have the student point out the capital letter at the beginning and the period at the end. Point out the spacing between words.

   Next, introduce the workbook page. **Look at the workbook page. Parts of the sentences are missing. The first word in each sentence is *the*. Fill in the missing letter. Will it be a small letter or capital?** (capital) **What goes at the end of a sentence?** (period) **Fill in the box at the end of each sentence. A letter is missing in the words that begin with the letter c. Use the picture to help decide what the missing letter is in the middle of each sentence.**

2. Use the handwriting paper to write and read the sentence: Pat is a cat. Have students read the sentence. Ask students which words are spelling words for this week. (is, cat)

3. Have the student read the word list and the First Step Reader *A Can*.
   Next, ask the questions:

   What was the first thing the cat did with the can? (tapped it)

   What did the cat do with the can next? (passed it)

   What was on the top of the can? (a tab)

4. Review the spelling list: the, is, cat, hat, sat.

   Ask students to spell each word. Say a word and the student should tell you how it is spelled. Next, spell a word and ask students to say the word. Finally, ask students to write the words.

Lesson 33

Lesson Objectives

1. Students will review sentence structure.
2. Students will write a sentence.
3. Students will read the First Step Reader *A Can*.
4. Students will act out the story.
5. Students will take a spelling practice test.

Preparation

* Workbook page, scissors and glue
* Handwriting paper with the sentence: The hat is tan.

Teaching

1. Show the student the sentence on the handwriting paper. Review the term sentence and period. Have the student point out the capital letter at the beginning and the period at the end. Point out the spacing between words.

   Look at the workbook page. Each sentence is missing a word. The missing word is either is or has. Read each sentence and try the word is and the word has in the blank. Pick the one that makes sense and glue it on the box.

2. Use the handwriting paper to write and read the sentence: The hat is tan. What words are spelling words? (The, hat, is)

3. Have the student read the word list and the First Step Reader *A Can*. Ask the questions:

   What happened to the cat at the end of the story? (The cat got sprayed from the can.)
   What do you think was in the can? (Answers vary.)
   Do you think this story could be true? Why? (No. Cats can't do these things.)
   Has this ever happened to you? (Answers vary.)
   Do you think a cat could really do these things? (No)
   Why couldn't a cat do these things? (Answer vary.)
   Could you do these things? (Yes)
   If the story had been about a person instead of a cat, could it have been true? (yes)

4. Students will act out the story *A Can*. Children should work in teams of two. One child will read the story. The other will act out the motions. Do not use props this time. In a homeschool situation, the parent can read the story. You may even do the story twice, reversing the roles.

5. Have students number paper from 1 to 5. Give the spelling dictation test:

   1. the 2. is 3. cat 4. hat 5. sat

Lesson 34

Lesson Objectives

1. Students will match words and pictures.
2. Students will write a sentence.
3. Students will read the First Step Reader *A Can*.
4. Students will create a story.
5. Students will practice spelling words.

T1

cat
pan
bat
can

Preparation

* Workbook page
* Handwriting sentence: A cap is a hat.

Teaching

1. Have the student match the pictures to the words on the workbook page. Trace the words.

2. Write the sentence: A cap is a hat.

3. Have the student read the word list and the First Step Reader *A Can*.
   Have the student look at the word list. Ask the following questions:

   What are things that you can touch? (can, cat, tab)
   What are things that you can do? (pass, tap)
   What word ends with two of the same letter? (pass)
   What word has a z sound at the end of it? (has)
   What word is on the list twice? (The, the)
   Why do you think it's on the list twice?
   (It's spelled with a small t and with a capital t.)
   What is a thing you lift to open something? (tab)

   A Can **word list:**
   a
   can
   cat
   has
   pass
   tab
   tap
   The
   the

4. **Pretend the cat in the story *A Can* is your cat. You come home and find that the house and your cat are a mess. What would you do? Make up a story that tells what happened after the story *A Can* ended.** Brainstorm ideas for the story. Perhaps the cat will need a bath. Maybe, the cat will clean up the mess. Maybe that cat will try to blame the dog.

5. Write a spelling word, but leave out a letter. For example, c__t, ha__, __s, __at, t__e.
   Ask students to fill in the missing letter, or have students write the words on their own paper.

Lesson 35

Lesson Objectives

1. Students will take an assessment.
2. Students will review missed concepts.
3. Students will write a sentence: The bass is tan.
4. Students will read the First Step Reader *A Can*.
5. Students will retell the story in their own words.
6. Students will share stories they created.
7. Students will take a spelling test.

Preparation

* Lesson 35 assessment
* Handwriting paper: The bass is tan.

Teaching

1. Students will circle the correct word on the assessment page.

   1. cat 2. is 3. as 4. pan 5. bass
   6. hat 7. ban 8. is 9. the 10. sap

2. Review any missed concepts on the assessment.

3. Write the sentence: The bass is tan.

4. Have the students read the word list and the First Step Reader *A Can*.

5. Have the students retell the story *A Can* in their own words.

6. Have students share the stories they created in Lesson 34.

7. Students should number paper from 1 to 5. Give the words as spelling dictation:

   1. hat 2. the 3. is 4. sat 5. cat

Lesson 36

Lesson Objectives

1. Students will learn the word *in.*
2. Students will distinguish between the words *is* and *in.*
3. Students will use the word ***in*** in a sentence.
4. Students will read the First Step Reader *The Hat.*
5. Students will learn spelling words.

T2

(in) <u>is</u>

1. Sap is in the can.
2. Pat is in a cab.
3. A bass is in the hat.
4. A bat is in the cap.
5. A can is in the pan.

Preparation

* Workbook page
* Handwriting paper with the sentence: A cat is in a can.

Teaching

1. Write the words *is* and *in.* **Point to the word you have already learned. What is the word?** (is) **What letter did it begin with?** (i) **What sound does short i make?** *(i)* **Today you will learn this word.**

   Point to the word *in.* **What letters are in this word?** (i and n) **Let's blend the letters. Say it with me *i-n.* The word is *in*, like in the sentence, You are *in* school.**

2. Use the workbook page. **Read the sentences. Circle the word *in* every time you see it in the first row. Underline the word is.**
   Ask questions about the sentences. **What kind of letters do all the sentences begin with?** (capital letter) **What is at the end of the sentences?** (period) **What words end with the *p* sound?** (sap, cap) **What word ends with the *b* sound?** (cab) **What words end with the *t* sound?** (Pat, hat, bat) **What word is a sticky stuff from a tree?** (sap) **What word is a kind of fish?** (bass) **What was in the pan?** (can) **What was in the hat?** (bass) **Where was Pat?** (In a cab)

3. **Look at the handwriting paper. Find the word in. Let's read the sentence together: A cat is in a can. Now you may write the sentence.**

   On another piece of paper, you may have the student draw a picture illustrating the sentence.

4. Have the student read the word list on the back of the reader. **Do you see a name in this list?** (Nat) **How do you know it's a name?** (It begins with capital N.) **In this story, Nat loses something, but he finds it again. Read the story to find out what Nat lost.**

5. Give the students a spelling pretest with the following words: in, can, has, bass, nab. This will be the spelling list for this week. These are words from the story *The Hat..*

Nat has a hat.

The bass has a hat.

Nat can nab the hat.
The bass is in the hat.

Lesson 37

Lesson Objectives

1. Students will read sentences using the words is and in.
2. Students will write a sentence.
3. Students will read the First Step Reader *The Hat.*
4. Students will practice spelling words.

Preparation

* Workbook page
* Handwriting paper with the sentence: A pan is in the can.

Teaching

1. **Can you remember the word you learned yesterday?** (in)
   How do you spell the word in? (i n)

   Look at the workbook page. A blue box with words is at the top of the page. Look at the sentences. In each sentence are two sets of lines. Above the lines are pictures. Write the words from the blue box on the lines to match the pictures. Read the sentences as you fill in the words.

2. Write and read the sentence: A pan is in the can.

   You may ask students to illustrate the sentence on another piece of paper.

3. Have the student read the word list and the First Step Reader *The Hat.* Ask the questions:

   Why do you think the name of this story is ***The Hat*****?** (Answers vary.)

   Who had a hat? (Nat)

   What happened to the hat? (It fell into the water.)

   Have you ever dropped anything in a lake or pond? Did you get it back? (Answers vary.)

4. Write the spelling words where the students can see them: in, can, has, bass, nab.
   Have students number paper from 1 to 5. Students may look at the list as you give clues as to which word to write.

   On line 1, write the word that begins with the same sound as ***cat.*** (can)

   On line 2, write the word that has two of the same letter at the end. (bass)

   On line 3, write the word that describes what I'm doing. Pantomime nabbing something, or actually nab an object. (nab)

   On line 4, write the word that begins with the same two letters as ***hat.*** (has)

   On line 5, write the word that begins with the same sound as the word ***is***. (in)

Lesson 38

Lesson Objectives

1. Students will identify words that rhyme.
2. Students will write a sentence.
3. Students will read the First Step Reader *The Hat*.
4. Students will act out the story *The Hat*.
5. Students will practice writing spelling words.

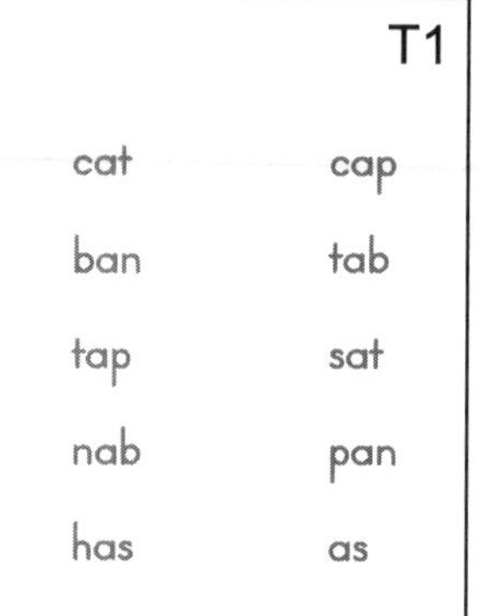

Preparation

* Any nursery rhyme that the student is familiar with
* Workbook page
* Handwriting paper with the sentence: A bat is in the hat.

Teaching

1. **Today we will talk about words that rhyme again. Remember, if two words have the same ending blend, they rhyme. Cat sat, the words rhyme. They both end with the ending blend *at*.**

   Say other pairs of words and ask the student if they rhyme. Read the nursery rhyme and have the student listen for words that rhyme. Have the student match the rhymes on the workbook page.

2. Have the student read the sentence. Point out the words that rhyme. Have the student write the sentence: A bat is in the hat. Students may illustrate the sentence on another piece of paper.

3. Have the student read the word list and the First Step Reader *The Hat*.
   Ask the following questions:

   What wore the hat in the story? (a bass)

   How did the bass get the hat? (It fell in the lake.)

   How did Nat catch a fish? (with his hat)

   How do you think Nat felt when he saw the fish? (Answers vary.)

   What do you think happened to the fish after Nat caught it? (Answer vary.)

   What would you do? (Answers vary.)

4. Have students act out the story *The Hat*. They may add to the story. What happens after the fish is pulled from the water? Have one student be the fish and one be Nat. Have students compare the different endings.

5. Have the students take a practice spelling test:

   1. in 2. can 3. has 4. bass 5. nab

Lesson 39

Lesson Objectives

1. Distinguish between the words is and in.
2. Write a sentence.
3. Read the First Step Reader *The Hat.*

T1

in	in	is	in	
is	in	in	is	
in	is	in	in	
is	in	in	is	
in	in	is	in	

Preparation

* Workbook page, crayons
* Handwriting sentence: Sap is in the can.

Teaching

1. Review the words is and in. Have the student do the workbook page. Say **See the box at the top of the page. An animal lives in the box. It is one of the animals on the right. You will find out what animal it is by coloring all the squares with the word *in* in it. The squares will make a path to the right animal.**

   The path does not move diagonally. It only moves vertically and horizontally. The squares will lead to the turtle. There are 2 paths.

2. Write and read the sentence: Sap is in the can.

3. Have the student read the word list and the First Step Reader *The Hat*. Have the student look at the word list. Ask the following questions:

   What word is a person's name? (Nat)
   What word is a kind of fish? (bass)
   Point to the new word you learned this week. (in)
   What word begins with the same letter? (is)
   What word means to grab? (nab)
   What word is something you put on your head? (hat)

   The Hat word list:

a	is
bass	nab
can	Nat
has	The
hat	the
in	

4. Students will create a story about dropping something in a lake. A fish (or other water animal like a turtle, snake, or frog) finds it. What was dropped? What did the animal do with it?

5. Write the spelling words where the students can see them: in, can, has, bass, nab. Students number paper from 1 to 5. Students may look at the list as you give clues as to which word to write.

   On line 1, write the word that rhymes with *as*. (has)
   On line 2, write the word that rhymes with *pan*. (can)
   On line 3, write the word that rhymes with *fin*. (in)
   On line 4, write the word that rhymes with *cab*. (nab)
   On line 5, write the word that rhymes with *pass*. (bass)

Lesson 40

Lesson Objectives

1. Students will take an assessment.
2. Students will review missed concepts.
3. Students will write a sentence: Pat is in a cap.
4. Students will retell the story *The Hat*.
5. Students will tell stories created in Lesson 39.
6. Students will take a spelling test.

Preparation

* Lesson 40 assessment
* Handwriting paper: Pat is in a cap.

Teaching

1. Students will circle the correct word on the assessment page.

   1. in 2. sat 3. pan 4. has 5. is

   6. nab 7. the 8. cab 9. pat 10. as

2. Review any missed concepts on the assessment.

3. Write the sentence: Pat is in a cap.

4. Have the students read the word list and the First Step Reader *The Hat*. Have the students retell the story in their own words.

5. Have students tell the stories created in Lesson 39.

6. Give students the spelling test:

   1. bass 2. in 3. can 4. nab 5. has

Lesson 41

Lesson Objectives

1. Students will learn the word on.
2. Students will review words.
3. Students will write the word on in a sentence.
4. Students will read the First Step Reader *Nan.*
5. Students will learn spelling words.

T1

on in

1. The cat is on the hat.
2. The bass is in the pan.
3. A tab is on the can.
4. A bat is in the cab.
5. Sap is on the cap.

Preparation

* Workbook page
* Handwriting sentence: A cat is on Pat.

Teaching

1. Write the words in and on. Point to the word in. **What word is this?** (in) **Next to it is a word we will learn today. Notice it looks like the word in, but the vowel is different.** Point to the o. **What letter is this?** (o) **What sound does o make?** (*o*) Point to the n. **What letter is this?** (n) **What sound does it make**? (*n*) **Let's blend the sounds together. Say this with me, o-n, on.** Have students read the sentences on the workbook page. Students should circle the word on and underline the word in.

2. You may have students respond to this review in several ways. They may write answers, say answers and spell the words, or take turns writing on a chalkboard. Read clues to the students and have them write the word. The clues given below will relate to the meaning of the words. If students still do not know the word, start giving phonetic clues such as, it starts with c. It ends with t. It rhymes with hat. You may also give students a word list of the answers.

   You wear it on your head. (cap or hat) **Another word for something you wear on your head.** (hat or cap) **Something you do with a salt shaker or a football.** (pass) **To hit or touch lightly.** (pat or tap) **Something someone did in a chair.** (sat) **A kind of rule or law.** (ban) **To sleep for a short time.** (nap) **Sticky stuff that comes from a tree.** (sap) **A small flap that helps you open a can.** (tab) **Something you need to play baseball.** (bat) **Something with a tail.** (cat or bass) **A light brown color.** (tan)

3. Write and read the sentence: A cat is on Pat. Have students illustrate the sentence.

4. Have the student read the word list. **There's an animal in this story. Can you look at the word list and guess what the animal is?** (bat) **There is a picture of a girl on the front cover. What do you think her name is? Look at the word list and make a guess.** (Nan) **What makes you think that Nan is a name?** (It begins with a capital letter.) **Let's read about Nan and the bat.**

5. Give the spelling pretest: **1. bat 2. pan 3. on 4. pass 5. tab**

The bat sat. Nan has the hat. The hat is on a can. The hat can pass Nan.

Lesson 42

Lesson Objectives

1. Students will read sentences using the word on.
2. Students will write a sentence using the word on.
3. Students will read the First Step Reader *Nan*.
4. Students will review spelling words.

Preparation

* Workbook page
* Scissors, glue, extra paper

Teaching

1. Have the student cut out the puzzle pieces on the workbook page and put together the two sentences. Have the student put a period after the last word in the second sentence. Each sentence can be glued on a piece of paper. Students can draw pictures to illustrate the sentences.

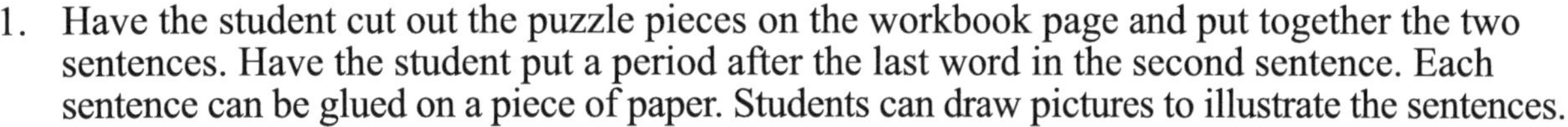

2. Have the student choose one of the sentences from the puzzle to write.

3. Have the student read the word list and the First Step Reader *Nan*. Ask the following questions:

   What was the hat sitting on at the beginning of the story? (a rock)
   What was in the hat? (a bat)
   Who took the hat? (Nan)
   Who do you think the hat belonged to? (Answers vary. - Nan)
   Do you think Nan knew the hat was on the can? (Answers vary.) **Why?**

4. Have students number paper from 1 to 5. Write the spelling words where students can see them: bat, pan, on, pass, tab. Have students write just the spelling word they hear in the following sentences.

   Listen to the sentences I say. In each sentence is a spelling word. Listen for the spelling word and write it on the correct line.

   1. Food is cooking in the pan. (pan)
   2. I will pull a tab to open the can. (tab)
   3. Can you please pass the peas? (pass)
   4. A cat is on the chair. (on)
   5. The bat flew over my head. (bat)

Lesson 43

Lesson Objectives

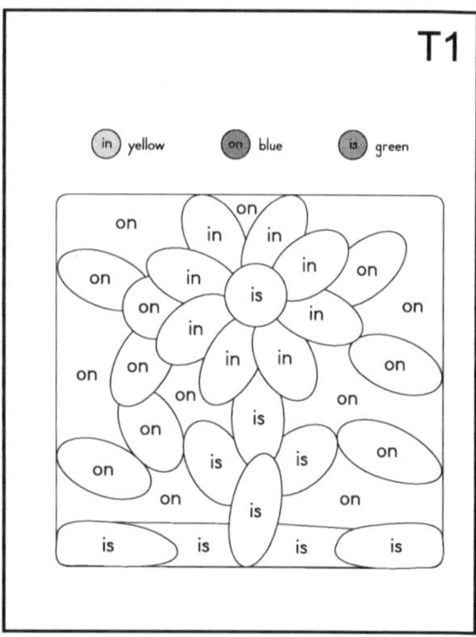

1. Students will review is, in, and on.
2. Students will review words.
3. Students will write a sentence.
4. Students will read the First Step Reader *Nan*.
5. Students will take a spelling test.

Preparation

* Workbook page, crayons
* Handwriting sentence: A bat can nap on the hat.
* Optional book or other information about bats.

Teaching

1. Review is, in, and on using the workbook page.

2. Review words with students to prepare them for the test. Do this on an erasable surface such as a chalkboard or dry erase board. Start with the beginning blend ca-. You or the students should add b and read the word. Erase b and add t. Erase t and add p. Read the word, then erase the c and leave the ending blend –ap. Add n, then s, then t.

   Do this kind of drill with other ending and beginning blends. The letters you will work with are a, b, c, h, n, p, s, t. Also review the words *the, is, in,* and *on*.

3. Read and write the sentence: A bat can nap on the hat.

4. Have the student read the word list and the First Step Reader *Nan*.
   Ask the following questions:

   Where did Nan put the hat? (on a can)
   Why was the hat able to fly? (A bat was inside.)
   How do you think Nan felt when her hat flew away? (Answers vary.)
   Do you think Nan got the hat back? (Answers vary.)
   Tell me what you know about bats.
   At this point you could share your book or information about bats.

   Nan word list:

a	Nan
bat	on
can	pass
has	sat
hat	The
is	the
nab	

5. Because of the phonics test, the weekly spelling test will be during this lesson. If students need more practice, you may continue to work with the list and give the test again during Lesson 45.

   1. on 2. bat 3. pan 4. tab 5. pass

Lessons 44 - 45

Lesson Objectives

1. Unit One Test.

Preparation

* Three test pages from the workbook for lessons 44-45.

Note:

You may continue reading the story *Nan* and have students act it out during these two lessons.

Teaching

1. The test may be given over a two day period. The student will fill in an answer on each line. The directions are as follows:

Part 1

Color the circle with the:

1. consonant in it **2. *b* sound** **3. *s* sound** **4. *t* sound**

5. *h* sound **6. *p* sound** **7. *n* sound** **8. vowel in it**

Part 2

Color the circle that has the:

1. beginning sound of bag **2. beginning sound of hat**

3. beginning sound of pat **4. beginning sound of sack**

5. ending sound of lap **6. ending sound of man**

7. ending sound of fit **8. ending sound of bus**

Part 3

Color the circle that has the word:

1. on 2. the 3. is 4. in 5. tab 6. pass 7. cap 8. pan

Lesson 46

Lesson Objectives

1. Students will read short i words.
2. Students will write a sentence using short i.
3. Students will read the First Step Reader *Cat in a Bin.*
4. Students will learn spelling words.

T1	
bat	b_t
pan	p_n
has	h_s
nap	n_p
sat	s_t
tap	t_p

Preparation

* Workbook page
* Write the words is and in on a piece of paper.
* Handwriting sentence: Pat hit the tin can.

Teaching

1. Use the paper with the words is and in on it. **What vowel do you see in these two words?** (i) **What sound does short i make?** (*i*) **Today we will begin using short i in other words.** Write the words has, sap, tan, pat. Ask students to read the words. Replace the a in has with an i. Have students read the new word. (his) Repeat with the other words.

   Workbook page 46: Students will read the short a words. Have students replace a with i and write the new words. Next, have students read the new words.

2. Have the student write and read the sentence: Pat hit the tin can.

3. Have the student read the word list and the First Step Reader *Cat in a Bin.* The word list includes the word tips with the blended ps. Blending s at the end of words is formally taught in Lesson 73. For now, just help the student read the word by saying tip and adding the s very quickly. Refer to Lesson 73 if you need additional ideas for helping the student.

   Talk about the meanings of the following words: bin, hip, tin, and tip. Ask students if they know the meaning of each word.

   A bin is something you can put things in, like a box. Bins are used to help organize things.

   Can you pat your hips?

   Tin is a thin piece of metal. What things can be made of tin? Bins can be made of tin.

   If I tip something what am I doing? (knocking or pushing something over)

   Look at the front cover. What is the cat sleeping in? It's a kind of box. It can help organize things. What is it? (A bin) **Some things happen to the cat while it's sleeping. Read the story to find out what happens to the cat.**

4. Give the spelling pre-test: **1. bin 2. his 3. hip 4. hit 5. tip**
   These words were used in the story.

A cat is in a bin. The cat has a nap.

The tin can tips.

The can hit the cat.

It is on his hip.

Lesson 47

Lesson Objectives

1. Students will discriminate between short a and i words.
2. Students will learn vocabulary words.
3. Students will write a sentence.
4. Students will read the First Step Reader *Cat in a Bin.*
5. Students will practice spelling words.

Preparation

* Workbook page, crayons
* Handwriting sentence: A bib is on the cat.

Teaching

1. Write the words bit and bat. **Point to the word that has the *i* sound. What vowel sound does the other word have?** (*a*) Have the student do the workbook page. Color the short i words green. Color the short a words purple.

2. Review the words bin, hip, tin, and tip. Introduce the words nip, pit, sin, sip.

   If something nips you, what has happened to you? (been bitten) **What might nip you? Have you ever seen a pit? What is a pit?** (a whole in the ground)
   Do you know what it means to sip? Pretend you're sipping something. What did you sip?

3. Write and read the sentence: A bib is on the cat.

4. Have the student read the First Step Reader *Cat in a Bin.* Ask the following questions:

   What was the cat doing at the beginning of the story? (napping)

   What was the cat in? (a bin)

   Where was the mouse? (on a shelf)

   Do you think the cat knows what is happening? (no) **Why?** (It's asleep.)

5. Students will spell their spelling words by relating them to short a words. **I will say some words. The words all have the short a sound. If you change the a to i, you will make a spelling word. I'll help you with the first one.**

   Number 1, has. Change the a to i and it becomes what word? (his)
   Write his on line one. 2. tap 3. ban 4. hap 5. hat

   Have students check and correct their own answers. Ask, **what did you write on line 2?** (tip) **Line 3?** (bin) **Line 4?** (hip) **Line 5?** (hit)

Game:

Ruff's Lunch - Slider Strip 2

Lesson 48

Lesson Objectives

1. Students will discriminate between short a and i words.
2. Students will recognize short i words in sentences.
3. Students will write a sentence.
4. Students will read the First Step Reader *Cat in a Bin.*
5. Students will act out the story.
6. Students will take a spelling practice test.

T2

1. The tin can tips.

2. The cat hit his hip.

3. A pin is in the bin.

4. A bat sits on the bib.

5. His hat is in the pit.

Preparation

* Workbook page
* Two index cards or index size pieces of paper per student
* Handwriting sentence: Pat is in the pit.

Teaching

1. Have students make two response cards. Use the two index cards or pieces of paper. Students should write an *a* on one and an *i* on the other. As you say the following words, have the student hold up the card with the vowel sound of that word: **bat, sit, pin, hat, bit, pan, hit, sat**

2. Students will read the sentences on the workbook page and circle the short i words. Ask questions about the sentences.

   What kind of letters do all the sentences begin with? (capital letter)

   What is at the end of the sentences? (period)

   What words have the *ip* blend? (hip, tips)

   What word ends with the *b* sound? (bib)

   What word is a hole in the ground? (pit)

   What word is a part of a body? (hip)

   What was in the bin? (pin)

   What did the bat sit on? (bib)

   What happened to the tin can? (It tipped.)

3. Write and read the sentence: Pat is in the pit.

4. Have the student read the word list and *Cat in a Bin.* Ask the following questions:

   How did the can tip? (The mouse pushed it.)
   Where did it hit the cat? (on the head)
   Where did the can end up? (on the cat's hip)
   What do you think the cat did next? (Answers vary.)
   Has anyone ever scared you while you were asleep? What did (or would) you do?

5. Students will act out the story. To prevent injury, they should not use a prop to drop on the cat. Students can supply sound effects. Ask what sounds might be heard. One student can read the story while the others act it out. Extend the performance by having students decide what would happen next.

6. Students will take a spelling practice test: **1. hip 2. bin 3. his 4. tip 5. hit**

Lesson 49

Lesson Objectives

1. Students will read sentences for meaning.
2. Students will write a sentence.
3. Students will read *Cat in a Bin.*
4. Students will create a story.
5. Students will practice writing spelling words.

Preparation

* Workbook page
* Scissors, glue
* Handwriting sentence: A pin is in the hat.

Teaching

1. Use the workbook page. **Look at the workbook page. Find the blue box. Read the words in the box. These words will be used to complete the sentences. The pictures are clues. Use the words in the blue box only one time.**

2. Have the student write and read the sentence: A pin is in the hat.

3. Have the student read the word list and the First Step Reader *Cat in a Bin.* Have the student look at the word list to answer the questions:

Cat in A Bin word list:	
a	hit
bin	in
can	is
cat	on
has	the
hip	tin
his	tips

What vowel is in the word *bin?* (i) **What sound does it make?** (*i*)
What other words have this sound? (hip, his, hit, in, is, tin, tips)
What word rhymes with bit? (hit)
What word is something like a box? (bin)
What is a part of your body? (hip)
What word means to push over? (tips)
What word is a kind of metal? (tin)
What word is something you can do with a baseball bat? (hit)

4. **In the story *Cat in a Bin* a mouse played a trick on the cat while it was asleep. One day, the cat saw the mouse sleeping. What do you think the cat did? Create a story telling what happened when the cat saw the mouse sleeping.**

5. Write the spelling words where students can see them: bin, his, hip, hit, tip. Students will need paper numbered 1 to 5. **I will say a word that rhymes with a spelling word. Write the correct spelling word on the line.**

One line 1, write the spelling word that rhymes with pit. What word did you write? (hit)

There are two spelling words that rhyme with sip. Write one on line 2 and the other on line 3. (tip and hip)

On line 4, write the spelling word that rhymes with fizz. (his)

On line 5, write the spelling word that rhymes with sin. (bin)

Lesson 50

Lesson Objectives

1. Students will take an assessment.
2. Students will review missed concepts.
3. Students will write a sentence.
4. Students will read *Cat in a Bin.*
5. Students will share stories created in Lesson 49.
6. Students will take a spelling test.

Preparation

* Lesson 50 assessment
* Handwriting sentence: It is his pan.

Teaching

1. Students will circle the correct word on the assessment page.

   1. bit 2. sit 3. tap 4. his 5. sip

   6. pat 7. nip 8. ban 9. pin 10. tan

2. Review any missed concepts on the assessment.

3. Have the student write the sentence: It is his pan.

4. Have the student read the word list and the story *Cat in a Bin.* Have the student retell the story in his or her own words.

5. Students will share stories created in Lesson 49. The author can then ask questions about the story to the other students, such as what happened to the mouse?

6. Have students take the spelling test:

   1. hip 2. hit 3. tip 4. bin 5. his

Lesson 51

Lesson Objectives

1. Students will learn the sound of m.
2. Students will write a sentence using m.
3. Students will read the *Map & Ham*.
4. Students will learn spelling words.

Preparation

* Workbook page
* Handwriting sentence: The man has a mitt.

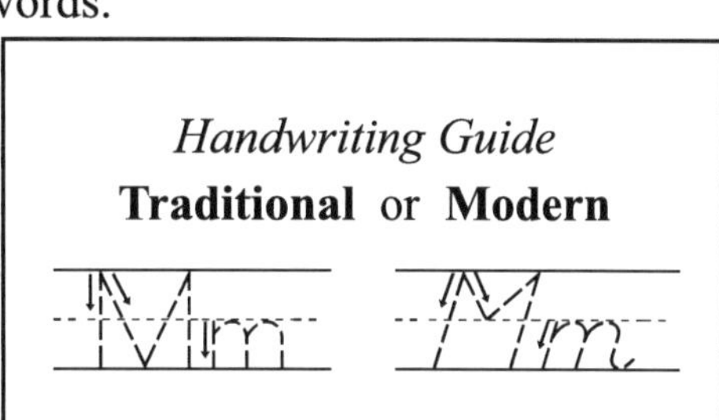

Teaching

1. **Today you are going to learn a new letter sound.** Write the words *tap*, *sat*, and *can*. Ask students to read the words. Next, write the letter m. **The letter m makes the *m* sound. Say the m sound.** (*m*) **Think of things that begin with the *m* sound.** Have the student say words that begin with m. **Now let's blend m and a. Look at the three words I wrote on the board. What if I replace the beginning consonants with the letter m? What new words would I make?** (map, mat, man)

   Write the words *miss* and *mitt*. Ask students to read the words**. What is the beginning blend?** (*mi*)

   Write the words *hit* and *hat*. **Read these words. What if I took off the ending sound and added m. What new words would I get?** (*him* and *ham*)

   Workbook page: Write the beginning sounds that match the pictures. Have students say the names of the pictures with you. **The pictures are a mouse, clown, mitt, magnet, moose, bug, milk, map and hat.**

2. Have the students write and read the sentence: The man has a mitt.

3. Have the student read the word list and the book *Map & Ham*. **What words are names on the back of the book?** (Sam, Tim). **What's the name of the book?** (Map & Ham) **The shape that looks kind of like an 8 between the words Map and Ham stands for the word and.**

   Sometimes we do this on signs, titles of books, or names of things like companies and stores. We don't use this mark when we write sentences. Why do you think this story is called Map & Ham? Read the story and find out.

4. Give the spelling pre-test:

   1. ham 2. map 3. him 4. miss 5. man

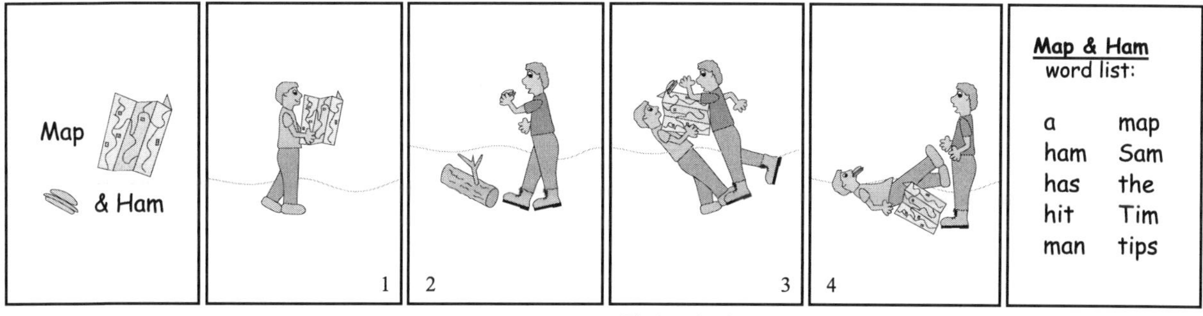

Lesson 52

Lesson Objectives

1. Students will review the use of m.
2. Students will practice handwriting.
3. Students will read *Map & Ham*.
4. Students will review spelling words.

	T1
Tim	ham
man	mat
Sam	sap
hat	him
map	tan

Preparation

* Workbook page
* Handwriting sentence: Tim has the ham.

Teaching

1. Review rhymes. Point out that for words to rhyme they have to have the same ending blend, not just the same ending consonant sound. Hit and bit rhyme, hit and bat do not rhyme. Have the student match the rhymes on the workbook page.

2. Have the student write the sentence: Tim has the ham.

3. Have the student read the word list and the book *Map & Ham*. Ask the following questions:

   Who had the map? (Tim)
   Who had the ham? (Sam)
   What did Sam trip over? (a log)
   How did the ham end up in Tim's mouth? (Sam dropped it.)
   What would you have done if you were Tim? (Answers vary.)
   What would you have done if you were Sam? (Answers vary.)

4. Write the spelling words where students can see them: ham, map, him, miss, man.

   I will give you a clue. You write the spelling word that matches the clue.

   Line 1. This can help you find your way if you get lost. What word did you write? (map)
   Line 2. A girl is a her. A boy is a _______. (him)
   Line 3. When a boy grows up he becomes this. (man)
   Line 4. You can make a sandwich with this. (ham)
   Line 5. You may feel this way about someone you haven't seen in a long time. (miss)

Game:

Wiggle Worm - 1

Handwriting Guide

Traditional or **Modern**

Mm Mm

Lesson 53

Lesson Objectives

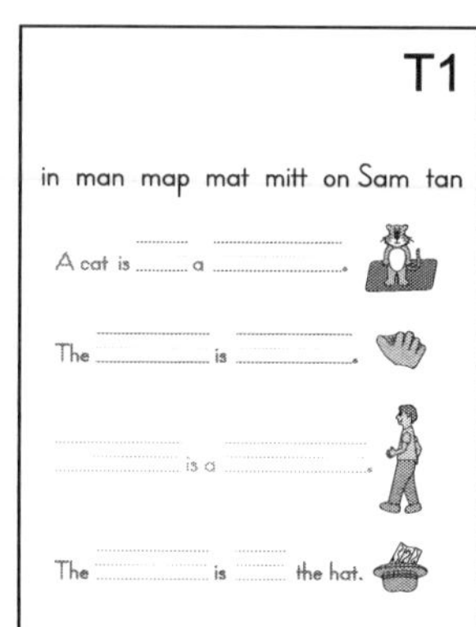

1. Students will read sentences using the letter m.
2. Students will practice handwriting.
3. Students will read the First Step Reader *Map & Ham.*
4. Students will act out the story.
5. Students will take a spelling pre-test.

Preparation

* Workbook page
* Handwriting sentence: Tim has the map.

Teaching

1. Use the workbook page. **Look at the red box at the top of the workbook page. Read the words. Use the words to complete the sentences. Use the pictures as clues. Use the words in the red box only one time.**

2. Write the sentence: Tim has the map.

3. Have the student read the word list and the book *Map & Ham.*

   What happened when the ham hit the map? (Sam tipped Tim.) Have the student find and read the sentence that says this on page 3.

   Who had the ham at the end of the story? (Tim) Have the student read the sentence on page 4 that says this.

   Why did Sam and Tim have an accident? (They weren't watching what they were doing.)

   What do you think happened to the ham sandwich after the story ended? (Answers vary.)

   Have you ever had an accident like this? (If yes: Tell us about it.)

   Could this story have really happened? Why do you think that? (Answers vary.)

4. Have students act out the story. What happened after the book ended? Students can add to the performance.

5. Give the spelling pre-test:

   1. ham 2. map 3. him 4. miss 5. man

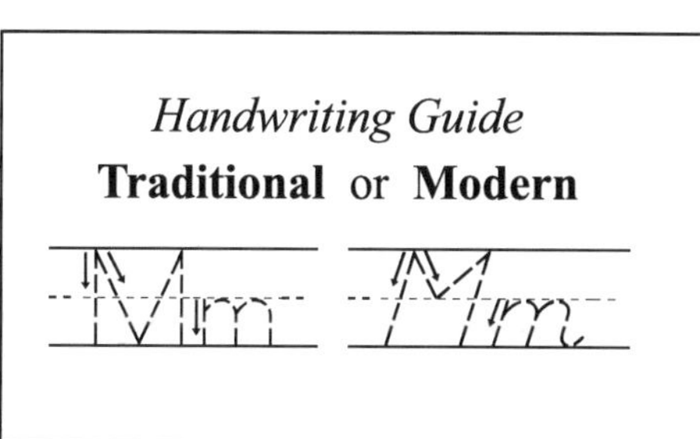

Lesson 54

Lesson Objectives

1. Students will be introduced to the question mark.
2. Students will write a question.
3. Students will read *Map & Ham.*
4. Students will create a story.
5. Students will practice spelling words.

Preparation

* Workbook page
* Handwriting sentence: Can Sam tip the can?

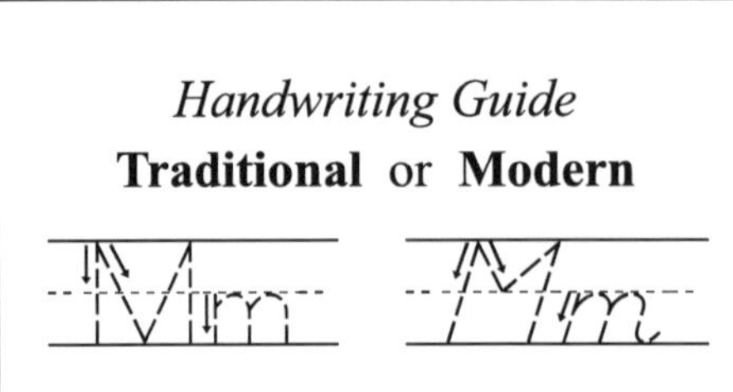

Teaching

1. **What comes after the end of a sentence?** (*a period*) **Sometimes we put a different mark at the end of a sentence. Today we will learn a new way to end a sentence.**

   Write a question mark. **This is called a question mark. We use a question mark at the end of a sentence that asks something. I always ask a lot of questions about the books we read. If I were to write those questions, I would put a question mark at the end of it. In the air, trace the question mark with your finger. Let's practice drawing a few question marks in our workbook.** Have the students trace the question marks at the top of the page and try to draw one of their own.

   Next, students will decide whether the first word in each sentence is the word Is or Can. **Look at the sentences. Each sentence has blank lines at the beginning and the end. The lines at the end are for question marks. The beginning lines are for the word Is or Can. You can decide which word goes in the blank by trying each one before writing. Look at the first sentence. Which sounds right? Is Sam the bass sit? or Can Sam the bass sit?** (*Can Sam the bass sit?*)

2. Write the sentence: Can Sam tip the can?

3. Have the student read the word list and the book *Map & Ham*. Have the student look at the word list and answer the following questions:

   What words have the *m* sound at the beginning? (man, map)
   What words have the *m* sound at the end? (ham, Sam, Tim)
   What word has *ps* at the end? (tips)
   What word is something that people eat? (ham)
   What is something made of paper? (map)
   What word rhymes with *sit*? (hit)

   Map & Ham
   word list:

a	map
ham	Sam
has	the
hit	Tim
man	tips

4. What if Sam and Tim had been carrying something different? What are some other things they could have been carrying that would have caused bigger problems? What could have happened? Create a story that tells what could have happened.

5. Write the spelling words where students can see them: ham him, man, map, miss

   Write the word that rhymes with:
   1. cap (map) **2. kiss** (miss) **3. sam** (ham) **4. tan** (man) **5. Tim** (him)

Lesson 55

Lesson Objectives

1. Students will take an assessment.
2. Students will review missed concepts.
3. Students will write a sentence.
4. Students will read the First Step Reader *Map & Ham*.
5. Students will share stories created in Lesson 54.
6. Students will take a spelling test.

Preparation

* Lesson 55 assessment
* Handwriting sentence: Is Sam a man?

Teaching

1. Students will circle the correct word on the assessment page.

    1. mat 2. Tim 3. Sam 4. hit 5. map
    6. sap 7. him 8. tab 9. mitt 10. Pam

2. Review any missed concepts on the assessment.

3. Write the sentence: Is Sam a man? **What is the mark at the end of the sentence**? (question mark) **Why is it there instead of a period?** (It is a question.) **Which one of these words is a spelling word?** (man)

4. Have the student read the word list and the First Step Reader *Map & Ham*. Have the student retell the story in his or her own words.

5. Have students share their stories. Encourage children to ask questions, such as why did you choose the things the people carried?

6. Have students take the spelling test:

    1. him 2. man 3. miss 4. map 5. ham

Handwriting Guide
Traditional or **Modern**

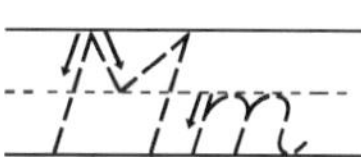

Lesson 56

Lesson Objectives

1. Students will learn the sound of r.
2. Students will write a sentence using r.
3. Students will learn vocabulary words.
4. Students will read the book *The Ram*.
5. Students will learn spelling words.

Preparation

* Workbook page
* Handwriting sentence: A rat ran on the rim.
* A can

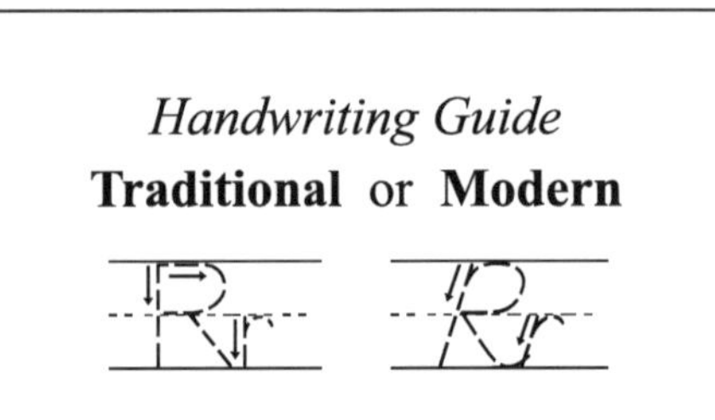

Teaching

1. Teacher's note: The letter r is only being taught as a beginning sound in this curriculum. The letter r changes or "controls" vowel sounds when it comes after a vowel.

   Today you are going to learn a new letter sound. Write the letter r. **What letter is this?** (r) **What sound do you think it makes? The letter r makes the *er* sound. Say the r sound.** *(er)* **Think of things that begin with the *er* sound.** Have the student say words that begin with r. **Now let's blend r and a.** Write an a after the r. **Read the blend.**

   Add a t to the end of ra-. Have students read the word. (rat) Switch the t with other letters. Make the words rap, ram, and ran. Repeat for the blend ri, and the words rib, rip, and rim. On the workbook page have the students read the words. Replace the beginning consonants with r. Write the new words.

2. Have the student write and read the sentence: A rat ran on the rim.

3. Introduce the vocabulary words: ram, rib, and rim. **Have you ever seen a ram? A male (or boy) sheep is a ram. Some rams have big curly horns. The word ram also has another meaning. If you hit or push something very hard, you ram it. The next word is rib. Can you point to a rib? The last word is rim.** (Hold up the can or other object) **Where is the rim on this?**

4. Have the student read the word list and the First Step Reader *The Ram*. **What animal is on the front cover?** (Ram) **Look at the word list. What other animals are in the story?** (cat, rat) **Read the story to find out what happens when the cat and rat meet the ram.**

5. Have students take the spelling pre-test: **1.rat 2. ram 3. rib 4. ran 5. rip**

The cat ran. The rat ran.
The rat sat on the ram. The cat ran.
The ram is at the can.
The cat is in the can.

Lesson 57

Lesson Objectives

1. Students will learn the words yes and no.
2. Students will practice handwriting.
3. Students will read the First Step Reader *The Ram*.
4. Students will practice spelling words.

Preparation

* Workbook page
* Handwriting: the words yes, no, and the question mark ?

Teaching

1. **When we ask a question, usually we want an answer. Answer this question. Are you 90 years old?** (no) **Right, the answer is no. Are you** (student's age) **years old?** (yes) **Right, the answer is yes.**

   Those are two possible answers to a question. You will learn to read the words yes and no. Write the word no. Point to the n. **What sound does n make?** (*n*) **What letter comes after the n?** (o) **The o does not make the short o or *o* sound. It just says its name. It says o. So is this word yes or no?** (*no*)

   Write the word yes. **What is this word?** (yes) **How is it spelled?** (y-e-s) **Look at the questions on the workbook page. Under each question are the words yes and no in ovals. Read the questions about the pictures and fill in an answer.**

2. Have the student write the words yes and no, then practice writing question marks.

3. Have the student read the word list and the book *The Ram*. Ask the following questions:

   What was the cat chasing on page 1? (a rat)
   What animals are on page 2? (rat, cat, ram)
   Which animal is the largest? (the ram)
   Which animal is the smallest? (the rat)
   What did the rat do to get away from the cat? (It sat on a ram.)

4. Write the spelling words where students can see them.

   Write the spelling word that rhymes with:

   1. ham 2. fib 3. man 4. hip 5. cat

Game:

Ruff's Lunch - Slider Strip 3

Handwriting Guide
Traditional or **Modern**

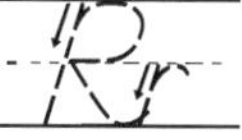

Lesson 58

Lesson Objectives

1. Students will learn the g sound.
2. Students will review beginning and ending blends.
3. Students will write a sentence using the letter g.
4. Students will read the book *The Ram.*
5. Students will act out the story *The Ram.*
6. Students will take a spelling pre-test.

Preparation

* Workbook page
* Handwriting sentence: A pig is in the bag.
* Double Slider
* Scissors, glue

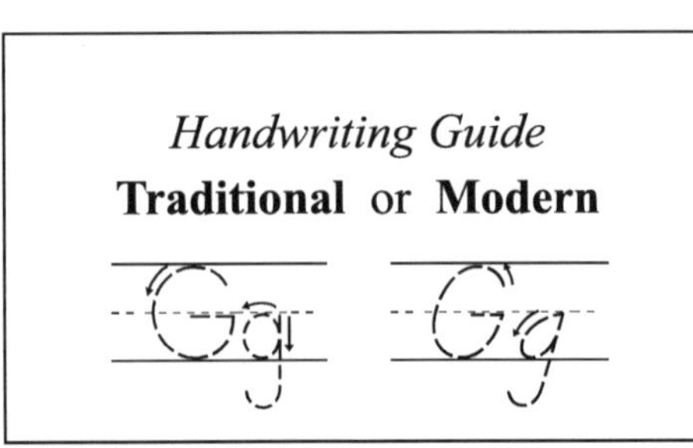

Teaching

1. **Today you are going to learn a new letter sound.** Write the letter g. **What is this letter?** (g) **What sound does it make? The letter g makes the *g* sound. Say the g sound.** (*g*) **Think of things that begin with the *g* sound.**

   Have the student say words that begin with g. **Now let's blend g and a.** Add ending consonants to make gap and gas. Repeat for the ending blends ag and ig to make the following words: bag, sag, tag, big, pig, rig.

   Look at the workbook page. In the past we have written the beginning sounds under the pictures. This time we will write the ending sounds under the pictures. (dog, ram, pig, bag, log, carrot, ham, bug, egg)

2. Have students cut out and assemble the slider. Ask students to make different words. Include questions that make the students think about the words. Following are some examples. **Which are real words, and which are nonsense words? Make a nonsense word. Read your nonsense word to me. Now make a real word.** Ask students to make rhyming words such as: **make the words that rhyme with wag.** Ask students to find words based on meaning. For example: **make a word that means to sleep.** (nap) Discuss any potentially unfamiliar words such as gab. **Make the word *gab*. What do you think it means? It means to talk a lot or talk too much.**

3. Handwriting sentence: A pig is in the bag.

4. Have the student read the word list and the First Step Reader *The Ram*. Ask the questions:

   Where did the cat hide? (in a can)

   Why was the can flying? (The ram hit it.)

   What do you think happened next? (Answers vary.)

   Why do you think the cat was chasing the rat? (Answers vary.)

5. Have students make puppets to act out the story.
   They can be simple paper puppets glued on sticks.

6. Give the spelling practice test:

   1. ran 2. rip 3. ram 4. rat 5. rib

Lesson 59

Lesson Objectives

1. Students will read rhymes.
2. Students will practice handwriting
3. Students will read the book *The Ram*.
4. Students will create a story.
5. Students will practice spelling words.

	T1
Pam	pig
rat	map
big	Tim
gap	Sam
rim	cat

Preparation

* Workbook page
* Handwriting sentence: Pam has a rag in the big bag.

Teaching

1. Review rhymes. Point out that for words to rhyme they have to have the same ending blend, not just the same ending consonant sound. Hit and bit rhyme, hit and bat do not rhyme. Have the student match the rhymes on the workbook page.

2. Students will write the sentence: Pam has a rag in the big bag.

3. Have the student read the word list and the First Step Reader *The Ram*. Have the student look at the word list and answer the questions:

   What words begin with the *r* sound? (ram, ran, rat)
   What words are things that the animals did? (ran, sat)
   What words begin with the *i* sound? (in, is)
   What words rhyme with hat? (at, cat, rat, sat)
   What words are things with tails? (cat, rat, ram)
   What words rhyme with pan? (can, ran)

The Ram word list:

at	ram
can	ran
cat	rat
in	sat
is	the
on	

4. The cat didn't learn its lesson. The next day the cat was chasing the rat again. This time, they didn't meet a ram. They met something else. What was it and what did they do? Create your own story to tell what happened.

5. Write the spelling words where students can see them: rat, ram, rib, ran, rip.

   I will read some sentences. One word in each sentence is a spelling word. Write the spelling word on the line.

   Line 1. A rib is a bone. What was the spelling word? (rib)
   Line 2. I ran to my house. (ran)
   Line 3. Did you rip your shirt? (rip)
   Line 4. The ram had big horns. (ram)
   Line 5. The rat ate the cheese. (rat)

Handwriting Guide
Traditional or **Modern**

Gg Gg

Lesson 60

Lesson Objectives

1. Students will take an assessment.
2. Students will review missed concepts.
3. Students will write a sentence.
4. Students will read the First Step Reader *The Ram*.
5. Students will share stories created in Lesson 59.
6. Students will take a spelling test.

Preparation

* Lesson 60 assessment
* Handwriting sentence: Is gas in the can?

Teaching

1. Students will circle the correct word on the assessment page.

   1. ram 2. big 3. gab 4. tag 5. rip

   6. pig 7. gas 8. rag 9. rib 10. ran

2. Review any missed concepts on the assessment.

3. Write the sentence: Is gas in the can?

   Review the use of the question mark.

4. Have the student read the word list and the First Step Reader *The Ram*. Have the student retell the story in his/her own words.

5. Students will share stories created in Lesson 59. Ask children why they chose the thing that the cat and rat met the next day. How did it change the story?

6. Give students the spelling test:

   1. rip 2. ran 3. rib 4. ram 5. rat

Handwriting Guide

Traditional or **Modern**

Gg Gg

Lesson 61

Lesson Objectives

1. Students will learn the d sound.
2. Students will read words that end with d.
3. Students will write a sentence using the letter d.
4. Students will read the book *The Big Pig*.
5. Students will learn spelling words.

Preparation

* Workbook page
* Handwriting sentence: Dan sat on the big pad.
* Slider 61, scissors, glue

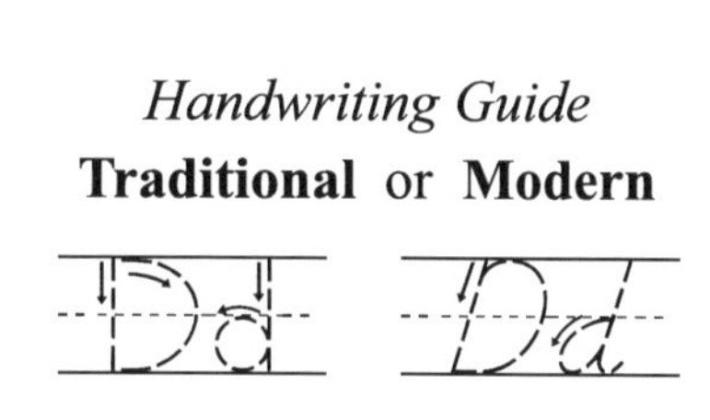

Teaching

1. **Today you are going to learn a new letter sound.** Write the letter d. **What letter is this? What sound does it make? The letter d makes the *d* sound. Say the d sound.** (*d*) **Think of things that begin with the *d* sound.** Have the student say words that begin with d. **Now let's blend d and a.** Write da. Add an n to make the word dan. Read this word.

   This is not quite right. What is wrong with this? (It is a name. It should be capitalized.) Change the d to D. Write the beginning blend di and make the words dim, dip, and dig.

   Repeat for the ending blends ad and id. Have the student make the following words: bad, dad, had, pad, bid, did, hid, and rid. Have the student write the beginning sound under each picture on the workbook page. The pictures are: ball, dog, turtle, bat, saw, duck, deer, ram, dish.

2. Use Slider 61 to practice words that end with d. Have students make words and read them. Next, ask students to move the slider to make various words.

3. Handwriting sentence: Dan sat on the big pad.

4. Have the student read the word list on the back of the book *The Big Pig*. **Can you find the name of a person on the back of this book?** (Dan) **Dan owns an animal. Can you guess what it is?** (A pig) **How did you know that?** (title, the word pig) **Owning a pig isn't always easy. Let's read the book to find out why.**

5. Give the students a spelling pretest: **1. dig 2. dim 3. dad 4. hid 5. bad**

   Ask students if they know what dim means. **If a light bulb is dim it is what?** (not too bright) You may ask students to act out the words dig and sad.

Dan has a pig.

The pig hid.
The pig is in the pit.

Can the pig nip Dan?

The pig did nip Dan.
The big pig is bad.

Lesson 62

Lesson Objectives

1. Students will discrimination between the letters b and d.
2. Students will practice handwriting.
3. Students will read the book *The Big Pig*.
4. Students will practice spelling words.

T1

b	d	b	d	b
d	d	d	b	b
b	b	d	d	d
b	b	b	d	d
d	b	b	b	d

Preparation

* Workbook page
* Handwriting sentence: Did Dad dig the pit?

Teaching

1. Use the workbook page. The student can use this sheet for as many lessons as necessary to develop rapid discrimination skills between b and d. Because the letters look so similar, students often confuse the two.

   To use this sheet, have the student make a letter b with their left hand and a d with their right. Do this by sticking the index finger straight up. Touch the middle finger to the thumb and curl the other two fingers.

   The student will match the left hand to the b's on the practice sheet and the right hand to the d's. Have the student make the letter sounds and lower and raise the correct hand as the student reads the letters in each row going across the page.

2. Write and read the sentence: Did Dad dig the pit?

3. Have the student read the First Step Reader *The Big Pig* and the word list on the back cover. Ask the following questions:

   Who had a pig? (Dan)
   Have you ever seen a real pig? Tell me about it.
   Where did the pig hide? (in a pit)
   What does nip mean? (to bite)
   Why do you think the pig nipped Dan? (Answers vary.)
   Would you like a pig for a pet? Why? (Answers vary.)

Handwriting Guide
Traditional or **Modern**
Da Da

4. Write the spelling words where students can see them: dig, dim, dad, hid, bad.

   I will give you clues. You write the spelling word that matches the clue.

   Line 1. He is not a mom. (dad) **Did you write *dad* on line 1?**
   Line 2. If you've done this you may be hard to find. (hid)
   Line 3. If a light is not bright it is ____. (dim)
   Line 4. If it isn't good it's this. (bad)
   Line 5. A shovel helps you do this. (dig)

Lesson 63

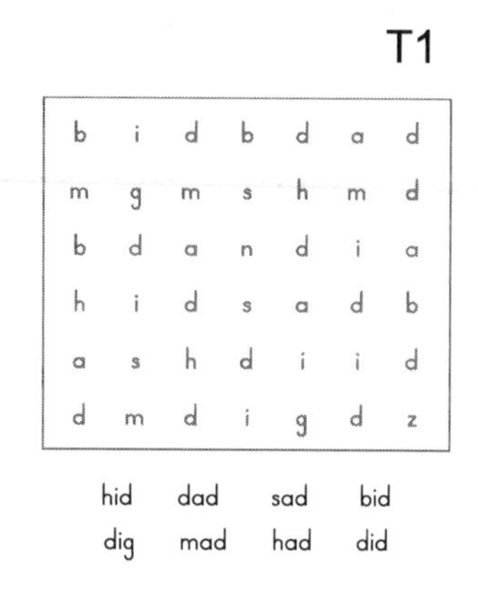

T1

b	i	d	b	d	a	d
m	g	m	s	h	m	d
b	d	a	n	d	i	a
h	i	d	s	a	d	b
a	s	h	d	i	i	d
d	m	d	i	g	d	z

hid dad sad bid
dig mad had did

Lesson Objectives

1. Students will practice visual discrimination skills.
2. Students will practice handwriting.
3. Students will read the book *The Big Pig*.
4. Students will act out the story.
5. Students will take a spelling practice test.

Preparation

* Workbook page
* Handwriting sentence: Did Dan bid on the pig?

Teaching

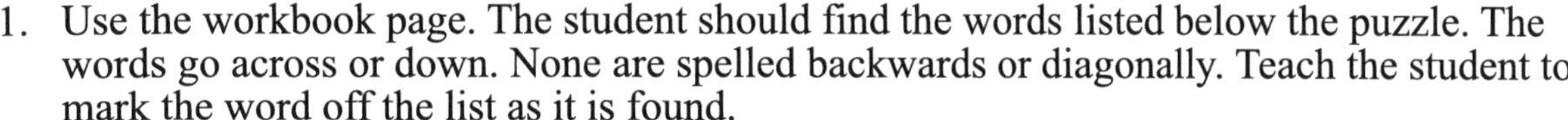

1. Use the workbook page. The student should find the words listed below the puzzle. The words go across or down. None are spelled backwards or diagonally. Teach the student to mark the word off the list as it is found.

   If the student has a difficult time finding words encourage him or her to look for the beginning sound first and see if the rest of the word is around it.

2. Write and read the sentence: Did Dan bid on the pig?

3. Have the student read the First Step Reader *The Big Pig* and the word list. Ask the questions:

   Did the pig nip Dan? (yes)
   Do you think the pig was sorry? Why? (Answers vary.)
   What do you think Dan should do to the pig? (Answers vary.)

4. Have students make puppets out of paper and perform the story.

5. Give the practice spelling test:

   1. dim 2. dad 3. hid 4. bad 5. dig

Handwriting Guide
Traditional or **Modern**

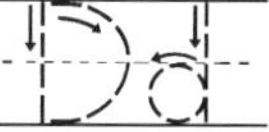

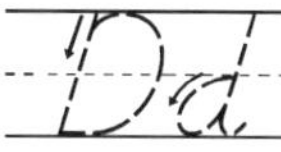

Lesson 64

Lesson Objectives

1. Students will read sentences for meaning.
2. Students will practice handwriting.
3. Students will read the book *The Big Pig*.
4. Students will create a story.
5. Students will write spelling words.

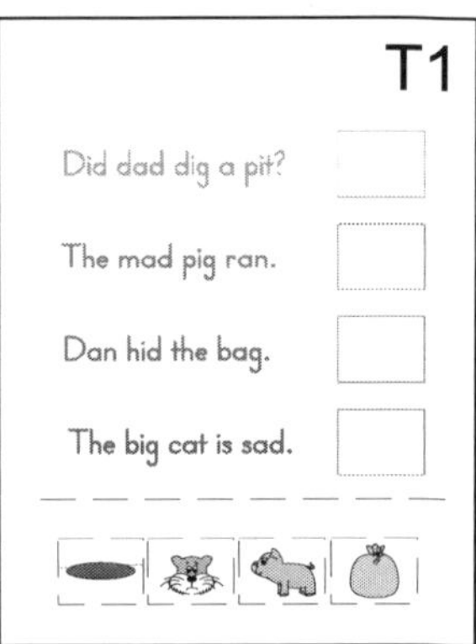

T1

Did dad dig a pit?

The mad pig ran.

Dan hid the bag.

The big cat is sad.

Preparation

* Workbook page 64
* Scissors and glue
* Handwriting sentence: The bad cat hid in the can.

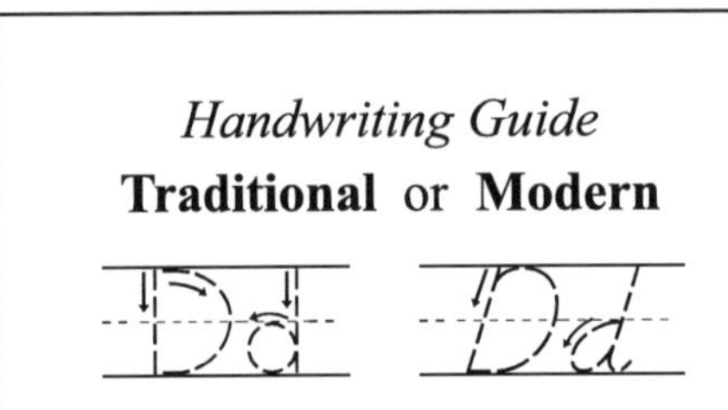

Teaching

1. Use the workbook page. Have the student cut and glue the pictures next to the correct sentences.

2. Write the sentence: The bad cat hid in the can.

3. Have the student read the book *The Big Pig* and the word list on the back cover. As the student looks at the word list ask the following questions:

   What words end with the *d* sound? (bad, did, hid)
   What words begin with the *d* sound? (Dan, did)
   What word means a hole in the ground? (pit)
   Find the word that begins with the *n* sound. What word is it? (nip)
   Change the vowel from i to a. What is the new word? (nap)
   What word describes the size of something? (big)

The Big Pig
word list:

a	hid
bad	in
big	is
can	nip
Dan	pig
did	pit
has	the

4. **The big pig was sorry he nipped Dan. It wanted to show how sorry it was. Have you ever done something wrong that you were sorry for later? What could the pig do to show Dan that it was sorry for nipping Dan? Create your own story.** Alternative idea: Students can create a story about a time they were sorry for doing something wrong. They should tell what they did about it.

5. Write the spelling words where students can see them: dig, dim, dad, hid, bad. Give phonetic clues to help students identify the words.

   On line 1, write the word that ends with the *m* sound. (dim)
   On line 2, write the word that begins and ends with the same sound. (dad)
   On line 3, write the word that begins with the same sound as hat. (hid)
   On line 4, write the word that begins with the *b* sound. (bad)
   On line 5, write the word that ends with the *g* sound. (dig)

Lesson 65

Lesson Objectives

1. Students will take an assessment.
2. Students will review missed concepts.
3. Students will write a sentence.
4. Students will read the book *The Big Pig*.
5. Students will share stories created in Lesson 64.
6. Students will take a spelling test.

Preparation

* Lesson 65 assessment
* Handwriting sentence: Dan had a tan mitt.

Teaching

1. Students will circle the correct word on the assessment page.

   1. did 2. big 3. rib 4. Dan 5. dig

   6. dip 7. bad 8. sad 9. pad 10. hid

2. Review any missed concepts on the assessment.

3. Write the sentence: Dan had a tan mitt.

4. Have the student read the First Step Reader *The Big Pig* and the word list on the back cover. Have the student retell the story in his or her own words.

5. Students will share the stories created in Lesson 64. Encourage students to ask questions about the stories.

6. Give the spelling test:

   1. dim 2. hid 3. dad 4. dig 5. bad

Handwriting Guide

Traditional or **Modern**

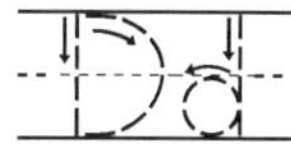

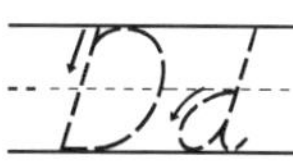

Lesson 66

Lesson Objectives

1. Students will read short o words.
2. Students will write a sentence using short o.
3. Students will read the book *Hot Dog*.
4. Students will learn spelling words.

T1

Preparation

* Workbook page
* Handwriting sentence: Ron has a hot dog.

Teaching

1. Write the words on and in. Point to the word in. **What vowel does this word have?** (i) **What sound does short i make?** (*i*)

   Point to the word on. **What vowel does this word have?** (o) **What sound does short o make?** (*o*) **Today we will begin using short o in other words.**

   Write the words bass, hip, map, and dig. Have students change the vowels to o and make new words. Use the workbook page to sound out short o words. Students fill in the missing o and read the words.

2. Have the student write and read the sentence: Ron has a hot dog.

3. Have the student read the back cover of the book *Hot Dog*. **What word ends with s? You will need to blend the b and s.** (sobs) **What does it mean to sob? Can you act it out? We know that something or someone sobs in this story. Can you guess who? Read the book to find out who sobs and what makes them sob.**

4. Give the spelling pre-test. Tell students that the vowel in all these words is o:

   1. dog
   2. got
   3. nod
   4. mop
   5. toss

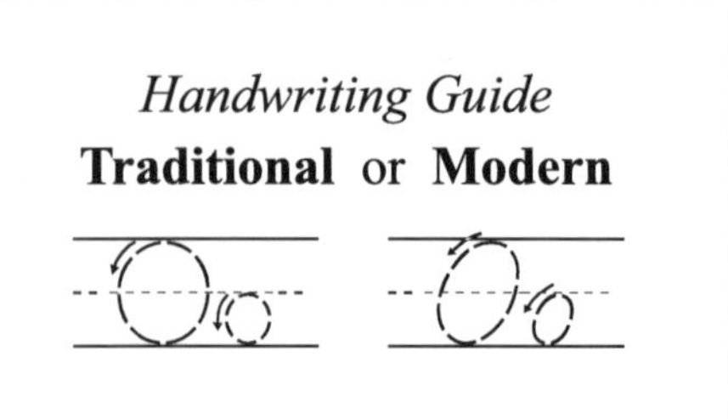

Todd bit a hot dog.

The dog bit the hot dog.

Todd sobs.

Dad got Todd a hot dog.

Hot Dog word list:

a
bit
Dad
dog
got
hot
sobs
the
Todd

Lesson 67

Lesson Objectives

1. Students will review rhyming words and short o.
2. Students will learn vocabulary words.
3. Students will practice handwriting.
4. Students will read the book *Hot Dog*.
5. Students will practice writing spelling words.

	T1
hog	mob
moss	dot
Bob	hop
not	boss
top	dog

Preparation

* Workbook page
* Handwriting sentence: Bob is not the boss.

Teaching

1. Review rhymes with the student. Then review short o. Have the student think of rhymes for these words: Tom (mom), nod (cod, rod), off (cough). Next, find the rhymes on the workbook page.

2. **Write the words cob, cod, hop, sod, nod, hot. What is a cob? Have you ever eaten corn on the cob? It's the part that's left over after you've eaten the corn. Pretend you are eating corn on the cob. Do you know what cod is? It's like a bass. So what is a cod?** (fish) **Act like a cod swimming in the ocean.**

   Act out the next word. (hop) **Do you know what the next word is?** (sod) **It's something you have to mow. It's another name for grass. Pretend you are mowing the sod. Can you act out the next word?** (nod) **The last word is the way it feels in the summer. Act out the word.** (hot)

3. Write and read the sentence: Bob is not the boss.

4. Have the student read the book *Hot Dog* and the word list. Ask the questions:

   What did Todd bite? (a hot dog) Have the student read the sentence on page 1.
   What ate the rest of the hot dog? (a dog)
   What word was used to tell what Todd did after the dog took the hot dog? (sob)
   What does sob mean? (to cry)

5. Write the spelling words where students can see them: dog, got, mop, toss, nod.

   On line one, write the word that rhymes with hop. (mop) **On line 2, write the word that rhymes with cod.** (nod) **On line 3, write the word that rhymes with moss.** (toss) **On line 4, write the word that rhymes with hot.** (got) **On line 5, write the word that rhymes with log.** (dog)

Game:

Ruff's Lunch - Slider Strips 4 and 5

Handwriting Guide

Traditional or **Modern**

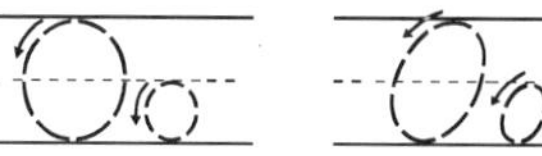

Lesson 68

Lesson Objectives

1. Students will discriminate between vowel sounds.
2. Students will practice handwriting.
3. Students will read the book *Hot Dog*.
4. Students will act out the story.
5. Students will take a spelling practice test.

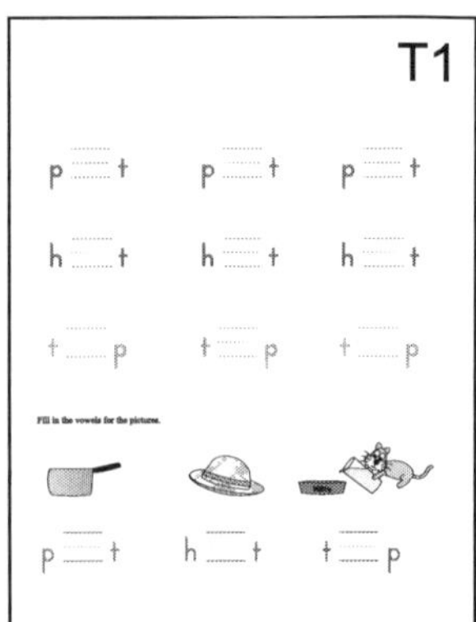

Preparation

* Workbook page
* Handwriting sentence: Pat hid the pot in a pit.

Teaching

1. Say the following words one at a time and have the student tell you the vowel sound in each word: **cat, big, cob, sip, sod, gap, moss, miss, mass, dot**

   Look at the workbook page. The words are missing vowels. Fill in a, i, and o to make different words. Say the words. Students will write in the vowels:

   pot, pat, pit, hat, hot, hit, tip, top, tap

   Write the words that match the pictures at the bottom of the page. You may say the words to students:pot, hat, tip.

2. Write the sentence: Pat hid the pot in a pit.

3. Have the student read the First Step Reader *Hot Dog* and the word list on the back cover. Ask the following questions:

   How did the dad help Todd? (He got Todd another hot dog.)

   What do you think Todd would do if he saw the dog again? (Answers vary.)

   Should Todd have sobbed? What would be a better thing to do?

   Why do you think the dog took the hot dog?

   Have you ever had an animal take food from you?

4. Have students act out the story. Students may add to the story. What would happen if the dog came back for the second hot dog? Maybe Todd's mom could help out.

5. Give the spelling practice test:

   1. got 2. toss 3. mop 4. dog 5. nod

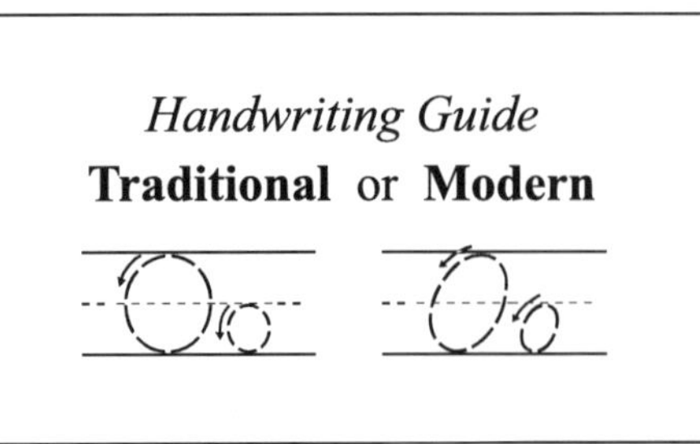

Lesson 69

Lesson Objectives

1. Students will complete sentences using short o words.
2. Students will practice handwriting.
3. Students will read the book *Hot Dog*.
4. Students will create a story.
5. Students will practice spelling words.

T1

hog Bob mop

___ the ___ has a ___.

on dog dot

A ___ is ___ the ___.

pot Ron hot

___ has a ___ ___.

Preparation

* Workbook page
* Handwriting sentence: Ross can toss the mop.

Teaching

1. Write a sentence with words missing: ___ can ___ on ___. Give students three choices for answers: moss, hop, Ross. **There are three words missing in this sentence. You have three choices to fill in the correct words. Fill in the blanks.** (Ross can hop on moss.)

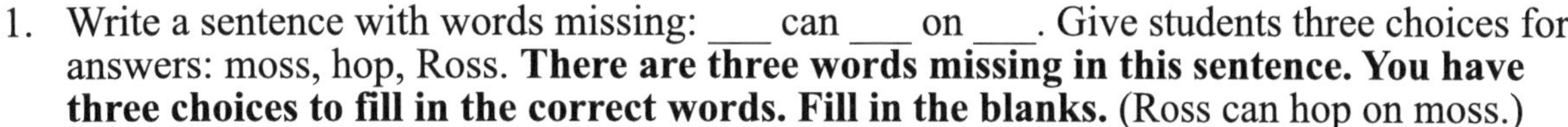

   Use the workbook page. Students will fill in the blanks to complete sentences. The boxes are the word choices for each sentence.

2. Write the sentence: Ross can toss the mop.

3. Have the student read the book *Hot Dog* and the word list on the back cover. As the student looks at the word list ask the following questions:

   What word is something a sad person does? (sobs)

   What words have the *o* sound? (dog, got, hot, sobs, Todd)

   What word is someone's name? (Todd)

   What kind of letter is at the beginning of names? (capital)

   Look at the word hot. What would the word be if I changed the o to a? (hat)

   What if I changed the o to i? (hit)

Hot Dog words

a
bit
Dad
dog
got
hot
sobs
the
Todd

4. Pretend you went to the zoo. You were eating your lunch when all of the sudden, something took your food. What took your food and what would you do? Create a story.

5. Write the words where students can see them: dog, got, mop, toss, nod.
I will say a sentence. One of the words is a spelling word.
Write the spelling word on the line.

   Line 1. I will mop the floor. (mop)

   Line 2. Can you toss a football? (toss)

   Line 3. The dog barked at the cat. (dog)

   Line 4. We got a new puppy. (got)

   Line 5. I will nod my head. (nod)

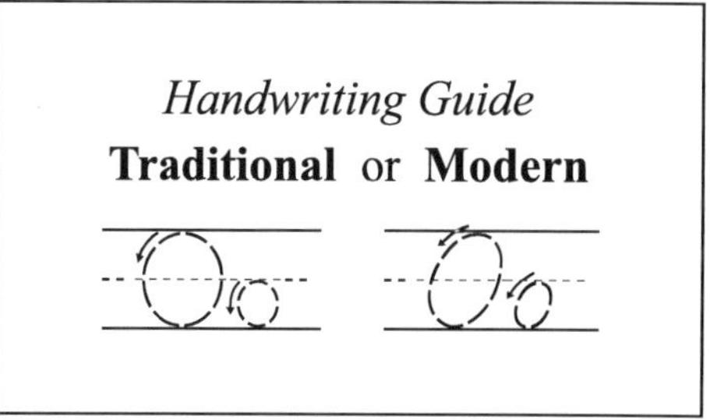

Lesson 70

Lesson Objectives

1. Students will take an assessment.
2. Students will review missed concepts.
3. Students will write a sentence.
4. Students will read the book *Hot Dog*.
5. Students will share stories created in Lesson 69.
6. Students will take a spelling test.

Preparation

* Lesson 70 assessment
* Handwriting sentence: The cob is in the pot.

Teaching

1. Students will circle the correct word on the assessment page.

   1. boss 2. Don 3. hot 4. top 5. dog
   6. cab 7. mop 8. rod 9. rot 10. Tim

2. Review any missed concepts on the assessment.

3. Write the sentence: The cob is in the pot.

4. Have the student read the book *Hot Dog* and the word list on the back cover. Have the student retell the story.

5. Have students share their stories. Encourage students to ask questions.

6. Give the spelling test:

   1. nod 2. dog 3. toss 4. got 5. mop

Handwriting Guide

Traditional or **Modern**

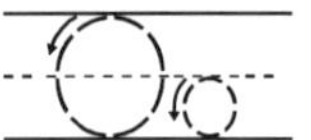
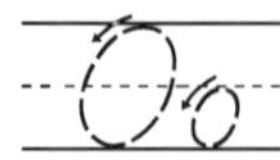

Lesson 71

Lesson Objectives

1. Students will learn the l sound.
2. Students will read words with the l sound.
3. Students will read and illustrate a story.
4. Students will practice handwriting.
5. Students will read the book *Lill.*
6. Students will learn spelling words.

Handwriting Guide
Traditional or **Modern**

Preparation

* Workbook page, crayons
* Handwriting sentence: A doll is on the lid.
* Slider 71, scissors, glue

Teaching

1. **Today you are going to learn a new letter sound.** Write the letter l. **What letter is this? The letter l makes the *ul* sound. Say the l sound.** (*ul*) **Think of things that begin with the *ul* sound.** Have the student say words that begin with l.

   Now let's blend l and a. Write the blend la. Have the students read the blend. Add ending consonants to make the words lad, lag, and lap. Repeat for the beginning blend *li*. Make the words lid, lip, and lit.

   Repeat for the beginning blend *lo*. Make the words log, lop, and lot. Next, do ending blends for *ill* and *oll*. Make the words hill, pill, and doll.

   Write the blend *all*. **Now look at this ending blend. This looks like it should say *al* like in alligator. It doesn't. It makes the same sound as o-l-l. Words like hall and ball are spelled with the letters a-l-l not o-l-l even though the words have the *oll* sound.**

2. Use Slider 71 to practice the *l* sound and to review short o.

3. Have the student read the story on workbook page. Have the student draw an illustration for the story in the box.

   T3
   A log is on a hill.
   A dog is on a log.
   Moss is on the log.
   The log can tip.
   The dog hit his lip.

4. Write the sentence: A doll is on the lid.

5. Have the student read the word list on the back of the book *Lill.* **What are the two names in this list?** (Lill and Pam) **How do you know they are names? What kind of letter do they begin with?** (capital letter)

   One of these names belongs to a little girl. The other name belongs to a doll. Which one do you think is the girl's name? Read the story to find if the girl is Lill or Pam.

6. Give the spelling pre-test:

   1. ball 2. doll 3. hill 4. lap 5. lid

Lesson continued on the next page.

Lill
Lill is a doll.
Pam has Lill.
1
2
The hog has Lill.
The hog sat on the log.
The log lobs Lill.
3
4
Pam has Lill.
Lill word list:
a
doll
has
hog
is
Lill
lobs
log
on
Pam
sat
the

Lesson 72

Lesson Objectives

1. Students will discriminate between vowel sounds.
2. Students will practice handwriting.
3. Students will learn vocabulary words.
4. Students will read the book *Lill.*
5. Students will practice spelling words.

Preparation

* Workbook page
* Handwriting sentence: Sal ran a lap.

Teaching

1. Say the following words one at a time and have the student tell you the vowel sound in each word:
   loss, lass, lip, lap, lop, lid, lad, log, Bill, hill

   Next, use the workbook page. Have the student write a word for each picture. Say the names for each picture. The pictures are: **ball, log, lip, tall (giraffe), doll, hill.**

2. Write the sentence: Sal ran a lap.

3. Write the words lap, lip, lob, hill, and call. Have students think of different ways to act out the words.

4. Have the student read the book *Lill* and the word list. Ask the questions:

   What is Lill? (a doll)
   Find the sentence that tells you this. Who does Lill belong to? (Pam)
   What took Lill away from Pam? (a hog)
   Did you like this story? Why or why not?
   How do you think Pam felt when she couldn't find her doll?
   How would you fell if you lost a toy?

5. Write the spelling words where students can see them: ball, doll, hill, lap, lid.

   I will give clues. Write the spelling word that matches the clue.

   Line 1. This is the top of a can. (lid)
   Line 2. This is something that bounces. (ball)
   Line 3. This goes away when you stand up. (lap)
   Line 4. This is something you climb. (hill)
   Line 5. This is a toy that looks like a baby. (doll)

Handwriting Guide
Traditional or **Modern**

Lesson 73

Lesson Objectives

1. Students will learn s as an ending sound.
2. Students will practice handwriting.
3. Students will read the book *Lill.*
4. Students will act out the story.
5. Students will take a spelling practice test.

Preparation

* Workbook page
* Handwriting sentence: Tim's pigs nap on the logs.

T1

1. The cat nap_ on the log.
2. Tom'_ dog bit the pill.
3. Pam had 3 doll_.
4. Dan can tap the can'_ lid.
5. The 2 lad_ sat on a hill.
6. Bill lob_ the ball.

Teaching

1. Although we have blended s at the end of words in a few stories, it has never formally been introduced. You may refer back to *Cat In A Bin*, *Map & Ham*, and *Hot Dog*. Write the letter s. **What letter is this?** (s) **What sound does s make?** (*s*) Write the letter p in front of the s. **We are going to blend the letters p and s.** Help the student blend the letters and repeat for g and s.

   Why do you think we have to add s to words like nap, bag, and pig? (Answers vary.) **Listen to this sentence: The rabbit hop. Did that sentence sound right?** (no) **Let me change it by adding an s to the word hop. The rabbit hops. Sometimes we add an s to a word that tells what one thing is doing. Sometimes we add s to words that tell us about things.**

   Listen to this sentence. The pig are in the pen. Did that sound right? (no) **I need to add an s to the word pig. Listen again: The pigs are in the pen. I need to change the word pig to pigs to show that there are many pigs.**

   Finally sometimes we add s to the end of someone's name to show that something else belongs to them. Listen to this sentence. I'll say it wrong the first time. This is (say the student's name without the possessive s and point to the workbook) **book. Now I'll add an s to your name and say the sentence right.** (Repeat the sentence correctly.)

   When I write that, (demonstrate writing the student's name with an apostrophe on the paper) **I have to put this little mark called an apostrophe between your name and the s. This shows that we're talking about something that belongs to you.** The student does not need to remember the word apostrophe. This was introduced just so the student will be aware of it when he or she encounters it while reading.

   There are sentences on the workbook page where one word needs an s. Students should read the sentences. Add an s on the blank lines and reread the sentence. Students should see how adding the s changes the sentence so that it sounds right. The first sentence is an example.

2. Write the sentence: Tim's pigs nap on the logs.

Lesson continued on the next page.

Lesson 73

3. Have the student read the First Step Reader *Lill* and the word list. Ask the student the following questions:

   Where did the hog sit? (on a log)

   Find the sentence that tells you that. (page 3) Have the student read the sentence.

   What word on page three means to toss or throw? (lobs)

   Who had Lill at the end of the story? (Pam)

   How did Pam get Lill back? (Answers may vary, but should include the idea that she caught the doll.)

   How do you think Pam felt about the pig at the end of the story?

4. Have students act out the story. You may point out that the book doesn't show us all the parts of the story.

   What did Pam do when the pig took Lill? Did the pig really grab it out of her arms? Maybe she set it down and the pig took it. Pam may have looked for Lill for a long time.

5. Give the spelling practice test:

   1. lap 2. hill 3. ball 4. doll 5. lid

Handwriting Guide

Traditional or **Modern**

Lesson 74

Lesson Objectives

1. Students will answer questions.
2. Students will practice handwriting.
3. Students will read the book *Lill.*
4. Students will create a story.
5. Students will practice spelling words.

T1

Can a doll sit?
yes no

Is the pig on a log?
yes no

Is a lid on the can?
yes no

Preparation

* Workbook page
* Handwriting sentence: Did the hogs tip the cans?

Teaching

1. **Look at the questions on the workbook page. Under each question are the words yes and no in ovals. Read the questions and fill in an answer.**

2. Handwriting sentence: Did the hogs tip the cans?

3. Have the student read the First Step Reader *Lill* and the word list. Have the student look at the word list and answer the following questions:

   What word is spelled l-o-b-s? (lobs)
   Say the word without the s (lob)
   What does it mean to lob something? (to throw)
   Act out the word.
   What word both begins and ends with the *l* sound? (Lill)
   What other words begin with the *l* sound? (lobs, log)
   What other word ends with the *l* sound? (doll)
   How many l's are at the end of the word doll? (2)
   You may explain that this is a spelling rule and does not change the way we say the word.
   What words are names? (Lill, Pam)
   What kind of letter do names begin with? (a capital letter)
   Besides Lill and Pam, what words are things you can see? (doll, hog, log)

<u>Lill</u> word list:

a	lobs
doll	log
has	on
hog	Pam
is	sat
Lill	the

4. **Lill was Pam's favorite toy. Do you have a favorite toy? Write a story telling about your favorite toy, or a toy you would like to have.**

5. Write the words where students can see them: ball, doll, hill, lap, lid.

   I will say sentences. In each sentence is a spelling word. Listen for the spelling word and write it on the line.

   Line 1. The doll had a pink dress. (doll)
   Line 2. The cat sat on my lap. (lap)
   Line 3. The ball bounces high. (ball)
   Line 4. A lid is on the tin can. (lid)
   Line 5. Can we climb the tall hill? (hill)

Lesson 75

Lesson Objectives

1. Students will take an assessment.
2. Students will review missed concepts.
3. Students will write a sentence.
4. Students will read the First Step Reader *Lill*.
5. Students will share stories from Lesson 74.
6. Students will take a spelling test.

Preparation

* Lesson 75 assessment
* Handwriting sentence: The cat tips Sal's doll.

Teaching

1. Students will circle the correct word on the assessment page.

   1. lad 2. mill 3. lop 4. lot 5. lass

   6. dill 7. lob 8. lag 9. bill 10. lip

2. Review any missed concepts on the assessment.

3. Write the sentence: The cat tips Sal's doll.

4. Have the student read the First Step Reader *Lill* and the word list.

5. Students will share their stories from Lesson 74. Ask students to tell more about their favorite toy. For example, **Why is it your favorite? How did you get it?**

6. Give the spelling test:

   1. hill 2. lid 3. doll 4. lap 5. ball

Reading Books

Beginning with Lesson 76 the student will read a new book every five lessons. A brief introduction will be included in the first lesson of the week. Follow the sequence below through each 5 lesson book unit. The sequence is much the same as the set of pre-readers. Follow this procedure:

Day 1:
a) Introduce the reading book and the word list on the back cover.
b) Have the student read the first half of the book.

Day 2:
a) The student should review the word list on the back cover.
b) Ask questions over first half of the book.
c) Have the student read the second half of the book.

Day 3:
a) The student should review the word list on the back cover.
b) Ask the student the questions over the second half of the book.
c) Have the student read the whole book.
d) Have students do a play or puppet show about the book. Additional ideas may be listed in the lesson plans.

Day 4:
a) The student should review the word list. Ask questions about the words.
b) Have the student read the book.
c) Do the workbook question sheet.
d) Students will create stories. Story ideas will be listed in lesson plans.

Day 5:
a) Have the student tell the book in their own words.
b) Have the student read the book.
c) Students may color the coloring page from the resource pack.

Feel free to change the structure as needed. The student may be able to read the whole book on the first day. You may also want children to read silently some days. The books will follow this order (the lesson it begins on is also listed):

Lesson	Book	Lesson	Book
76	*Cat Nap*	126	*Sam and the Shark*
81	*Sam and Kit*	131	*Rose the Mole*
86	*Pup in Mud*	136	*Quack and Quill*
91	*Mop, Mop, Mop*	141	*The Mule Ride*
96	*Vic's Van*	146	*Kate's Nest*
101	*Red and Bess*	151	*Can a Deer Steer?*
106	*Fuzz the Yak*	156	*Ruff Camps*
111	*The Ape and Cake*	161	*Goat and Toad*
116	*Jane's Jet*	166	*Kay and the Ray Gun*
121	*Ruff's Cab*	171	*Greg's Grape Ride*

Lesson 76

Lesson Objectives

1. Students will learn the f sound.
2. Students will practice visual discrimination.
3. Students will practice handwriting.
4. Students will learn spelling words.
5. Students will begin reading *Cat Nap*.

T2

f	i	n	f	i	l	l
a	f	o	g	f	f	f
n	i	f	f	o	f	a
f	t	f	f	a	d	t
f	f	o	l	l	o	f
i	a	h	f	f	i	g

fan fit fog fill fin
fad off if fat fig

Preparation

* Workbook page
* Handwriting sentence: Bill's fan fits in the can.

Teaching

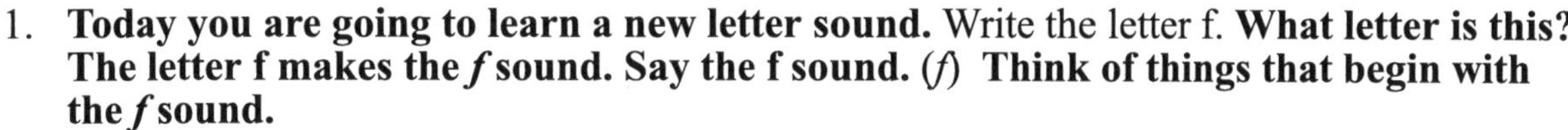

1. **Today you are going to learn a new letter sound.** Write the letter f. **What letter is this? The letter f makes the *f* sound. Say the f sound.** (*f*) **Think of things that begin with the *f* sound.**

   Have the student say words that begin with f. **Now let's blend f and a.** Write the blend fa. Help the student form the words fad, fan, and fat. Repeat for the beginning blend *fi.* Make the words fib, fig, fin, and fit. Repeat for the beginning blend *fo.* Make the word fog.

2. Use the workbook page. The student should find the words listed below the puzzle. The words go across or down. No words are spelled backwards or diagonally.

   Remind the student to mark the word off the list as it is found. If the student has a difficult time finding words, encourage him or her to look for the beginning sound first and see if the rest of the word is around it.

3. Write and read the sentence: Bill's fan fits in the can.

4. Give the spelling pre-test:

   1. fan, 2. fall, 3. fog, 4. fill, 5. off (You may tell students it has two f's at the end.)

   After completing the pre-test, have students think of an action to go with each word. Decide as a group on one action for each word. Students should be able to perform the action while sitting down. In the next lesson, you will give the action and students will write the spelling word.

5. **A cat takes a nap and goes for a wild ride. How do you think the cat will like it? Read the story *Cat Nap* to find out.**

Games:

Ruff's Lunch - Slider Strip 6
Wiggle Worm 2

Handwriting Guide
Traditional or **Modern**

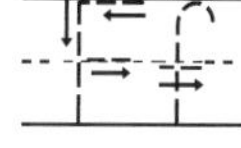

The cat sat.

1

The cat naps.

2

The cat sags.

3

The cat falls off.
The cat is in the bag.

4

The cat fills the bag.
Pam has the fat bag.

5

The fat bag fills the can.

6

The man has the bag.

7

The bag falls off.
Can the cat pass the bag?

8

The cat is on the cab.

9

The cat falls off the cab.
The cat fits on Pat's cap.

10

The cat naps on a cap.

11

The cat sat.

12

Cat Nap word list:

bag	fat	off
cab	fits	on
can	has	Pam
cap	in	pass
cat	is	Pat's
falls	man	sags
fills	naps	sat
		the

Lesson 77

Lesson Objectives

1. Students will review rhyming words and f.
2. Students will learn vocabulary words.
3. Students will practice handwriting.
4. Students will answer questions about the book.
5. Students will practice writing spelling words.

Preparation

* Workbook page 77
* Handwriting sentence: The bass hit his fin.
* Optional: fig and/or fig cookies.

Teaching

1. Review rhymes with the student. Then review the f sound. Next, find the rhymes on the workbook page.

2. Write the words fib, fad, and fig. **What is a fib? If you don't tell the truth, you are telling a fib. What is another name for fib?** (lie)

   Let's look at the next word. If a toy becomes very popular for awhile, then after a while it's not as popular, it's called a fad. Can you think of a fad?

   What does fig mean? Is it something you do or see? A fig is a fruit. (You may share the fig or cookies at this point.)

3. Write and read the sentence: The bass hit his fin.

4. Questions over the first half of *Cat Nap*:

   What was the cat sitting on at the beginning of the story? (a table)

   What did the cat fall into? (a bag)

   Did Pam know that the cat was in the bag? (No)

   What do you think a real cat would have done?

   What do you think will happen next?

   Students can now read the second half of the book.

5. Write the spelling words where students can see them: fan, fall, fog, fill, off.
   Act out the spelling words and have students write them on the lines in the following order:

   1. fill 2. fan 3. fall 4. off 5. fog

Handwriting Guide
Traditional or **Modern**

Lesson 78

Lesson Objectives

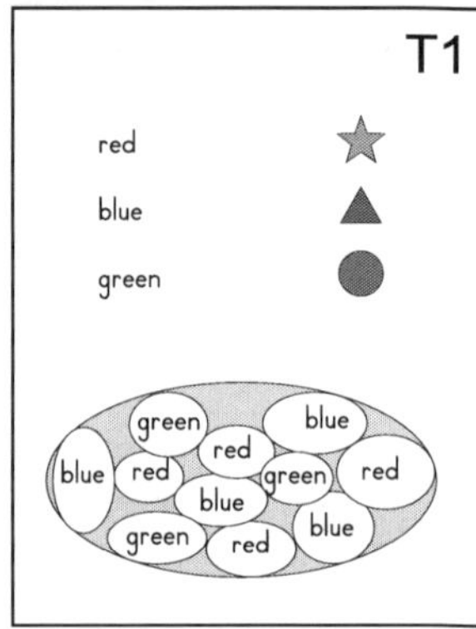

1. Students will learn the color words red, green, blue.
2. Students will practice handwriting.
3. Students will answer questions about the book *Cat Nap*.
4. Students will act out the story.
5. Students will take a spelling practice test.

Preparation

* Red, green and blue construction paper
* Workbook page, crayons: red, blue, and green
* Handwriting sentence: The red bag is fat.

Teaching

1. Although most of the color words can not be spelled with the phonetic knowledge the student has already learned, point out as many phonetic elements as possible that the student can use as clues for decoding the words.

   Write the words red, green, and blue. **These words are all names of colors.** Point to red. **What sound does this word begin with?** (*r*) **What color begins with *r*?** (red) If the student can't answer the question, use the construction paper as a clue. Match the color word to the color (construction paper). **How do you spell red?** (r-e-d) **What vowel is in the word red?** (e)**What letter does red end with?** (d)

   Repeat the procedure for the words green and blue. After all three colors have been introduced, drill the student by mixing up the words and having the student match them to the construction paper. Have the student match words to colors on the top of the workbook page. Next, students will color the ovals at the bottom of the page to match the words. Review color words daily as they are learned.

2. Handwriting sentence: The red bag is fat.

3. Questions over the second half of *Cat Nap*:

   How did the bag get in the truck? (A man put it in.)
   How did the cat get out of the truck? (It flew out.)
   Who was in the cab? (Pat)
   Do you think this story could really happen? Why or why not?
   Did you like this story? What did you like? What would you change?

4. Have students act out the story. They may want to use paper puppets.

5. Give the spelling practice test:

   1. off 2. fill 3. fog 4. fall 5. fan

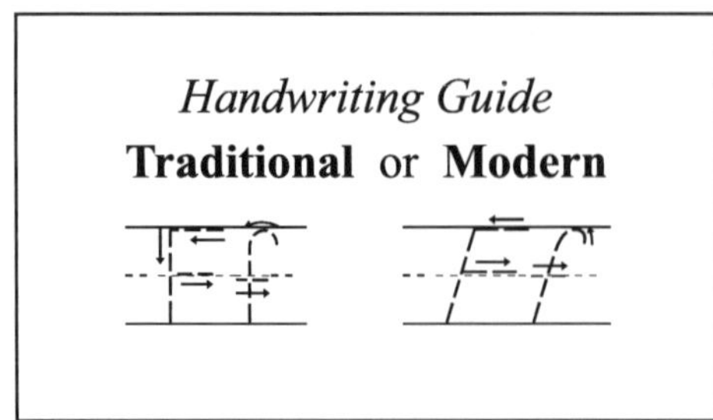

Lesson 79

Lesson Objectives

1. Students will use reading comprehension skills.
2. Students will practice handwriting.
3. Students will answer questions about the word list on *Cat Nap*.
4. Students will create a story.
5. Students will practice writing spelling words.

T1

Cat Nap

Did the cat sag? ◯ ◯

Did the cat pass the cab? ◯ ◯

Did the cat nap on a cap? ◯ ◯

Did the cat sit on a dog? ◯ ◯

Preparation

* Workbook page
* Handwriting sentence: The blue pan is in a green can.

Teaching

1. Have the student read the questions on the workbook page. The questions are about the story *Cat Nap*. The student should answer the questions by filling in the correct oval.

   Answers: 1. yes 2. no 3. yes 4. no

2. Handwriting sentence: The blue pan is in a green can.

3. Students will look at the back of the book and answer the questions about the list.

   What words have two different consonants at the end? (falls, fills, fits, naps, Pat's, sags)

   What is something you wear? (cap)

   What is something you ride in? (cab)

   What words have the short o sound? (off, on)

   What four words have the short i sound? (in, is, fills, fits)

   What word rhymes with bass? (pass)

Cat Nap word list:

bag, cab, can, cap, cat, falls, fills

fat, fits, has, in, is, man, naps

off, on, Pam, pass, Pat's, sags, sat, the

4. **Pam and Pat were going on a trip. They were packing a suitcase. The cat was asleep on the dresser. What do you think happened next? Make up a story.**

5. Write the words where students can see them: fan, fall, fog, fill, off.

   Line 1. Write the word that rhymes with call. (fall)

   Line 2. Write the word that rhymes will pan. (fan)

   Line 3. Write the word that rhymes with hog. (fog)

   Line 4. Write the word that rhymes with cough. (off)

   Line 5. Write the word that rhymes with bill. (fill)

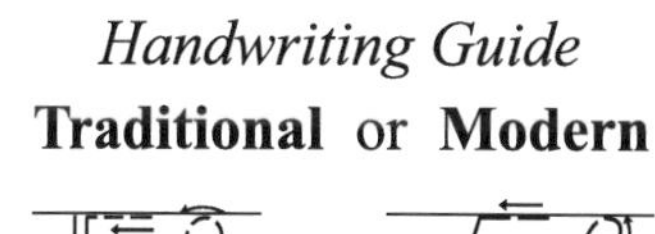

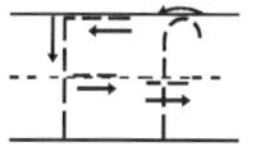

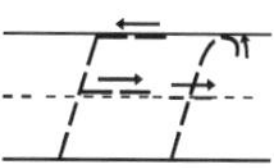

Lesson 80

Lesson Objectives

1. Students will take an assessment.
2. Students will review missed concepts.
3. Students will write a sentence.
4. Students will share stories.
5. Students will take a spelling test.

Preparation

* Lesson 80 assessment
* Handwriting sentence: A green dot is on the fan.

Teaching

1. Students will circle the correct word on the assessment page.

   1. fad 2. fin 3. red 4. fog 5. fat
   6. blue 7. fill 8. green 9. got 10. off

2. Review any missed concepts on the assessment.

3. Handwriting sentence: A green dot is on the fan.

4. Share stories from Lesson 79.

5. Give the spelling test:

   1. fall 2. fog 3. off 4. fan 5. fill

Lesson 81

Lesson Objectives

1. Students will learn the k sound.
2. Students will learn the spelling rule for c and k.
3. Students will practice handwriting.
4. Students will begin reading *Sam and Kit*.

Note: The spelling list will not be given until Lesson 82

T2

☐id	☐ot
☐ap	☐en
☐it	☐iss
☐ob	☐an

Preparation

* Workbook page
* Handwriting sentence: Kim can kiss the cat.

Teaching

1. **Today you are going to learn a new letter sound.** Write the letter k. **What sound does the letter k makes? It makes the *k* sound. Say the k sound.** (*k*) **It has the same sound as c does in the word cat.**

2. Note: You may want to write the spelling examples given in this section to illustrate the spelling rules. **Why do you think we have two letters that make the same sound?** (Answer vary.)

   We have words in our language from all over the world. A long time ago people used different letters to stand for different sounds. Words whose next letter is short a, o or u are spelled using the letter c. Cat, cod, and cup begin with c.

   Words whose next letter is short i or e begin with the letter k. Kit and Ken begin with K.

   When the *k* sound is at the end of a word with a short vowel sound, it is spelled with both a c and a k. Write the words back and sick as examples.

   Have the student practice the beginning letter spelling rules using the workbook page.

3. Write and read the sentence: Kim can kiss the cat.

4. **We have another story about a cat this week. This time, the cat is trying to catch something. Look at the word list on the back of the book. What do you think the cat is trying to catch? Read the book to find out if you are right.** Point out the words on the back of the book. Help students blend the letter s at the ends of the words *kicks, licks, lips, rams, Sam's,* and *sits*.

Handwriting Guide

Traditional or **Modern**

Kk Kk

Sam and Kit

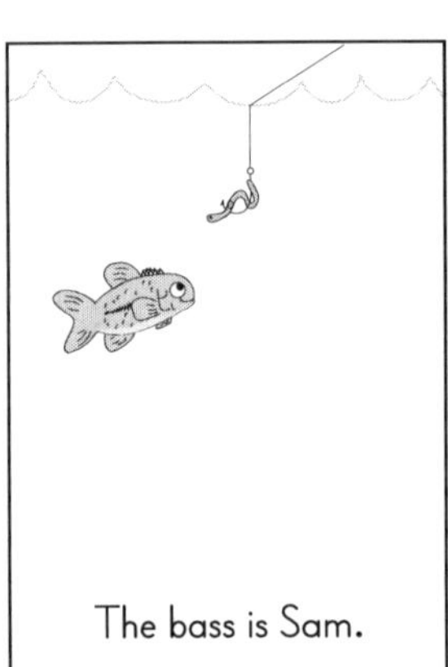

The bass is Sam.

1

The cat is Kit.
The fat cat has Sam.

2

Sam is in the pan.
Kit licks his lips.

3

Sam can nip Kit.
Kit kicks the pan.

4

Kit has Sam's fin.

5

Sam is in the can.
Kit can pick on Sam.

6

The can is on Kit.

7

Sam rams Kit's back.

8

Sam sits on a rock.
Kit is in the pan.

9

Sam and Kit word list:

and	his	on
back	in	pan
bass	is	pick
bit	it	rams
can	kick	rock
cat	kicks	Sam
fat	Kit	Sam's
fin	licks	sits
has	lips	the

Lesson 82

T1

Lesson Objectives

1. Students will learn the ck ending.
2. Students will practice handwriting
3. Students will answer questions.
4. Students will learn spelling words.

Preparation

* Workbook page
* Handwriting sentence: A rock is in the sock.
* Slider 82, scissors, glue

Teaching

1. **Yesterday you learned the k sound. Say the k sound.** (*k*) **What other letter makes this sound?** (c)

   When words that have short vowels end with the k sound, we write the c and the k together. Look at the workbook page. The pictures are: a rock, a tack, a sock, a pick, a sack, and a lock. Fill in the missing vowels.

   Now write the words that tell what Ruff has is carrying. (back pack)

   Use Slider 82 to practice reading words that end with ck.

2. Handwriting sentence: A rock is in the sock.

3. Questions over the first half of *Sam and Kit*:

   What was the cat doing at the beginning of the story? (fishing)

   Why would a cat be fishing?

   Who is Sam? (the bass)

   Where did the cat put Sam? (in a pan)

   What is the cat's name? (Kit)

   How did Sam get away? (He nipped Kit.)

   What does nip mean? (bite)

   What do you think will happen next?

   Do you want the fish to get away or the cat to have a good meal?

   Have you ever gone fishing?

   Students can now read the second half of the book.

4. Give the students a pretest.
   Remind students of the two k spelling rules:

   1. kiss 2. kid 3. back 4. sick 5. rock

Handwriting Guide

Traditional or **Modern**

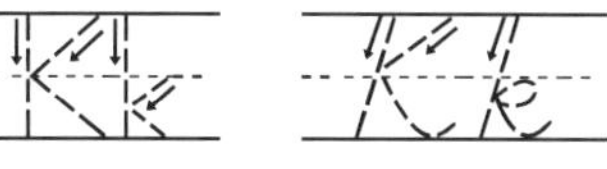

Game:

Wiggle Worm 2

Lesson 83

Lesson Objectives

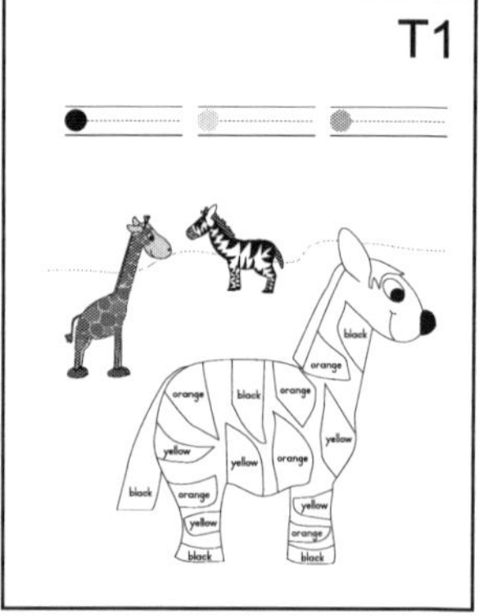

1. Students will learn the color words black, yellow, and orange.
2. Students will practice handwriting.
3. Students will answer questions.
4. Students will act out the story.
5. Students will practice writing spelling words.

Preparation

* Construction paper - red, blue, black, green, yellow, orange – small squares for each student.
* Workbook page, crayons: black, yellow, and orange
* Handwriting sentence: A tack is in the black sack.

Teaching

1. Write the color words red, green, and blue. **Say these words. Match the words to the construction paper. When I point to a word, hold up that color.** Point to the word black. **What two letters does this word end with?** (ck) **You know all the sounds in this word. Try to sound it out.**

   Point out the phonetic elements in yellow and orange. Have the student practice matching the words to the construction paper.

   On the workbook page students will write the names of the colors of the dots. The student should color the large zebra on the workbook page using the color words.

2. Handwriting sentence: A tack is in the black sack.

3. Questions over the second half of *Sam and Kit*:

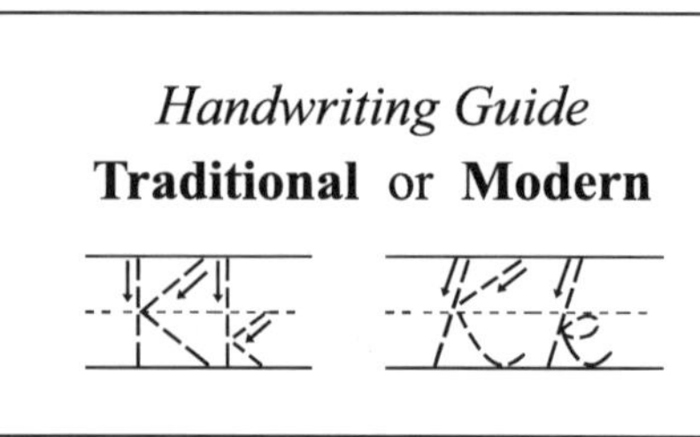

   What did Kit get stuck in? (a can)

   How did the cat get out of the water? (Sam rammed it.)

   Where did the cat end up? (in the pan)

   Where did Sam sit? (on a rock)

   Do you think this story could really happen? Why or why not?

   Did you like the way this story ended?

4. Have students act out the story using people or puppets.

5. Write the spelling words where students can see them: kiss, kid, back, sick, rock.

   Write the word that rhymes with hid on line 1. (kid)

   On line 2 write the word that rhymes with sack. (back)

   Line 3. miss (kiss)

   Line 4. clock (rock)

   Line 5. pick (sick)

Lesson 84

Lesson Objectives

T1

Is Sam the cat?

Is the cat fat?

Did Kit kick Sam?

Did Sam ram Kit?

Did Sam kiss Kit?

1. Students will use reading comprehension skills.
2. Students will practice handwriting.
3. Students will create a story.
4. Students will answer questions about the word list.
5. Students will practice spelling words.

Preparation

* Workbook page
* Handwriting sentence: Bill's sock is yellow.

Teaching

1. Have the student read the questions on the workbook page. The questions are about the story *Sam and Kit*. The student should answer the questions by filling in the correct oval.

2. Handwriting sentence: Bill's sock is yellow.

3. Have the students create their own fishing story. It can be about a real fishing experience or students can make one up.

4. Have students look at the word list on the back of the book *Sam and the Cat.*

   What word described the size of the cat? (fat)

   What word rhymes with it? (cat)

   What words end with ck? (back, kick, lick, pick, rock)

   What words begin with k? (kick, kicks, Kit)
   What words have a k sound and end with s? (kicks, licks)

   What word is a kind of fish? (bass)

   What word means it belongs to Sam? (Sam's)

   What helps a fish to swim? (fin)

Sam and Kit word list:

and	has	on
back	in	pan
bass	is	pick
bit	it	rams
can	kick	rock
cat	kicks	Sam
fat	Kit	Sam's
fin	licks	sits
his	lips	the

5. Write the words where students can see them: kiss, kid, back, sick, rock.

   I will say clues. Write the spelling word that answers the clue.

   Line 1. If you take *l* out of the word black, you get this word. (back)
   Line 2. If you take *t* out of the word stick, you get this word. (sick)
   Line 3. This is something you might call a child. (kid)
   Line 4. This is something you do with lips. (kiss)
   Line 5. This is something that is very hard. (rock)

Lesson 85

Lesson Objectives

1. Students will take an assessment.
2. Students will review missed concepts.
3. Students will write a sentence.
4. Students will share stories.
5. Students will take a spelling test.

Preparation

* Lesson 85 assessment
* Handwriting sentence: Kim has an orange hat.

Teaching

1. Students will circle the correct word on the assessment page.

   1. pack 2. lock 3. cat 4. yellow 5. orange
   6. kiss 7. rock 8. tick 9. sack 10. black

2. Review any missed concepts on the assessment.

3. Handwriting sentence: Kim has an orange hat.

4. Have students share stories from Lesson 84.

5. Give students the spelling test:

   1. back 2. kid 3. rock 4. kiss 5. sick

Handwriting Guide
Traditional or **Modern**

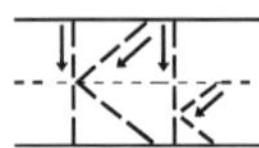
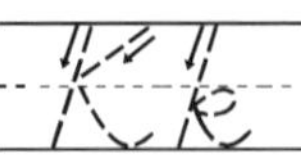

Lesson 86

Lesson Objectives

1. Students will learn the short u sound.
2. Students will practice handwriting.
3. Students will begin reading *Pup in Mud.*
4. Students will learn spelling words.

Preparation

* Workbook page
* Handwriting sentence: Mud is on the cups.

Teaching

1. **Today you are going to learn a new letter sound.** Write the vowels a, e, i, o, and u. **Are these letters vowels or consonants?** (vowels) **Today we'll begin using the short u sound. Short u says *u* as in umbrella. Say the short u sound.** (*u*) **Can you think of any words that have the *u* sound?**

   I'll say some words. Raise your hand if you hear the short u sound, *u*. Fan, bus, dig, hot, cub, cap, hug, mud. What word would I get if I changed the a in fan to u? (fun) **What about the a in cap?** (cup) **The i in dig?** (dug) **The o in hot?** (hut) **Which word still means about the same thing even after we changed the vowel?** (dig – dug) **The vowel sound changes to tell us when the digging happened. Can you think of some words we can change just the vowel to u to make new words?**

   Have the student do the workbook page by filling in the missing letters. The pictures are: cup, bus, sun, bug, nut, duck, pup, bun, tub.

2. Write and read the sentence: Mud is on the cups.

3. **What would you do if you had a pup that got into mud? Look at the word list on the back of the book. Who do you think the pup belongs to?** (Tom) **Read the story to find out what Tom does when his pup is muddy.**

4. Give the students a spelling pre-test. Tell students that all these words have the short u sound:

   1. bus 2. duck 3. pup 4. hug 5. fun

Game:

Wiggle Worm 2

Handwriting Guide

Traditional or **Modern**

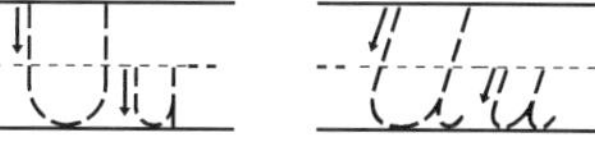

Pup In Mud

Pup In Mud word list:

a	hugs	pup
back	in	suds
bit	is	the
bug	mud	Tom
digs	not	Tom's
dug	picks	tub
hog	pit	tugs
		up

Lesson 87

Lesson Objectives

1. Students will review rhyming words short u.
2. Students will practice handwriting.
3. Students will answer questions.
4. Students will practice spelling words.

T1	
tub	pup
cut	rub
sup	sun
hug	mug
run	but

Preparation

* Workbook page
* Handwriting sentence: The pup is not a mutt.

Teaching

1. Review rhymes with the student. Then review the short u sound. Next, find the rhymes on the workbook page.

2. Write and read the sentence: The pup is not a mutt.

3. Questions over the first half of *Pup in Mud*:

   What happened in the first half of the story?

   Who did the pup belong to? (Tom)

   What was Tom doing to the pup? (giving it a bath)

   Do you think the pup liked taking a bath? (Answers vary.)

   What did the pup do? (It ran away.)

   What do you think will happen next?

   Students can now read the second half of the book.

4. Write the spelling words where students can see them: bus, duck, pup, hug, fun. **I will say sentences. A spelling word is in each sentence. Listen for the spelling word and write it on the lines.**

   Line 1. The pup is very cute. (pup)

   Line 2. It was a bumpy bus ride. (bus)

   Line 3. Reading is a lot of fun. (fun)

   Line 4. The duck quacked at us. (duck)

   Line 5. I like getting a warm hug. (hug)

Handwriting Guide

Traditional or **Modern**

Uu Uu

Lesson 88

Lesson Objectives

1. Students will learn the color words brown, pink, and purple.
2. Students will prepare for Test 2.
3. Student will practice handwriting.
4. Students will answer questions.
5. Students will act out the story.
6. Students will practice spelling words.

Preparation

* Construction paper - red, blue, black, green, yellow, orange, brown, pink, purple
* Workbook page, crayons
* Handwriting sentence: Pink gum is fun.

Teaching

1. Write the words red, blue, black, green, yellow, orange, brown, pink, and purple. **I will point to color words. Match the words to the construction paper.** Point out the phonetic elements in pink, purple, and brown. Point out the differences between pink and purple.

   Point out the differences between the words blue, black, and brown. Have the student practice matching the words to the construction paper.

   Workbook page: Write the names for the colors of the dots. Color the ice cream cones using the color words.

2. Test 2 will be given in Lesson 90. Preview the test and see if there are any concepts students need to review.

3. Handwriting sentence: Pink gum is fun.

4. Questions over the second half of *Pup in Mud*:

   What did the pup tug? (a hog)

   What happened to the hog? (It fell in the pit.)

   How did the pup get out of the pit? (Tom picked it up.)

   How do you think Tom felt about the pup?

   How would you feel?

   What do you think the pup was thinking during the story? (Answers vary.)

5. Have students act out the story. Encourage students to add dialog. What was the pup thinking in the story? Have students speak it out loud.

6. Give the students a practice test. (The final test will be in Lesson 89.)

   1. bus 2. pup 3. fun 4. duck 5. hug

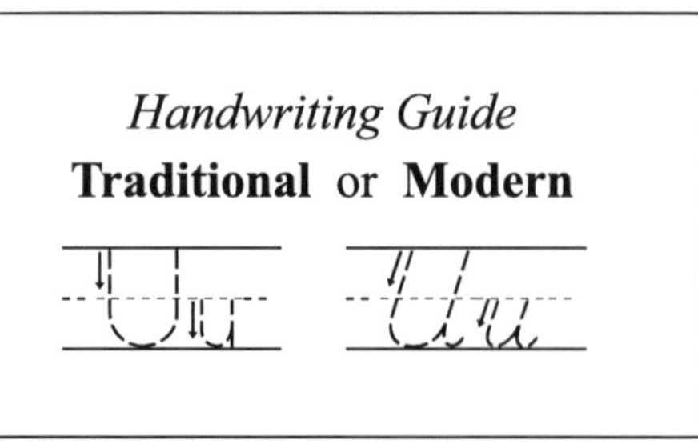

Lesson 89

Lesson Objectives

1. Students will use reading comprehension skills.
2. Students will practice handwriting.
3. Students will answer questions.
4. Students will create a story.
5. Students will take a spelling test.

T1

Pup in Mud

Is the pup Tom's?

Did the pup dig up a bug?

Did a cat dig in the mud?

Did the hog tug the pup?

Did Tom pick up the pup?

Preparation

* Workbook page
* Handwriting sentence: A brown duck is on the purple bus.

Teaching

1. Have the student read the questions on the workbook page. The questions are about the story *Pup in Mud*. The student should answer the questions by filling in the correct oval.

2. Handwriting sentence: A brown duck is on the purple bus.

3. Students should look at the back of the book to answer the questions:

   What two words rhyme with lugs? (hugs, tugs)

   What word means tiny bubbles? (suds)

   What word means a hole in the ground? (pit)

   What word rhymes with it? (bit)

   What is something you take a bath in? (tub)

   Why is there an s at the end of Tom's?
   (It shows something belongs to Tom.)

Pup In Mud word list:

a	hugs	pup
back	in	suds
bit	is	the
bug	mud	Tom
digs	not	Tom's
dug	picks	tub
hog	pit	tugs
		up

4. **Do you have a pet? Has it ever tried to run away from you? Write a story about a runaway pet. It doesn't have to be a pet you really have. It can be any animal. What kind of problems would it cause if it ran away? What would you do?**

5. Give the students the spelling test:

   1. pup 2. duck 3. bus 4. fun 5. hug

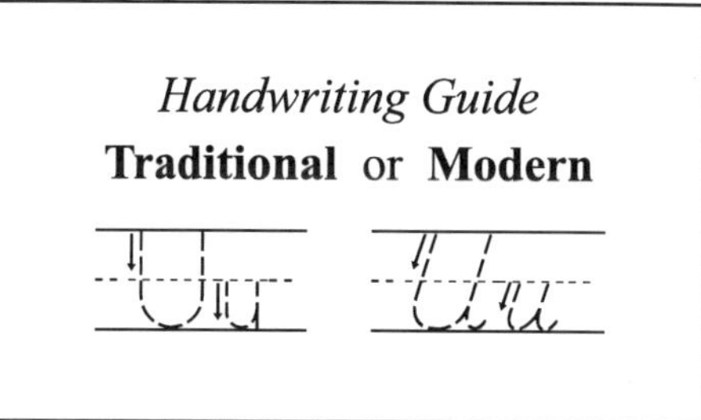

Lesson 90

Lesson Objectives

1. End of unit test

Preparation

* Workbook pages (Parts 1 and 2) for Lesson 90, crayons

Teaching

Unit Test

Part 1:

Top section: **Fill in the vowel that you hear in each picture.**
cat, fish, log, duck, dog (The teacher may say the names of the pictures.)

Bottom section: **Color the circles using the color words.**

Part 2:

Top section: **Fill in the missing ending mark.**

Bottom section: **Fill in the missing letters to make the following words:**

1. mud 2. gum 3. fat 4. dig 5. log 6. ran
7. kiss 8. duck 9. ham 10. big 11. sad 12. doll

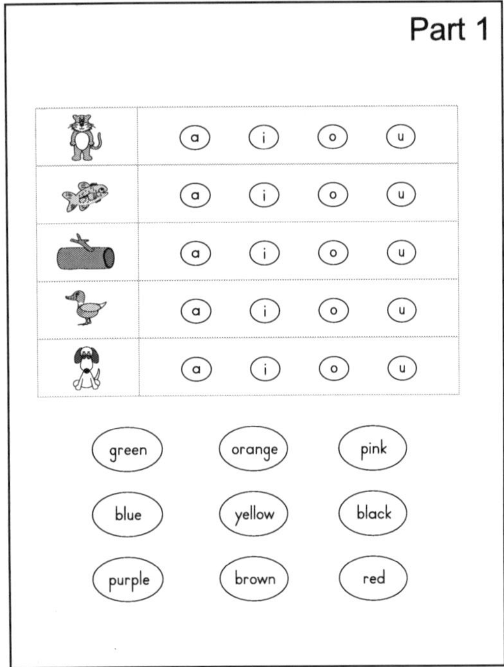
Part 1

a i o u
a i o u
a i o u
a i o u
a i o u

green orange pink
blue yellow black
purple brown red

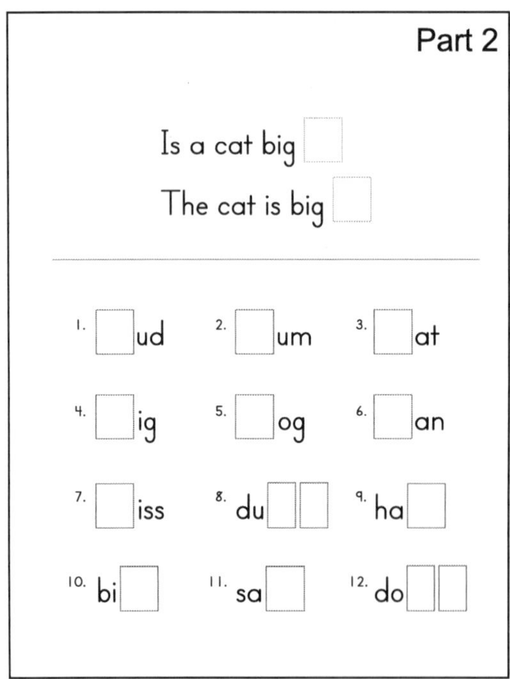
Part 2

Is a cat big
The cat is big

1. ud 2. um 3. at
4. ig 5. og 6. an
7. iss 8. du 9. ha
10. bi 11. sa 12. do

Answers

Lesson 1
b
a
a
a
b
a
b
b
a
b
a
b
a

Lesson 2
b
a
a
b
b
b
a
a
b
a
b

Lesson 4
ba ab ba ba ab ab

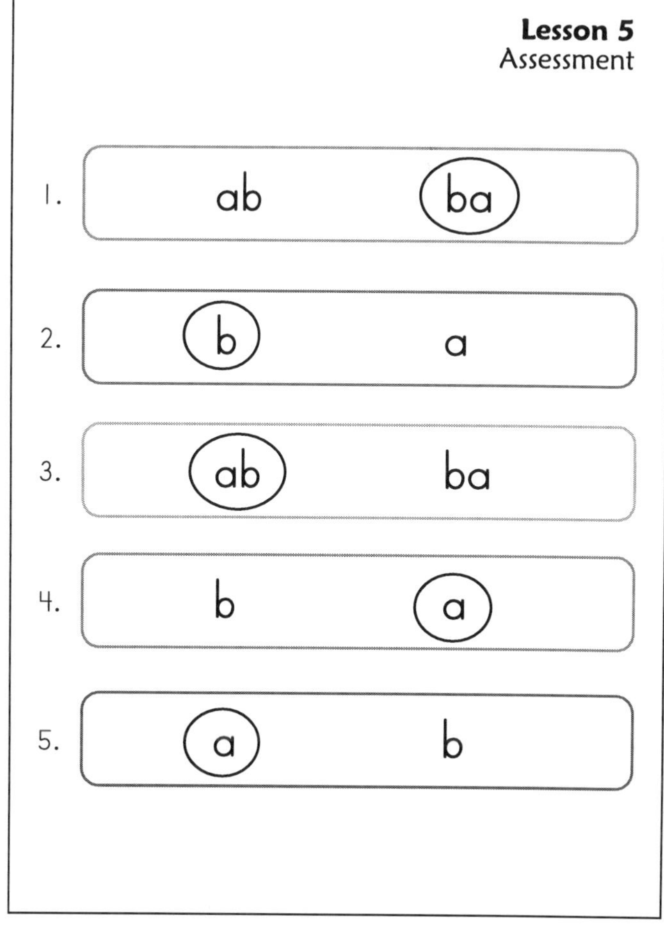
Lesson 5
Assessment
1. ab ba
2. b a
3. ab ba
4. b a
5. a b

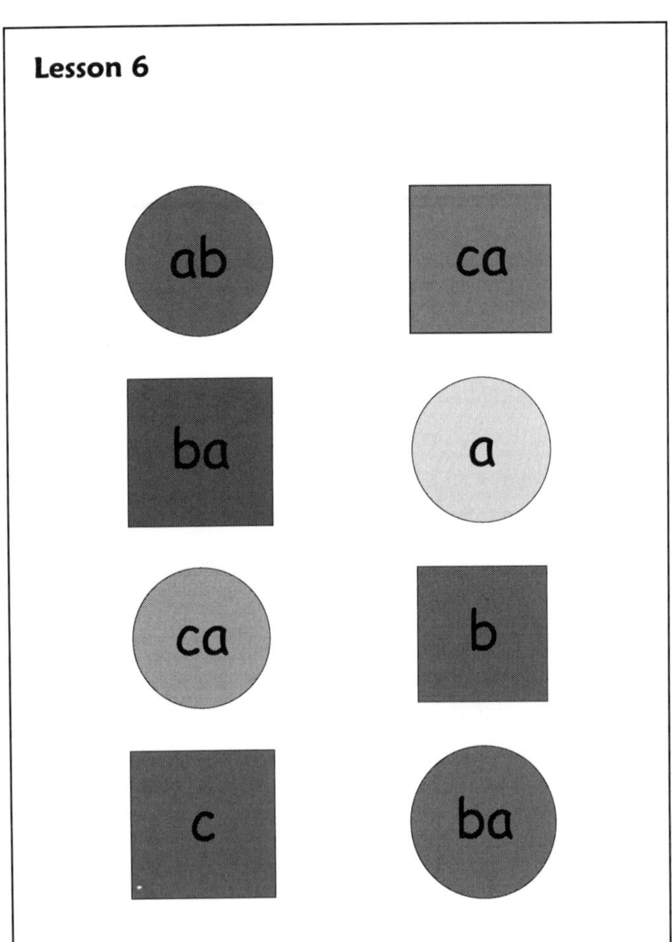
Lesson 6
ab
ca
ba
a
ca
b
c
ba

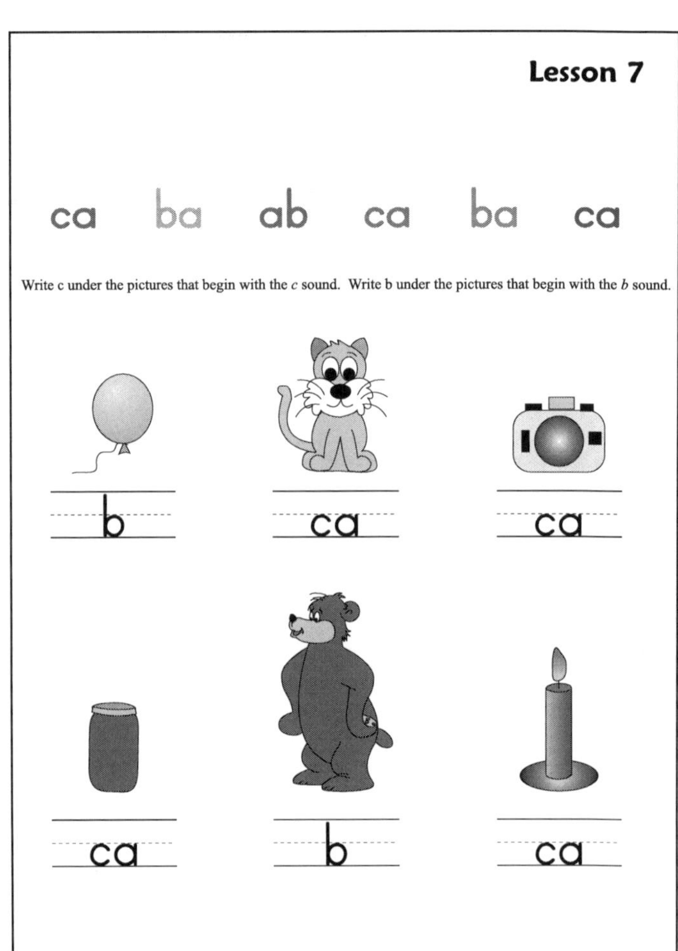
Lesson 7
ca ba ab ca ba ca
Write c under the pictures that begin with the c sound. Write b under the pictures that begin with the b sound.
b
ca
ca
ca
b
ca

Lesson 8
ta ba ab ca at ca
ba ta at ca ta at

Lesson 9
c a
a b t b
a
a a c t
a c a

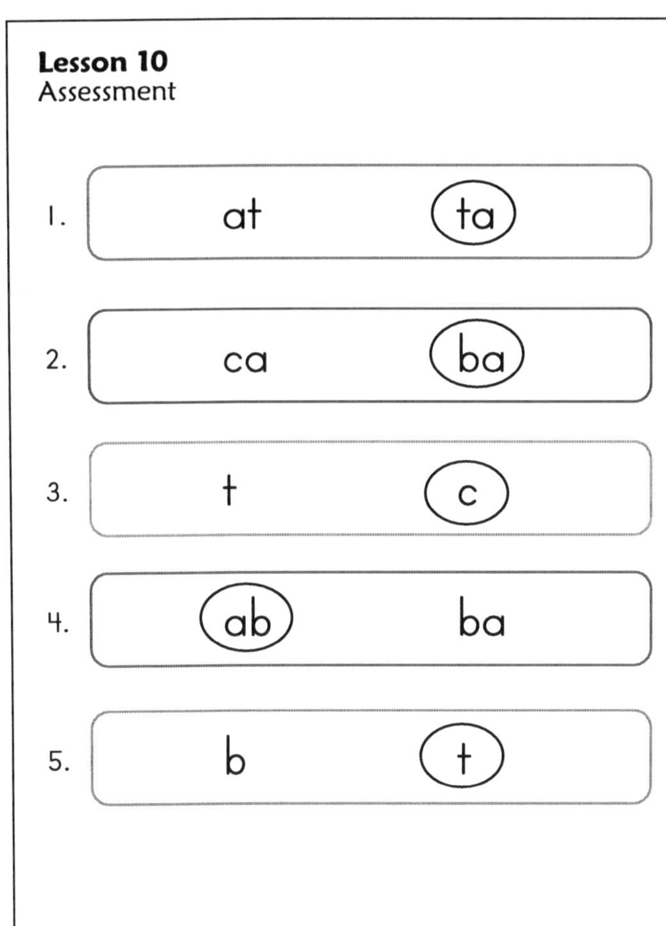
Lesson 10
Assessment
1. at ta
2. ca ba
3. t c
4. ab ba
5. b t

Lesson 12
ta ca pa ba ca pa ta
b c p t
p
c
b
t

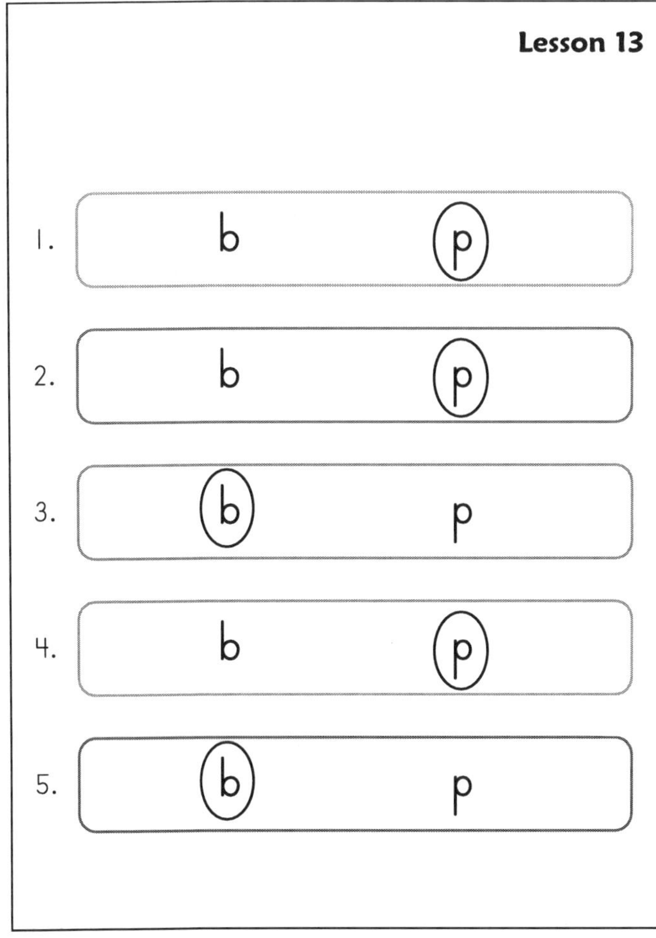
Lesson 13
1. b p
2. b p
3. b p
4. b p
5. b p

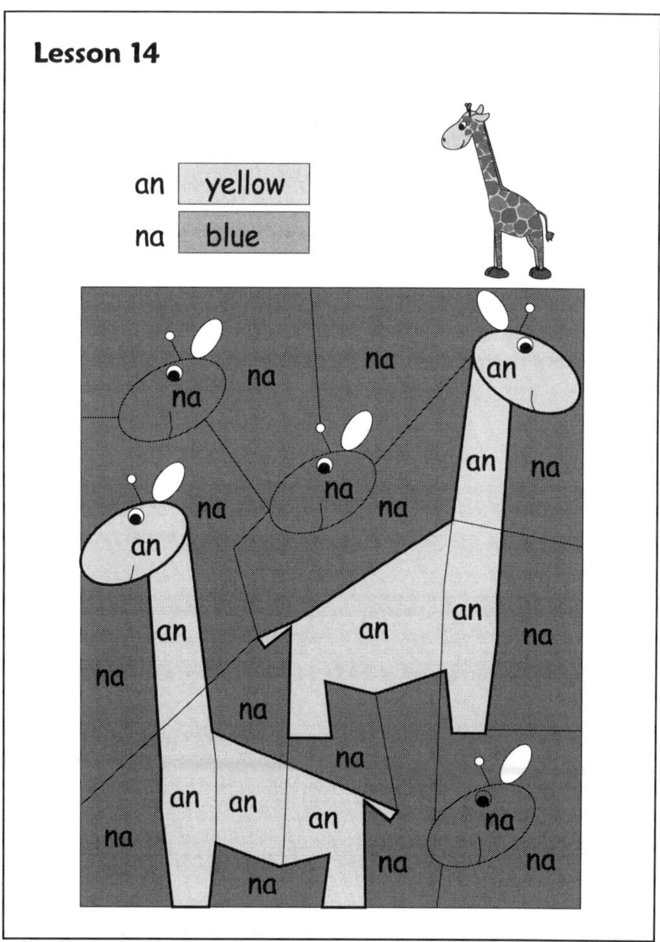
Lesson 14
an yellow
na blue

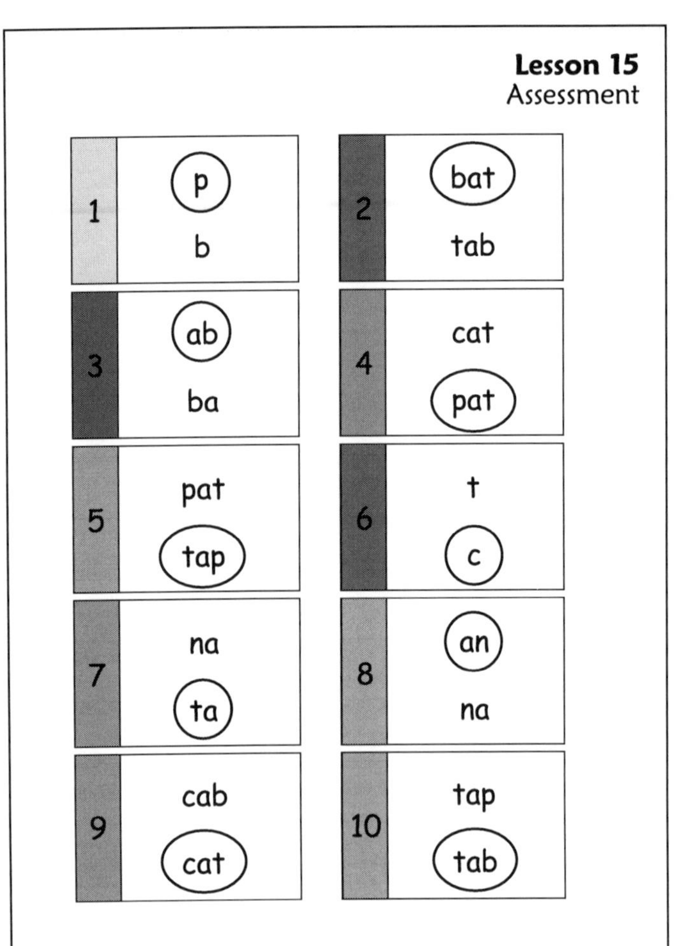

Lesson 15
Assessment

1	p b	2	bat tab
3	ab ba	4	cat pat
5	pat tap	6	t c
7	na ta	8	an na
9	cab cat	10	tap tab

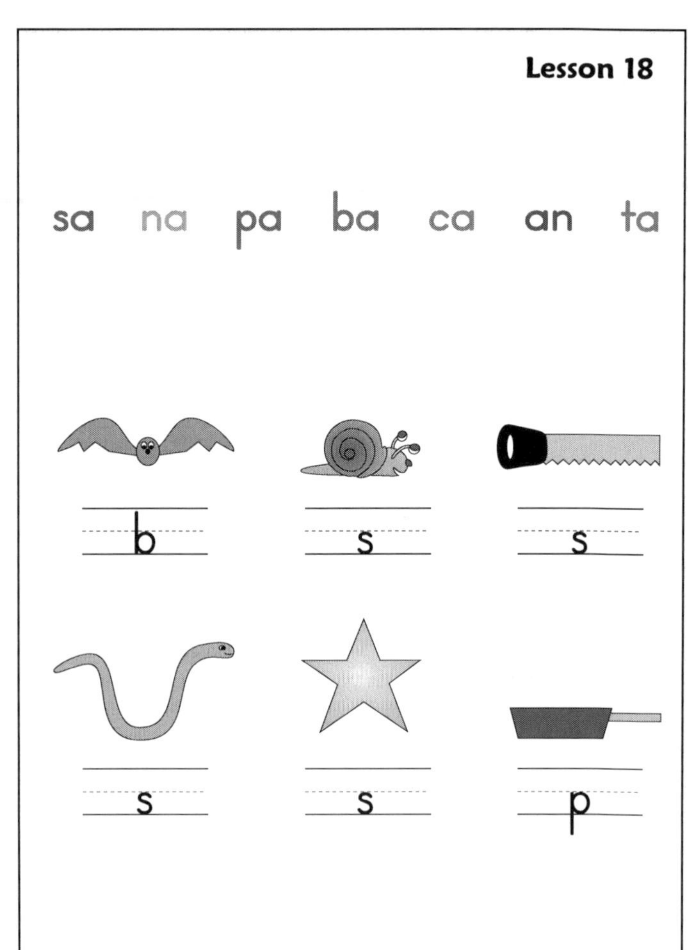

Lesson 18

sa na pa ba ca an ta

b s s

s s p

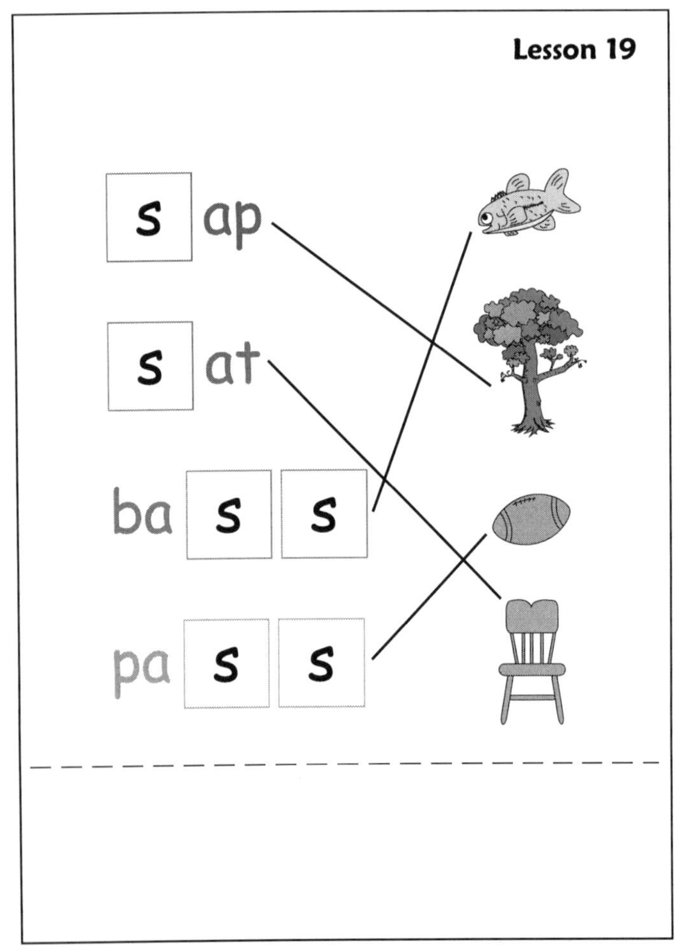

Lesson 19

s ap

s at

ba s s

pa s s

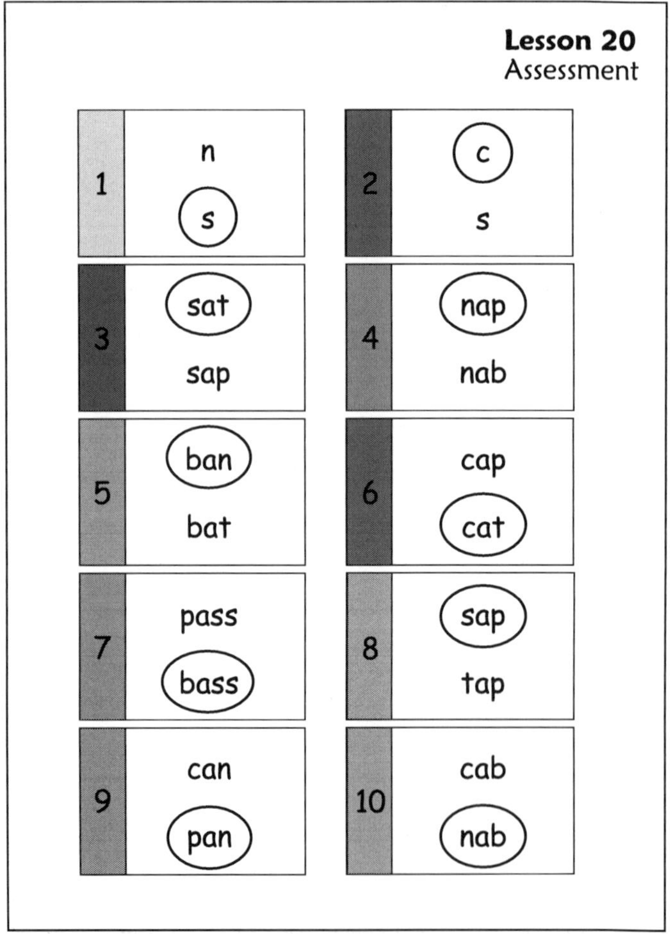

Lesson 20
Assessment

1	n s	2	c s
3	sat sap	4	nap nab
5	ban bat	6	cap cat
7	pass bass	8	sap tap
9	can pan	10	cab nab

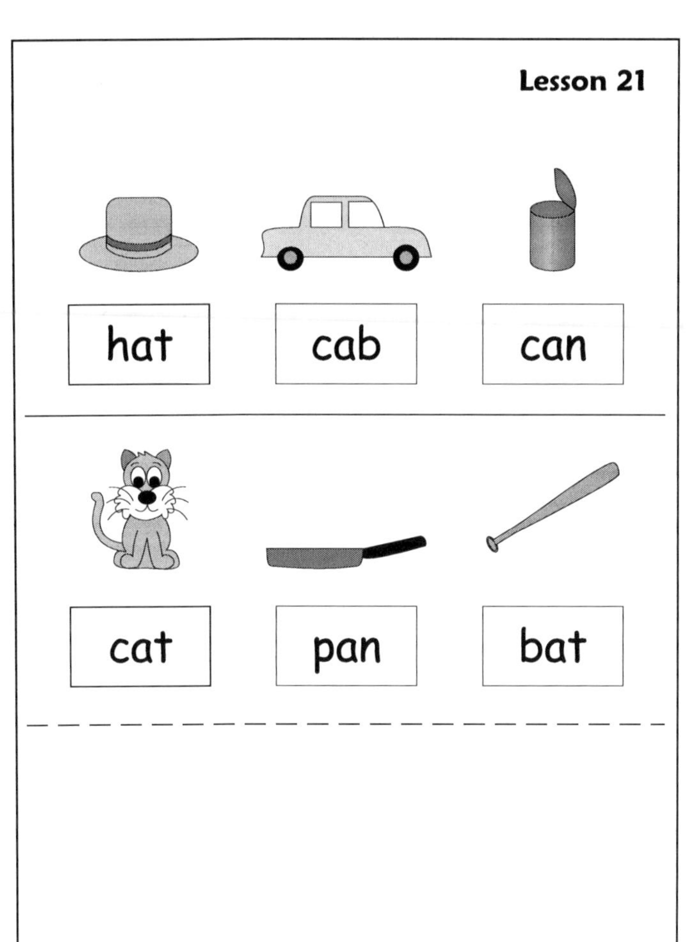
Lesson 21

hat cab can

cat pan bat

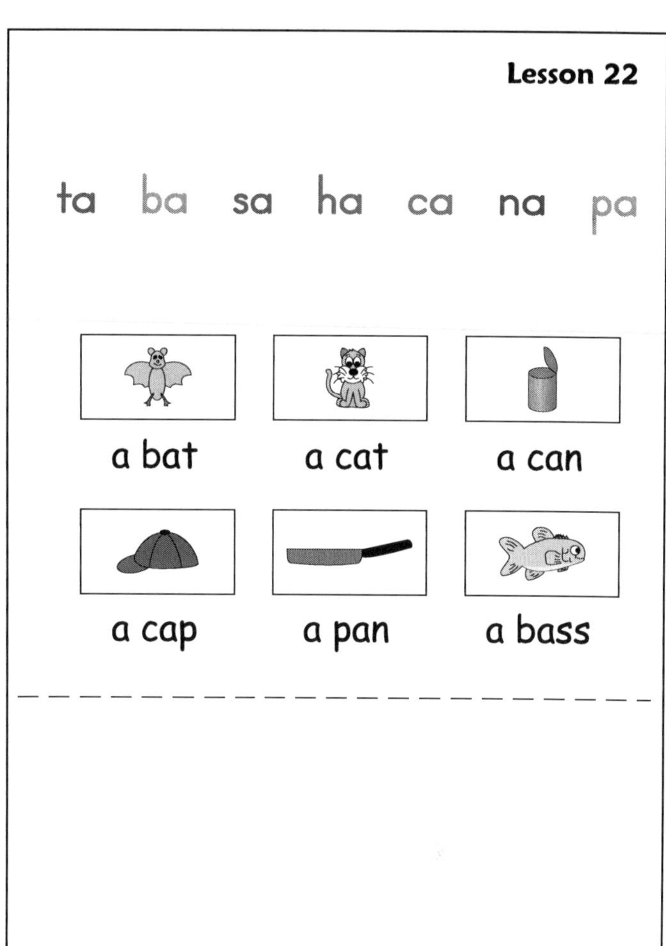
Lesson 22

ta ba sa ha ca na pa

a bat a cat a can

a cap a pan a bass

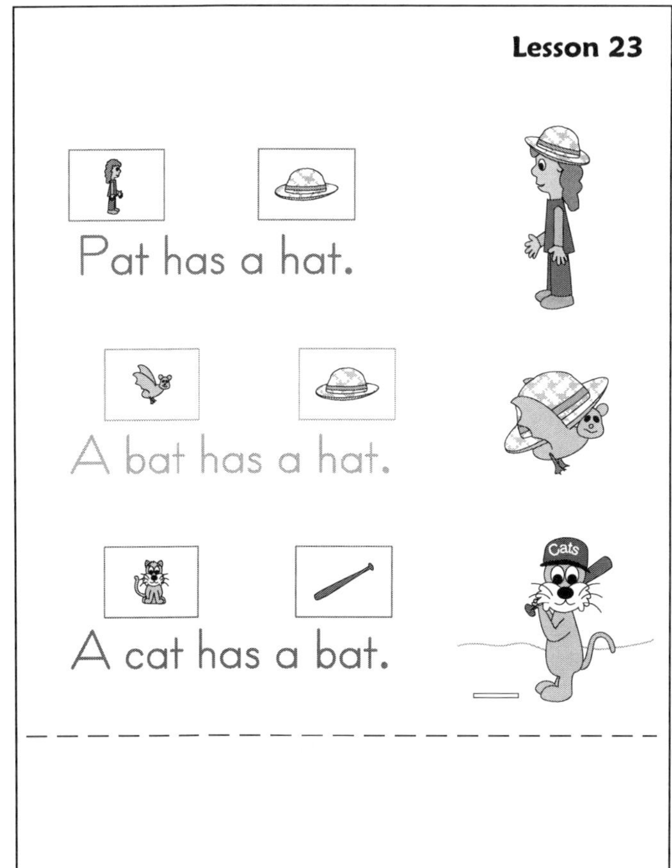
Lesson 23

Pat has a hat.

A bat has a hat.

A cat has a bat.

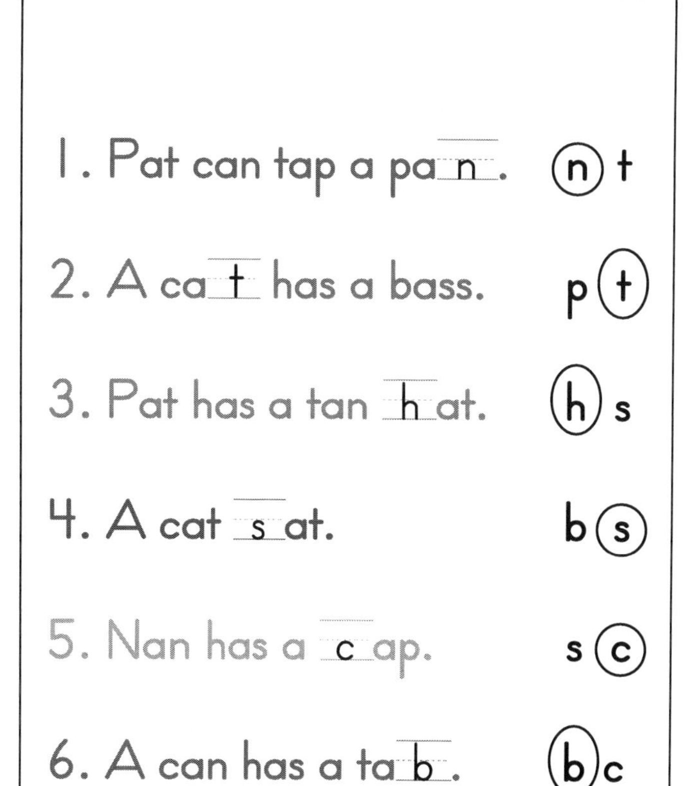
Lesson 24

1. Pat can tap a pa n . n t

2. A ca t has a bass. p t

3. Pat has a tan h at. h s

4. A cat s at. b s

5. Nan has a c ap. s c

6. A can has a ta b . b c

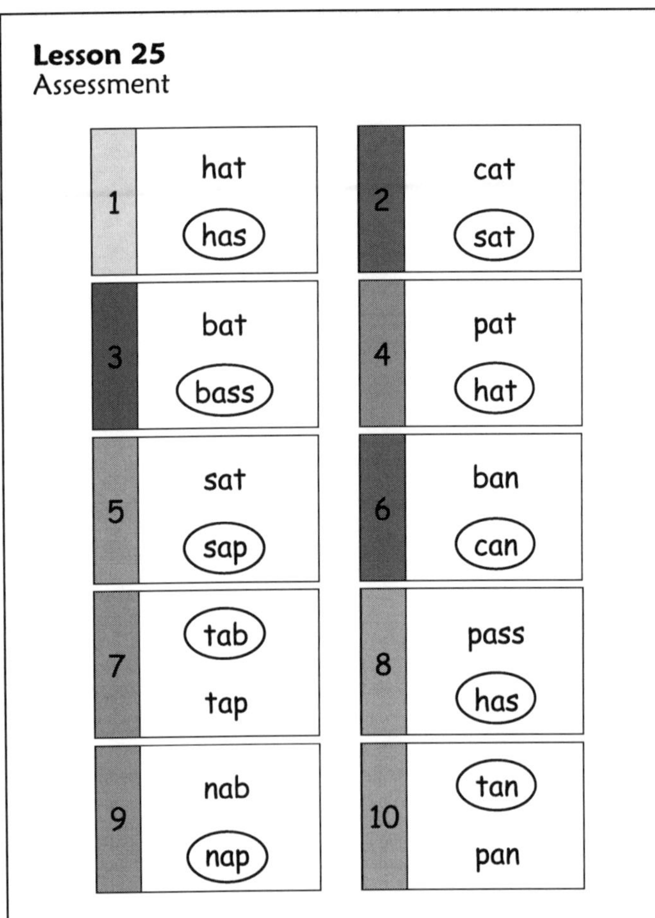
Lesson 25
Assessment
1
hat
has
2
cat
sat
3
bat
bass
4
pat
hat
5
sat
sap
6
ban
can
7
tab
tap
8
pass
has
9
nab
nap
10
tan
pan

Lesson 28
The the
1. The cat sat.
2. The bat can nap.
3. Pat has the hat.
4. Nan has the tan can.
5. The cab can pass the cat.

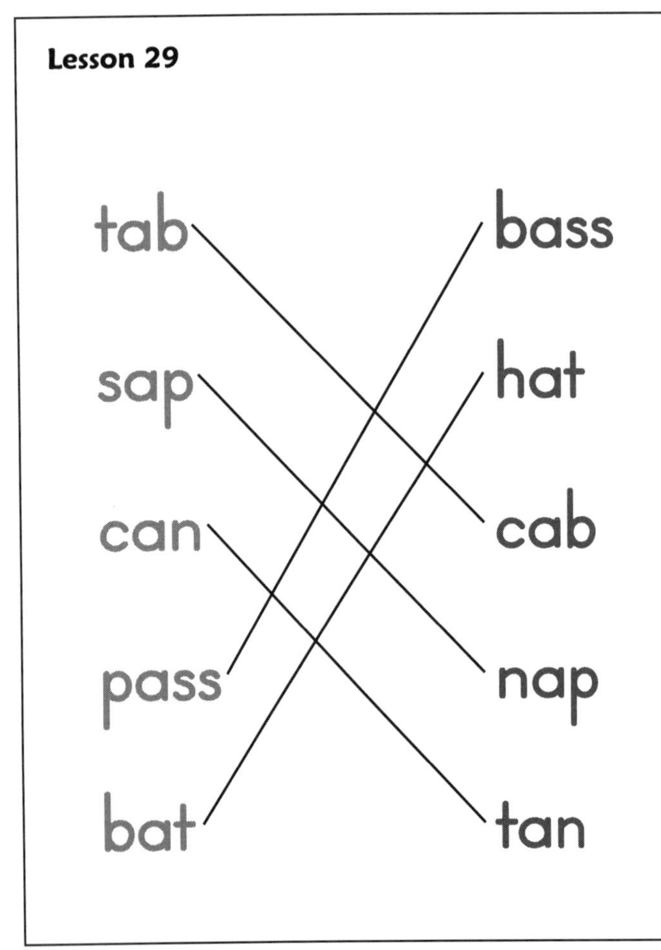
Lesson 29
tab
sap
can
pass
bat
bass
hat
cab
nap
tan

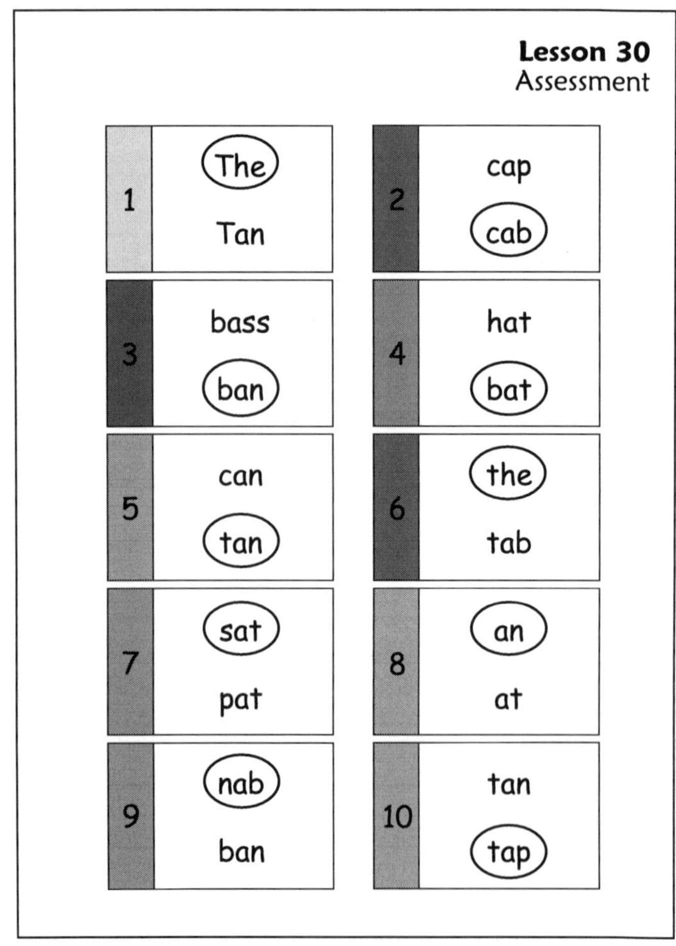
Lesson 30
Assessment
1
The
Tan
2
cap
cab
3
bass
ban
4
hat
bat
5
can
tan
6
the
tab
7
sat
pat
8
an
at
9
nab
ban
10
tan
tap

Lesson 31
as
s
is
is
i
as
is
s
is
is
i
as
is
is
s
is

Lesson 32
The can is tan.
The cat is tan.
The cap is tan.

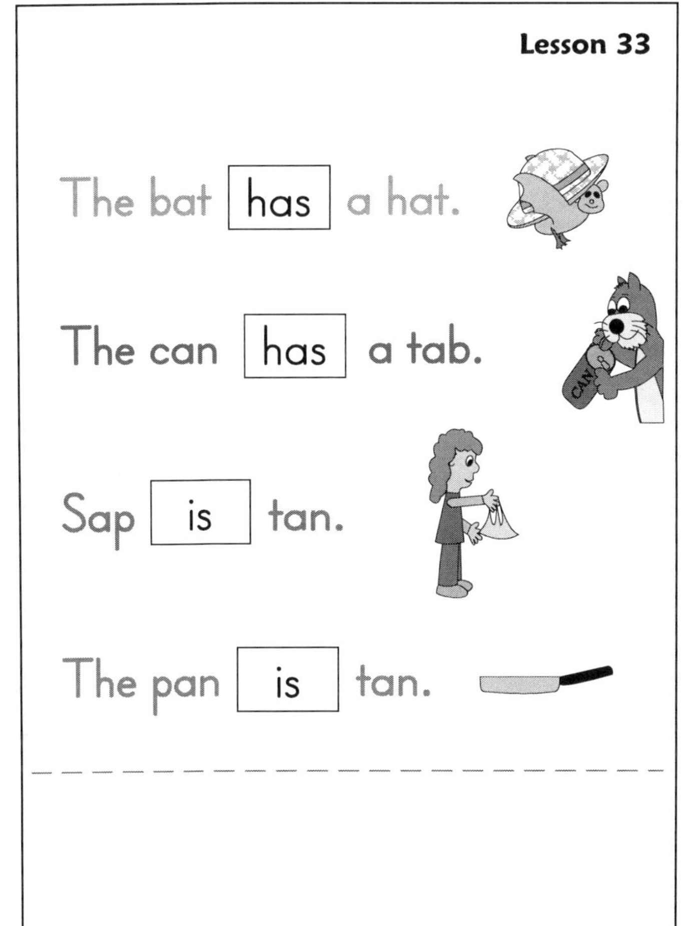
Lesson 33
The bat has a hat.
The can has a tab.
CAN
Sap is tan.
The pan is tan.

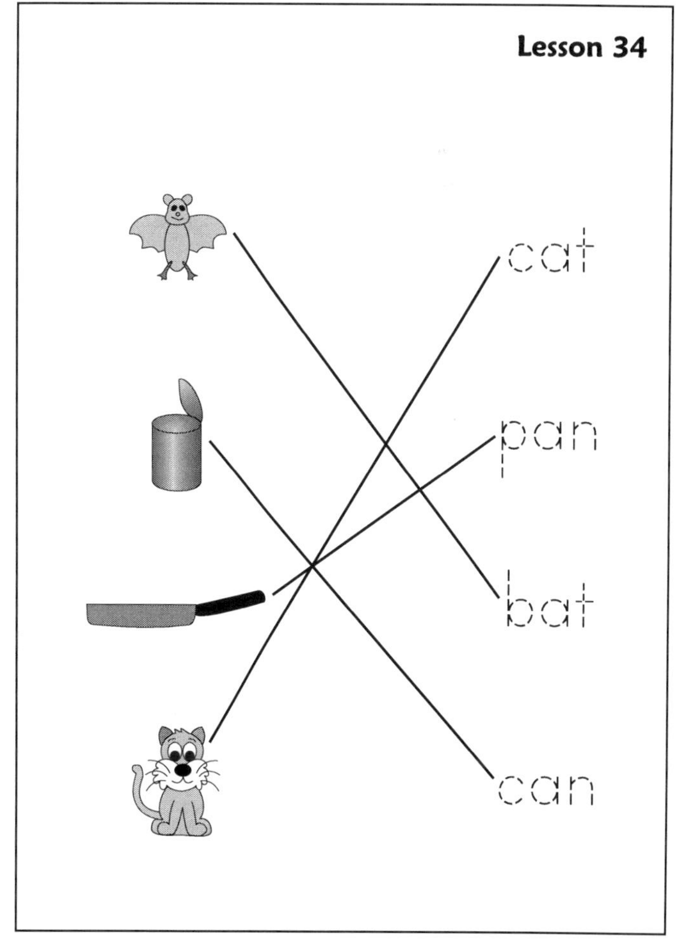
Lesson 34
cat
pan
bat
can

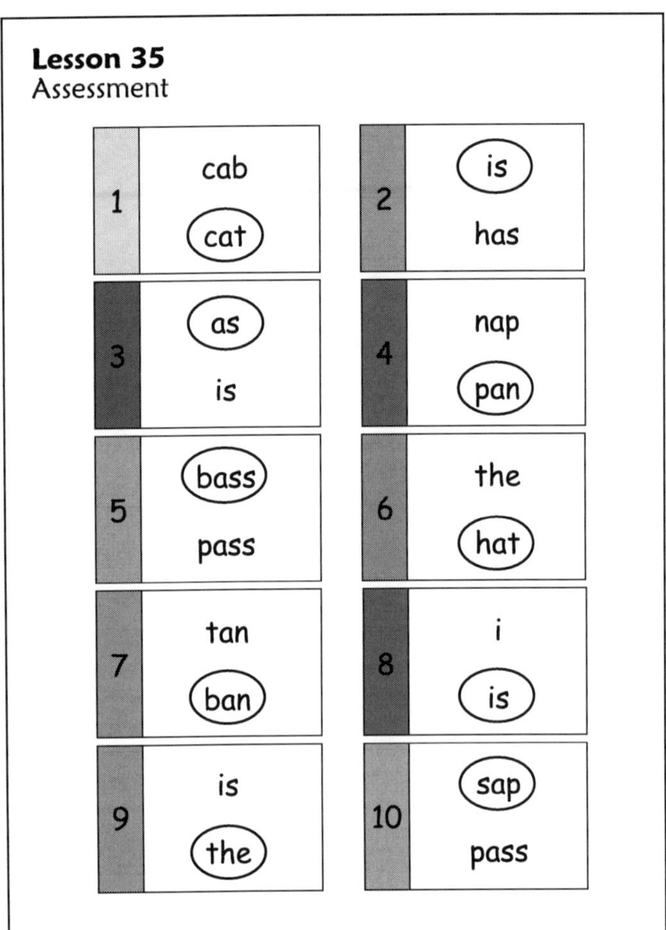

Lesson 35
Assessment

1	cab	cat
2	is	has
3	as	is
4	nap	pan
5	bass	pass
6	the	hat
7	tan	ban
8	i	is
9	is	the
10	sap	pass

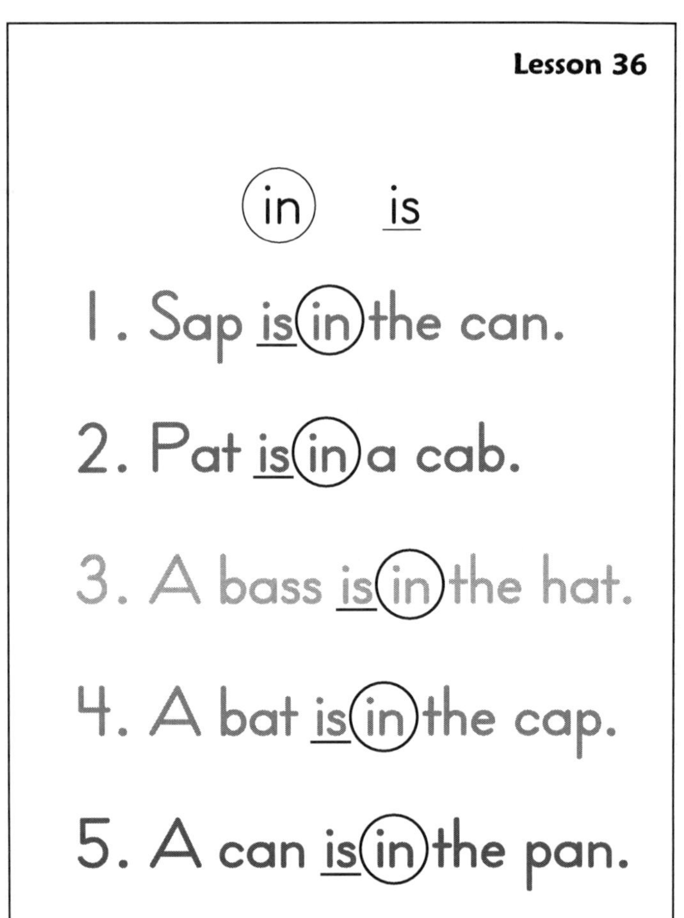

Lesson 36

in is

1. Sap is in the can.
2. Pat is in a cab.
3. A bass is in the hat.
4. A bat is in the cap.
5. A can is in the pan.

Lesson 37

bass bat can cat hat pan

A cat is in the hat.

A bat is in the can.

A bass is in the pan.

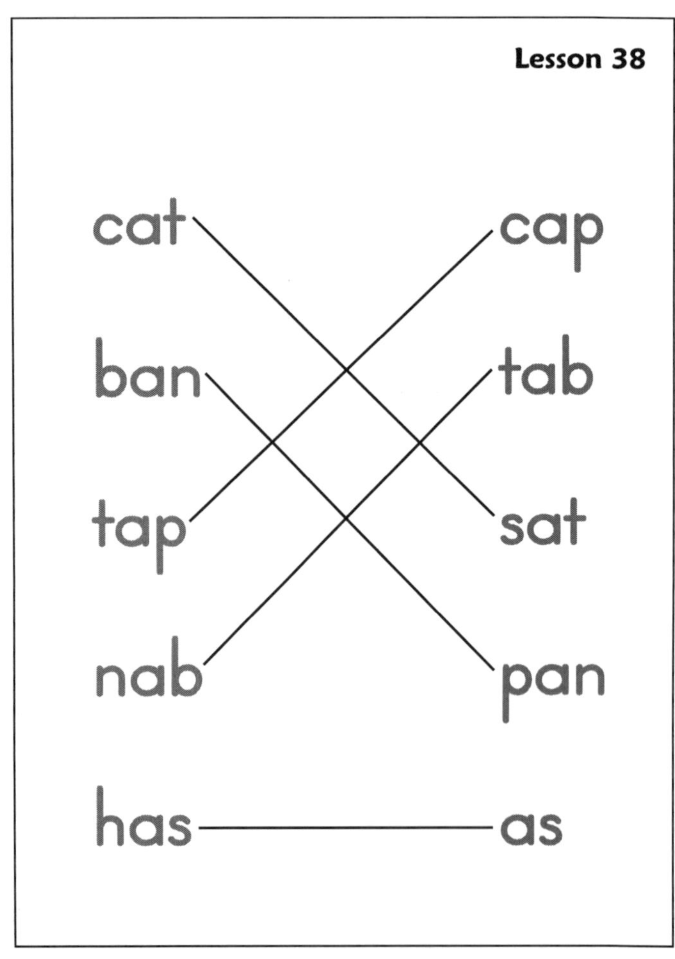

Lesson 38

cat	cap
ban	tab
tap	sat
nab	pan
has	as

Lesson 39

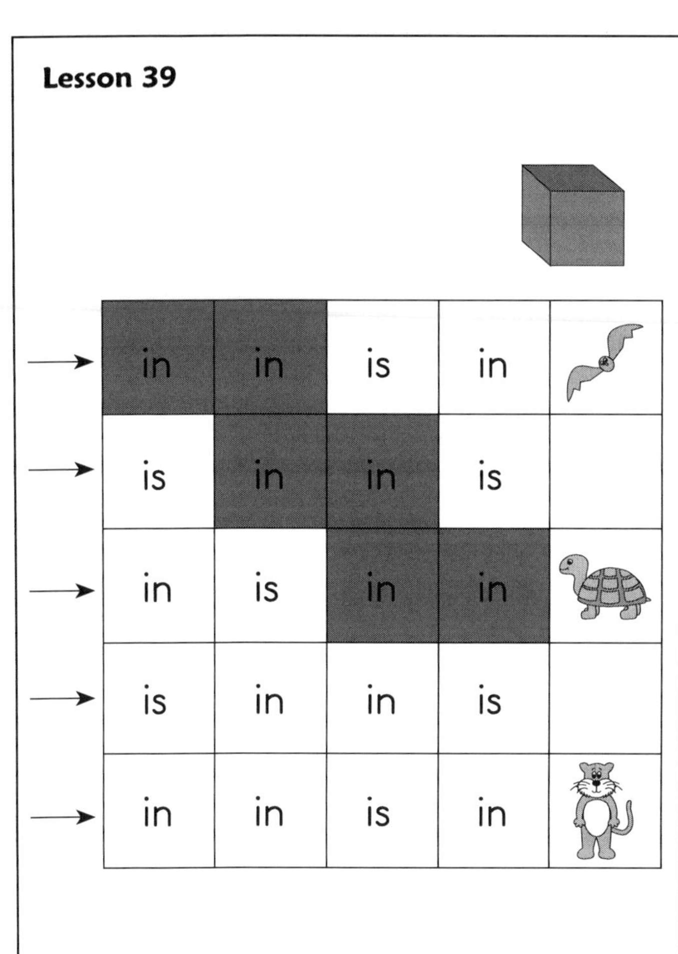

Lesson 40
Assessment

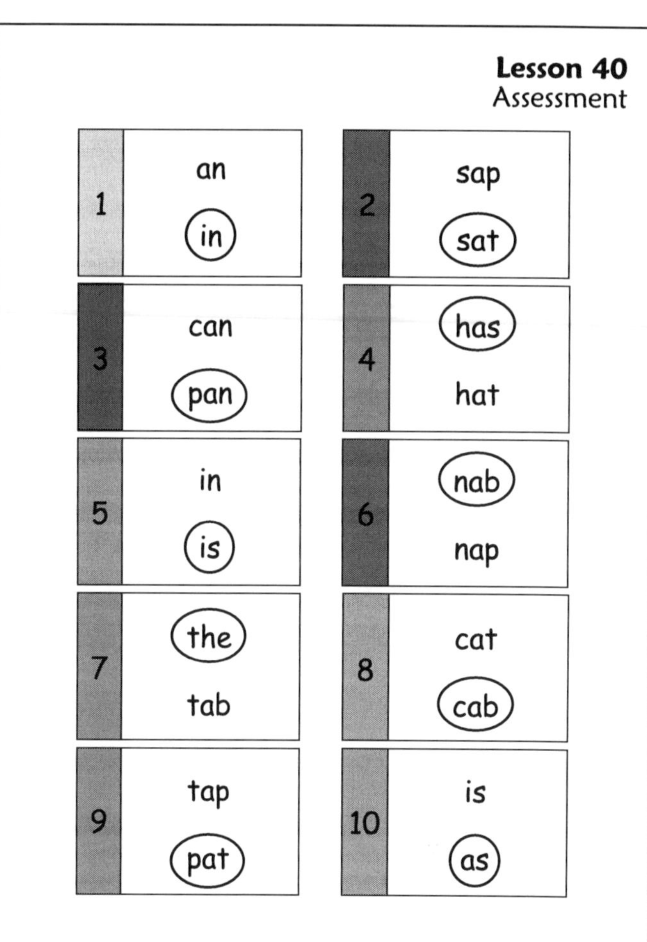

Lesson 41

on in

1. The cat is on the hat.

2. The bass is in the pan.

3. A tab is on the can.

4. A bat is in the cab.

5. Sap is on the cap.

Lesson 42

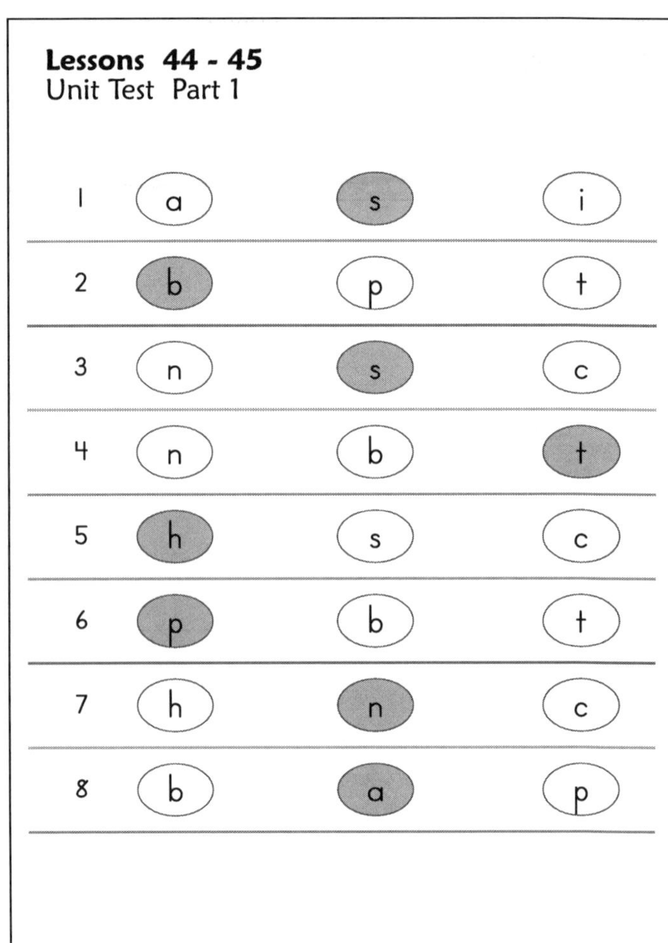

Lessons 44 - 45
Unit Test Part 1

1	a	s	i
2	b	p	t
3	n	s	c
4	n	b	t
5	h	s	c
6	p	b	t
7	h	n	c
8	b	a	p

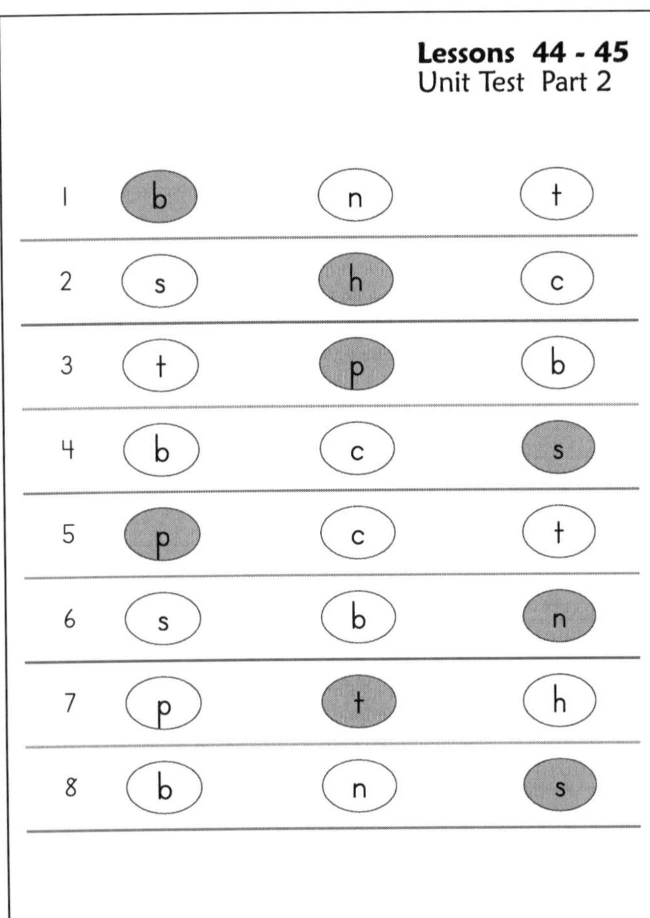

Lessons 44 - 45
Unit Test Part 2

1	b	n	t
2	s	h	c
3	t	p	b
4	b	c	s
5	p	c	t
6	s	b	n
7	p	t	h
8	b	n	s

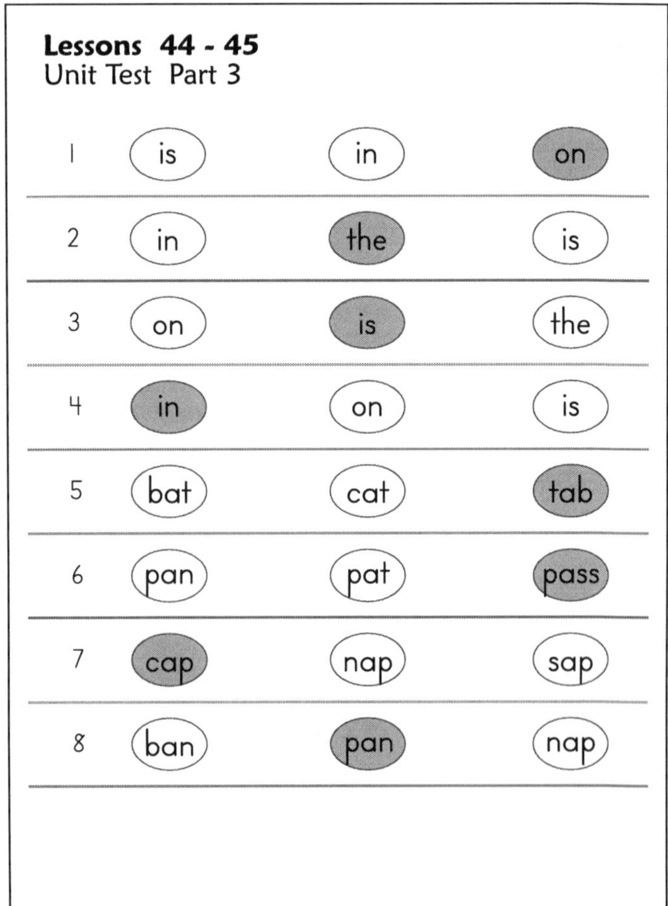

Lessons 44 - 45
Unit Test Part 3

1	is	in	on
2	in	the	is
3	on	is	the
4	in	on	is
5	bat	cat	tab
6	pan	pat	pass
7	cap	nap	sap
8	ban	pan	nap

Lesson 16

bat	bit
pan	pin
has	his
nap	nip
sat	sit
tap	tip

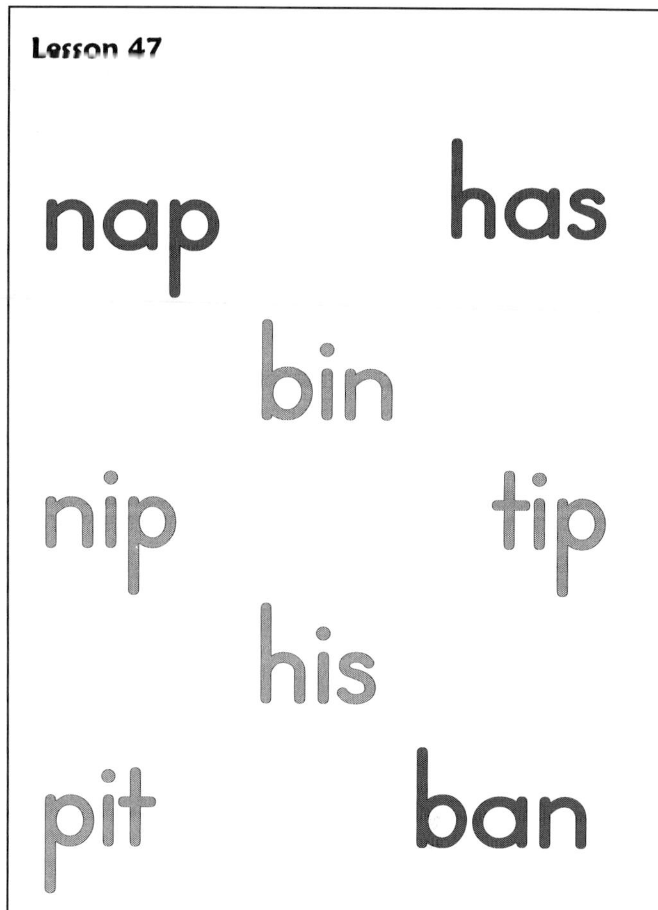

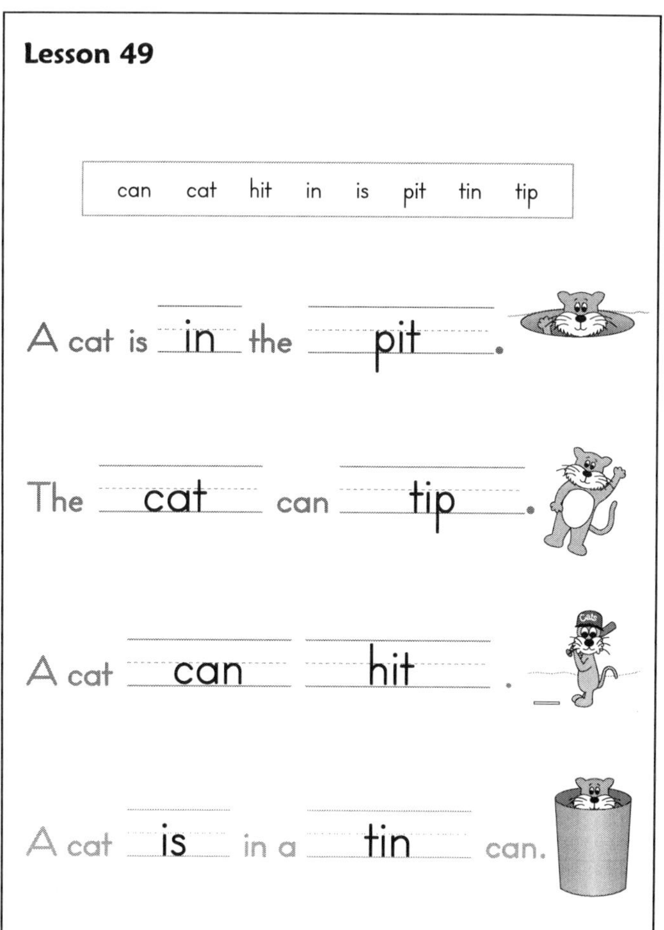

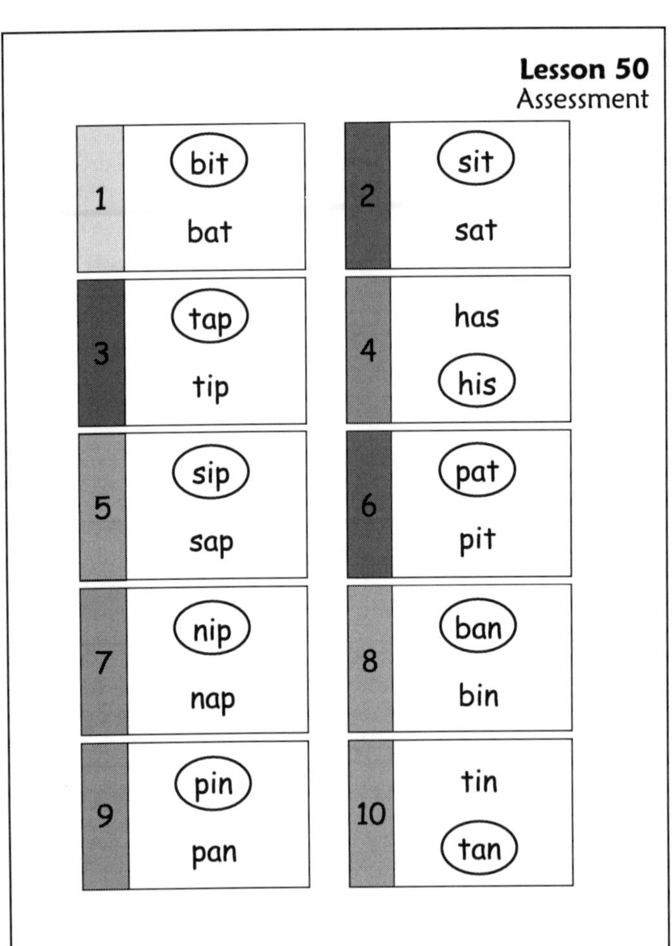
Lesson 50
Assessment
1 bit bat
2 sit sat
3 tap tip
4 has his
5 sip sap
6 pat pit
7 nip nap
8 ban bin
9 pin pan
10 tin tan

Lesson 51
m
c
m
m
m
b
m
m
h

Lesson 52
Tim
man
Sam
hat
map
ham
mat
sap
him
tan

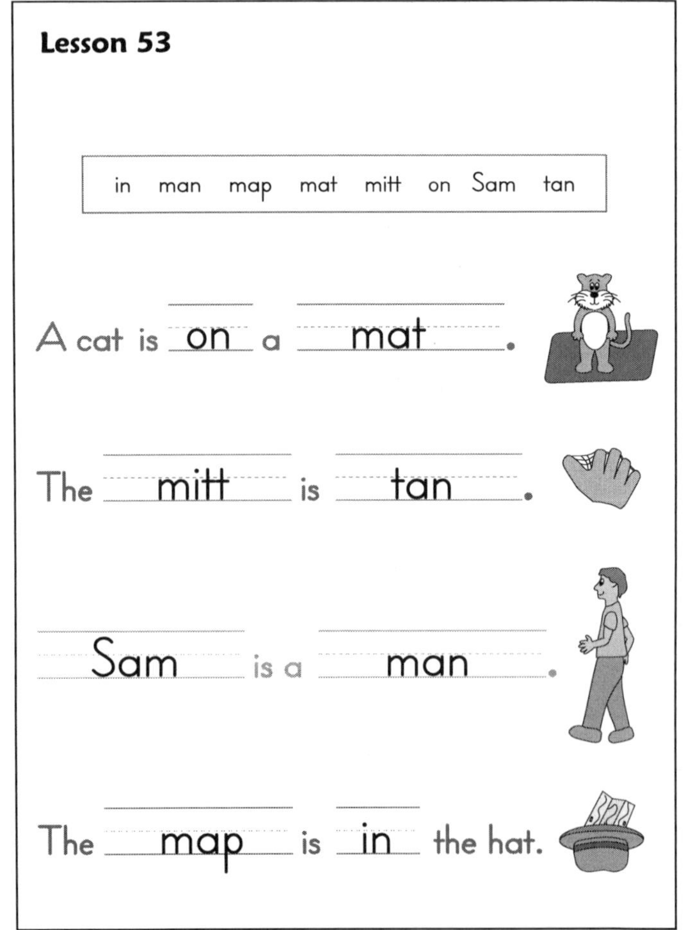
Lesson 53
in man map mat mitt on Sam tan
A cat is on a mat.
The mitt is tan.
Sam is a man.
The map is in the hat.

Lesson 54

? ? ? ? ? ? ? ? ?

Is Can

Can Sam the bass sit ?

Is Tim a man ?

Can a cat bat ?

Is the pan his ?

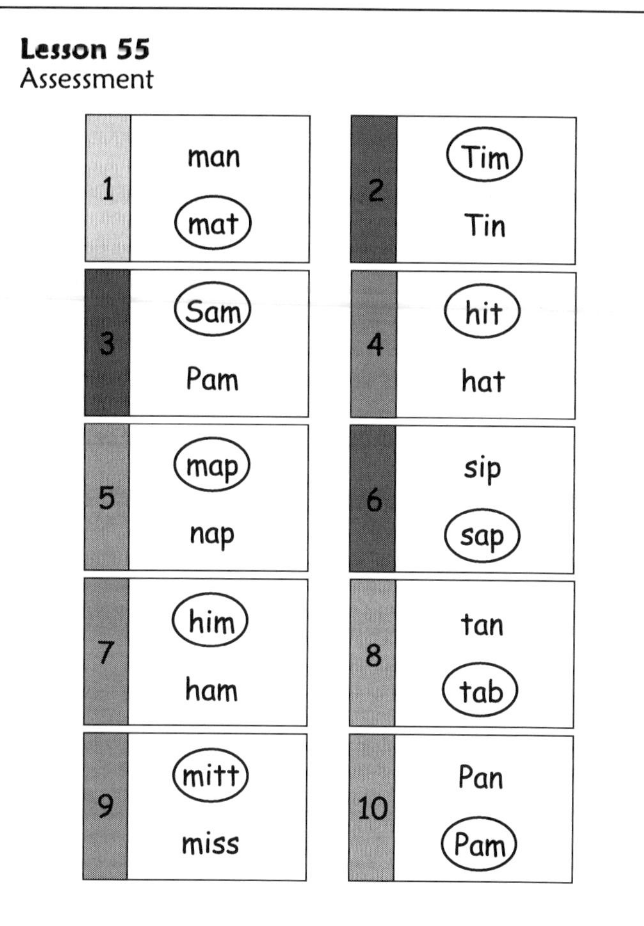
Lesson 55
Assessment

1	man / (mat)	2	(Tim) / Tin
3	(Sam) / Pam	4	(hit) / hat
5	(map) / nap	6	sip / (sap)
7	(him) / ham	8	tan / (tab)
9	(mitt) / miss	10	Pan / (Pam)

Lesson 56

can	r an
map	r ap
pat	r at
ham	r am
bib	r ib
sip	r ip
him	r im

Lesson 57

Is a rat in the pit?
yes no

Is a hat on a ram?
yes no

Is a ram in the can?
yes no

Is a rat on the ram?
yes no

Lesson 58
g
m
g
g
g
t
m
g
g

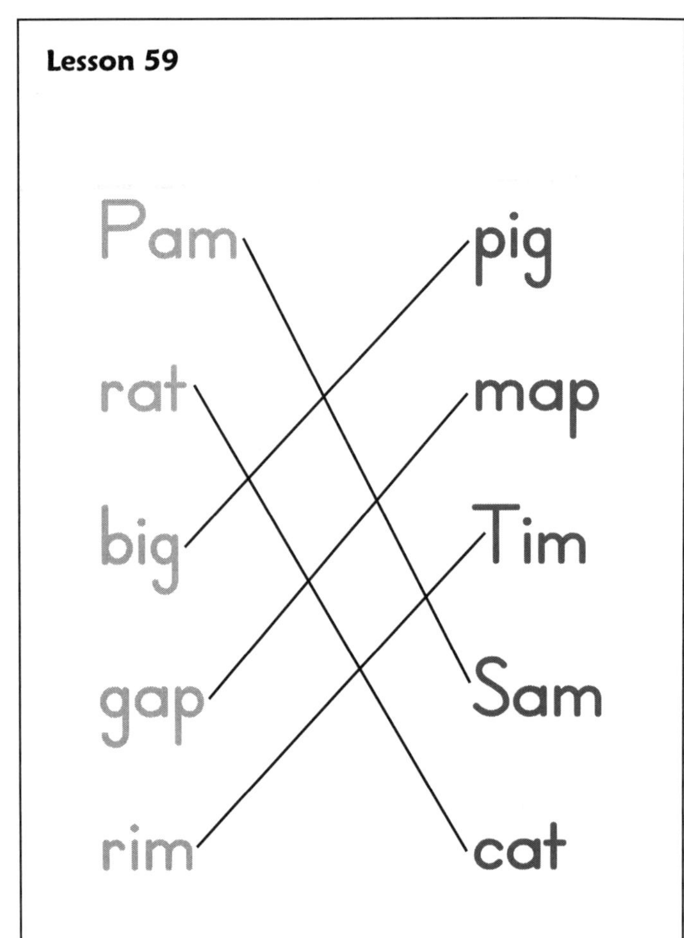
Lesson 59
Pam
rat
big
gap
rim
pig
map
Tim
Sam
cat

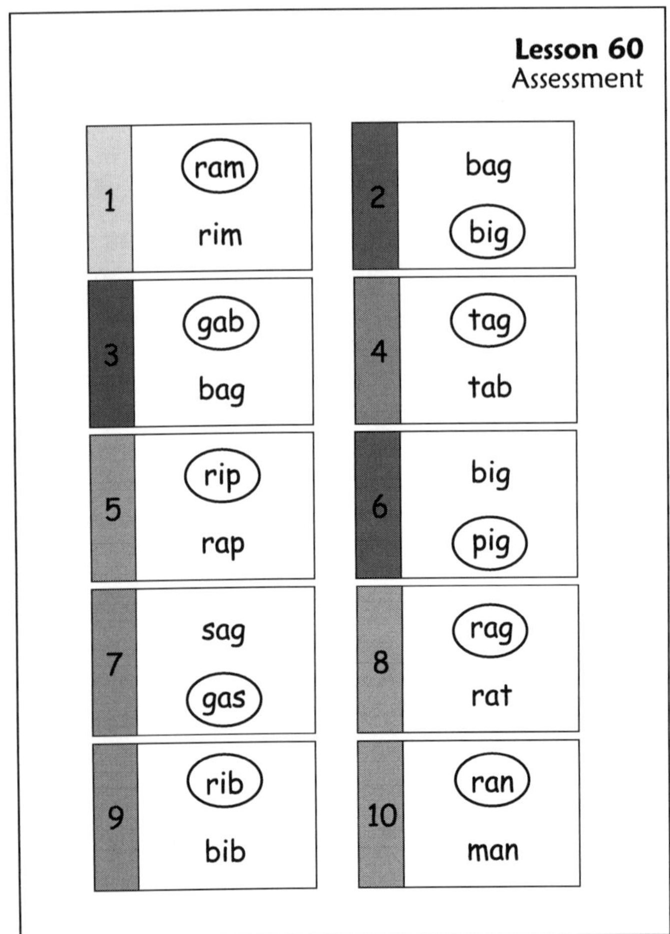
Lesson 60
Assessment
1
ram
rim
2
bag
big
3
gab
bag
4
tag
tab
5
rip
rap
6
big
pig
7
sag
gas
8
rag
rat
9
rib
bib
10
ran
man

Lesson 61
b
d
t
b
s
d
d
r
Ruff
d

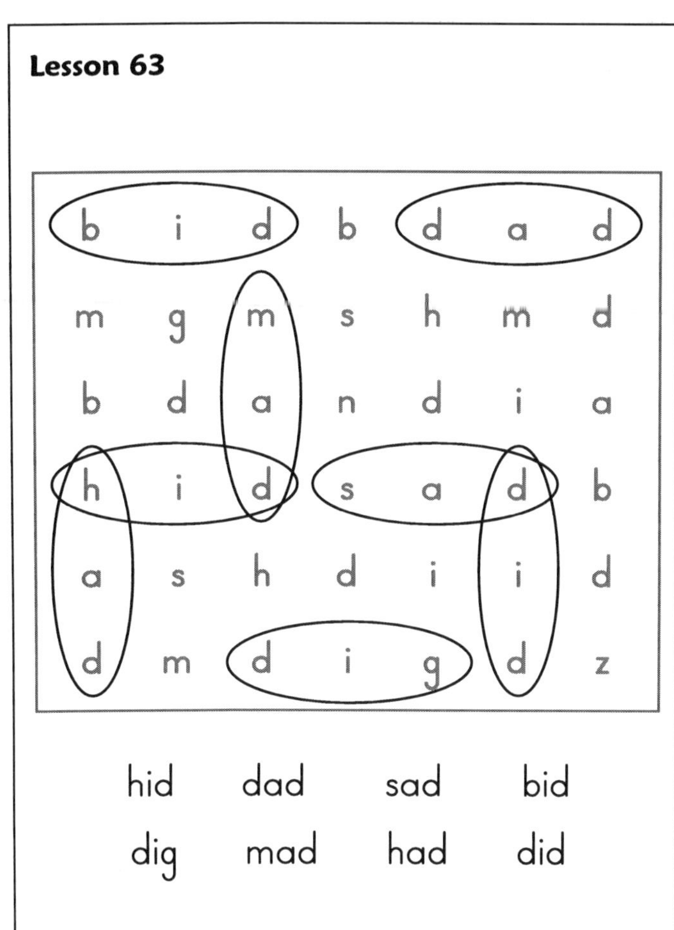
Lesson 63
b i d b d a d
m g m s h m d
b d a n d i a
h i d s a d b
a s h d i i d
d m d i g d z
hid dad sad bid
dig mad had did

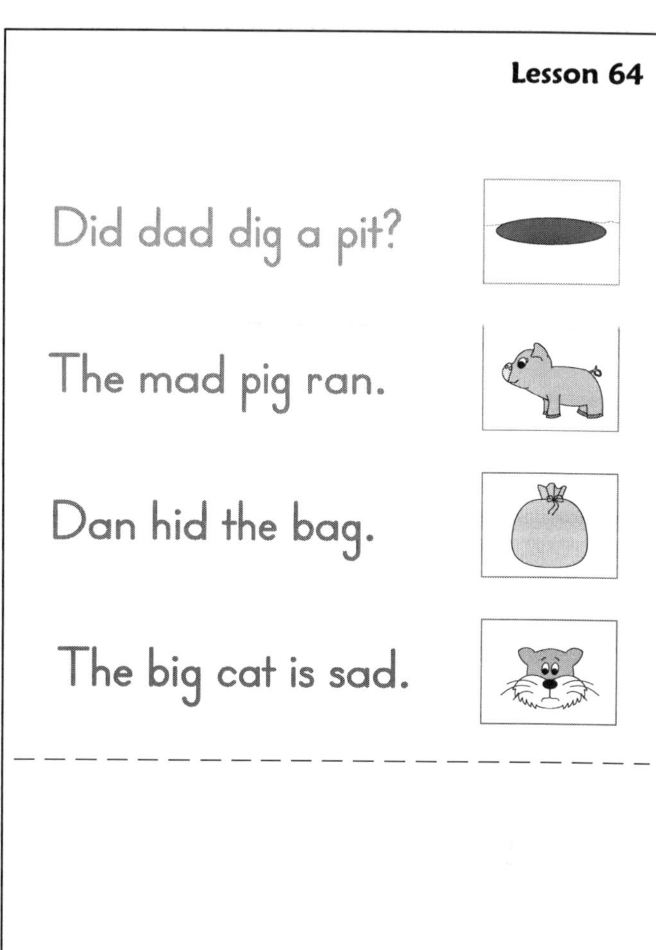
Lesson 64
Did dad dig a pit?
The mad pig ran.
Dan hid the bag.
The big cat is sad.

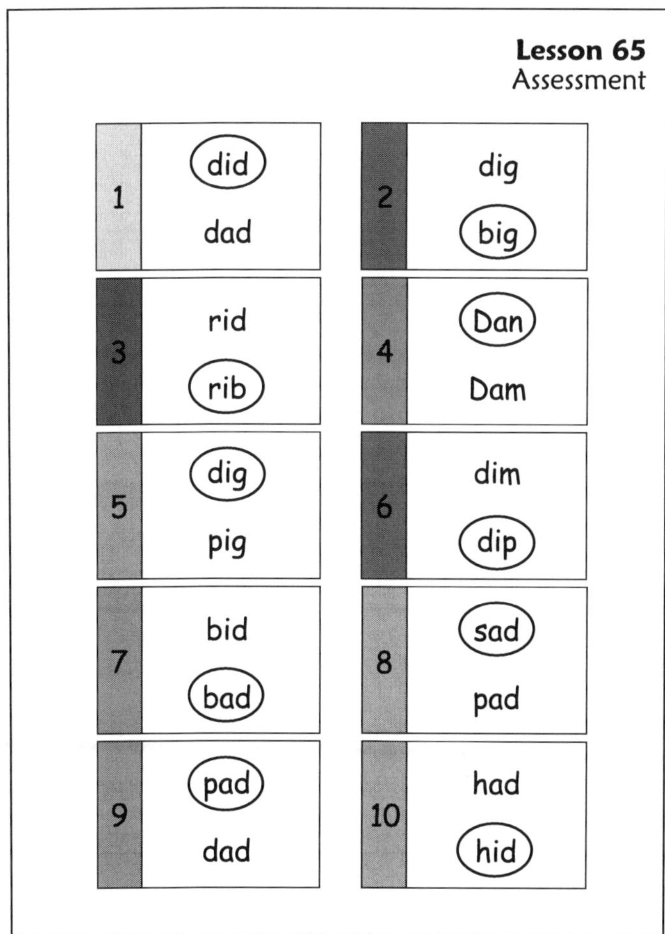
Lesson 65
Assessment
1 did dad
2 dig big
3 rid rib
4 Dan Dam
5 dig pig
6 dim dip
7 bid bad
8 sad pad
9 pad dad
10 had hid

Lesson 66
h o g
m o p
d o g
r o d
c o b
p o t
hot dog

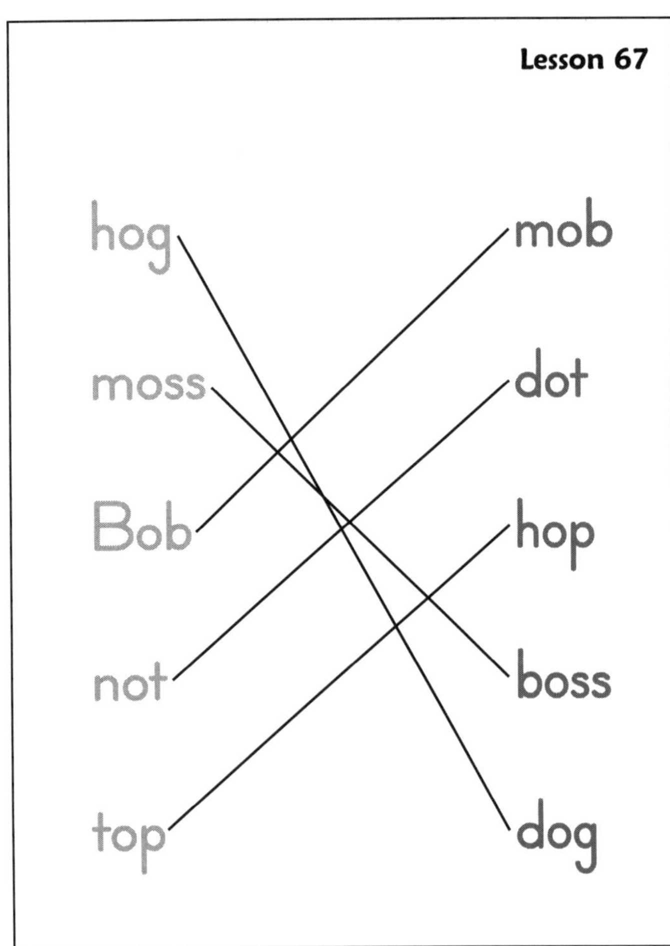
Lesson 67
hog
moss
Bob
not
top
mob
dot
hop
boss
dog

Lesson 68
p o t
p a t
p i t
h a t
h o t
h i t
t i p
t o p
t a p
Fill in the vowels for the pictures.
Kitty
p o t
h a t
t i p

Lesson 69
hog Bob mop
Bob the hog has a mop.
on dog dot
A dot is on the dog.
pot Ron hot
Tom has a hot pot.

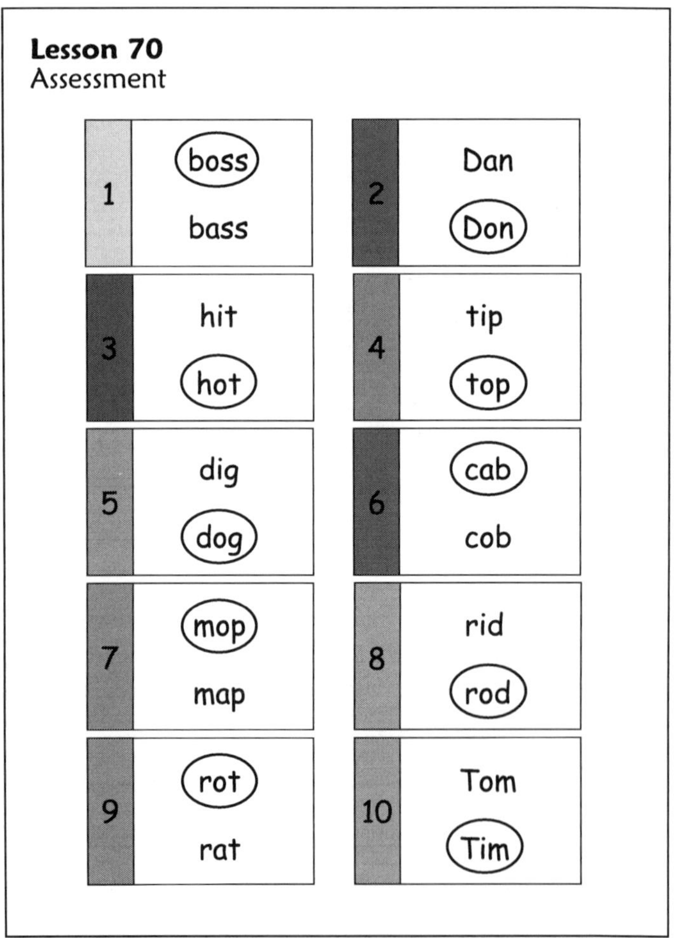
Lesson 70
Assessment
1 boss bass
2 Dan Don
3 hit hot
4 tip top
5 dig dog
6 cab cob
7 mop map
8 rid rod
9 rot rat
10 Tom Tim

1. The cat nap s on the log.
2. Tom's dog bit the pill.
3. Pam had 3 doll s.
4. Dan can tap the can's lid.
5. The 2 lad s sat on a hill.
6. Bill lob s the ball.

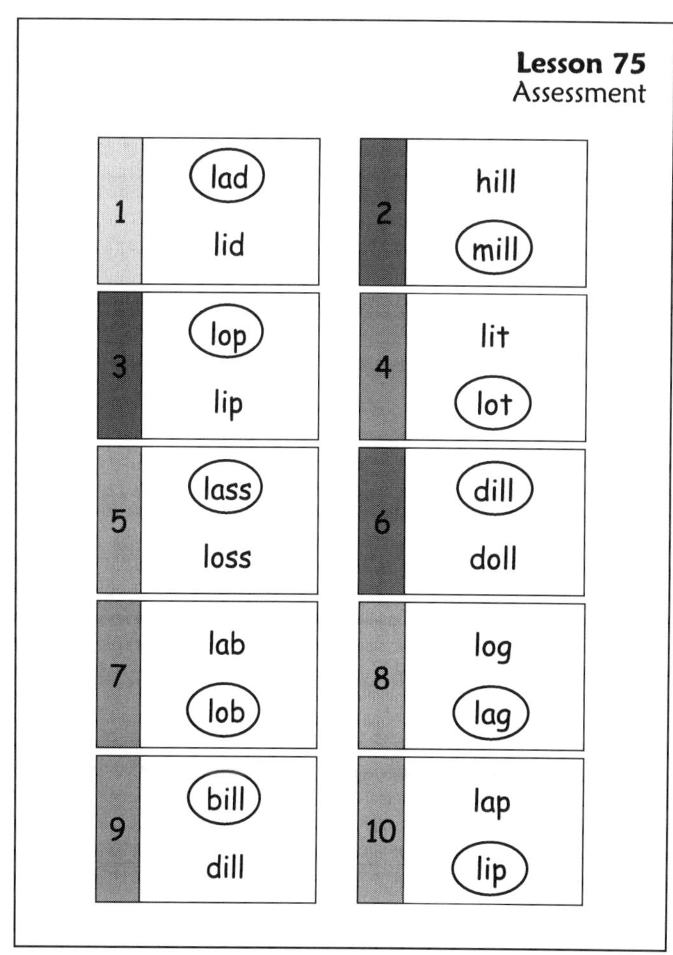

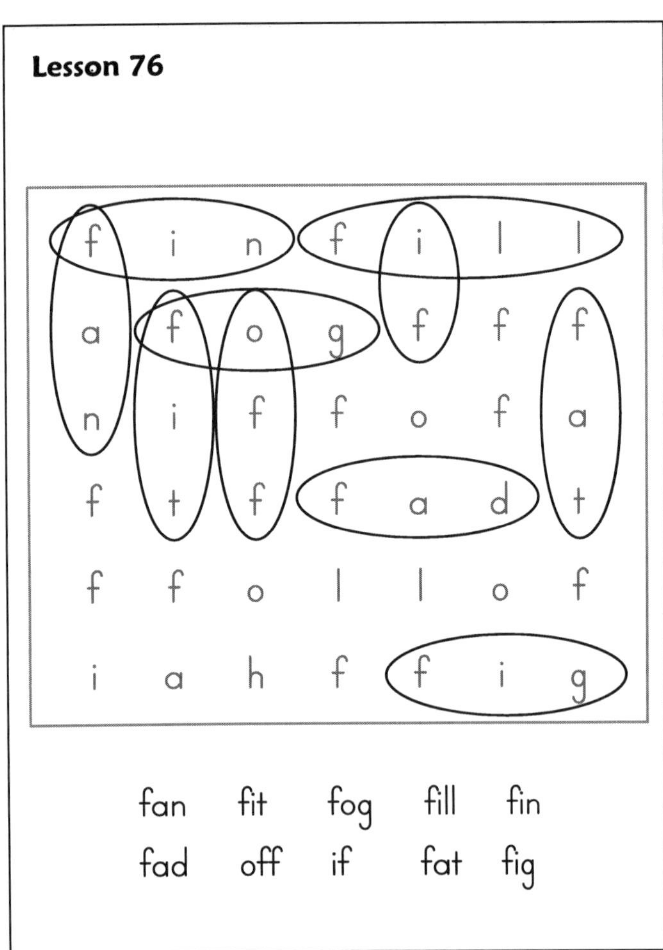
Lesson 76
f i n f i l l
a f o g f f f
n i f f o f a
f t f f a d t
f f o l l o f
i a h f f i g
fan fit fog fill fin
fad off if fat fig

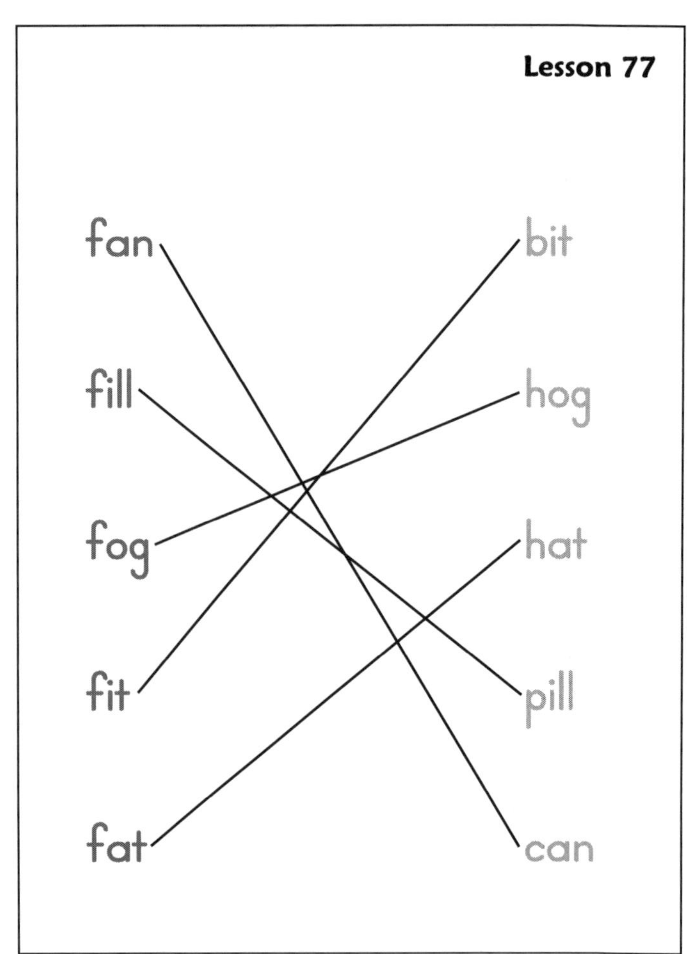
Lesson 77
fan
fill
fog
fit
fat
bit
hog
hat
pill
can

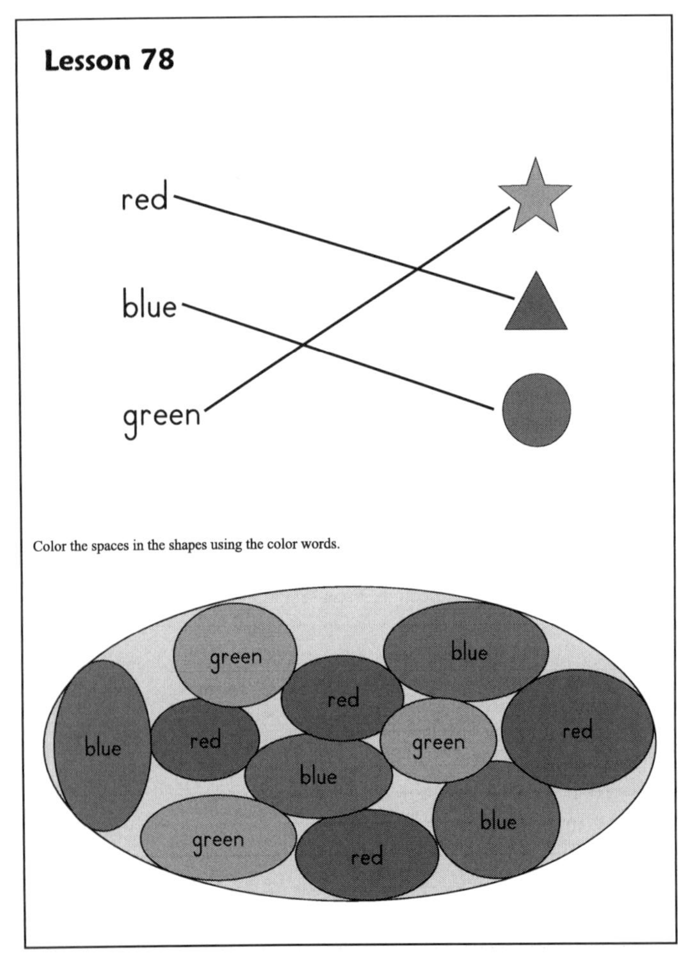
Lesson 78
red
blue
green
Color the spaces in the shapes using the color words.
green
blue
red
red
blue
green
red
blue
blue
green
red

Lesson 79
Cat Nap
Did the cat sag?
yes no
Did the cat pass the cab?
yes no
Did the cat nap on a cap?
yes no
Did the cat sit on a dog?
yes no

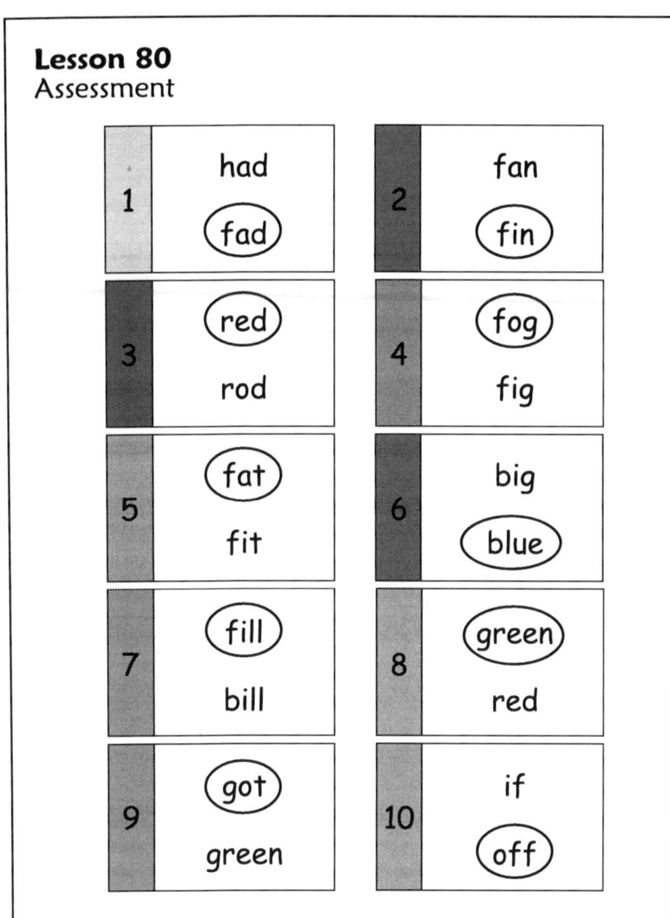
Lesson 80
Assessment
1 had fad
2 fan fin
3 red rod
4 fog fig
5 fat fit
6 big blue
7 fill bill
8 green red
9 got green
10 if off

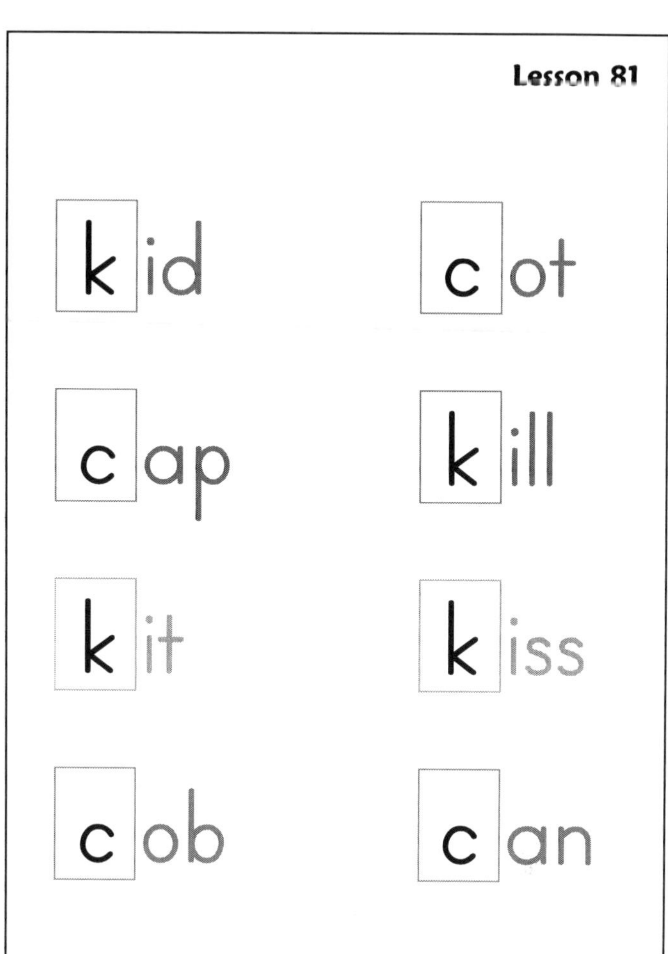
Lesson 81
k id
c ot
c ap
k ill
k it
k iss
c ob
c an

Lesson 82
r o ck
t a ck
s o ck
p i ck
s a ck
l o ck
back
pack

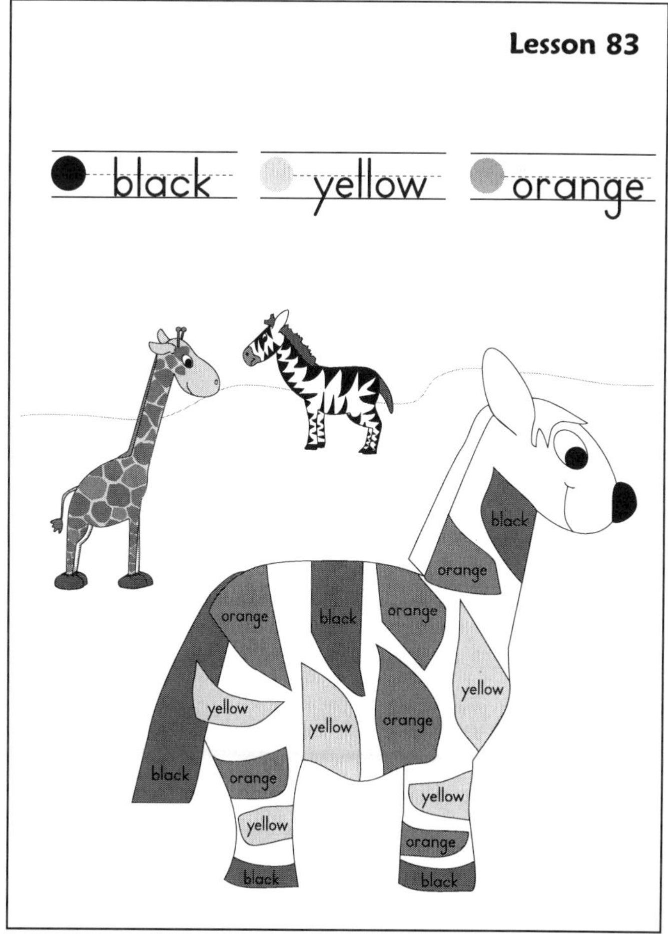
Lesson 83
black
yellow
orange

Lesson 84
Sam and Kit
Is Sam the cat? yes no
Is the cat fat? yes no
Did Kit kick Sam? yes no
Did Sam ram Kit? yes no
Did Sam nip Kit? yes no

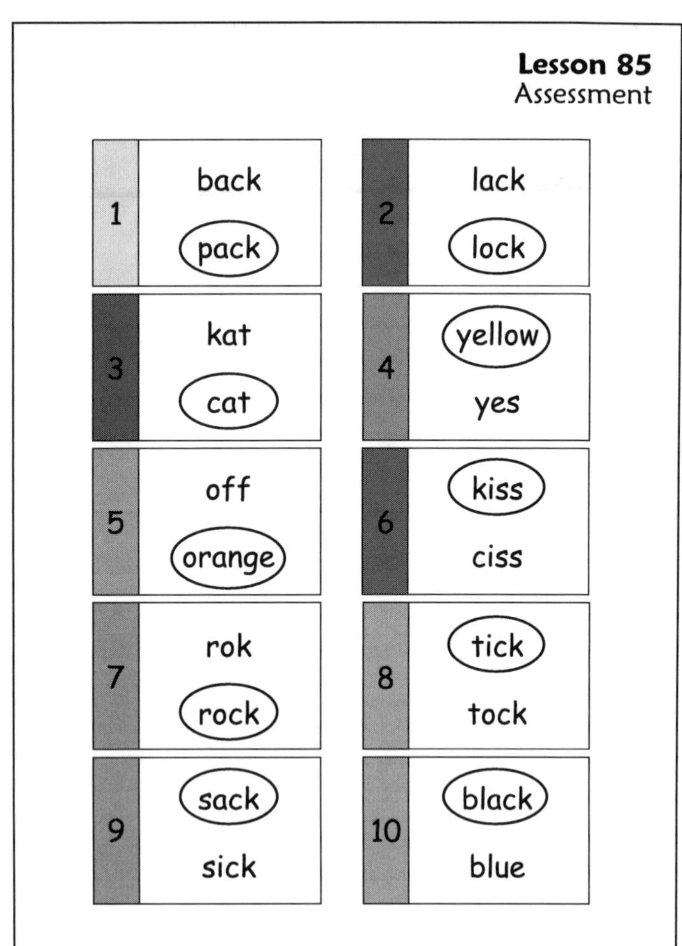
Lesson 85
Assessment
1 back pack
2 lack lock
3 kat cat
4 yellow yes
5 off orange
6 kiss ciss
7 rok rock
8 tick tock
9 sack sick
10 black blue

Lesson 86
c u p
b us
su n
b u g
nu t
d u ck
pu p
b u n
t ub

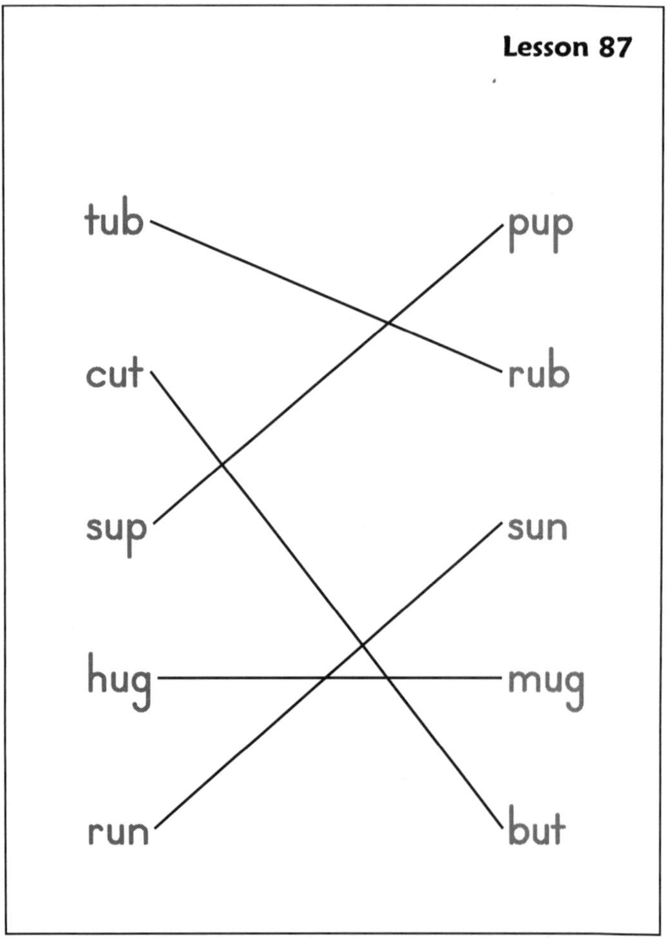
Lesson 87
tub
cut
sup
hug
run
pup
rub
sun
mug
but

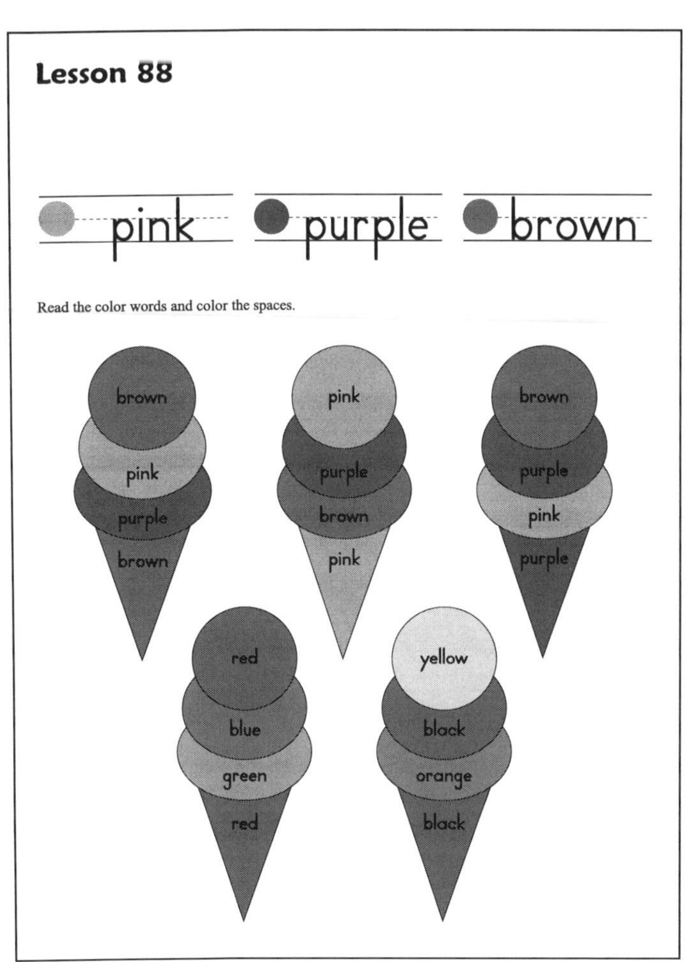
Lesson 88
pink
purple
brown
Read the color words and color the spaces.
brown
pink
purple
brown
pink
purple
brown
pink
brown
purple
pink
purple
red
blue
green
red
yellow
black
orange
black

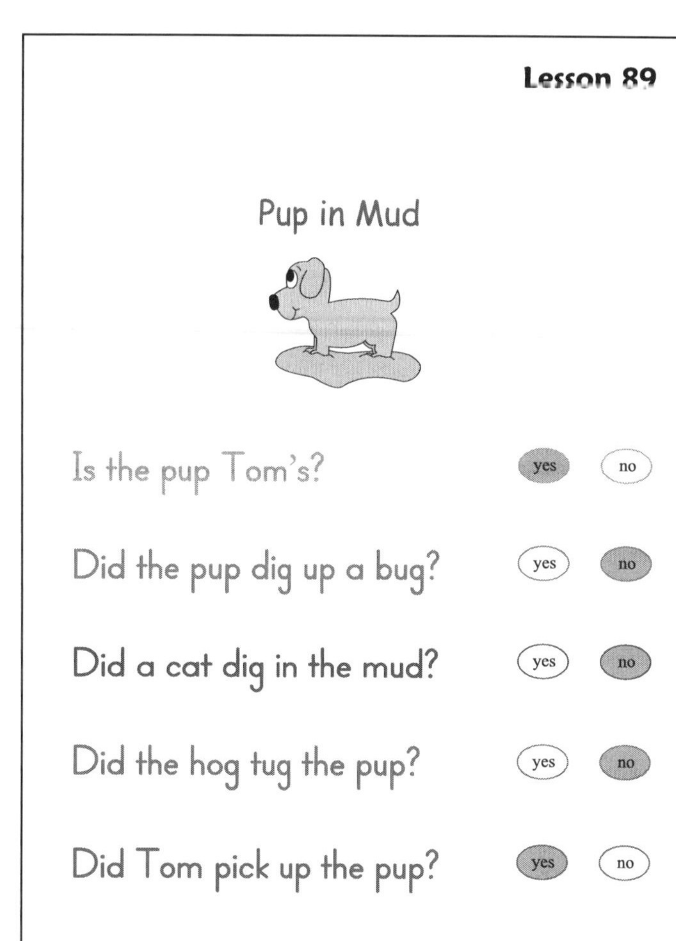
Lesson 89
Pup in Mud
Is the pup Tom's? yes no
Did the pup dig up a bug? yes no
Did a cat dig in the mud? yes no
Did the hog tug the pup? yes no
Did Tom pick up the pup? yes no

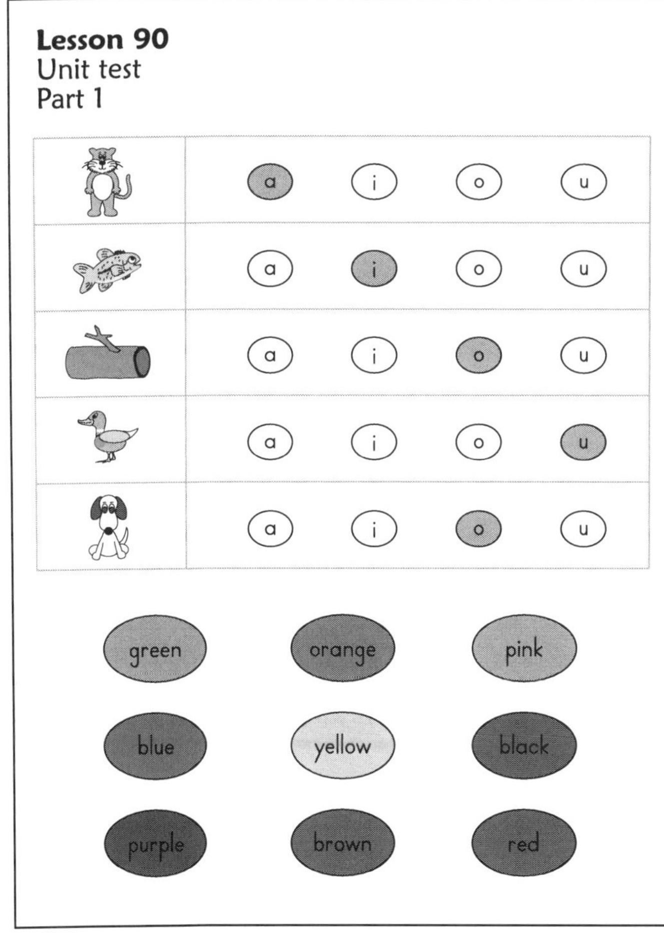
Lesson 90
Unit test
Part 1
a i o u
a i o u
a i o u
a i o u
a i o u
green orange pink
blue yellow black
purple brown red

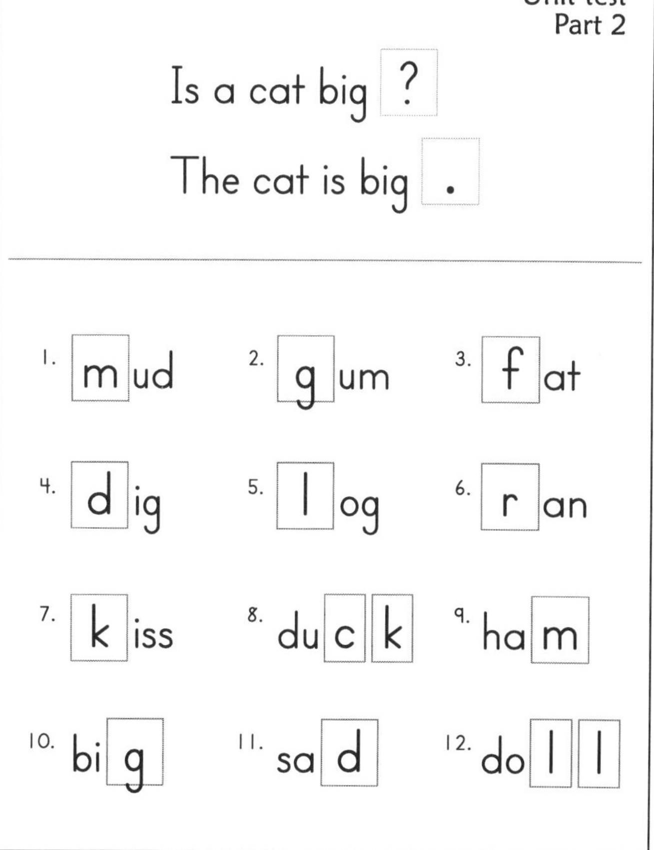
Lesson 90
Unit test
Part 2
Is a cat big ?
The cat is big .
1. mud
2. gum
3. fat
4. dig
5. log
6. ran
7. kiss
8. duck
9. ham
10. big
11. sad
12. doll

Made in the USA
Monee, IL
06 June 2023

MW01633236

“One sees clearly only with the heart.

Anything essential is invisible to the eyes.”

Antoine de Saint-Exupery from “Le Petit Prince”

Who Should Read This Book

If you can imagine a kitchen that is the heart and soul of your home, where friends and family are drawn into a setting of warmth and comfort that captures both the mind and the heart, then you will find this book is written especially for you.

Here are true stories of clients who imagined a new design and found a richer connection than they could ever have thought possible. They ran the gamut from those who didn't cook to executive chefs. Each of them started with the most common fear, *"What if I do everything right and it still doesn't come out the way I hoped?"*

Not only did they end up with a new space that became their favorite place to be, they also enjoyed themselves along the way. In helping you move from where you are to where you want to be, this book will provide not only unique design insights, but the knowledge, expert perspective and road map you will need to navigate smoothly through the remodel process.

Table of Contents

Introduction

If your kitchen is to be the heart and soul of your home, then it's too important to be limited to just working well and looking great. That's why I created the **Design Pyramid** shown below.

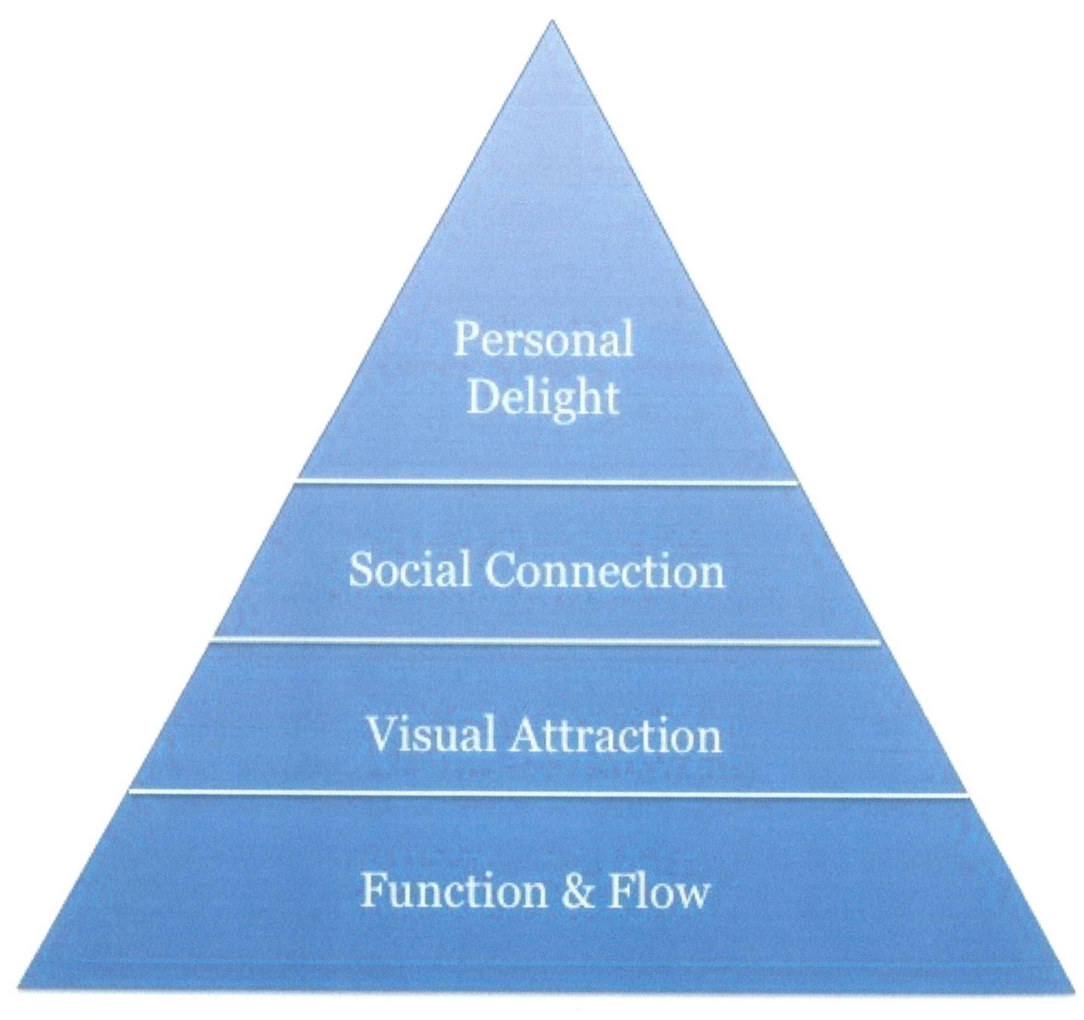

Function & Flow: Whether the activity is preparation, cooking, storage or clean up; efficiency and ease of movement form the foundation of good space planning. Achieving a high level of organization and good ergonomics are the twin objectives that ensure ease of use.

Visual Appeal: Everyone wants to end up with a great looking kitchen. While choices often revolve around issues of style and décor, they still must incorporate the basics of matching color, texture and finish with aspects of form, scale and proportion. Properly addressing natural and artificial lighting is always of primary importance.

Social Connection: The reason the kitchen is so often referred to as the heart and soul of the home is because of its role as a social gathering area. Providing areas of smooth interface between the work and non-work areas, creating good lines of sight and conversation, and having multiple landing areas to handle the various types and levels of social interaction are all important. Just as important is aligning a client's sense of personal space to the physical space surrounding them.

Personal Delight: Walking into a room where you instantly connect with in an emotional way – the kind of place that feels so good, so magical you don't want to leave, is an experience most of us have had at least once. The captivation we feel is difficult to put into words because we're unable to separate the space around us from the way we are feeling. It's helpful to keep in mind as you read the stories that likes (or dislikes) are emotional and immediate, while preferences are rationally considered. That's why "Personal Delight", which is at the top of the pyramid and is all about emotional response, is supported below by more rational objectives.

My Design Pyramid intentionally borrows from Abraham Maslow, the renowned behavioral psychologist who posited a pyramid of human needs. His hierarchy showed personal fulfillment or self-actualization at the pinnacle, representing an achievement that was only possible when the needs lower on the pyramid (e.g. food, shelter, and security) had already been met. In your kitchen, reaching personal delight requires first tending to the building blocks below.

At the bottom level of the pyramid things are very straight-forward. There are clear guidelines for us to follow when it comes to flow, efficiency, organization and ergonomics. But, at the top level, things are very subjective. We are caught in the gap between what something will look like and how it will make us feel. This is never more evident than when you are asked, *"What do you like?"*. Your response is probably *"I don't know, but I can tell you if I see it."*.

This is usually unhelpful because your designer, builder or architect has asked you for a rational explanation of something that is being driven by an emotional connection. What you might more accurately respond with is, *"I don't know, but I can tell you when I feel it"*. These exchanges often prove fruitless because we don't have the tools or language to understand and explain how something has to look in order to excite our emotions. Most of us consider our tastes to be wide-ranging and somewhat disparate and unconnected. The good news is that beneath the surface are consistent and well-defined patterns of preference that shed light on *why* we like the things we do.

As you'll see in the stories that follow, finding where you have a strong emotional connection and then looking for the *whys* is essential. When you fully understand why you are in love with, say, a piece of art or furniture, a car, a picture frame or piece of sculpture; those same factors will directly correlate with achieving an emotional connection and sense of personal delight in your new space.

This book is intended to help you imagine more and gather the understanding and tools to move your design from one that merely renovates to one that transforms. To be honest, it has taken me almost twenty years to discern that there was a clear structure and process about what for me had been an intuitive process. After sifting through hundreds of my projects, I found the same steps were taken in each case. These steps often occurred in different sequences; some even happening simultaneously, but collectively they remained the same. I refer to them as the **Design Formula**. Here are the five steps in the process.

1. **Identify your design area by its physical, visual and social connections.**

2. **Find your passions and their underlying patterns.**
3. **Identify your goals and challenges.**
4. **Determine your boundaries for personal space, visual structure, and ambiguity.**
5. **Modify the physical and perceived space to match each level of the design pyramid.**

Business consultants who assist companies with strategic analysis actually have a somewhat similar list; it has a nifty acronym. They call it a **SWOT analysis– (S) Strengths, (W) Weaknesses, (O) Opportunity, (T) Threats.** The common element is developing a strategic vision of your goal.

As the stories unfold you'll see how these steps are put into practice. You will also notice that my role changes between custom builder and kitchen designer because the stories are presented thematically rather than chronologically. In the first chapter (**Musical Chairs**), my career designing and building custom homes had taken me to a point where I felt so strongly about needing a higher level of design in the kitchen, I undertook the role myself.

I started off thinking of design as a means of reaching the obvious end- the new space. But I was wrong. The real finished product would turn out to be the joy and delight my client could experience and the newly designed space was just how I would get them there. The end product wasn't the room(s), it was the client!

A Buddhist maxim states, "*When the student is ready, the teacher will appear.*" As often as that might have described my own circumstance, I could never have imagined how such clear and powerful lessons would consistently arrive, each one packaged with surprise and serendipity. As you read the stories in Part One, you will see how each successive client seemed to show the way to a broader understanding of what kitchen design could be.

In Part Two, I relate the stories of other clients whose experiences richly illustrate the powerful and transformational role design can play in our lives. My client's environments

moved so far beyond dysfunction and renovation, they were able to inspire the mind, energize the body and nourish the spirit. Most thought they had started with a remodel and ended up with a new home.

In Part Three, I address how to get the answers you are seeking by asking the right questions. You'll see how to break free of the many barriers that make this difficult. Outlined in detail are the three elements essential for your design to reach its full potential as well as the patterns that underpin all the different design styles. I also review the emotional and personality characteristics that most commonly drive these patterns. These will enable you to see where your own preferences place you in the larger scheme.

Part Four tackles the mechanics of just how you can navigate your journey from *Before* to *After*. Each of the four stages of remodeling are covered in detail. The planning stage follows a sequence of 12 questions that you and everyone must address along the way. How to prepare a budget, choose product, select builders, designers and cabinet suppliers are all covered along with schedules and contracts. You'll learn how to see things from an insider's perspective, avoid the most common pitfalls, and develop the knowledge and tools that will help you make better decisions.

In addressing the pre-construction stage you will learn the correct early preparations for a smooth transition to construction. The sections on construction and post construction will take you through the entire remodel process of one of the kitchens presented in Part One. The text and many photos give you the context and perspective to develop a good conceptual framework from which to work. Rather than a glossary, terms and language you will encounter are explained in their actual context. At the end, I have provided an index of the book's most "Essential Ideas". All of these ideas are bookmarked to allow you to navigate with ease to each of the areas where they are covered

My hope is you will finish with the knowledge, insight and tools needed to create your own completely personal kitchen, enjoy the process, and say at the end,

"It came out just the way I hoped!"

Part One - The Lessons Learned

1

Musical Chairs

I'd been designing and building custom homes for some time when an upcoming remodel/addition offered my first opportunity to take responsibility for the kitchen design. In the past, I'd worked with the assistance of my regular vendors; but increasingly, their efforts seemed sterile and mechanical.

I couldn't put my finger on the problem or solution, but I knew the kitchen was too important a part of the home just to settle for working well and looking good. Efficiency and visual appeal were always desirable in their own right; but an inner voice was telling me these were only a good start on something that could become much more.

My clients for this first opportunity were Ellen and Sean. Ellen was a full-time mom and her husband, Sean, was one of three partners in a corporate insurance business. Sean's work kept him out of town much of the time so most of my contact was with Ellen. Both turned out to be some of the most engaging and gregarious people I would meet. I didn't realize it at the start, but this facet of their personalities would play a significant role in the outcome of their project.

On my first visit, Ellen led me to the back of the house where their existing kitchen/family room/nook area was located. The barely-organized chaos I encountered reminded me of Grand Central Station. The area was filled with adults and kids of every age, coming and going. You needed a scorecard in order to match up who belonged to whom. If there was an unofficial neighborhood community center, I had just found it. In the few minutes I saw Ellen interact with the kids in the group, it was clear she was a second mom to most of

them. Inadvertently, I'd also stumbled onto what was to become my first lesson in the essentials that make for great kitchens-

Social connection can be every bit as important as function and efficiency.

The kitchen is often regarded as the heart and soul of the home, but never more so than here. Everywhere I looked people seemed fully engaged with each other. The entire area was permeated with a sense of belonging. My immersion into such extraordinary richness and depth of social connection left me changed. I knew I could never go back to the mechanics of kitchen design without first identifying and understanding the dynamics of how friends and family would gather and interact.

Both Sean and Ellen wanted to remain in their present home and neighborhood; but existing building regulations prevented any expansion of the home's footprint. Finding a solution would be no easy task. To find an answer, I borrowed a maxim from Conan Doyle's fictional character, Sherlock Holmes:

"When you have eliminated the impossible, whatever remains, however improbable, must be the truth?

In our case, the improbable was that we would have to eliminate the dining room. It was the only area from which we could get the space required for Ellen's new and much larger kitchen. The good news? It was immediately adjacent to the kitchen and the wall separating these rooms was not load-bearing. The bad news? ..... no more dining room!

We couldn't stop there because both the size and value of the home as well as Sean and Ellen's love of entertaining dictated there be a formal dining room. That left us eyeing the living room. This was a viable option because this was a room that was almost never used. The old dining room had been modest in size and just barely contained hutch, table and chairs for six. The newly created dining space would be spacious and better suited

for entertaining. With extra chairs and table leaves the table could easily accommodate eight to ten people. The larger room also offered some great amenities - a fireplace with mantelpiece, a large bay window, and lots of room for art. (See photo below).

Because we felt some form of living room space was required for future resale (this was 1987 and the living room hadn't yet become a vestigial room that could be easily sacrificed), it was decided we could adapt the first floor study just off the foyer. It could become the new parlor- an intimate area for reading a book or greeting company. To make it large enough for even this, we would have to remove a wall of built-in bookcases.

If you've ever played the game, Musical Chairs, you may now be thinking the music is about stop just as we were ending up with a missing room and no place else to turn. You'd be correct. With this plan we'd have no study, and Sean, who was already short on the space needed for his books; now found us talking about taking away the room that held them as

well as his computer and his prized cherry desk. The study was Sean's sanctuary and taking it way meant that when the music stopped he would be the the one standing with no chair. We were going to need a more complete solution than what we could get from repurposing various rooms.

Fortunately, we were planning an addition to the second floor to create a separate bedroom for the older daughter; and, in this case, I could see there was room to expand further to create a library/study. Sean was excited about this because he would have twice the area, the space could work as a home office and library, and this room would be separate from the bedroom areas. The new space for Sean's library was the turning point in our planning because our new plan would be meeting everyone's needs.

Creating space for the library was unlike that of the kitchen because it would involve some engineering work and significant new construction. Because of this, we decided to focus on the library design first. It was just at this time that I ran across a plaque in the second-floor hallway. Up to this point, all I actually knew about Sean was that he was very outgoing, casual in style and he sold insurance for a living. Whenever I'd seen him at home he was always dressed in shorts and one of his favorite rugby shirts. Was I in for a surprise; the plaque had been given to Sean in recognition of being the top insurance agent in the world! I actually read it twice before grasping its import. As soon as I did I couldn't help but think, "If he is the best in the world at what he does, what level of effort he is expecting from me?"

I was pleased with the work I'd been doing, but I decided I needed to raise the bar even higher by doing everything I could to give Sean a library that was world class. I got ahold of every book I could find on the great libraries of the world so he and I could find the right look and feel. We did just that and for reasons still unknown, he decided he was going to call it his *Winston Churchill* library. (See photos below)

With the library under way we started the tear out of the old kitchen and dining room. kitchen. When we were done, we had a 13' x 22' area in which to create our new kitchen. This space still had the home's best view of the golf course and mountains and it would be fully open to the family room, nook and sunroom. With the view to the outside and the long site lines inside, this new area would certainly feel expansive. But given the kind of social connections I had experienced, it had to feel intimate at the same time. I needed a new and broader term that would integrate my enriched understanding of the area being designed. It had to be something that made it easy for me to integrate interior, kitchen and architectural design.

To better serve Ellen's needs, without getting trapped in old constructs, I finally came up with the term *platform for living*. As soon as I did I could see its real benefit:

The *platform for living* is defined less by its physical boundaries than the visual, social and emotional elements that pull it together.

The new kitchen itself, would have two islands, a multitude of cabinetry and bells and whistles of all kinds. My problem was that success, in traditional terms, would end up with people walking in and saying, *"Wow, look at all the cabinets."* or *"What a lovely kitchen."*. If that were to happen it wouldn't be a success at all because it would diminish the success of the room as whole. The reaction I would be shooting for was, *"This feels so good I never want to leave."* It was a classic case of making sure the proverbial trees didn't obscure the view of the forest. The next lesson was this:

All visual elements must be blended in a manner that supports the emotional appeal of the room(s).

When framing was complete, Ellen and I walked the new space to get a feel for how it was going work. I watched as she moved pensively back and forth. Finally she settled comfortably on the particular spot that was to become the center of the first island. This was a location equidistant from the family room, nook and sun room and would afford an easy connection with each of these areas. What she said then as her eyes panned across the room, envisioning it populated with family and friends, was this:

"If I stand right HERE, I will feel like I'm part of what's going on."

Like so much of what had already occurred, the clarity and profoundness of her simple statement could not be missed. Her words found recognition in my brain, but the emotions with which she spoke; her look, tone and body language all combined to leave an indelible imprint. The insight that followed would change everything I would do from that moment forward:

The kitchen design should always allow those in the work area to remain connected to the people, happenings and the view that surrounds them.

How many work triangles had I seen over the years, where the person cooking or preparing food was forced into a position where their back was facing others? Too many, for sure. In Ellen's case there was an added dimension. She wasn't trying to avoid feeling excluded as much as she was thrilled she could be in the midst of what was happening. Connecting strongly with others was at the core of who she was and how she found joy.

The sense that kitchen design could deliver much more potential had been with me for some time and now Ellen was lighting the way forward. Without any conscious intention, she was helping me peel away layer after layer of accumulated blindness.

In the weeks following completion, Ellen was gracious in allowing me to bring by several prospective clients. I stayed in the background when it came to the kitchen because she insisted on giving the tour. For its time, hers was a show kitchen. Just like many luxury-estate kitchens, the larger of the two islands had 2.25 inch thick granite top, fully circumscribed by a large brass towel rail. Four panels with leaded, beveled glass in adjacent upper cabinet doors were backlit with interior cabinet lighting; this gave us a dramatic visual focus on the wall furthest away. There was even a TV concealed behind two retractable pocket doors in the upper part of an oven cabinet. So, with each tour I anticipated comments about these items, as well as the many other *bells and whistles* we had included. (See below)

At the end of the visit with the third prospective client, I suddenly realized each of the women had exited Ellen's house and made the same comment. And, it had nothing at all do with the cabinetry, granite, appliances countertops, etc. In their own words they all said,

"Wow, she is really in love with her kitchen."

What they were all reacting to was the overall joy she was feeling in her special space. Each of them were craving and wanted to capture the same feeling for themselves. This had all happened about two years before the movie "When Harry met Sally" was released, but to cite from the movie, each of the prospects was saying *"I'll have what she is having!"*

Here came another important lesson, perhaps the most important of all:

The *finished product* is not the rooms, materials or finishes; it is the personal joy of the client.

And just as I was thinking about the irony that this show kitchen had been created for a woman who seldom cooked a meal, the next lesson came into focus:

Your kitchen should be your favorite place to be, even if you never cook a meal.

Many years after Ellen's project was completed, I conceived the **Design Formula** mentioned earlier in the Introduction. Because the five steps are so important, I'll recap them and illustrate how they applied to Ellen and Sean's project.

1. Identify the design area (*platform for living*) by its physical, social and visual connections.

(In Ellen's case the design area included a conclave of adjacent gathering areas – kitchen, family room, nook and sunroom. Focusing just on the kitchen would have meant missing what the larger area was about)

2. Find the client's passions and uncover the underlying patterns.

(For Ellen as well as Sean, the one thing they were most passionate about was interacting with others.)

3. Identify the goals and challenges.

(In Ellen's case it was how to find space for the larger kitchen and allow her to maintain her connection to others and the space around her.)

4. Determine the client's boundaries for personal space, visual structure, and ambiguity.

(Ellen and Sean were such strong, confident and outgoing personalities personal space and ambiguity didn't factor at all. Visual structure for Ellen was driven by her desire to expand her existing décor. The white cabinetry, polished brass accents and glass accents gave her a bright clean background that allowed her extensive use of accessories to remain in the forefront. For Sean, his library was designed almost entirely around his favorite desk.)

5. Modify the physical and perceived space to match each level of the design pyramid.

(Ellen didn't cook much, so function and flow were done more *by the book.* Visual attraction was driven by her existing décor. Social connection and personal delight were so strongly aligned they actually became one and the same.)

In only a few weeks, Ellen's project had taken me from a vague perception that "There must be more." to a the more intriguing question: *"How much more is there?"* I was now on a journey and headed in the right direction. Still a long way from having all the answers, I took comfort in knowing that going forward I would be working with better questions.

The most pressing question for me now was "*Could it happen again?*" In the next story, you'll see the answer presented itself to me in a round-about and almost surreptitious way.

2

The Dysfunctional Kitchen

Finishing up Ellen's project left me exhilarated. I couldn't wait to start designing and creating more welcoming environments that would bring together family and friends, while also being visually exciting and emotionally engaging. At the same time, I was feeling a little unsettled. What if Ellen's results were a one-time occurrence, a fluke? What if these results couldn't be duplicated with a new client?

The chance to find out came quickly. I was starting the remodel of an existing kitchen for Ted and his wife, Maria. Their suburban two-story home was about twenty years old and had reached the point where the original finishes were starting to look worn and dated; but it wasn't the look or the wear that was the concern.

Maria had an Italian heritage and loved to reconnect and express this in the meals she cooked for her family; but there wasn't enough storage or counter space. The dysfunctional kitchen layout also kept her from being able to have things in the right place. Something she loved doing was now turning into a daily chore. In our first meeting we convened in the kitchen. To picture the room, see yourself looking into a 'U' formed by the cabinetry. (See drawings below).

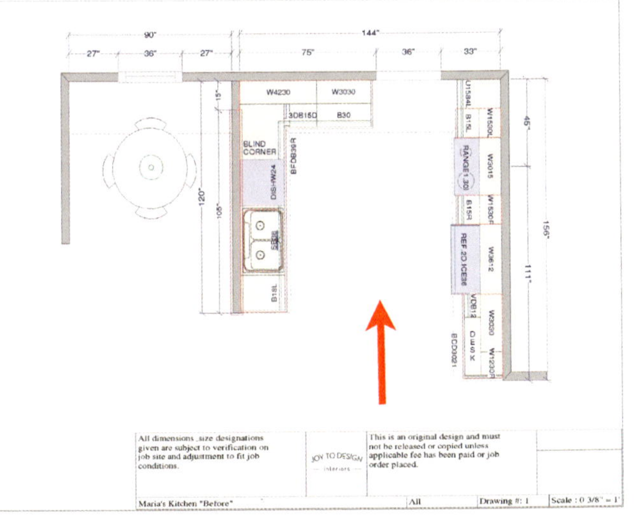

On the left was a peninsula counter with no upper cabinets; it was completely open to the adjacent eating area (further to your left) where the lighting consisted of a window and a hanging lamp centered above a round table and four chairs. This peninsula held the sink and dishwasher; so if you were rinsing dishes, you'd be looking into the dinette area.

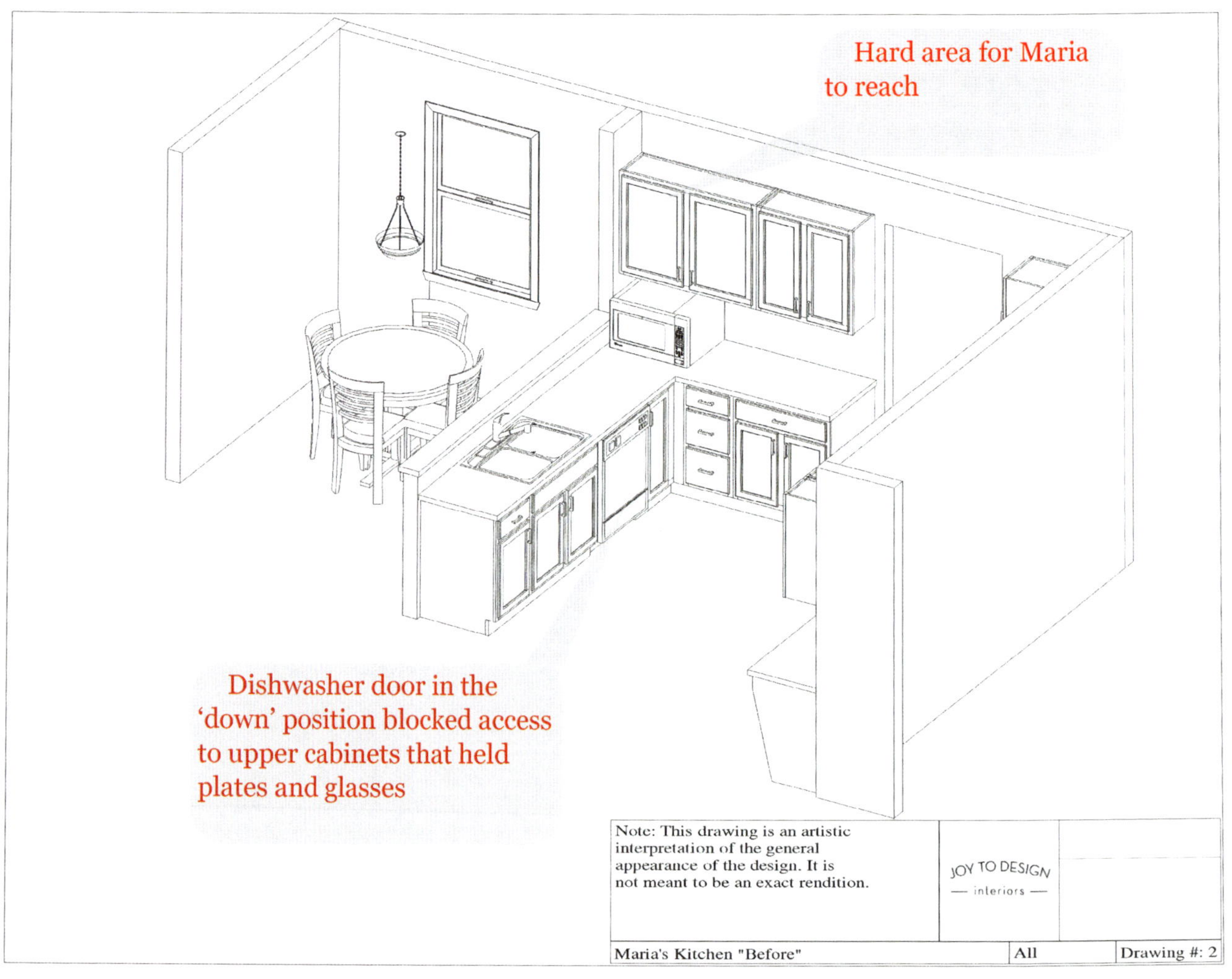

Back at the top of the 'U' was a full-height wall, broken up just right of center, by the door opening to the family room. The counter to the left of the opening contained a microwave oven. On the right side of the kitchen was another full-height wall which contained a pantry cabinet, a range with hood above and flanking upper and lower cabinets, a refrigerator, and finally a small desk area.

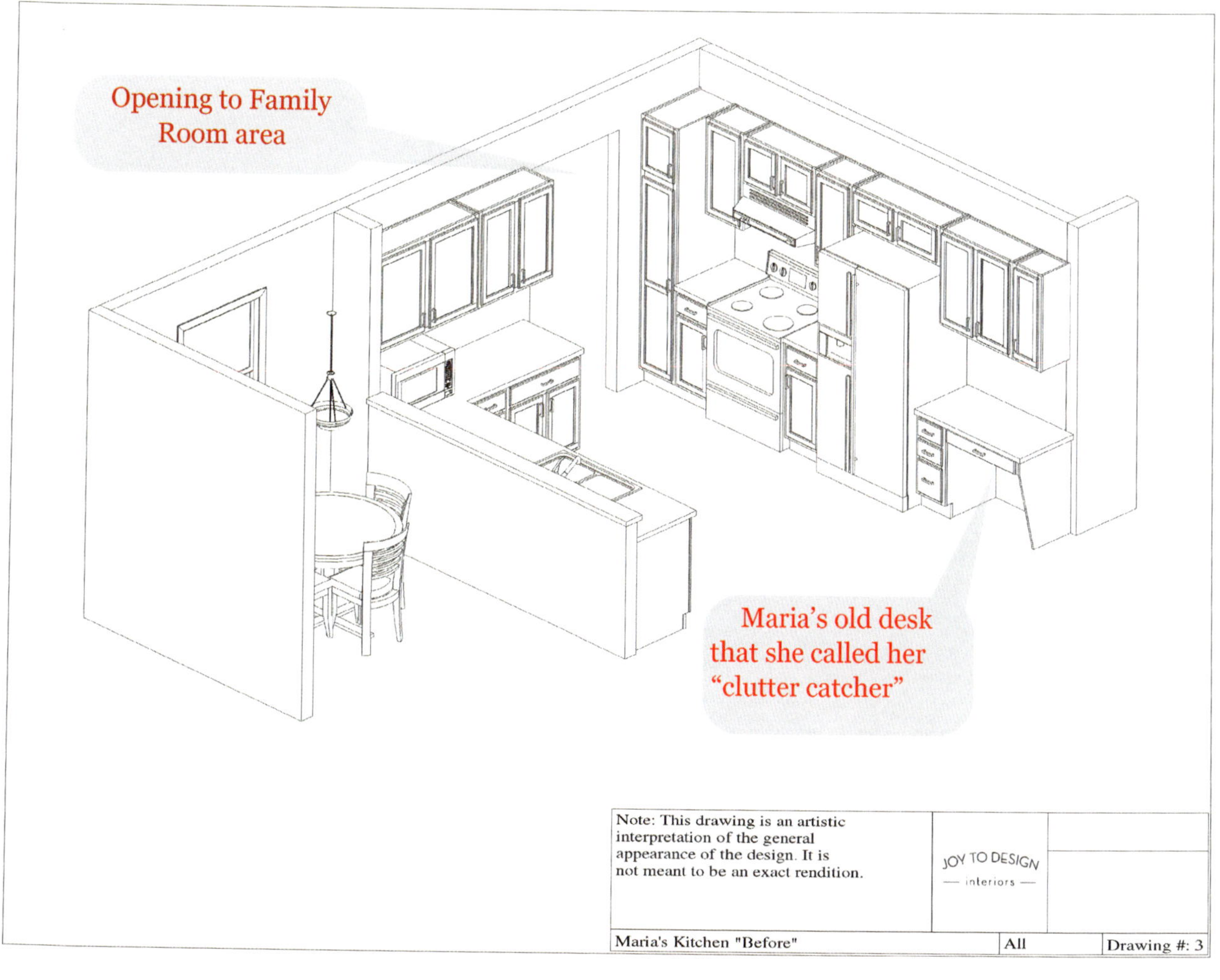

Besides the obvious shortage of storage, drawers and counter space I could spot many functional problems. There were five prominent issues to be solved:

1. **Storage for glasses and plates** was limited to two cabinets to the right of the sink. Of these two, the one on the left was almost impossible for

Maria to reach and the one on the right was three steps from the sink location.

2. **Unloading the dishes** from the dishwasher to get to the cabinets mentioned above was another big problem. With only fifteen inches of room between the dishwasher door (when in the down position) and the counter to the right, there was not enough room for Maria to stand while unloading. In most cases, she unloaded the dishes from the front of the dishwasher to another counter and once the dishwasher door was closed she put things away in the cabinets.

3. In the cooking area, the two 15 inch cabinets flanking the range didn't provide enough **room for lids, pots and pans**; and the two drawers were not enough to handle spices, utensils and hot pads.

4. With the exception of a small 15 inch counter to the right of the range, there was **NO counter space available to serve the refrigerator** (the desk area was always cluttered). Returning from the market to put away groceries was a major chore for Maria.

5. Because a counter-level microwave and the coffee pot occupied counter space to the far right of the sink, there was **no prep space** anywhere in the kitchen.

These issues were addressed by a number of changes in the new design: (See Drawing Below)

- A 24" x 36" **island was added** to the center of the kitchen. The resulting counter space provided another work area as well as the perfect *landing* area for the refrigerator. It also provided a 24" base cabinet with two roll-out shelves and an open cabinet for storage of cook-books.

- Maria thought the desk area just attracted clutter and she never used it. We eliminated it, giving us **room for a large pantry.** Maria's would later comment,

"I can just open the door and see right away what I need to get at the store."

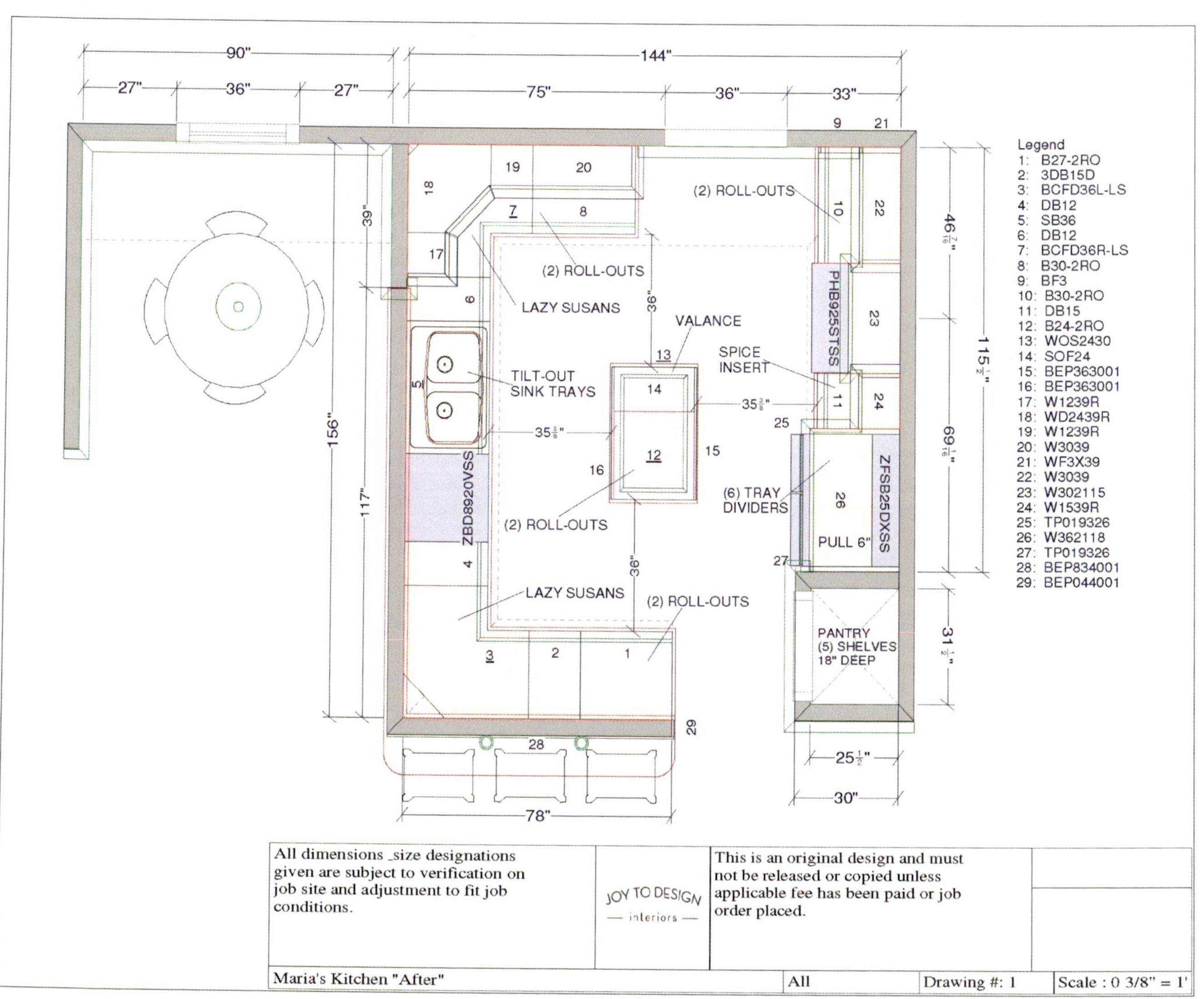

- Because we could now eliminate the small pantry cabinet, we were able to add extra room to the left of the range. We now had a 30" base cabinet and 2 roll-outs that would give us terrific **storage for pots and pans** as well as a large drawer for cutlery. The cabinet to the right was now a four-drawer cabinet. The top drawer contained a spice drawer insert to help Maria keep her spices organized and the others were available for trivets, hot pads, measuring cups, and other items. (See Drawing Below).

- A **peninsula was added** at the end of the sink run of cabinetry to provide an eating bar with seating for three. It also provided enough counter space for the perfect prep area as well as added storage.

- The **dishwasher location was moved to the left of the sink** and a return wall was added to allow us to add upper cabinets to the right. The wall corner diagonal cabinet greatly increased the amount of storage and, combined with the dishwasher move, Maria could now put away all her dishes in one operation without taking more than one step.

The kitchen also suffered from deficiencies that were simply related to the cabinets themselves:

- Because the old cabinetry style was *framed*, the construction reduced both the width and depth of the drawers. It also presented Maria with wooden center supports in both base and upper cabinets. This was alleviated by **changing to frameless cabinetry**. This meant easier access and increased storage.

- The upper cabinets were increased in height from 30" to 39". Because this **added a third shelf in each cabinet**, the storage was increased by 33%.

- The old base cabinets had fixed shelves that were only 12" deep. Because we put **roll-out shelves** in all the new base cabinets, the storage was increased 33% and Maria would not have to scrunch down to retrieve items. This was part of our effort to **keep the most used items between knee and shoulder height** (good ergonomics).

- All of the drawers in the new cabinets were given **full-extension glides** so Maria would have easy access to the whole drawer (like a file cabinet). With her old framed cabinets and ¾ glides, Maria was always scraping the top of her hand on the cabinet frame when she reached into the back of a drawer.

- The old cabinet above the refrigerator had been too small and set back too far to have any practical use. When we gave the refrigerator a built-in look, we added an 18 inch deep and 18 inch tall cabinet with **six vertical tray dividers.** This handled all of Maria's storage needs for trays, muffin tins, cookie sheets, and cutting boards. Because these items were stored vertically they could be pulled out as easily as taking a book off shelf.

- Just to the right of the old dishwasher was something called a blind-corner base cabinet. Although not the real reason, I always thought the name might have derived from the fact that access was so limited you could barely see what you after! You had to get down on your knees and stretch your arm way out to reach items in the back of this cabinet. In the new layout we were able to change this out for a **lazy susan cabinet** that allowed Maria full access to two revolving shelves that she could move with just the tips of her fingers. A second lazy susan was also included at the peninsula.

- To open up even more counter space, the **old microwave was replaced** with a model mounted above the range that doubled as a vent.

Cumulatively, the impact all of these changes had on storage and counter space was staggering. Here they are, by the numbers (desk cabinets are excluded because the only kitchen items they contained were cookbooks which were relocated to the island):

- Drawers – increased from 7 to 16 (up 129%, with drawer space up 171%).
- Wall Cabinet Shelving – 17 to 32.75 lineal feet (up 93%)
- Counter Space – 31.52 to 76.2 square feet (up 142%)
- Base Cabinet storage – (121 % increase)
- Pantry Storage - (100% increase)

Back in that first meeting, the problems noted above weren't the only ones I'd noticed; there was no real place for any social interchange. None of the three of us had any sense about where we should stand, and our discomfort showed in our fidgeting and awkward body language. When I called attention to our collective unease, Ted and Maria seemed slightly startled and that is when I knew their kitchen had never been a place where the

family hung out together. I asked them if they might consider adding an eating bar to the end of the peninsula in order to create an area where the social and the business aspects of the kitchen could coexist. They were both amenable. Ted said it would be good because there was never any place he could stand without getting in the way.

The main attraction to Maria was she could get more counter and cabinet space. The design deficiencies were so severe in her mind that all of our efforts became singularly focused on anything and everything that could give her more efficiency and a better place for meal preparation. Maria's approach was all business and no detail was too small.

Because of this, ideas I had about giving the bar a strong visual appeal that would draw everyone to it and create a place for relaxed and easy social interaction were never brought forward in our discussions. I had learned years earlier, you do not sell answers to clients who do not have questions. That was a big reason that I kept silent about my broader objectives.

Before we placed the cabinet order Maria and I were both confident there would be a place for everything, and that she could look forward to the ease and efficiency that comes from being able to keep everything in its (correctly located) place. Visually we also had a much more attractive kitchen.

Three months after the project's completion I stopped by to visit and ask Maria how she liked her new kitchen. I suspected that if it was anything but great to cook in, I would have already heard; but there was no way at all I was prepared for what she said:

"I love my new kitchen so much I don't even
want to go out to eat. After dinner, Ted and
the two boys always used to go into the family
room to watch TV. Now, no one wants to leave!"

I was dumbfounded. Her first two comments weren't about function or efficiency; they were all about the social and emotional transformation. She was in love with her kitchen, and the physical changes had brought the family together in ways not previously possible. Here was the validation I'd been seeking, and in case I'd missed it before, there was an additional lesson:

When you reach the top of the design pyramid, renovation moves into transformation.

With my confidence restored, I knew going forward I would begin to shape conversations with the kind of questions that would lead to better answers. I would also owe Maria a debt of gratitude. It was her determination that spurred me on in our efforts to gain effectiveness and efficiency. We had kept the same footprint (no additions) and yet we had seen **improvements ranging from 93 to 142%.** Without her laser focus I might never have understood just how much was possible.

3

Room for One More

The owner of a cabinet manufacturer, who I knew well, had heard me talk about how Ellen and Maria had fallen in love with their new kitchens; and he had met another user who he thought shared the same feelings and excitement. He asked if I could assist him by going out to the recently-supplied job, interview the owner, Deborah, and write her story in a way that would capture her feelings about the result. Because I thought this might provide further validation for my new insights on kitchen design, I readily agreed.

Deborah and her husband had recently moved into their new custom home. It had been constructed on an upward-sloping, heavily-wooded site. The home's exterior was finished with large beam constructions and finely-fitted stonework. It almost seemed like a lodge. The builder and architect had taken such great care to position the home that I had to wonder if the house and the surrounding trees had all grown up together.

Entering the home for the first time, I could see an expansive kitchen, living and eating space. A wooden-beamed ceiling towered above all of this area like a great canopy. Everything emanated warmth and a casual opulence. I had no part in the design, but I sure wished I had. Deborah welcomed me and led me directly from the foyer to kitchen/family room area. The kitchen itself, was anchored by a large rectangular island, roughly 5' x 12' in size. Four pendant lights dropped from a beam and aligned symmetrically above its three-ply (2.25 inch thick) granite top. The pendant lamps were made with a ribbed glass that created pools of soft diffused light that drew you naturally toward any one of the leather-topped bar stools.

The cabinetry was used plentifully throughout the kitchen and the family room. In contrast to so many designs, it blended seamlessly with the architectural style of the home. Deborah was clearly ecstatic about her new kitchen and she was also enamored with the beauty of the Cherry wood used in all of the cabinetry.

Over the years, my clients who preferred Cherry all had an emotional connection to the wood. Those who selected other species like oak, pine, birch, alder, or walnut usually expressed their approval by saying they liked the look. But those who chose Cherry had been unanimous in saying, *"I don't know what it is, but I just (like/love) the wood"*. In addition to its natural warmth and emotional appeal, it would darken over time and take on a rich patina. In Deborah's home it was the perfect complement for the interior motif.

Deborah and I talked for well over an hour as she explained in detail how she and her family used the kitchen and how much joy she and others felt when they gathered in this area.

"Finding just the right recipe for creating my new kitchen meant blending convenience and beauty into a special gathering place for friends and family- a place where everyone would experience the warmth, comfort and security of the hearth. This must be why I chose the soft, nostalgic finishes and beautifully simple look I remembered from my Grandma's farmhouse kitchen. It was there she served up equally generous portions of love and home-cooked meals to her family, friends and farmhands.

Now for after-school snacks or homework for my six children, neighbors dropping in, birthday parties, or pancakes served from the griddle on Saturday morning– the warm, comfortable feeling draws everyone in and no one ever wants to leave! And it is fabulous I can prepare, cook and serve meals in the prettiest room in the house, while remaining part of what is going on.

Even though the island seats nine, not a day has gone by that it hasn't been full. For my family, the kitchen is both the heart and the soul of our home. And, as I carry on the traditions of childhood, Grandma would be proud that in our hearts and in our kitchen– there is still room for one more".

The beautiful sentiments expressed by Deborah were additional validation we can all create a place in our home that provides a sense of warmth, comfort and sharing that blesses both host and guest; where we feel uplifted and inspired; where we can make wonderful memories to last a lifetime.

In this kitchen, which I didn't design and with a client I didn't know, I discovered the very same feelings expressed by both Ellen and Maria. With Ellen, Maria, and now Deborah, a pattern had begun to emerge. I was seeing just how transformational the spaces in which we live can become. The message to me was this:

When key design elements all come together, our everyday living spaces can support and energize both ourselves and our relationships.

The Bristlecone Pine

An area once part of an ancient seabed is now a high-plains desert running up and down the foothills of the Southern Colorado Rocky Mountains. This barren, arid expanse is home to tumbleweed, sagebrush, piñon trees and cactus. A boom in residential development was beginning to add roads, homes and lawns to the mix. It was the opportunity to design and supply kitchens to the builders and owners of these new homes that had drawn me to the area.

After a two-hour commute and a busy day of work I was ready to return home. I had pulled up to a stop sign when something quite unexpected caught my eye. It was a Bristlecone Pine, with its unmistakable sinuous and twisting trunk and limbs. (See photo from higher elevation)

(Photo Courtesy of itwikipedia.com)

The Bristlecone is one of our planet's oldest living organisms, some being almost five thousand years old. Because I'd often hiked at higher-elevations, up to and above tree line (9,000 ft. elevation), I'd been privileged to see a handful of these rare and beautiful trees; but I was amazed to see one four thousand feet lower than its normal habitat. I had to drive over and get a closer look.

The tree was growing in front of a new home that was under construction, and that is how I first met Steve. He was the owner of the property and was building a new home for himself and his wife, Jill. Their home was situated atop a slight rise; and, in contrast to most other lots that were dead-flat, it enjoyed a relatively unobstructed view of the foothills to the west.

Hearing my enthusiasm and delight in having discovered the pine, Steve said he felt the same as I did; and, with a beckoning smile, he directed me to the back of the home where he showed off two more Bristlecones. He explained the three ancient pines were a big reason he purchased the property in the first place. As a former custom builder I could see great care had been taken not to have them disturbed by construction.

It wasn't long before we were soon working together on a design for his new kitchen. He had a good deal of curiosity coupled with such an engaging personality; I could see he was going to be one of my most interesting clients. Steve exhibited a strong analytical bent, but his strong emotional connection to the Bristlecones hinted a dormant but deep level of intuition that would show itself before we finished his kitchen.

Steve owned and operated a commercial business in the area. Some years before, he had relocated from Chicago, where he was a motivational speaker and shared the same stage with the legendary Zig Ziglar. I was impressed because I had read many of Zig's writings when I went through a *power-of-positive-thinking* stage.

Steve told me about the first time he was going to be speaking to a large group. With no one else on the stage he would be solo; but Zig was supposed to be close by if needed. Zig, however, had decided to go off for a smoke break; and Steve, awash in a tangle of nerves, was left to swim or sink on his own. Afterward, Steve asked Zig how he could speak

so easily to such large crowds. He'd said, *"I still get the butterflies, just like you, but mine are flying in formation!"*

Often during construction, in order to help my clients visualize, I mock up the kitchen layout with materials from the job. For Steve and Jill, I gathered loose 2x4's that were being used to frame the walls and laid them out on the subfloor so they formed an outline of the cabinet fronts. The kitchen was in the center of the house with the nook straight ahead, and the family room just off to the right.

Jill was troubled as she studied the layout. She told me, *"It looks really small"*. I thought about some possible changes, then moved things around to create a new island configuration. She was delighted with the result and said, *"It feels so much larger"*.

This presented a good opportunity to clarify the difference between measurable, physical space versus the same space as we actually perceive it. When I showed Jill that the change had actually shrunk the physical dimensions of the space, she was incredulous because the new and smaller layout felt so much larger. We had started off with her feeling penned in, but the change was allowing her to feel fully connected to the adjacent eating and family room areas. What it was (physical) and how it felt (perceived) were dramatically different.

The demonstration helped Steve and Jill see that in instances where we couldn't change the physical attributes, we could still control how things would be perceived. Rectangular spaces could be made to seem square, ceilings could go up or down, sharp outside corners and ceiling drops (soffits) could be made to disappear – even entire walls. As Jill and Steve managed to get their heads around how things had just gotten bigger, none of us could anticipate then how much larger *big* was about to become.

Looking outward from our new island location, the view was dominated by the Western foothills. It was made even more expansive because we were looking through an outside wall filled with floor-to-ceiling windows, in the center of which was a large,

fixed-glass picture element. With our interior color scheme in desert neutrals the visual connection between inside and out was strong and seamless.

Doug West, who has painted so many landscapes of the American Southwest, is a favorite artist of mine. Looking westward out of Steve's window, I realized the view we were working with was right out of one his paintings. (See Photo Below)

(Photo Courtesy of Doug West and Blue Rain Gallery)

Early on in design I learned when nature gives you something extraordinary to work with, it is important not to get in the way. If our design could enhance the emotional connection Steve and Jill had with the landscape, then for the first time, the *platform for living* could extend not only beyond the kitchen to surrounding rooms, but outside the building- all the way to the base of the hills. And, here came the next insight:

Visual perception and social connection occur across dimensions not perfectly aligned with our physical space. They are all more like a series of overlapping planes.

Confining a design merely to the physical space can severely limit its potential. Jill had been connected perceptually with the larger living space inside the home. But now, if the emotional pull was strong enough, we could take her from looking out at a Doug West setting to feeling like she was in the midst of the setting. If it worked, she and Steve would experience something inside their home most of us only find when we are outside, and wrapped up in a panoramic view. We could deliver an experience that was at once both expansive and intimate.

We were just one key element away from that goal, and that would be the granite chosen for the island. The island top with its angled form and asymmetric curves was going to be uniquely positioned between viewer and view. If the right granite could be found, it could act as a sort of *stargate* or *worm hole*, allowing Jill to move back and forth between the inside and exterior realities.

Lest this sound like science fiction, it is not so different from common everyday experience. If you have enjoyed *al fresco* dining at a restaurant whose outdoor seating area is well designed; you can probably recall not only the intimacy of dining with your partner, but also how effortless is was to shift your focus to the street scene for people-watching and then back again to either your partner or your group of fellow diners. When these transitions across different levels are seamless and appear to happen unconsciously, it is a big part of the magic we experience.

Full of passion and enthusiasm about my new insight, I shared it with Jill and Steve. I told them how imperative it would be, when choosing their granite slabs, to find ones that had the same feel and energy as the view. I went on to explain how previous clients had described a common experience. They would look at hundreds of granite slabs, but when the right one appeared, it was as though the granite had picked them rather than the other

way around. The lists they had made of their top picks suddenly became meaningless when a loud voice inside them said, *"That's it!"*

No sooner had I used this metaphor when I realized I had forgotten who my audience was. Steve rolled his eyes and gave me a look that made me think I must have grown two heads. He seemed to think I was saying the law of cause and effect would reverse. Steve had always been upbeat as well as eager and receptive to new ideas, but his worldview was strongly grounded in empirical reality and he needed language to be clear and direct. Not sure what else to say at the time, I moved on to other topics.

Only much later did I realize I should have explained the range of granite patterns and colors is enormous; and, like snowflakes, no two are exactly alike. The way in which people respond is much like artwork, because there are so many subtleties of depth, form, light, and motion that come into play. It is similar to looking at paintings in a gallery. With some pieces you begin by looking at the artist's work, only to realize some moments later, there was a power and resonance that launched you into a sort of reverie; almost as though you had been transported to another place and time. After the fact, my previous clients would all have said when they found the right granite slab, they knew it in their gut before the realization hit their heads. In other words, **if they had to think about it, it wasn't the right choice.**

Jill had definitely chosen the right granite. Often during the finishing stages of construction she and Steve would find themselves caught up in the view toward the west. They told me whenever this happened they felt a remarkable connection to the land and its history.

Six weeks later, I found myself back at Steve's house. He was telling me Jill thought she'd found the perfect granite, but it was more than a little pricey. Trying to be cost-conscious and wanting to make sure it was worth the extra expense, Steve had made the two-hour trip to the distributor's warehouse to have a look for himself. As I sat there and listened, Steve told me how he'd been looking at that particular granite for a few minutes

when he turned and started to walk away. He said he'd gotten only twenty feet before he was compelled to turn and look back. In his words:

"It was almost like the granite reached out
and yanked me out of my socks!"

This was the cue I'd been waiting for. I smiled and said,

"You mean it was almost like the granite
chose you instead of the other way around?"

Steve's reaction was palpable. I could tell goose bumps were running up and down his arms. His neatly-ordered view of reality had just developed a little fissure. That moment turned out to be just the first of several such occurrences to follow. There was one in particular however, where I was the one caught by surprise.

It was early morning out on the job site and Steve had been talking to me as I followed him to the back of the house. We had just exited the walk-out basement, next to one of those ancient bristlecone pines, and begun walking under the partially-completed deck above. With only the framing members above me, it gave the appearance of a trellised walkway.

At this juncture, it is important to explain that I am *always* attentive to what my clients are saying; so I was shocked to find I was looking ahead to see Steve facing me. He asked if I was okay. It was then I realized there had been a point where my forward motion, my hearing and time itself had stopped. Somewhat embarrassed, I apologized and told Steve I had been entirely overcome by a feeling of being in the Appian Way in Rome. He said it was a favorite place of his and he could understand. What he didn't know was that, of the two of us, only he had actually been there. I wasn't going to mention it to Steve, but I was starting to wonder if those ancient pines had mystical powers.

This and other smaller things took on more meaning as the home progressed toward completion. About two months after Steve and Jill moved in, I stopped back to visit. Having designed and built custom homes years earlier, I'd been wanting to ask Steve for some time; how his beautifully-designed home had actually come to be. Early on I learned Steve had no previous building experience, but only toward the end of the project did I realize the design had been entirely his.

Steve explained that for two years prior to construction he would come to the property almost every evening to look out to the west and get lost in the view. He had set up a bench on the higher ground and would just sit there, sometimes for hours. After that, he said, he just knew what needed to happen; and from that point forward, all the right people kept finding him at just the times he needed. Steve said to me:

"It is almost like the house was building itself,
and I was just coming along for the ride."

Being a big believer in serendipity, I responded,

"Maybe it was not an accident all
those people showed up just when needed."

After all, it had been a Bristlecone Pine that called out to me on that very first day.

5

Finding Malibu

Imagine you'e just toured a builder's show home and are so enamored you want the builder to construct the exact same model for you. Now, imagine your new home is built and you've moved in all of your furnishings, only to discover what you thought you wanted is completely wrong!

This almost happened to one of my homebuilding clients. Only the most fortuitous of circumstance kept me from building them the wrong home. It also brought new insights and clarity that would greatly augment my ability to help my future kitchen design clients reach their goals.

Tom and Nancy were both in their early fifties and owned and operated a large medical device company. Tom was an engineer by training, typically dressed in a short-sleeved white shirt. He possessed such a good-humored nature it seemed to be forever pushing itself outward into a broad smile. Nancy had always worked on the business side of the medical field. She was affable but carried herself in a more reserved manner. You could immediately pick up on their confident but self-effacing nature; but working with them in depth also revealed their keen appreciation for the subtlest of design issues. Since I was always absorbed in the smallest of details, it's not surprising they were some of my most interesting clients.

Tom and Nancy initially contacted me to talk about building a new custom home in the same community where I'd just finished one for another client. To give them a sense of the detail and quality they should expect, I arranged a tour of that house. It contained five-bedrooms and a total living area of 6500 square feet, all of which reflected a contemporary

southwest look. The stucco exterior was done in a sandstone color. Staying true to style, the front of the home was set off with a 20' x 25', brick-paved courtyard, the entrance to which was heralded by a gate with two 3' x 7' custom made doors. Each 3.5 inch thick door was banded in ornamental iron and was so heavy it took four men to lift into place. Atop the home terra cotta-colored, double-barrel concrete tiles covered the roof structure. (See courtyard below)

On the inside, the floors of the main living areas were covered in a burnt-orange Saltillo tile (terra cotta tile from Saltillo Mexico). Bath walls, kitchen backsplash and stair risers were adorned with a variety of hand-made Talavera tiles. All of the interior walls were finished with a special *pooled* wall texture; the hand troweling created the look of old-world plaster. A *bee-hive* fireplace gave the family room an authentic look and feel.

After touring this home, Nancy and Tom were excited about all of the things they had seen; so much so, they wanted me to design and construct something similar for them. They asked me to get things in motion as soon as possible.

To gain a sense of my prospective client's style and décor, I usually started a project by arranging an early meeting at their home. When I suggested this to Tom, he told me they had already sold their home and he and Nancy were renting a small townhouse to use during construction. However, because they'd used some of their things to furnish the rental, I set up an early meeting with them, myself and Bill, who was the person I was using to draw up the blueprints.

I'd built custom homes that met the functional and aesthetic objectives of each client as well as opportunities and limitations that were posed by the individual building sites. As a result, I'd never built two homes that were even remotely alike. Now, because Tom and Nancy had such a strong emotional connection to the home they'd just seen, I was worried this was becoming a real possibility. I didn't realize at the time that there was more than that to be concerned about.

As soon as Bill and I entered the rental townhouse, red flags started popping up, letting us know something was amiss. In the dining room, to the right of the foyer, I could see a table with six chairs. Instead of rustic wood with hand-carved details, I saw clean straight lines; and where I would have expected a low-sheen, glazed finish, I was staring at high-gloss black lacquer and polished brass inlays. From the foyer we turned right and headed down a short hallway that led to the family room. At the end of the hall we found ourselves passing a serigraph by Erte. Up to this time, I'd seen only sculptures by this 1920's Art Deco artist. I asked Tom about it and he said he and Nancy were big fans of the artist. I made a mental note that it matched the contemporary styling of the table.

As we took our seats, I scanned the furnishings and accessories. Nothing remotely resembled the Southwest - no sign of pottery, Kachina dolls, muted desert colors, or richly-textured fabrics. Zip! We'd been getting input from Tom and Nancy for only a few minutes when I felt compelled to pause our discussion. Looking at Bill, I said,

"Are you thinking the same thing I am?"

He nodded his head in agreement, so I asked Tom to confirm my initial impression about how strongly he and Nancy had been attracted to the Southwest home. They both answered affirmatively, and their tone made it clear their emotional connection was as strong as ever.

Dilemmas and conundrums seem to jump out at the most unexpected times. The couple in front of me were enthusiastic and eager to get started on their new southwestern home. The problem was that the southwestern style was not the correct fit and I didn't have a clue where they were coming from. Previous experience with other clients had taught me that those who liked clean lines, and slick, high-gloss finishes would never be asking for Saltillo tile, pewter metals, or other time-worn finishes. Southwest and ultra-modern styles just don't mix; yet my client's reaction appeared to be telling quite a different story.

I knew we needed to dig deeper to find the underlying reasons they liked the Southwest house. Because I trusted the integrity of their emotions, I sensed there must be a way to ferret out what was driving their feelings. If I could discover this, we could get back on firm ground and find a way forward. After an hour of questioning and discussion, the answers began to emerge. We discovered four things that had resonated strongly with Tom and Nancy; and the good news was that not one of them was uniquely peculiar to southwest design.

First, they were attracted to the **openness**. The main living area of the home had flowed together beneath a vaulted ceiling. The seamless visual transitions allowed them to use their thoughts and actions to define the space, rather than having it imposed on them by a design that might feel rigid and contained. Tom and Nancy wanted to be surrounded by space that came alive with their participation rather than observation; in effect, the wanted a design that said, *"What do you want me to be?"* rather than, *"Here I am!"*

Second, they liked the curved sweeping walls which we had utilized in the nook, the courtyard and elsewhere. Their strong attraction to the **curvilinear elements** was telling us even though they liked clean lines and smooth surfaces, they wanted to keep things relaxed and with a sense of motion, rather than the straight-lined, rectilinear style prevalent in many contemporary homes.

Third, the interior exuded **softness** because rounded drywall forms were used for dropped ceiling elements (interior soffits), outside wall corners, and had even replaced the more traditional wood and window door casings. Without any sharp edges to catch their eye, Tom and Nancy were better able to experience the whole rather than just the parts.

Finally, they were impressed by the strong **connection to the outside**. We'd achieved this, in part, with floor-to-ceiling windows that were blended together into an overall wall design. The effect was two-fold. It not only let the light and beauty of the outside in, but allowed those on the inside to feel part of the larger landscape beyond.

Having probed deeper, we could now see all of the things that created the attraction for Tom and Nancy. Avoiding an expensive and time-consuming wrong turn at the beginning, we took away a critically important lesson:

> ***What* you like is not nearly as important as *Why*. Many people can like the same things, but for entirely different reasons. Understanding the underlying reasons is essential to helping you achieve your goals.**

This realization would have a major impact on everything that followed. Going forward, I would seek out items to which my clients had a strong emotional attraction and then apply the scrutiny needed to grasp the forces that were driving those emotions. In the case of Nancy and Tom, here is how we applied what we learned at that early meeting:

•**Soft elements** to provide visual flow, a more relaxed ambiance, as well as an increase in the perceived size were used in every detail –reeded, wood

inserts on the front door, bull-nosed edges on drywall corners (90 degree turn, 1 inch radius), rounded edges on window and door surrounds, cylindrical, 24 inch diameter, one-and-a-half story interior columns, cabinet and drawer fronts with rounded edges and curved door fronts, even rounded profiles on the window jambs and the wall thermostat.

In the kitchen, smooth, flat, hi-gloss door and drawer finishes, bull-nosed black granite, and rounded cabinet forms combined to create interior design elements that were as visually arresting as the space around them. Wall cabinets became a backdrop for the kitchen island whose reeded back, asymmetric shape, and pendant lighting reached out to the adjacent family room.

•**Curvilinear design elements** were highlighted everywhere. On the full-width exterior deck, rolling and sinuous shapes were created with horizontal, tubular railings. In the main living area a curved railing of etched-glass panels was illuminated by a light source hidden inside the top and bottom, gloss-black rails. It wrapped itself around the end of the dining room that was open to the floor below. In the master bath rounded sink vanities floated above a marble floor and a curved glass block wall, adorned with colored, fused glass, enclosed the walk-in shower.

•**Openness** was enhanced by limiting interior walls to a bare minimum and using transparent elements wherever possible. In the case of the stairs to the lower level, we used glass railing elements and the stairs themselves were designed to be supported by a single center beam to eliminate vertical stair risers. Each stair tread appeared to be floating in space. An island configuration was used for the two-way, bar that separated family and dining areas.

•**Connection to the outside** was assured because the entire rear of the house had a 26' high, south-facing, glass curtain wall that allowed light to flood deeply into the entire structure. From everywhere on the main floor you were afforded an expansive view of Pike's Peak and the plains that rolled away toward the south. (See photos below)

In retrospect, I never should have worried about having this home become a copy of another. Each home I built was tailored to clients with unique backgrounds, personalities and

design tastes, providing solid insurance against that ever happening. In the case of Tom and Nancy, they ended up with their dream home and were ecstatic with the results. The finished design was an ultra-contemporary style and looked as if it were plucked right out of the California Big Sur country. Even though we had figuratively started in Santa Fe and ended up in Malibu, we were right where needed to be to meet their needs.

In subsequent years, I would look back to that meeting in the townhouse as a seminal moment because it launched me into an earnest and on-going study of the subtle and intricate connections people have with those personal things for which they have strong emotional attachment. It also helped clarify previous client behavior. For as long as I could remember, clients had always answered the question of *"What do you like?"* with the same answer, *"I don't know, but I can tell you if I see it."*

Now I could see that the reason they couldn't tell me was because they were not aware of the underlying reasons for their likes and dislikes. No wonder all my building and kitchen clients over the years had been harboring the same unspoken, but #1 fear:

What if, after doing my best to get things right, it doesn't come out the way I hoped it would?

In the past, good performance on a construction project had centered on budget, schedule, finishing detail, working relationship, etc. But, I could see now, that a superlative effort would also require delivering an emotional result most aptly described as exuberant delight. This would prove true over and over again, but years would pass before I could discover the tools and methods to achieve such results.

Once I started listening and looking for areas of emotional attachment, clues were plentiful. And, once I could discover the driving force, it was impossible not to notice it showing up in numerous other areas.

I found that one of the fastest ways for me to find inner motivations was to take clients out to **look at granite slabs at a very early stage.** Not surprisingly, clients ran the

gamut in their preferences. Some loved patterns imbued with lots of motion while others eschewed this. Some were enthralled with slabs that had great depth or irregularity in their design, while others would find comfort in slabs that were uniform and homogeneous.

Before long, I could see that the former group was often more comfortable with issues of ambiguity, change, openness and flexibility. It was common to find a desire for homogeneity to also be linked with stronger preferences for symmetry, rectilinear shapes, closed cabinetry, visual structure and strong definition between the work and social areas of their kitchen. From a decorating standpoint, these preferences often indicated how strong a role would be played by the client's furnishings, art and accessories.

Generalizing about personal preferences can be tricky, but early on I could sense that clients who exhibited the strongest preference for motion and asymmetry, tended to also be more outgoing, more accepting of changes and more excited by design elements that exhibited whimsy. Perhaps because they tended to be more extroverted, they also sought less protection of their personal space, were more comfortable with ambiguity, and wanted to keep the structure of their kitchen designs more relaxed.

I've illustrated the extremes, but in reality, each client's motivations were as unique as their personality. Just like a good tailor, it was imperative to take careful measurements in order to craft a design each client would find intensely personal. For years I labored under the impression people were all over the place in what they liked; and I couldn't see the constancy lying just below the surface. The lesson:

In our conscious realm, we all like a number of different things, but in the *why* category we exhibit a marked consistency.

Tom and Nancy had been the perfect example of this. They liked both the Southwest home originally toured and they liked the contemporary home we built for them. Outwardly, these two homes represented radically different styles. Yet, when we viewed the underlying motivations, it was clear that they liked both homes for exactly the same

reasons. Coming to this realization and understanding that my clients would always let me know how much emotional attachment they had by their tone and words was a real turning point. The trick was to start listening to both the words as well as the emotional content with which they were delivered.

As a kid I had seen TV game shows measure their audience's reaction by using what they called an applause meter. I adapted this term for my own use and called it the *Emotional Meter*. Seldom did my clients show their excitement about something by actually clapping, but they would make it known in their tone, inflection, body language and word choices. For example, every time I heard a client say, "*I don't know what it is, but ....*", I knew they were about to relate an important clue that would have everything to do with how something made them feel.

In regard to my own experience this was just as apparent. I drove a Chevy SUV and struggled for years to give an adequate answer when asked, *"How do you like your Tahoe?"* In my mind there were so many factors that I finally started answering, *"How much time to do you have?"* The heart of the problem was I needed to describe an experience rather than an object. I liked it so much because of the comfort, freedom and euphoria I felt whenever I drove it.

When motivations would rise to the surface where clients could recognize them, they began to see patterns and connections that allowed their heads and heart to work together. Miraculously, **it removed both the guesswork and fear out of the design and selection process.** For the first time, my clients were able to remain consistently enthused and energetic throughout the design, product selection and construction process.

The best part for me was that this new approach completely ended the heavy anxiety for my clients. It also ended the second-guessing and *cold feet* about decisions already made that had stemmed from their uncertainty. Before building for Tom and Nancy, every client had required regular contact and reassurance. It was as though they were always holding back a kind of emotional lava flow. If we hadn't met or spoken for more than three days, day four always produced an explosive outburst of worry and concern!

Going forward, my clients and I could share a new confidence and surety in approaching their vision of the future. The fear was now gone, and that made all the difference.

Part Two

(Transformations)

6

Trundle Beds in the Kitchen

This is the story of Michelle's kitchen and how its transformation seemed to spark changes in both her work and personal life. When we first met, she was a young single, professional running a large project group for a leading company in the field of technology consulting. Michelle owned a home in an urban neighborhood where the rapid influx of young, move-up buyers as well as older couples down-sizing from the suburbs was setting off a remodeling boom.

Her two-bedroom bungalow had good bones, quaint charm and terrific potential. Michelle liked to entertain as well as cook, but her existing kitchen and eating area weren't conducive to either. If she had people over while she was cooking they always ended up in the way and whenever she entertained friends and colleagues, serving food and drinks was a problem because there was no counter space available. The look and finishes of her old kitchen did nothing to enhance the charm present in the rest of the home. And, the kitchen design heralded back to a much earlier time when the kitchen was intended to be strictly functional and social gatherings occurred in other parts of the home. Her project is best described in her own words, written in a note she sent to me a couple of years after completion:

"Young, single and successful, I had purchased an 80-year old historic bungalow home. I loved the architectural details of the house; grand sweeping archways, hardwood floors, and beautiful stained glass – all original to the house.

But the kitchen – what a disappointment!

There was a wall cutting off the tiny kitchen from any connection to the rest of the house. I always felt suffocated, as my dinner parties would end up with people jockeying for position in my kitchen as I did final prep. The layout was so poor that the fridge door could not open 90 degrees, and the pantry (originally the spot for milk delivery on the back side of the house) jutted out into the middle of the room. Cleanup was a nightmare.

After an initial contact with a big box store, I realized that I would prefer a less generic, and more personalized approach to my new kitchen. I was fortunate enough to find a designer whose passion for kitchens was amazing and so very infectious. I began to dream that my kitchen would not only be "updated", but that the feel of my entire house would be transformed to reflect me, my tastes, and my lifestyle.

My kitchen went from the worst spot in my home, to the absolute best. Walls were removed and the kitchen layout was reconfigured. Cabinets were designed to maximize every square inch of my limited storage space. A bar-height counter was put in to give me a connection to my guests while also keeping them at bay. A prep island with excellent lighting was installed at the center of the kitchen.

It is now five years later, and I am married with one child. With my new kitchen, I now love hosting both smaller gatherings and larger parties. I love my kitchen and wouldn't change a thing. When I work from home, I setup my office in the kitchen, simply because it is my favorite place. I would sleep in here if I could.

Perhaps my designer could add a roll-out trundle bed to the cabinet line? Then I would never have to leave the kitchen!"

What Michelle would subsequently say was that the transformation of her home started, or at least was a catalyst for, significant changes that began happening in her life. She told me that the remodel also had a deeply-personal impact on her and she thought it even played a role in finding the man she eventually married.

Ironically, it also led her away from corporate life where she was in line to become the next vice president. Looking ahead at her career she could see more supervision, less hands-on work, as well as large sacrifices if she wanted to raise a family. Contemplating

diminished psychological rewards from work, she couldn't stop thinking about **how much fun she had with her remodel and how enthused she had become about the power to make a difference through design.** (new kitchen photo below)

Three years had elapsed since completion when Michelle phoned me with a most unusual proposition. She said that if she could take a leave of absence from her job, she would like to do an unpaid internship with me. She did, and she now has her own design business as well as four children.

The upshot is that we all have experienced things so special that it is difficult to put into words because the whole is so much more than the sum of the parts. Michelle hit the highlights as well as anyone I know, but having worked closely with her for a long period, I

know that she could have gone on and on and still feel she was coming up short in describing her joy and satisfaction with her kitchen.

As is the case with most kitchen remodels, the functional problems of Michelle's old kitchen provided a strong motivation to make changes. Her desire for a fresh modern look was also compelling. The key to finding more was to also think of the kitchen as a strong architectural and interior design element that could provide greater social connection as well as personal inspiration.

7

Chain Saws in the Kitchen

The home was located in a neighborhood where I'd already done two other kitchen remodels. All of the lots were one to five acres. Many properties had outbuildings or stables and backed up to large tracts of public land. No one was growing crops, but the feeling was certainly pastoral.

My most recent project in this neighborhood had been for Richard and Diane. Their ten-year old home had been one of the newer ones. Their house had a traditional exterior style, but after we finished the family room and kitchen area, the inside looked as contemporary as a SOHO nightclub. Two years had gone by and I hadn't thought about it much since, until I got a call from one of their neighbors. Susan and Dan lived just a block away in a thirty-year-old, 3000 square foot ranch-style home that still had almost all of its original finishes. It was on one of the larger lots and there was a 30' x 60' storage building 75 feet from the residence.

It was early evening in mid-summer and I had just arrived at their home for our first meeting. Standing on the front porch, I was looking for a doorbell when I was jolted by loud, low-pitched growling and fierce barking on the other side of the door. It was the kind of sound that could only come from a pack of angry guard dogs. An instant later, the commotion ceased abruptly and I heard someone say, *"Hang on just a minute, while I put the dogs out back."*As I started coming down from the adrenaline rush, I thought to myself, "Who needs a doorbell?"

It was Dan who had corralled the dogs. When he opened the door, he apologized and offered a warm welcome. His wife Susan, who seemed just as charming, had just stood up

from her chair to shake hands. In spite of their warm welcome, I felt taken aback. I was barely inside when I realized that I had walked directly into their informal living area. There wasn't really any foyer. I felt like I needed to excuse myself, go back outside and try again. The little seating area was actually a small part of a much larger open area, but it was tightly grouped around a TV that sat no more than seven feet from the entry door.

Directly behind this grouping sat one of the largest dining room tables I'd ever seen. It was about four feet in width and nine feet in length and its construction was massive. It was sitting alone in a somewhat nondescript space, but it would have been more at home in a castle. We actually sat down at that table to start things off and what occurred during the next twenty minutes was so remarkable, it has remained fixed in my mind ever since.

The living area around us was about 28' x 40' in dimension and the only full height partition anywhere was the wall that divided the kitchen from the living room area. I'd never seen such openness in a home of this age. Another thing I found fascinating was the feeling in the room. The eight foot ceiling height was out of proportion to the large floor area. This would have normally created a sort of squashed and heavy feeling coming from the ceiling. But it didn't!

On reflection, I could see that this was being mitigated in large part by the fact that each of the outside walls had numerous windows near the corners. This was softening the natural light as well as increasing its penetration into the interior. The light effect was essentially reducing the perceived size of the floor area to the point that it seemed balanced with the height.

I called this to the attention of Dan and Susan and told them I could visualize this space as a great, social gathering area that would accommodate any number of activities, people, and levels of social intimacy. I wasn't picturing this on an exaggerated scale, but the size of the space was significant and it would therefore have a large impact on any renovation plans. If we focused only on updating the kitchen area with new cabinets, counters and appliances, it would cast a poor light on all of the areas surrounding it. It would also squander an opportunity to develop something special.

As for the kitchen, we'd yet to even mention it when I began sensing that something was a little off. For a number of years I'd been working in cabinet sales and design; but I now got the feeling that this couple had no idea what I did for a living. I couldn't help but ask them,

"What exactly did Richard and Diane say to you before you called me?"

Dan answered,

"Not much. They just said don't do anything until you meet with Chris."

That settled two things immediately. One was that Richard and Diane were still pleased with their results, and the other was that we could continue exploring the design potential of this home without getting prematurely lost in the details of cabinetry and kitchen mechanics.

In the short time we had left, we talked about the bigger picture. Dan and Susan were becoming as eager and enthusiastic as a couple of kids going to the circus. Dan even asked if he could give me a check to get started, and we hadn't even worked our way to the kitchen. This was just another reminder of what I had seen in that first kitchen with Ellen. It's not about the product, it's about the client experience.

When Dan, Susan and I made our way to the kitchen. Two things jumped to me. First, it was large, almost 15' x 16' in size. This was somewhat obscured by the fact that in the middle of the room there was a full-sized oval dinette table, surrounded by four upholstered arm chairs. Dan and Susan explained that they liked to play cards there with their friends. Second, the view toward the family room was blocked. Between the kitchen and the rest of the family room area, there was a long peninsula with both upper and lower cabinets. The upper cabinets hung down from the ceiling to a point just 24 inches above the counter.

Adjacent to the kitchen was a large rectangular room, devoid of furniture and clearly unused. Furthest from the kitchen was a long wall that held a massive stone fireplace and mantle. Without giving it much thought, I casually asked Dan and Susan if they'd ever

considered moving the dining table parallel to the fireplace. Doing so would allow them to move their family room furniture more toward the rear of the house where it could connect with their kitchen and outdoor patio area. They had't. I mentioned that the mass and texture of the fireplace and table would complement each other and form a dining area with character and a strong sense of place. By now, almost three hours had elapsed, it was dark outside and our time had run out before I could do more than take measurements in the kitchen. We agreed to meet in three days when I could come back with preliminary concept drawings.

If I was taken aback the first time I entered the house, the second was no less shocking. Everything was different. The dining room table (which must have taken four men to move) was now happily ensconced in the room with the fireplace, the family room seating area was

at the rear, and I now found myself standing in a foyer/parlor area that felt completely welcoming! And Dan and Susan? They were excited about the changes and were gung-ho about moving forward. With no apparent attachments to the old layout, we seemed to have a clean slate from which to work. The old saying, *It's hard to move ahead when your eyes are always on the rear-view mirror* definitely didn't apply to this couple.

Susan was most interested in more storage and counter space, so I'd put together a design that moved the dinette table out of kitchen. This left room for a large 54" x 66" island in which I'd included a prep sink, seating for three, and a plethora of drawers and cabinets with rollout shelving. Opposite the main sink there was now also room for a trash compactor that Susan wanted. These drawings showed the floor plan, perspective and birds-eye views, giving us a great start. Susan was enthralled with the possibilities that the island offered, but she wasn't sure about relocating the dinette table. She said to me, *"When we play cards with our friends, we love being in the kitchen."*

I thought about that and realized we could alter the kitchen design to create an alternate seating area. Adding just 18 inches to the length of the wall between the kitchen and *new* dining area would make it possible to pull the peninsula out far enough from the island to allow a rounded, bulb-shaped counter area at the end. With the counter lowered six inches to match the table height, we just needed to float the last four feet of counter and support it with a center pedestal instead of base cabinets. This would create a space that would seat four adults comfortably.

I told Dan and Susan that this kind of a change would require getting rid of the upper cabinets above the peninsula; but by doing so, we could change the entire feel of the kitchen by connecting it visually and socially into the larger space. They were warm to the idea, but Susan was concerned about losing storage space. I told her I could see a way to recover the lost space by moving the existing doorway leading into the dining room. The iteration of drawings would show these changes; and I told them that it would make it easy to visualize the changes and give us a solid basis for making the decision. There would also be a few minor tweaks on the island, on the sink wall and also on the oven wall. In four days the drawings were complete and I was back at the house to present the changes.

As soon as I entered the house, I realized that I must have been operating in slow-learner mode because I obviously had still not picked up on their true level of enthusiasm and their desire to be done with the old and start with the new. When I looked toward the kitchen, I could see that the upper cabinets that once blocked the view were gone! They had been so excited about the idea of opening things up that they had emptied things out of the cabinets the next day and Dan had taken them down. The change was dramatic and they loved the new look and feel. I told them we normally finished the design before construction commenced, but I had to agree that the openness made a huge difference.

The new plan for peninsula seating was shown with four captain's chairs; but, to make sure we had this critical element nailed, we marked it out on the floor with blue painter's tape. After taking some measurements, we realized the width of the island would need to

shrink, but only six inches. As I was about to leave, I said that since the new dining area looked so fantastic, we might want to consider creating an arched opening that would visually connect the dining room with the kitchen. It would open up a view of the fireplace wall and we could have a pass-through area for serving. As I sketched it out their faces lit up, showing me how much they liked the idea. Before I left however, I made Dan promise me that he would not get out the chain saw and start cutting out the pass-through before we could work out its exact size and location. He agreed, but the look in his eyes told me that he had already thought of doing just that.

By the time the project finished we had in place the arched opening and pass-through to the dining room and a low peninsula for eating or playing cards with friends. With twenty-seven drawers and 50% more storage in the kitchen, Susan was able to put away all of her kitchen items including five boxes she had been storing in the basement. (See photos).

Dan and Susan were thrilled and felt like they had ended up with a new home rather than a renovated kitchen. Sharing in their excitement and joy reminded me once again how important it is to take a broad view that allows kitchen design to blend into good interior design; where you can move beyond just fixing problems to transform space into its fullest potential.

8

What's a "Funk-meter"?

Linda and her husband, Ken, were having a custom home built by one of my regular homebuilders for whom I furnished kitchen design and cabinetry. Linda and I were in the middle of our third meeting and were finalizing design details for her new kitchen. Ken's busy work schedule had kept him out of these meetings, but things had been proceeding well. Linda and I had been exploring the whys behind the things she liked, and we were using that information to tailor everything closely to her kitchen requirements as well as her personality. The new kitchen would have a vaulted ceiling but whenever she mentioned it, Linda's unease was sending me signals that this was going to be disruptive to her sense of place and her personal space.

Voluminous space, when created with good proportion, can energize some clients with a sense of freedom and possibility, but for others, it can be alienating. Both impacts, diametrically opposed, are illustrated well by my two Norwegian Forest cats. They are sisters, but couldn't be more different. For Lily, the *princess*, every change, every new space, every new sound that comes into her world is filled with possibility. For her, it is all about discovery and adventure and it always sends her bounding forward with enthusiasm. Her sister is named Heidi, and is so named because she is a scaredy-cat who wants to hide. In spite of her large size and 21 pound weight she is a bundle of nerves. The same external events so wondrous to her sister cause her to retreat to safety with her eyes dilated and her breathing and heart-rate amplified. For her, constancy, control and security trump everything else.

From the beginning I could sense that Linda was a little more like Heidi than Lily. Spaces that were too open, materials that had a sense of motion or flow, finishes with depth– anything that might speak of ambiguity, could work against her feeling secure and comfortable. For her the vaulted ceiling was going to be problematic.

The need to achieve a human scale and feeling of intimacy in a large vertical space had come up years before with a Victorian home I was building. The plan called for a two-story great room. Twelve foot ceilings had been common in many of the original homes, but in our newly-constructed replica, the seventeen foot family room ceiling height could be jarring, overwhelming or both. To create the illusion of a lower ceiling, I wainscoted all the walls up to ten feet and capped the paneling with an overmantle that protruded about six inches from the wall. This small detail had the dramatic effect of greatly lowering the perceived height of the room as well as giving it a sense of comfort and warmth. Subconsciously, the height

of the crown overmantle would be read as the actual height of the room. (See photo, above)

With this in mind, and since I had seen this issue come up before in the kitchen, I was able to suggest to Linda that we select a large, coved crown moulding for the top of the cabinetry. Much like the overmantle, the large forward projection of the crown moulding would give the illusion of a lower ceiling height. And, because it mimicked the sheltered feeling we get when moving along a street that has large overhanging tree branches on each side, it would afford a subtle, yet solid feeling of security. (See Photo below)

(Photo Courtesy of www.Simplypoet.com)

As soon as I demonstrated how the moulding would work, I could see her relax. Just as with Steve's kitchen where shrinking the size made it look larger, we were changing the perception of the vault to make it seem more like a flat ceiling. In Linda's case I found myself trying to address not only her need to protect her personal space but strong preferences when it came to clarity vs. ambiguity, flow vs. structure, order vs. whimsy, etc. Doing this required me to think of her kitchen in multiple ways:

Physical space = empirical space based on actual measurement (size and shape)

Perceived space = visually, how big or what shape the space seems to be.

Social space = the area defined by its influence on our interactions with others.

Psychological space = how the space actually feels to us personally; our emotional connection.

In working with Linda, other preferences had also come to the fore. She was expressing a strong desire for balance and symmetry in the design as well as avoiding any elements that might be draw her away from a simple visual perception and into an (uninvited) emotional connection. With granite countertops, wood graining, and all surfaces she was most strongly inclined toward homogeneity. Granite slabs with strong patterning or motion as well as woods with marked grain patterns would induce a negative rather than a neutral response. It was not surprising when we looked at metal surfaces to find that she favored surfaces that were clean, crisp and lacking in any patina. Finishes like oil-rubbed bronze that could elicit a strong emotional response in some clients, were a turn-off for Linda. Honed granite, tumbled marble, weathered and glazed finishes were completely off the table.

As with all my clients, I wanted Linda's new kitchen to offer a design that would provide her a continual source of visual surprise and delight. Because of her strong negative

reaction to so many items, I was becoming concerned that her *safe* choices would preclude the opportunity for dynamic elements she would need to bring it to life. So, I decided to convey my concern in a light-hearted manner and told Linda that I was troubled that we were missing opportunities to introduce a sense of whimsy into the design. In what I thought was mock-earnest I said,

"I am afraid that after your kitchen is complete, that if we go in with a funk-meter, we will not even get a reading!"

I had expected a smile or at least a grin, but the serious and concerned look on Linda's face, told me I had missed my mark completely. I quickly explained that I was just kidding and there was not anything called a funk-meter. We didn't explore this further before wrapping up our meeting. She returned home and, that evening, related our conversation to her husband, Ken. I found out the next day that Ken, the engineer, had unambiguously proclaimed to both Linda and the builder:

"We are not paying for whimsy!"

Fate must have stepped in to keep me from digging an even deeper hole, because that meeting with Linda was the last time I saw or talked with her. I never did meet Ken; and most strange to me, I never saw the kitchen- even though my team did the installation.

The epilogue to this story is that when the home was complete the builder told me Linda and Ken had actually added some uniquely personal touches to the finishes and that they were thrilled with the outcome. He said that he thought that in all the homes he had built, this kitchen was one of the best he had ever seen. I was pleased to hear the news, but still deflated that I had mishandled the process. It was a hard lesson to learn, but humor is like a wielding a double-edged sword when you end up embarrassing your client.

No more "funk-meters" for me!

9

Lawyer John's "Kick-Ass" Kitchen

Hillary, an interior designer and colleague, had called me about doing the cabinetry on a remodeling project. She said I would enjoy working with her client, an attorney and real character, whom she referred to *Lawyer John*. John and I did hit it off right away; but even though I thought the moniker was a good fit for this likable and good-hearted client, I never used it in his presence. Hillary, on the other hand, had known John for years, and could more easily take the liberty of being informal.

John was living in a one-story bungalow, in what was fast becoming a very desirable urban neighborhood. Forty-yard construction dumpsters could be found on almost every street; a clear indication that this area was undergoing a major gentrification process as people started moving back into the city. Every block had several homes that were either being remodeled or being torn down to make way for the larger new homes that would soon take their place.

John's architect had designed a "pop-top"; where a one-story home is expanded by removing the roof and adding a second level. His design brilliantly took a rather nondescript structure and recast it into what would soon become one of the best-looking homes in the neighborhood. And, he was able to fully capture and enhance its 1950's vintage character.

On the interior, the old house had some wonderfully-aged walls of exposed brick, beautiful hardwood flooring throughout, and oversized woodwork in every room. The existing kitchen however, had suffered one poorly designed and executed remodel along the way. It had resulted in dull-white, slab-door, laminate cabinetry with white Corian counters

that were now in poor condition and quite at odds with the feel and style of the home. The good news was that the old kitchen would disappear from its current location. As the master bedroom was moved to the new second floor level, we would have a 20' x 33' area in which to create the new kitchen/family room. Located at the rear of the home, this area was infused with tree-filtered light from three sides and perfectly proportioned for the task at hand.

As I am visualizing and trying out different designs in my head, my enthusiasm sometimes can push me into flights of ethereal language (my wife would say *woo-woo*). This is fine for creative clients, but not at all helpful for lawyers and others with a more analytical bent. In this case however, I was able to contain the urge. In my head I could envision a magical space that would radiate a warmth and comfort and capture the emotion of all who entered. With a quick mental gear change, I ended up telling John that we could create a really "Kick-Ass" kitchen. I knew I had hit the mark when he gave a fist-pump and said, *"Yes, that's what I want!"*

In developing a design for the room, a key aspect would be to complement two strong elements that were already present. The first was the exposed brick that comprised the full length of the south and north walls. The face of the brick was a mottled red with brown accents and the brick faces had a

slightly irregular surface. The mortar joints were "struck" (flush) rather than raked (indented), (See photo above).The effect was to give the walls a time-worn, relaxed and somewhat artistic look. The new oak flooring, No. 1 oak, would match the rest of the original, main-level flooring and with its small knots and irregular grain.

The baseboard and window casings were large by modern standards and the moldings matched the arts-and-crafts style that had been used originally. To allow the trim color to bring out the warmth of both the flooring and the brickwork, we chose a creamy, off-white color, 'Mascarpone' by Benjamin Moore (AF-20). It is warmer than parchment, but it steers away from any grey or beige tones. This color's hidden power lies in its uncanny ability to bring out and amplify the warmth of any finishes nearby (including furniture pieces).

There was going to be a large amount of custom cabinetry in both the kitchen and living room areas; so as an added complement we chose alder as our wood specie and our finish was a brown, honeyed glaze. Our cabinet moldings mimicked those already in the home and we used an oil-rubbed bronze finish to give the hardware an old-world patina. Pulling together all of these finishes would magnify the effect of the brick, but we had another key element with which to work.

This element was the natural lighting. The large windows in the room would direct sunlight deep into the room from mid-morning until dusk. The location of trees on the exterior would provide a filtered quality to the light, creating a dappling effect as it hit the finish of the wood floor. Because the trees also afforded visual privacy, the amount of light could be enhanced by forgoing window coverings. We also benefited from the fact that our light was coming into the room from multiple directions. As the light comes in from opposing directions it eliminates glare and the light is diffracted into a much softer, ambient glow.

Bill Alexander, a noted architect, authored one of my favorite books– A Pattern Language. In the book he calls attention to the fact that humans are most attracted to rooms that have light coming in from more than two directions. The book does not delve into the science behind this fact, but it makes the sagacious observation that softer light

allows us to more easily make out facial expressions of others in the room; hence, putting us more at ease and thereby enhancing the room's social attraction (Our earliest strategies for survival has bred into us the instinctive need to immediately assess friend or foe).

Artificial lighting was also used for the same purpose. We created an island with a work area and cabinetry on one side and a raised curved bar on the other. Above the bar we placed hanging pendant lights so that we could create a *pooled* light effect where there was a subtle gradient between dark and lighter areas. Since people tend to be drawn toward this lighting configuration, it augmented our efforts to have the raised bar act as a social magnet that would help bring people together. The *draw* of the island was also enhanced because the curved shape of the top and its rounded edge would allow everyone to approach in the most relaxed manner. With no real visual markers, I compare it to being able to bring your boat up to the beach rather than guide it into a slip. In other words, you could keep your focus on the person on the other side of the island without having to think at all about how or where you were going to *land* at the island. (See Photo below).

The island was also instrumental in our efforts to create the feeling of one large gathering area; as opposed to a space split into a kitchen on one side and a informal living area on the other. Finishes on the kitchen side of the island matched the rest of the cabinetry, but on the side facing the seating area we used a finish that would be complementary to the cabinets, but also reach out to become part of the décor of the seating area. We chose vertical beading in a matte black finish. The black was neutral and the beading created the visual perception of motion that complemented the flow of curved top above. Without any visual markers, you could be certain when you were in the kitchen, certain when you were in the living area, but never sure about when you had made the transition from one to the other. And, of course, because we had raised the counter at the bar, the range top and cooking implements were screened from view.

There was one circumstance however that threatened to disrupt our efforts. John wanted double ovens. Even though he didn't cook, he thought that two ovens would be important one day for resale; but we were short of wall space. Our sink wall contained two large windows and once we had placed the refrigerator and other upper cabinets, there was *zero* space left for an oven cabinet. The only place left was the family room. My mind formed a picture of John inviting his guests into the family room with the admonition, *"Oh, don't mind the ovens. We couldn't find any place else to put them."* Ouch!

Fortunately, we found a great solution. We did have to move into the family room space, but the ovens were only three steps out of the kitchen work area. Since we couldn't literally hide them, the next best thing was to fool everyone into not noticing they were there. Our solution was to place a nine foot line of cabinetry on an adjacent family room wall that had two tall cabinet elements flanking a bar area in the center. We wrapped the tall columnar elements with fluted pilasters, added glass upper doors and flush toe kicks below for more of a furniture look (think armoire). The tall unit on the left of center contained the ovens. (See Photo Below)

But the real key to making the ovens disappear actually came from John. He showed us an old rusted, metal frontispiece found in the basement that had been part of the original fireplace. Since it was hinged, his idea was to use it as a door for the upper cabinet above the center of the bar and have the liquor stored on shelves behind it. The door was very heavy, but the builder worked out a support mechanism that was independent of the cabinetry. When it was all finished it worked like a charm. The rusted metal finish couldn't have been a better complement for the glazed alder and the aged-brick walls. It, of course,

became a great showpiece for John, but its visual attraction was so strong and it was supported so well by the flanking tall elements, that no one ever noticed that there were two ovens in the family room! (See photo below):

John was a courtroom litigator and his summation at project's end said it all:

> *"My team helped me pull together the entire design; including finishes, lighting, and accessories. As the new home came alive, there was a part of me that did the same".*

I believe this was more true however, than even he realized. He had been divorced and living alone with his dog in the old house for twelve years; but only six months after completion, John found himself in love and married to a wonderful woman that he hadn't even known previously. I met her once, and while I would certainly say that she liked the new home, it was clear that she liked the new John even more.

There is no guarantee that a remodel is going to result in both physical and personal transformation, but John's project identifies two salient elements that should be considered on any project:

1. **Identify, complement and enhance the strengths that already exist.** In John's project, these included the architectural character of the home, exposed brickwork, period moldings, and the exceptional quality of the natural lighting.

2. **Seamless Transitions.** If the kitchen area is going to be integrally linked to an adjoining social area, ensure that the design elements as well as the finishes flow into one another.

10

The First House Call

Tim was a friend and an architect with whom I'd worked several times in the past. We were catching up on the phone one afternoon when he told me about his frustration in trying to develop a design for a husband and wife who were planning the remodel of their kitchen. In each of several meetings with his clients (David and Anne), he said he came away with inputs so different that he didn't see how they could be reconciled into a workable design.

I suggested my experience with a previous client might offer some hope. I explained how digging into the *whys* behind my client's likes and dislikes had opened up common ground when none was apparent. He said that he would keep that in mind, but wanted to make one last attempt. About a week later, Tim had hit another dead-end and given up. He called to ask if I could call this couple and set up a meeting. He was pretty pessimistic about any positive outcome, but thought it couldn't do any harm to try.

David and Anne were the original owners of a twenty-year-old ranch style home of about 3200 square feet. It had a walk-out basement and a large rear deck with a wide, unobstructed mountain view. Anne had worked for years helping couples with Chinese adoptions and David was a doctor, renowned for his ability to treat patients with asthma. Anne was the more outgoing; David had a mild-mannered and kind presence about him.

Early in our first meeting Anne expressed her preference for modern design; but David was clearly a traditionalist. Both of them wanted to change to a new look from what they had, but their individual attachment to their preferred style was holding them back. They both thought that giving ground to the other would diminish the results that they had in

mind. To start them moving in a more positive direction, I explained that clients who liked the same design styles often did so for entirely different reasons. I suggested that a good first step would be to explore their underlying motivations.

Anne's taste for modern design elements turned out to be rooted in her attraction to curvilinear rather than rectilinear lines as well as colors that were clean (not muted) in appearance. She also wanted to feel a sense of flow between the rooms that was currently missing.

David's fear had been that moving to a more modern or contemporary style was going to result in sharp lines, hard edges, primary colors and highly reflective surfaces. It didn't take long before they could see that they had plenty of room in which to work without giving up on the things they found most important.

We settled on a modern, southwest look that was still in harmony with the home's exterior design. We would take the dark wooden posts and beams that separated the kitchen and family room and turn them into old-world Spanish-style, arched openings. All of the corner edges were kept rounded for visual flow. The finish would be hand-troweled stucco and we would apply this same treatment to the mocha-brown brick fireplace wall; all with a goal toward having the kitchen and family room space shed their separate identities and start working as a single, visually exciting and emotionally appealing gathering area. Both of them were excited about getting rid the dark beams and replacing the coffee-colored oak cabinetry with a lighter painted finish. David loved the traditional style while Anne liked the curved lines, the flow and openness. Remarkably, they became so excited about the vision for their kitchen/family room that they decided to update and modernize the entire home, including baths, closets and bedrooms.

Just two weeks after our first meeting, Tim was called back to draw up the plans. He called me to ask, *"What did you do to them? These are not the same people. And how did the scope of work expand from just the kitchen to the entire house?"* Before I could try to explain, he said, *"Never mind. They are both excited and we're finally moving forward"*.

Since we'd made plans for every other room in the house except David's study, I asked him why we were excluding it. He said pointedly,

"That's my favorite room, I spend a lot of time in there, and there is no reason to change it."

I didn't detect actual curtness in David's reply, but the way he said it that sounded off.

As construction moved forward, David became my main contact. The more time I spent with him, the more I found myself liking and respecting him. One afternoon he waved me into his study as he was finishing up a phone call. His voice suddenly got louder and took on an edge like hardened steel. I looked at his face. He was more serious than I'd ever seen him. And whoever was on the receiving end had clearly earned his extreme disfavor. To my surprise it turned out to be another doctor. I was thinking, "Do doctors actually talk to each other in such blunt terms?"

As soon as David put down the phone, his normal demeanor returned and he explained that a doctor who'd been on call for him during the previous two days had dropped the ball in a big way with one his patients. No harm had resulted, but the patient had been put in jeopardy; and that was a situation that David would not condone or tolerate. The other doctor must have gotten off the call feeling about two inches tall.

Seeing first-hand how deeply David cared for his patients had piqued my curiosity to learn more about his work as a doctor. I asked him how he got started in his profession. He said only a few knew, but he offered to tell me.

"I was serving my internship at a Manhattan hospital. Interns didn't have much money, and while it wasn't kosher and we didn't have much free time, moonlighting for the residents was a common practice. My first such job was also going to be my first house call. Being rather nervous, I packed everything in my bag but the kitchen sink.

My directions that evening took me to a part of the city I'd never been to before. With street address in hand, I'd driven around the block twice without seeing any such number and was stopped at a traffic light,

wondering what to do next. Just then two of the largest, burliest men I had ever seen appeared on each side of my car. Before I had time to think, the one on my side said, "Are you the Doc?"

I nodded my head and before I could open my mouth he had grabbed open my door with such force that it was loosened from its hinges. He pulled me out of the car and said, "Come with us!"

I grabbed my bag, and with these hulks holding each of my arms, I was escorted to a building that I could see didn't even have an address; and instead of being taken through the entrance, I was pushed and prodded up three flights of a fire escape and told to enter through a window.

The room was dimly lit, so as I crawled inside, I could see very little. That's when I was greeted cordially by an elderly gentleman who thanked me for coming and said he had called me to look at his sick grandson in the other room. I went into the bedroom and found the boy having considerable trouble breathing. After examining him, I returned to the larger room to tell the grandfather that the boy was very ill and in immediate need of a hospital where he could receive adequate care.

The grandfather said, "We don't do hospitals! You need to fix him here." My eyes had now adjusted to the low level of light and for the first time I could see about fifteen other men in the room. And, most were armed with a variety of hand guns and what appeared to be automatic weapons. Now, even more terrified than when I was yanked out of my car, I returned to the bedroom to see what, if anything, I could do. I also couldn't help thinking about what might happen to me if the boy died.

At the hospital I'd been studying a new experimental treatment for respiratory ailments. And because I had packed so many things in my bag, I actually had what was required to perform this technique. My problem was that I had only seen it done, hadn't practiced it, and couldn't be certain if it would alleviate the boy's breathing difficulty.

Two hours later, I walked back into the main room and was able to tell the grandfather that the boy was breathing more easily and was stable. The man's relief was palpable and he invited me to stay for dinner. I tried to beg off but quickly realized that it would be unwise and possibly insulting to refuse the invitation. After dinner the older man handed me $300 cash, which was more than I would have seen in a month. I tried to refuse, but to no avail. He said that I was welcome back any time, everyone now knew who I was, and I could be assured I would never

have a problem. I was escorted back to my car and to my astonishment; the broken door had been completely repaired.

Two things I knew then that I hadn't known before – one, that I had just saved the grandson of a grandfather who was a Mafia don and two, my medical path would now focus on helping patients with breathing difficulty".

David's story marked the beginning of my really getting to know him. As our remodel project neared completion, I learned for the first time that, when the house was originally constructed twenty years earlier, David had designed every detail of the house and had even determined exactly how it would be sited on the lot. While it occurred to me that this would've been good to know during our first meetings, it was only was only a matter of weeks before this information would help me understand David's connection to his home as well as the real reason we hadn't touched his study.

When the remodel was complete, I was invited to stop by for a private celebration. With wine glasses in hand, David and I walked into the family room/kitchen area and sat at the island admiring the result. David was ebullient and almost glowed with a joy I hadn't seen before. We moved from room to room and found ourselves sitting and conversing in several locations. The home now had so many wonderful areas to enjoy, we wanted to try them all out for size.

Then it hit me, two decades ago when David had first designed it, the home had been a perfect fit; but as the years passed, David had changed and grown to the point that he and the home had lost that original connection. It no longer resonated with who he was. That was why he spent so much time in his study; not because it was his favorite place to be, but because the rest of the house seemed almost foreign. Without David realizing it, the study had become a refuge from the rest of the house. With the new house reaching out to him as it once had long ago, David was a person transformed. I didn't say anything at the time, so it seemed ironic that only two days later, he must have realized the same thing. He was calling to say,

*"Can you come over to the house and look at the study with me?
I think we need to redo it too."*

11

Comfort and Ease

Amanda and her husband, who was a family doctor, resided in a suburban two-story home with their two children. They'd moved in fifteen years earlier when they were just starting their family. When I first met Amanda, she was working as a life coach and ran her business out of the house. She also worked with her husband, who was operating an urban medical clinic for low-income patients. Between both businesses, and two teenagers at home, life had become rather hectic.

Adding dysfunction to the mix, her kitchen was too small and cramped to meet the current needs of the family. There was limited storage, no prep area and no real area for social connection. The one place to talk to Amanda in the kitchen, without finding myself in the way, was the dinette table in the nook. With the table ten feet from the main kitchen, this was awkward and I could quickly feel my voice start to strain due to the distance. The work triangle compounded the issue because it was set up in a way that forced Amanda to keep her back to the nook and family room when cooking. Attempts to find a solution had also proved frustrating. Amanda said,

> *"I never anticipated we would outgrow our kitchen so soon. For three years we looked for a kitchen designer, but every new plan glorified the old kitchen".*

Earlier design efforts had all focused on rearranging cabinet and appliance elements within the current space; but it took only a cursory look at her kitchen to realize that without finding more room, just changing the layout would be like trying to rearrange the

deck chairs on the Titanic. So the question was not whether additional space would be required, but where to find it.

From the home's foyer, a hall led past an open staircase and straight into the kitchen area. And to the right of the entry was a living room. Since Amanda said this was a largely unused space, it became the logical area from which to *borrow* the space we needed to create the new kitchen. Because this would require moving a wall that was load-bearing, I called in a builder and and an engineer who confirmed the feasibility and rather minimal cost of opening up the wall by using a dropped beam across part of the span. It also unlocked the space needed to transform the kitchen. (See drawing below)

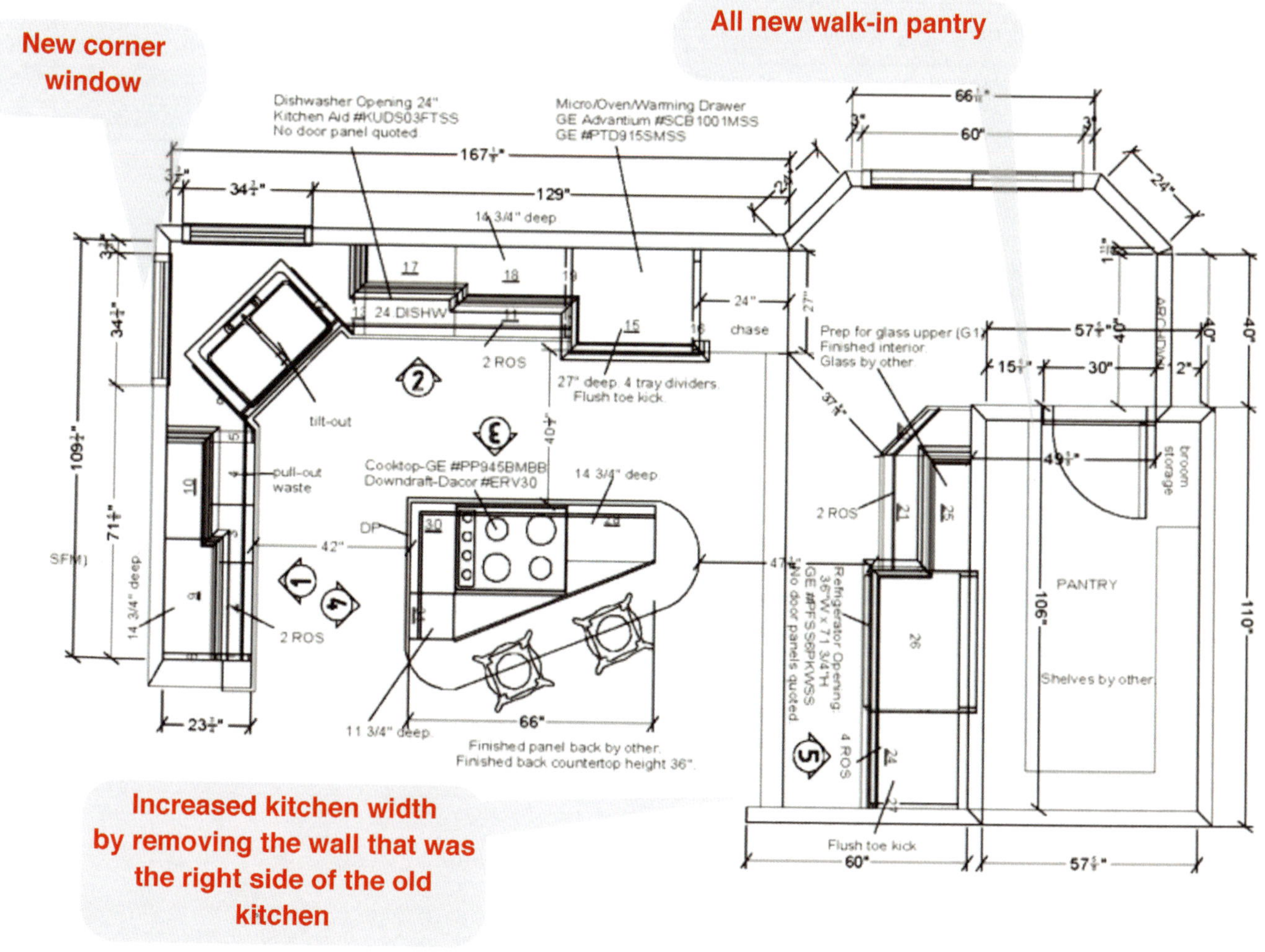

Even though we borrowed space from the living room, the space remaining was still large enough to function as a parlor/music room. Of the eight feet of newly-acquired space, we used five feet to create a walk-in pantry that would comfortably meet Amanda's storage needs. The remaining three feet went into the new kitchen and gave us room to create a center island with seating for two.

The island provided the missing prep area, as well as a place for social connection. Because we had added an extra window to open up the corner at the new corner sink location, the 60 degree angle at the bar stool area allowed those seated to direct their view easily toward the corner windows as well as the family room. The shape of the island top utilized two curves of different radiuses. This asymmetric element allowed the kitchen to appear larger than it actually was. Finally, we finished the back of the island in stone that complemented the new walnut flooring. This allowed the island to be in harmony with the décor of the family room and it helped make the transition between the two areas more seamless.

Unlike the planning of Maria's kitchen, our discussions had always gone beyond merely solving issues of work flow, storage, and organization. In all of our conversations the key words that kept popping up were comfort, ease and family. We were in agreement that the new kitchen should not only be a delight in which to work, but also draw family and friends into a warm and welcoming environment, while allowing Amanda to work and still connect with people and events around her. For a person who was continuously looking after the needs of family, friends, and clients – we needed to create a personal space that could energize her and even help her refill her emotional well.

The upshot was we were able to effect a dramatic, transformational change that showed up as much in Amanda as it did in the new space that was created. In her thank you note to me, she summed it up well,

"I was helped to see the big picture and to create a space that has made my life EASY. I can't explain the nagging irritation it had become to work in my old, outgrown kitchen.

My home is now free of congestion and clutter, and people have room to move around. I not only got a beautiful space, but the icing on the cake is the sense of ease and relaxation that I never dreamed I could have in a home. Because of the care put into the design process, my home fits my family like a glove. I'm tickled pink!"

12

The "Ugly Duckling"

Tina and her husband, Steve, lived in a thirty-year-old home. It was a bi-level and, as is customary with the style, the entrance brought you into a narrow landing with a split staircase going down to the garden level or up to the main living area. Ascending the stairs would bring you directly into a family room area with a vaulted ceiling that ran the full length of the living area. To the left and toward the front of the house was a small dining area with the kitchen area adjacent.

Tina and Steve had lived in the home for six years and were planning to update the kitchen from its original finishes. Actually, *update* is too kind. The kitchen consisted of a range, a refrigerator, a sink and about ten extremely worn and dilapidated, Thermofoil cabinets; all crammed into a 9' x 10' space. It was unlike anything else I had seen. (See photo left)

Before

My first thought was that the kitchen was the result of an early do-it-yourself remodel gone awry. As an upside, I certainly didn't need to ask Tina about her likes and dislikes about the old kitchen. Tina had left her job a few months earlier to have their first child. As a result she now found herself spending much more time in the home. With new needs to be met, there was a strong impetus not to delay dealing with the home's deficiencies.

When I asked if there were parts of the house she liked or felt strongly about, she took me downstairs to the recently remodeled nursery. Rather than the carpeting that I'd been expecting, it had planked bamboo flooring. It was a non-carmelized variation, so it had a light honey color tone and it conveyed a feeling of warmth and comfort. Bamboo is considered *green* because the speed and ease with which it grows makes it easy to replenish. As a flooring material, it is very durable because of its extraordinary hardness and dent resistance. It also has a natural feel and its patterning provides visual interest without being distracting. As Tina talked about the finishes in the room, it became clear that her emotional meter really amped up whenever she talked about the bamboo floor.

Now aware of something that she was strongly attached to, I needed to find other connections. When we went back up to the family room, I asked her about the furnishings. There was nothing about the furniture pieces that could help. Her comments were so emotionally detached, she could easily have been talking about the garage floor. I noticed that in the corner of the room there was a didgeridoo. This is a long, wooden-tubed musical instrument of Australian aborigines. Hers was made out of an exotic wood with a cherry-like appearance. It was displayed prominently in the corner of the family room; and like the bamboo floor, it suggested another connection to nature. She said she and Steve both fell in love with the piece when they were on a trip, so I chalked up clue #2.

A short walk to the rear of the house revealed an expansive raised deck that overlooked a large, level backyard surrounded by trees. When I asked about it, Tina said it was one of the things that had initially attracted her and Steve to the house. We when we walked outside the feeling was incredible.

As Tina talked to me about the backyard, something in her voice made me think that this area resonated with her in the same way as the bamboo flooring and the didgeridoo. If anything, this connection was even stronger. The dominant color of the many trees and shrubs was a yellow-green. It was impossible not to notice that this formed the perfect complement for the color on Tina's bamboo floor. I now had clue #3 and there was a definite pattern. I suggested that going forward we take our lead from the outside and make the interior open and sunny. Handling the transition properly could make the inside and the exterior an extension of each other.

Tina very much liked the idea, but we needed to find more room in order to create the new kitchen. We were starting with only about 90 square feet, and we would need much more than that to do the job. When I asked about the adjacent dining room space, Tina said their lifestyle didn't involve formal dining. She would be glad to give up this space if it could be used to create a better kitchen. Fortunately, the wall separating the dining room and old kitchen was not load-bearing, so removing it was easy. Its removal increased the space available to 190 square feet. There was also unused floor area, in the center where we could place a new island that would seat three adults. With almost 230 square feet we would even be able to incorporate a walk-in corner pantry.

As soon as the kitchen area had been expanded, I suggested to Tina that we could make it seem even larger. The concept was to expand our *platform for living* not only across the main living area, but all the way to the rear fence line (much like Steve's kitchen in **The Bristlecone Pine**). The key would be to create a completely seamless connection between these areas. Tina and Steve were already thrilled with change in the kitchen area so they were completely on board for taking it further.

What we did to make this work were the following:

- We **switched two of the windows** on the exterior wall. The one to the far end, where the dinette was located, was actually oversized for the space and the one in the center was on a scale that would better fit the dinette area.

- The door and window casings had hard edges and, with their dark stain finish were in stark contrast to the white walls. You couldn't connect with the outside without catching your eye at the transition. **We removed all the wood casing and substituted soft, drywall returns.**

- The pale, buttery yellow wall color that we chose for the **interior walls picked up the color palette on the outside as well as the new bamboo flooring** that now covered all of the main level. The hue and color value gave us a perfect match. To get just the right selection, we had used what I like to call the **Goldilocks Effect**. We put up several different, but closely-related shades. Of the five samples, two were eliminated immediately. With the remaining colors in a bracket of three, it was just like the little girl in the fable who found one bowl of porridge too cold and one too hot and one just right.

- The vaulted ceiling with its dark-stained wood beam running the length of the apex was a strong visual distraction. It actually created a *silo effect* by drawing the eye upward when our objective of connecting the interior and exteriors required us to **keep the visual focus at eye-level.** To correct this we flattened out the peak with short, wooden 2x4 cross-members, framed horizontally and then finished with drywall. Voila! The perceived height of the ceiling dropped and no longer pulled our eyes upward. Its **new shape almost made the old ceiling seem to disappear.** (See Photo below)

Tina chose a contemporary style for her new kitchen. To give it clean simple lines and strong visual structure we kept the main L-shaped work area rectilinear by using a simple shaker style door. For our wood finish we chose a maple with a warm, honey-colored finish. Our accents were largely brushed stainless which we used for all the appliances, the cabinet pulls and the pedestal leg that supported the seating area on the island.

As a counter-point to the rest of the kitchen, we gave the island an asymmetric shape outlined with a granite countertop that had warm tones and flowing motion. It would provide a great space for prep work, serving and entertaining and informal seating for two to three adults. The resulting juxtaposition between the sinuous and asymmetric curve of the island and the straight lines of the cabinetry gave us terrific visual excitement as well as

a perfect harmony between visual structure and relaxed flow. The island was supported on a combination of cabinetry and a stainless cylindrical post, which tied it into the appliance finishes.

A final touch was added by using a full-glass insert in the door of the corner pantry. We chose *rain glass* which is a decorative, semi-opaque glass with a wonderful texture and a look that mimics falling rain. To the right of the pantry was a large window with a decorative furniture piece that we designed using our cabinet line. When the glass was installed on the pantry door, everyone's eye moved past the corner toward the window. A solid wood door on the pantry would have created a hard visual stop, but with the glass, the entire corner just disappeared and there was nothing to break the visual flow. (See photos below)

08.04.2003

Tina and Steve now had a great room that felt three times larger, and the inspiration and joy they received from the new kitchen was too great to measure. We had simply taken the feature they liked most about the home (the backyard) and doubled down. The change in the home's look and feel was so great that it always reminded me of the story of the ugly duckling (before) that turned into a beautiful swan (after).

About two months after completion, I got an email from Tina telling me how happy she and Steve were in their new home.

"We had decided to remodel, even though our plans were to be in this home for only four or five more years. Now, neither of us can ever imagine moving away!"

13

The Boardroom

Ted and his wife Patty had been living in their suburban, ranch-style home for about twelve years. They were tired of their existing kitchen and wanted to renovate it. When I first saw it however, my impression was that it was laid out well and didn't appear to be suffering any dysfunctional elements. When I asked about their current likes and dislikes with the kitchen, there response was the most unusual I'd ever heard. They said

> *"We are both business consultants and like to entertain friends and clients. We know we need a kitchen, but we really don't want it to look like a kitchen."*

It was at that moment I remembered Yogi Berra once said, *"When you come to a fork in the road, take it."* I'd never been entirely sure what that meant, but strangely, it now felt entirely apropos.

As we explored design options in detail, I learned that their style was ultra-contemporary with sleek, glossy finishes and clean lines. With this in mind, we selected a slab cabinet door style that had a two inch, outside bevel of 15 degrees on each door side. The finish was a high-gloss polyester finish (think shiny plastic and you will be close). The cabinets were frameless so the gaps between door and drawer fronts were only 1/8". This gave us great visual flow (no interruption of frame, door, frame, etc.). It also allowed us to concentrate on using the cabinets to create art designs for the walls. Cabinet knobs and pulls were definitely out, so we dropped the upper doors an inch so they could be opened by

pulling the bottom edge, and we used touch latches (push to open) on all the lower doors and drawers. The single oven was chosen because it had all electronic controls with no knobs (entirely new at the time). The refrigerator and dishwashers were paneled to blend in with the cabinetry.

To maintain the desired look, a normal range was out of the question. We turned our focus to cook-tops, but we were running into a problem. GE had introduced a contemporary, slick-looking cook-top that used magnetic induction. At the time, it was the only completely smooth model on the market. Its thin profile and slightly beveled frame would allow it to disappear into the countertop; that is, if we could find one. GE had pulled this new product off of the market temporarily and no local suppliers had inventory. We started calling all over the country (pre-internet days), and two weeks later finally found one. This appliance was expensive and it also meant that the clients would need to buy all new cookware that would work with the induction process. For Ted and Patty, look was everything. They were thrilled that a solution had been found and the added expense seemed to be a minor issue.

The kitchen and family room were both getting the same flooring- a tight-woven, light gray, commercial-grade carpet. For the kitchen, this choice wasn't that practical, but they insisted. They said that since they didn't cook in the kitchen, it was not going to be a problem (they ate out often and their gatherings were usually catered). The cabinet color was mauve and was highlighted by the highly polished black granite used for the counters as well as the full backsplash that ran from the counter to the underside of the cabinets. To tie this all together, we put the same 15 degree bevel on the countertop edge that was on the cabinet doors.

We were also using granite for a large custom table I'd designed. The top was gray with a mauve veining that flowed and swirled across the slab. The table's support pedestals were done in the same black as the kitchen counters. The ultra-modern look when we finished gave the appearance of a custom-designed conference table.

I'd been up to the design challenges, but well into this project an entirely new thought made me wonder if I was up to speed with what my clients were wanting. I said,

This may sound odd, but it seems that the look we are going to end up with is more of an executive boardroom than a kitchen."

Their immediate answer arrived in unison,

"Exactly!"

Well, the good news was that we were on track. The bad? It had taken me much longer than normal to visualize the essence of what my clients were looking for.

When the project was complete, Ted and Patty were delighted with the outcome. But for me, there was an added bonus. Because we had created a kitchen that was functional but didn't look anything like its normal counterparts, I saw that the distance between form and function could break free from stereotypes and still be in harmony. This new-found insight became invaluable as I was able to apply it in many different instances; none more so that in the next story.

14

The $6.5 Million Dollar "Fixer-upper"

My wife, the publisher of a national lifestyle magazine for real estate agents, was setting up a photo shoot for an upcoming cover. It would highlight five top women CEO's of real-estate brokerage companies. She was going for a *Vanity Fair* look and had chosen an exceptional location recommended by a friend.

The selected residence was a palatial replica of an Italian Villa. The home had a heated 4-car garage, marble floors and fountains, two-feet thick stone and plaster walls, a two-story fully paneled library, etc. But most perfect for the current occasion, it was fully furnished and unoccupied. The owner and his wife had built it four years prior, and had modeled it after a home they visited while traveling in Italy. Unfortunately, both the home and the marriage finished up about the same time. They'd gotten divorced shortly after moving in. They both moved out and the home had now been for sale for some time.

My wife happened to meet the owner at the photo shoot and they struck up a conversation. He mentioned that he was surprised that the home hadn't yet attracted a buyer. My wife, who can be quite direct, said,

"You may have trouble trying to sell a house that doesn't have a kitchen."

The owner's ex-wife had handled almost all of the decisions during the construction of the home; and, since the divorce had occurred just after they moved in, the kitchen was an area that had somewhat escaped his attention. The *kitchen* was a large, 17' x 31' room with 11' tall ceilings and had a 7' x 6', ornately-carved stone fireplace, Saltillo tile flooring,

salmon-colored plaster walls and massive cherry doors and woodwork. The room's appointments were spare and consisted of a 60 inch commercial gas range with an oversized metal hood above and single base cabinets flaking it sides. A stone sink was set in the only other cabinet and just above the sink was a single wooden shelf. Where one might have expected to see an island there was only a card table; and in the rest of the room, lots of open space. Like so many upscale homes today where caterers are used almost exclusively, this home also had a large butler's pantry located just off the passage to the dining room. In it were a prep sink, fifteen feet of counter space, storage cabinets, extensive shelving, a microwave, and separate Sub-Zero refrigerator and freezer units.

Never one to bring up a problem without offering a possible solution, my wife said to the owner, *"I know someone who can help you fix this."* That's when I entered the picture. I made my first visit to the house to meet the owner and to look at the kitchen. My wife had tried to describe it in advance by saying:

"It's like walking into a small basketball court. There is no dishwasher, no upper cabinets, no refrigerator and no prep space. There's a massive range and even bigger fireplace, but to do anything you have to walk into another room. If anyone wants to cook, forget it."

I couldn't imagine it until I saw it for myself. My first glance told me there would be a long way to go if I were to develop a design that would meet the needs of the most discriminating cook, provide a place for informal socializing and eating (the home had a dining room but no area for casual eating) and still maintain the architectural integrity of the home. The latter issue posed the greatest challenge because the spartan appearance of the kitchen was in stark contrast to the attention to detail and exquisite ornamentation that was evident in every other room in the house.

To develop the design, I looked to the *unfitted* styles characteristic of old-world kitchens (and re-popularized by the British kitchen designer, Johnny Grey). Long before there was a cabinet industry and modular cabinetry, kitchens consisted of work tables, and

an array of furniture pieces used to store dishes, silverware, and cookware (Dry goods were stored in a larder instead of a modern pantry and perishable items were preserved and stored in cool cellars). While there are different interpretations of the term 'unfitted', I use it as a way to describe a kitchen design that consists of an assemblage of furniture pieces or cabinetry that have a unique character of their own and that are not assembled together in wall-to-wall configurations. Visually, this is somewhat similar to the difference between an ornamental area rug versus wall-to-wall carpeting. My strategy was to create **signature furniture pieces** out of cabinet elements that would meet the functional needs of the kitchen and also embody the style and character of the home.

The easiest part of the process was selecting a cherry door style in the same finish, style, color and scale as the interior doors and trim. The choice also ensured we would have compatibility with the light salmon color on the plaster walls. Because the color was part of the plaster mix rather than something added later, it would be almost impossible to have any patches blend in. That meant extra care was required to make sure wall cuts for new wiring were made behind cabinetry or tile work where they wouldn't show.

Not so easy was the owner's request made half way through the design process. He decided the kitchen should have a location for a TV and computer. I could see the practicality, but everything about the home's styling and decor read *old world*. That meant both locations would have to be entirely concealed.s

To keep the furniture look, I went back to the lesson learned on the Boardroom kitchen where form and function were allowed to go their separate ways. To address the owner's specific request for a computer area, I created a piece that consisted of a central armoire element with attached, flanking bookcase units. In the upper and lower center sections were decorative *pocket* doors (they are retractable and disappear as they slide into the cabinet). The upper doors were arched with opaque art glass installed behind wood grilles. When these opened and slid back, they revealed a desk space for a monitor and keyboard as well as shelves above. The lower portion operated the same way, except that when the doors were opened and slid back they revealed a desk top and a knee space that would also hold a computer tower. (See Photo below).

The sink wall was twenty-one feet long and its size alone would be a challenge. To minimize this, I need a strong visual focus at the center. I chose to use tall cabinetry elements, 36" in width, on each end of the run. The refrigerator was going to be placed on the far right. A Sub-zero model was chosen because it could be fully

paneled and the configuration would give it the look of another armoire element. And, on the far left, I created a matching piece, the upper portion of which concealed a TV behind more pocket doors. The center section was now reduced to a width of 10.5 feet and with the dishwasher paneled with a cabinet front; the entire assemblage resembled a large sideboard flanked by two armoires. It was all enhanced horizontally with a 2-piece, coved crown moulding and vertically with fluted columns terminating in bun feet. These details also matched the computer area piece. (See Photo Above).

The new island was designed to look like a stand-alone bar and was trimmed out with beadboard, corbels, and exotic spiral-turned columns- all finished in a distressed, matte black paint. Its addition provided comfortable seating for four and a great place to locate a wine cooler and second dishwasher. (See photo above)

In the end, we had great functionality as well an authentic style that honored the home's architectural integrity. The kitchen now had all of the modern conveniences but looked as though it were hand-crafted in the same style as the home.

Because the owner had originally moved in and right back out of the home, it was also missing the kind of landscaping that was appropriate to the neighborhood. Installation of a massive fountain, numerous large specimen trees and a variety of plantings began at the same time as the kitchen remodeling. That is why, when he summed his total project cost, he referred to it as his $6.5 million dollar "fixer-upper". The good news was that the home, having been on the market for years, was sold only two months after the kitchen and landscaping were completed.

My client was delighted with the kitchen work and that fact actually segues into the next story. He was in a committed relationship with a woman who was a business associate of my wife. Within the next two years they would become engaged and married, but at the time he was focused on her upcoming birthday, and he wanted to do something very special for her. You can imagine my surprise when he told me,

"I want to surprise her with the gift of a new kitchen and I need you to prepare the design drawings in time for me to gift wrap them as her gift!"

15

The Birthday Gift

When working with a referral I want to satisfy both the current client as well as the one making the recommendation. But being asked to do a kitchen design as a birthday gift does have a way of amping up the pressure to a new level.

Paul, whose kitchen I had just completed, wanted to give his girlfriend a new kitchen for her birthday. The design drawings he wanted from me would be intended to please and impress a woman I had never even met; and to keep this a surprise, it would be impossible for me to meet her beforehand. He also wanted a sample cabinet door. The birthday was only three weeks away.

His girlfriend, Robin, lived in a sprawling ranch-style home on a one-third acre lot. It was surrounded by stately, tall oak and maple trees and was located in a twenty-five year-old neighborhood with similar home sites scattered over gently-rolling terrain. Paul took me to see the home when he was sure Robin would be at work and her two teenagers would be in school. As soon as we entered the foyer, I could see that most of the interior materials and finishes were original. The living room rugs and furniture fabrics all had rich textures and muted colors. The home had a comfy feel and was well cared for.

When I reached the kitchen, I found two treasures that gave me my first shot of optimism about my prospects for success. One was a beautiful 60 inch round, tile-topped table, with a mosaic pattern done in 1/2 inch terra cotta and accent-colored squares. It looked as though it belonged in an Italian villa. (See Photo Below).

(Photos in this chapter courtesy of Phil Mumford Photography)

A few feet to the right was a fascinating five foot tall chest with styling that placed it somewhere between a secretary and a chinoiserie. It had soft, parchment-colored, painted “wash” finish with green accents. The two doors that sat atop the desk and two drawers below were scalloped and peaked at the center. There was also a matching, ornate crown moulding above. The cabinet sat 10 inches off the floor on four Queen Anne legs. With its washed finish and detailing, it felt right at home with the table. (See Photo below).

It was now clear that the new kitchen needed to be Old World in character and all of the finishes would be patinized– glazed paint, oil-rubbed bronze, tumbled marbles, etc. I envisioned a kitchen that would create the perfect setting for the two furniture pieces. Fortunately, I already had in my mind the right door style and finish. It was a square raised-panel design with an off-white painted finished with a light, brown glaze. The more difficult problem was that the rectangular kitchen/ eating area suffered from numerous problems:

• **The work and eating areas were cut in two** by a peninsular eating bar. Its placement disrupted any chance of flow and the area around the table was so cramped, you almost had to turn sideways to get seated. It created a *shoehorn effect.*

•These two areas were also separated in another important way. The light streaming into the nook from windows on the east and south was soft and filtered and the effect was wonderful. In sharp contrast was the **glaring light** pouring into the kitchen from a large, overhead skylight (see Photo above).

•The oven location was just inside the room's main entry. If an oven door were open, access to the kitchen was blocked. With the refrigerator in the same area the **entrance felt choked off**.

•The kitchen sink was centered on a wall with no windows. Working at that location left you turned away from the eating area and instead of being able to look out to the backyard through the south-facing windows, you were **staring at a blank wall** (See Photo below)

•The cooking area consisted of a cooktop with microwave above. It was centered into an alcove that was so small that there was **no pot and pan storage,** little counter space, and only two narrow drawers.

•There was **no pantry storage** for dry goods (flour, cans, cereals, etc.) The closet in the photo shows what was a broom closet.

With only one week remaining till Robin's birthday this was going to be my first and last visit to the home. Before Paul and I left, I took measurements as well as some photographs of the old kitchen and furniture pieces. Fortunately, the design for the new kitchen turned out to be relatively easy to formulate. Here is what was proposed:

• **A pantry cabinet with rollout shelves** would replace the small broom closet; and the double oven that had been crowding the cooking alcove and

blocking the entrance, would be replaced with a **professional range**. This would visually opened up the cooking area and provide lots of **room for cooking utensils, spices, hot pads, oven mitts, and pots and pans.** (See Photo Below)

• The old **microwave** which had been directly above the old range was moved to the other side of the room where a newer model with convection cooking would be installed between three inch fluted pilasters. This would leave room for a **modern hood** above the range and as well as a **beautiful mural** of wine and fruit done in a tumbled marble and set in field of old world tile. The mural itself would be bordered with a 3/4 inch tile rope moulding. This was a artistic element that could perfectly complement the two furniture pieces on the other side of the room. The look of the tiles left the impression that they had been reclaimed from a villa in the Italian hill country.

The old cooking area had been indistinct from the adjacent counters and cabinetry. The visual focus of the new area would give it a real sense of place. This was accomplished by creating a strong vertical, visual

relationship between the range (at the bottom – bumped out 2.25 inches and flanked with fluted pilasters), the tiled backsplash and mural (center location) and the stainless hood (upper element). The field tile on the backsplash would run up to the ceiling. The style of the hood had an Italian influence and its narrow profile would minimize visual obstruction of the tile work. The cooking area would go from being a nondescript, visual interruption of the countertop line, to an element with strong visual focus and emotional pull.

• The **peninsula** would remain but be **moved six inches** into the kitchen, shortened slightly in length and given an **elliptical-shaped end**. This would uncrowd the eating area and allow for a much improved traffic flow between the kitchen and eating area. (See photo below)

I turned in the drawings and sample door to Paul, crossed my fingers and began the wait to find out how the *gift* would be received. As it turned out, I needn't have worried. Robin was delighted with the design. (See Drawing Below)

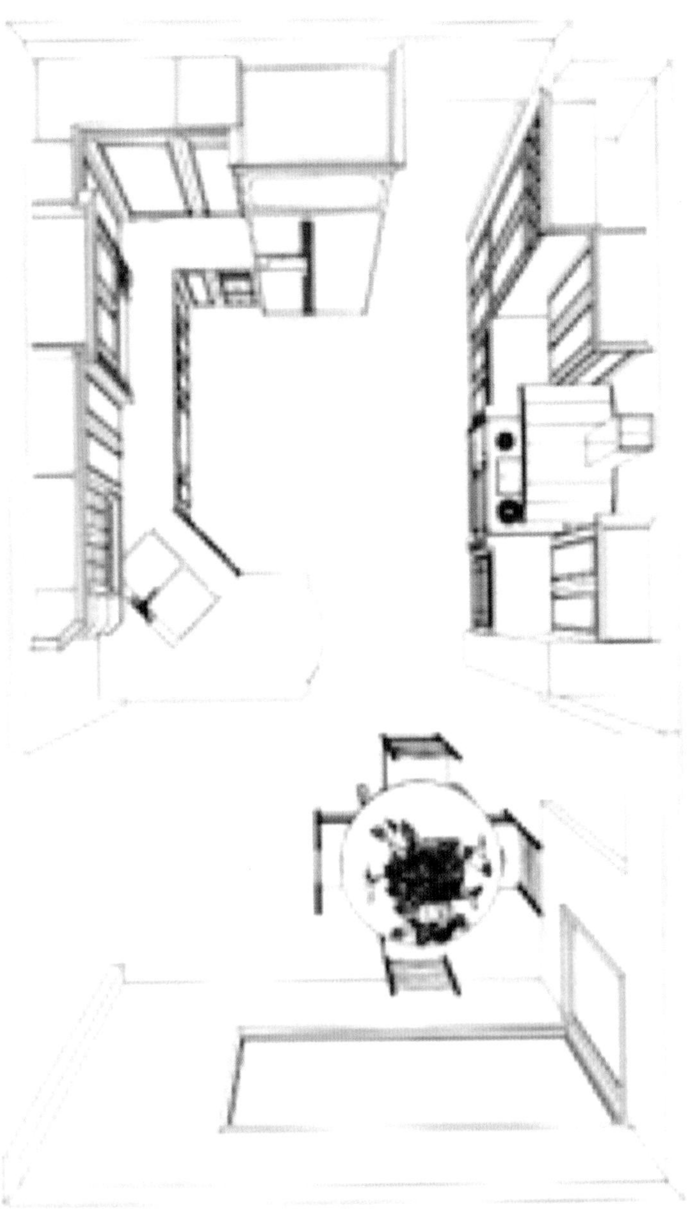

Robin actually made only minor changes to the design before we started working on product selections. As I helped her pick counters, flooring, wall color, etc., we were able to come up with two items that would prove helpful. We chose an old-world, chiseled-edge tile for the floor. Since it came in multiple sizes, we were able to have it laid in a random pattern that made the room look bigger and more unified at the same time. The problem with the harsh light from the roof skylight was solved by installing a sheer fabric (tulle) that was effective in diffusing and softening the light in the room.

For projects involving extensive work, it was common for me to assist my clients with referrals to subcontractors or general contractors. With my years of building experience, my contacts were extensive and current. But, this project was different. There would be lots of extra eyes watching. This included Paul who was paying for the kitchen and wanted it to be very special; Robin, who we wanted to end up delighted with the results; and my wife, who was a friend and business associate of Robin.

My over-riding concern was how to help Robin put this project together in a manner that would guarantee success. Balancing the demands of being a high-level publishing executive and single-mom with two teenagers left Robin with little extra time. Given the fact that she had no prior experience in remodeling, I needed a fool-proof plan.

I already had control of the design as well as the cabinet quality because I worked directly for the cabinet manufacturer. I also had my own seasoned install teams. Ten years had elapsed since I'd stop building custom homes, but to fill in the last piece of the puzzle, I decided to put my contractor hat back on and run the job myself. With approval from Paul and Robin, I pulled the building permit.

Throughout the years, I had seen enough projects suffer from manufacturer errors, install errors, or builder issues. But I was determined this time wouldn't be one of those. As a matter of fact, I decided it was a perfect laboratory to test out some of my theories on how to build surprise and delight into a process where most considered just getting through unscathed to be a success.

Robin was good-humored, effervescent, and great fun to work with. These qualities would help her navigate the changes ahead, but I knew from experience that they wouldn't make her immune to the strains and stresses that come with even the best-run remodel. Normal routines are turned upside down, strangers are coming and going, and there is mess and disorder. Just before we started, Robin said, *"I am so anxious to get started. I can't wait."* I didn't even have to think about my response, *"Does that mean that by tomorrow you will be just as anxious to be done?"*

She broke into a smile and we both laughed; but I knew just how quickly clients could start off, metaphorically skipping along the yellow brick road, only to soon find themselves in an impenetrable forest of darkness and despair. I had observed that each client starts their project with a tank of gas (i.e. hope, energy and goodwill) – some, like Robin, with more gas in the tank than others. Unfortunately, there is almost always a time when the client runs of gas and says, *"Talk to my hand, my head hurts!"* In other words, they just want it to be done and to return to a sense of normalcy.

Previously, things that had been helpful for my clients had included keeping my sites super clean, having everything organized with activity always proceeding, separating the construction as much as possible from the family to protect privacy and belongings (e.g. temporary kitchen areas and separate entrances).

With Robin's project I would have a chance to test out a radical new theory. I'd been toying with what I thought could tilt the odds even further toward a positive client experience. My hypothesis was that it would be possible to **manage a client's perception of time** as well as space!

I had noticed that whenever I found myself waiting in either a checkout or ticket line, it was not the length of the line that would trigger feelings of impatience and frustration, but the speed with which the line was moving. If I got into a short checkout line, but there was a slow-down ahead (price check, new register tape, or payment by check), it often sent my blood pressure rocketing skyward. In contrast, when I was in a long line, if it was moving quickly, I could remain calm. As long as I could see daylight at the end and could picture

myself moving on to other things instead of feeling trapped and even victimized, my blood pressure was stable.

What had taken me years to ascertain was that these feelings of elation or rage could occur in situations where the actual time to get through the check-out process was the same. The number of minutes on the clock was the same; the perception on my end was not.

My new supposition was that this *checkout-line psychology* could work the same way with remodeling. If I was correct, it would mean Robin's job could be managed to appear faster than it might otherwise seem. Certainly, the converse was true because even a project that is fast by industry norms may not feel that way to the client.

In order to test my theory, I set a goal to not only to give Robin a clear road map of what would be happening, but to structure the work in a manner that would allow her to come home and see demonstrable progress. We used this technique a lot on Fridays, so that Robin could go through the weekend admiring another visual milestone and also have something to show off to friends and family who might stop by. With one or two day's exception, we kept her feeling that the project was moving quickly. This was in contrast to the fact that in most cases we were very close to the schedule we had given her at the beginning. Reviewing our written schedule would allow her to measure our efforts rationally, but it was her **emotional clock** that we were more focused on.

When we reached the end of the project, Robin still couldn't believe how fast it had moved; nor could she believe that we had taken just the number of days we had scheduled. Her natural get-it-done spirit could have easily created great impatience on her part, so this was an important success for all of us.

The remodeled space had become the perfect complement for Robin's two unique furniture pieces and with the new layout she found that she loved preparing meals in her new kitchen. I was tickled with the personal note she had sent at the end... It said, *"I love my new kitchen... it is perfect. Thanks for all the special attention and for the fabulous outcome."*

As fate would have it, Robin had only about four months to enjoy her new kitchen. She and Paul became engaged and they bought a new home together. On the investment side of the ledger, her home sold before it could even be listed. The buyer was a neighbor who had seen and admired the new kitchen!

16

The "Interior" Window

Nestled in a wooded lot in the Colorado foothills, Ted and Maria lived in a 5800 square foot, two-story home. It had a walk-out basement and from the elevated rear deck they looked out at a killer view. The backdrop was a jagged mountain peak; and in the foreground, lay a meadow of protected open space that was part of an elk migration route. None of the area's home sites had fencing, so it was quite common for members of the herd to wander up into the yards.

At the time I started working on this project, my teenage stepson, Wil, was working as my driver and assistant. Being essentially a nocturnal animal, and not accustomed to rising early, he was perpetually tired in the mornings. On one early trip, I'd told him he could stay in the car to catch up on sleep while I went inside to talk with Ted. He'd fallen soundly asleep with his head leaning against the driver-side window when an odd noise woke him. He was shocked to find himself eyeball to eyeball with an 8-point bull elk that had been licking the window glass with his tongue. Needless to say, he was wide awake for the entire rest of the day.

At the rear of Ted's house were four large windows and two patio doors. This large expanse of glass created ample opportunity to enjoy the view from the dining and family room areas. The problem was the kitchen. As Ted initially explained it to me,

"We had this beautiful view but our eating area was this cramped spot that looked out across the street. We wanted to take advantage of the southern exposure and great views out the back."

The view to the rear was almost completely blocked by a wall of cabinetry. (See Photo below). He'd thought about taking out the rear-facing, south wall of the kitchen, but, being a serious cook, he felt it would mean giving up too much counter and storage area. Ted had conducted what he deemed a very arduous search for five years without finding a solution.

Armed with physical measurements and a computer generated design, I was able to show Ted how, with the right use of cabinetry and newer and more efficient storage options, he could open up the kitchen's south wall without actually losing counter area or storage space. That clinched the decision. When the wall came down the effect was dramatic. Southern light flooded deep into the room and the view toward the formal dining area and the outside completely opened up. (See Photo below)

With the new design, Ted's cooking area became wider and much more useable (counter space actually increased). There was now comfortable seating for four at the island, where before there had been none at all. With the new layout, the kitchen became an integral part of the living area where he and Maria could cook and entertain. The connection with the outside was enhanced, not only with the new openness and flow, but also with all new finishes, which included a color wash on pool-textured walls and ceilings (look of old-world plaster), a travertine pattern on porcelain floor tile, glazed knotty alder cabinetry and oil-rubbed bronze metal finishes. (See photo below)

(Photos in this chapter courtesy of Phil Mumford Photography)

As the first design drawings were developed, I could see that there was another concern that had not been apparent. The informal eating nook at the front of the house (north side) adjoined the kitchen. If the south wall were removed, the kitchen/dining area

would be so long in relation to its width, it would take on a *bowling alley* effect. This turned out to be a legitimate concern, but we solved it in a unique manner. We wanted the kitchen to stop where the front eating nook began, but we didn't want to close it off with a partition wall. To get rid of the long skinny look, we placed a peninsula with double glass door upper cabinets above, creating an 'L' formation. This continued to let light enter the kitchen during the day. And, at night, the interior cabinet lighting gave the same effect. We designed the upper cabinet assembly so that it would act like the window on the outside wall, except that it was seven feet inside the room. We referred to it as our *interior window.* (See photo above)

As you can see in the photo, we bull-nosed the edges on the granite island bar top. We did this because we had a narrow walkway on the seating side of the island and needed to make it feel wider than it was. With countertops, one's eyes will always *catch* on the sharp edge of a countertop. Rounding shuts this down and allows one's view to spread out to create a feeling of greater width. Psychologically this turns off your subliminal navigation system. You are no longer unconsciously measuring up the space. You can see the dramatic difference in your body language. In one case there is a slight stiffness that is part of *walking between* and in the other you observe a relaxed gait or amble that signifies *walking through.*

Achieving this was important also because it allowed those inside to keep their eyes focused on where they were headed, so the distance felt shorter or even non-existent. Anyone who has spent time on a National Forest Service hiking trail can relate to portions of the trail where your eyes are focused intently on steep, uneven, or rocky ground and then remember how the smooth flat sections allowed for the full appreciation of your surroundings and the natural beauty. In Ted's house we had eyes now focused forward and onto the mountain view at the rear.

Creating a strong connection to the outside and the beautiful view was our primary focus, but removing the wall of the old kitchen was just a start on completing this task. All the window casings were removed and replaced with rounded drywall returns, and the sharp, square drywall edges at outside corners and ceiling soffits were bull-nosed (rounded

in shape) to soften their look and feel. The soffits actually became invisible and there was no longer anything to disconnect the inside and outside. It had become seamless and you could definitely feel it. In Ted's words,

"We picked up the energy of the mountains, the view and the trees and incorporated it into the house. We had no idea we could open that room up."

Ted's remodel is another example of how thoughtful design can move the end result from renovation to transformation. The psychological satisfaction is enormous, but there is an economic value as well. Ted and Maria had a close personal friend in the area who was a realtor that specialized in Ted's subdivision. After seeing the finished remodel, she summed it up in these words:

"The design opened up the entire area, brought in wonderful light and created a kitchen/entertaining area that people will want to gather in. Kitchens and baths are the most important aspect of a home for buyers, and the attention to detail and the quality of the design and construction certainly increased the value of this house by twenty-five percent".

17

The French Country Kitchen

Ken and Andrea were homebuilding clients of mine. Ken had the longest commute to work of anyone I had ever met. He was a United Airlines pilot living in Denver, but he flew out of Atlanta. But this was in an earlier time when pilots enjoyed higher salaries and lighter work schedules.

The new home I was building for them was in the foothills west of Denver. It was located in an exclusive, heavily-wooded subdivision. Working with both Ken and Andrea through the site selection, design and early construction process had been a total delight. But when we got to the point we needed to determine interior finishes, everything took a sharp turn in the wrong direction. Ken had been easy going and open to new ideas, but suddenly he made it clear that no idea was going to be a good one unless he was the person who thought of it. I was suddenly dealing with a person that was both opinionated and short-tempered.

Things were compounded as Ken also started to referring to the project as *his* house. Andrea was finding herself increasingly shut out of the conversation. This was all happening as both she and Ken were expressing remarkably different opinions on interior appointments. Ken was still committed to rustic mountain finishes like knotty alder, natural fieldstone, aspen-paneled ceilings, and warm color tones. (see photo below). But Andrea was looking for a French Country kitchen with bright white tiles with cobalt blue decoration. I hadn't seen this coming and now I wondered how I could deliver a home where they could own both the process and the outcome?

As the tension between husband and wife ratcheted up, I pictured myself as a boxing referee who might get hit by getting too close to the action. Looking for a way out of the middle, I was quick to recommend to Ken and Andrea that they work with a local vendor who had a flooring and tile showroom. This vendor had been helpful to my clients in the past, so I was confident they could do a great job. Using a neutral party would be my chance to step away and avoid any appearance of taking sides.

"For every complex problem, there is a simple solution – that doesn't work." That's what was playing back in my head as I listened to Ken's immediate response to my suggestion,

"We don't need help. What's the big deal? We can just go there and pick everything out in twenty minutes!"

Hearing Andrea's kitchen design goals as well as Ken's thoughts about the selection process left me dumbfounded. We decided to adjourn our meeting and reconvene the next day. I had a 24 hour reprieve and absolutely no idea how to pull things back together. I did know that before I could address Andrea's discordant design request, I would have to find a way to deal with Ken.

Over many years, I'd learned that people most often come up with the wrong answers; not because they are not smart enough, but because they are not asking the right questions. Too often when they would see an A or B outcome, I could give them another way to look at things, so that they could then see C. Because I was able to help them reset the criteria by which a good decision could be judged, the best answer always seemed to jump out without so much as a nudge.

With Ken, I knew I'd have to do something similar. In his case however, I'd make sure that he always found himself with at least three possibilities for each decision, any of which would fit with the overall plan for the home. The added element, and this was essential, would be that he'd think all of the final decisions were his. The downside was this would't happen without an enormous amount of work on my part.

Solving the French kitchen issue for Andrea posed an entirely different challenge. Ken was begrudgingly willing to allow her to take the lead in this room, but the issue was how to meet her goals for the kitchen while still having it blend with the overall look and feel of the home. Fortunately, rustic and country styles have some affinity. The issue was how to deliver a kitchen that didn't become too refined in its finishes or too formal and stiff in its look. What I needed were materials that could provide a buffer, so that I could keep the transitions between the finishes and between the rooms in harmony.

My previous to trips to Aspen actually suggested a solution. Certain clothing pieces can be dressed up or down and this was a town with a plethora of examples. I used to be amazed by how people could be so smartly dressed and yet have their outfits be so casual at the same time. Taking a blazer and dressing it down with jeans and snakeskin cowboy boots and still wearing lots of bling (e.g. loud jewelry) was a common way to pull it off.

In Andrea's kitchen the bling was clearly going to be her tile backsplash with hand-painted deco tiles. For the blazer effect (cabinetry), I chose a New England cherry because it has a rich look, works with white or off-white, and can be as informal or formal as you want it to be. And for the jean/boots (flooring), I selected American Cherry. Unlike its cousins, it's not at all uniform in appearance, but has a highly patterned look with off-white and brown tones mixed in with the reds. It is also informal and somewhat rustic. The reds reached out wonderfully to the cabinetry while the brown and off-white tones captured the colors and feel of the home's knotty alder woodwork which was done in warm, golden brown tones. (See Photo Below).

Andrea got her French Country kitchen with the white backsplash and blue deco tiles, and it now fit in well with the house. Ken got to tell me that he had been right all along; that making the selections really was a piece of cake, and I finished the project feeling satisfied but in need of a well-earned rest.

18

Two Chefs in the Kitchen

When I first met Lance and Betty, my cooking experience was limited. I was great at clean up and pretty good as a helper, but I hadn't learned the satisfaction and creative fulfillment you can find in planning and preparing great meals. Our first meeting was to talk about their kitchen remodel plans. As we were getting started, I asked if they both worked and what they did. I was glad I did because Lance was an executive chef who had studied at the Cordon Bleu in Paris and Julie was a sous-chef. Both were working for local restaurants. This was going to be interesting!

Fortunately, most of my work with clients involved listening carefully for both functional and emotional requirements and providing properly-framed questions so they could reach the answers needed to achieve their goals. Even so, with this couple, I was hoping not to display my ignorance. Going through my head was a quote attributed to Abraham Lincoln, *"Better to remain silent and be thought a fool, than to speak and remove all doubt."*

When it came time to discuss spices and how they wanted to store them, they told me that they kept their *hot* and *cold* spices apart. For *hot*, red pepper or cayenne was coming to mind; but to play it safe, I asked if they could give me an example. It turned out that they were referring to *hot* spices as those they used at the range as opposed to *cold* that were applied during prep. It made total sense, but was completely new to me. Having dodged a bullet, my luck seemed to hold, because before I could jump in to explain how other clients enjoyed the convenience of spice drawer inserts, where spice bottles could be lined up in alphabetical order, Julie pulled out four plastic bags from an upper cabinet. Each of the

bags contained cinnamon harvested from a different part of the world. She let me smell them and the rich aromas were incredible. Each was recognizable as cinnamon but had a subtle, yet distinctive difference. Julie also explained to me that the aromas were so pungent because the spices were shipped while they were still fresh. This was eye-opening for a person who had yet to appreciate the difference between garlic powder in a jar and fresh chopped garlic. So much for spice drawers and McCormick's ® spices in a bottle.

Even with my client's experience in commercial kitchens, it turned out the normal guidelines for optimal work flow and organization would still hold sway in their new kitchen. I was able to introduce them to a term I had come to call the **dish triangle**. As with work area triangles (sink, stove, refrigerator), the idea was to keep the shortest distance between three points- the storage location for plates and glasses, the place they land when serving, and the clean-up location where they go before moving back to where they are stored.

Another concept just as useful for this project was one that I'd come to call **free counter space**. This is an area of counter where a project can be halted or left while attending to another cooking activity. The sense of it is simple, to not to have to put away your first project in order to free up space for your next. This was a sine qua non in Ken and Andreas work world, but surprisingly, they hadn't considered it for their own kitchen.

A third concept concerned how to site the refrigerator. Sometimes the location cannot be changed, but many times there are one or more alternate locations. For families where there is going to be considerable interaction between the social and business sides of the kitchen, I tend to look for a location where the refrigerator can be **out on point**. This is a term I use to indicate a point of the work triangle where the refrigerator is equally accessible to those cooking and those not. The idea is for those outside the work area to be able to get what they need from the refrigerator, such as drinks or snacks, without going into or across the work triangle.

I'd once worked with a remodel client whose existing refrigerator location couldn't be accessed without a major disruption occurring in the work area. With a sardonic smile she

shook her head in agreement when I said: "*I bet whenever any of the family show even the slightest indication that they might want something from the refrigerator, you immediately jump to offer to get whatever they need.*"

The drawing below (**Lawyer John's "Kick-Ass" Kitchen**) shows the refrigerator located conveniently close to the person cooking as well as anyone that might approach from the family room. This is a perfect example of the refrigerator being **out on point**.

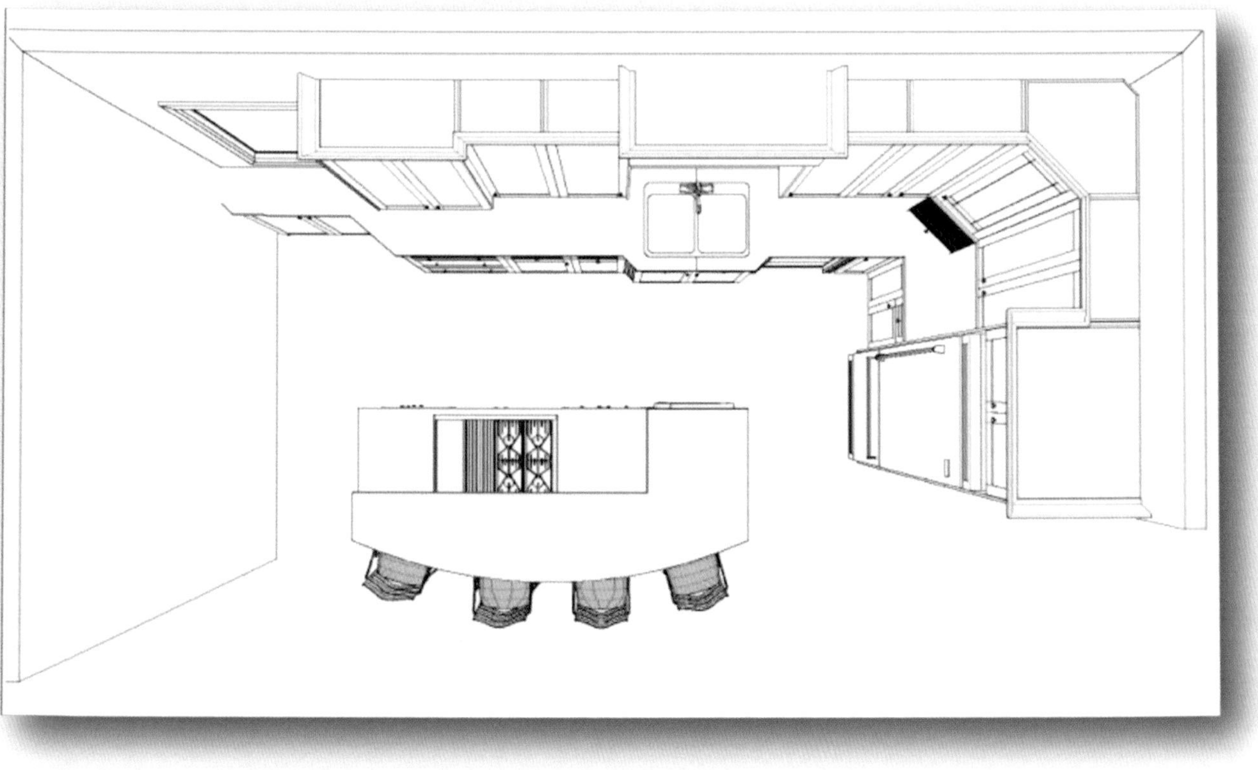

The drawing below shows an alternate location (**The Birthday Gift**). The old refrigerator location was kept so that we could provide the desired enhancement of the range area. As you can see, it is not convenient to someone approaching from the sitting area. It is however easy to reach when approaching from the family room, living room and dining room and this was also a consideration for not moving the location.

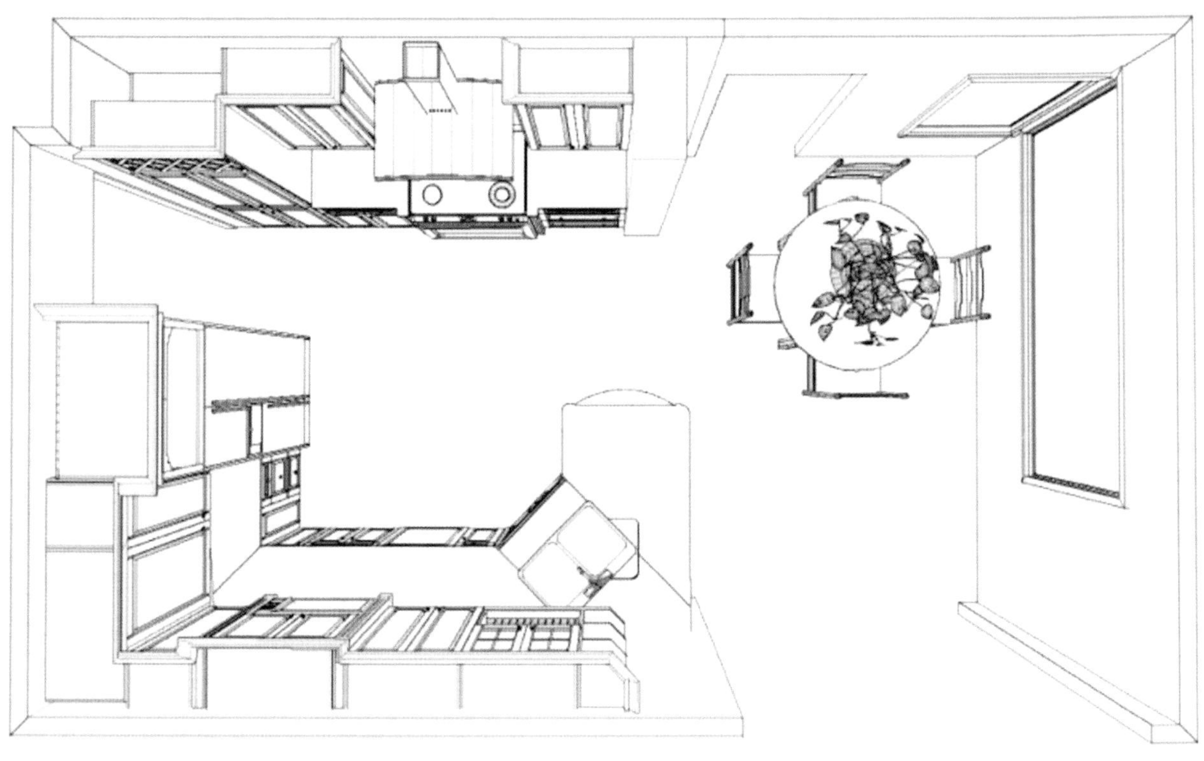

With Lance and Julia I was also able to share some other design concepts that became valuable as we worked through appointments and finishes. One of the most helpful was given to me years ago by one of my clients and I've used it ever since. She had described **finishes with depth** as those that have the power to draw you in emotionally.

On opposite sides of the spectrum you have finishes with depth like oil-rubbed bronze, pewter, and satin-nickel while on the other are others like chrome and polished brass. The first group, like other textured finishes, can easily elicit oohs and aahs, whereas the latter group is about appearance and form. Again, the first can elicit a gut reaction where the latter is more cerebral.

The reason this is so useful is that clients who are strongly attracted to textured finishes in one area, such as metal (e.g. Brushed nickel, rust, verdigris) will usually gravitate toward the same thing in other materials (tumbled marble, honed countertops,

leathers, muted colors, tapestries, ornamental rugs, glazed walls or cabinetry, distressed woods, etc.).

All of the concepts mentioned were put to good use in our design discussions and when their project was finished, Lance and Julie were thrilled with the results. It left me encouraged to see that addressing the pertinent zones for cooking, baking, warming, clean-up as well as storage for perishables, dry goods and implements followed the same path for these professionals as it did for my other clients.

19

"Feeling is Believing"

Computer assisted drawings (CAD) can generate numerous three dimensional views that help you when trying to visualize what your new kitchen will look like. This is especially true when a new home is involved; because, unlike a remodel, there is no prior frame of reference. Also, because architectural floor plans are two-dimensional and are filled with dimensions and building notes, they offer most clients little assistance in imagining the outcome.

Such was the case with Wendy who was building a new home with her husband. When we had our first kitchen design meeting, I asked her how construction was coming along. She said the walls of the kitchen had just been framed, but lamented that her inspection that morning was disappointing. She said,

"When I walked into the kitchen space there were studs everywhere and it just looked like a bunch of spaghetti!"

Her food analogy was unusual, but I understood how difficult it can be to get a good feel for any room in a house where drywall has not been installed. Your eyes are always going past any particular wall and into the space of another room. As part of my presentation that afternoon, I'd brought along CAD drawings of the kitchen that had numerous perspective views and even a top-down or birds-eye view (all 3 dimensional). The latter view looked as though it was created with a photographer shooting straight down while strapped to the ceiling.

More often than not, this one drawing seemed to be most helpful because the client could see the entire kitchen at once. I'd worked hard to make Wendy's drawings as photorealistic as possible. It was the first time that I'd been able to enhance the drawings by including tables, bar stools, overheard lighting and accessories. I was excited and could hardly wait to see if these new inclusions would make a difference. (See Drawings Below)

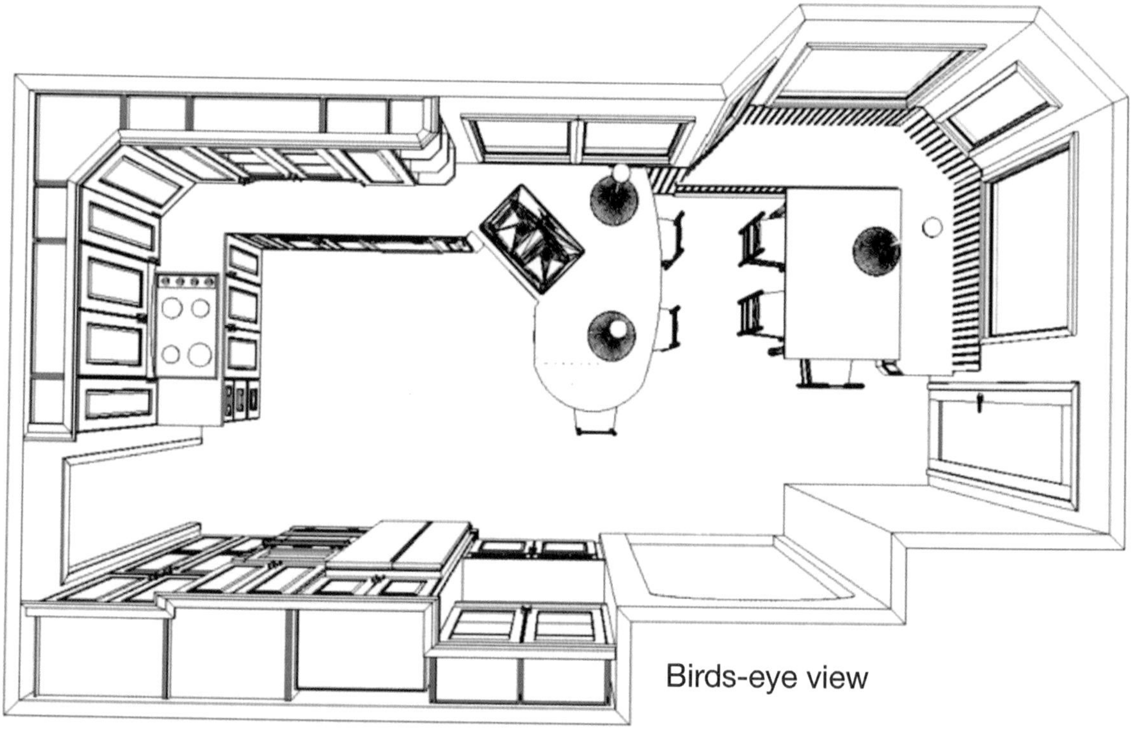

Birds-eye view

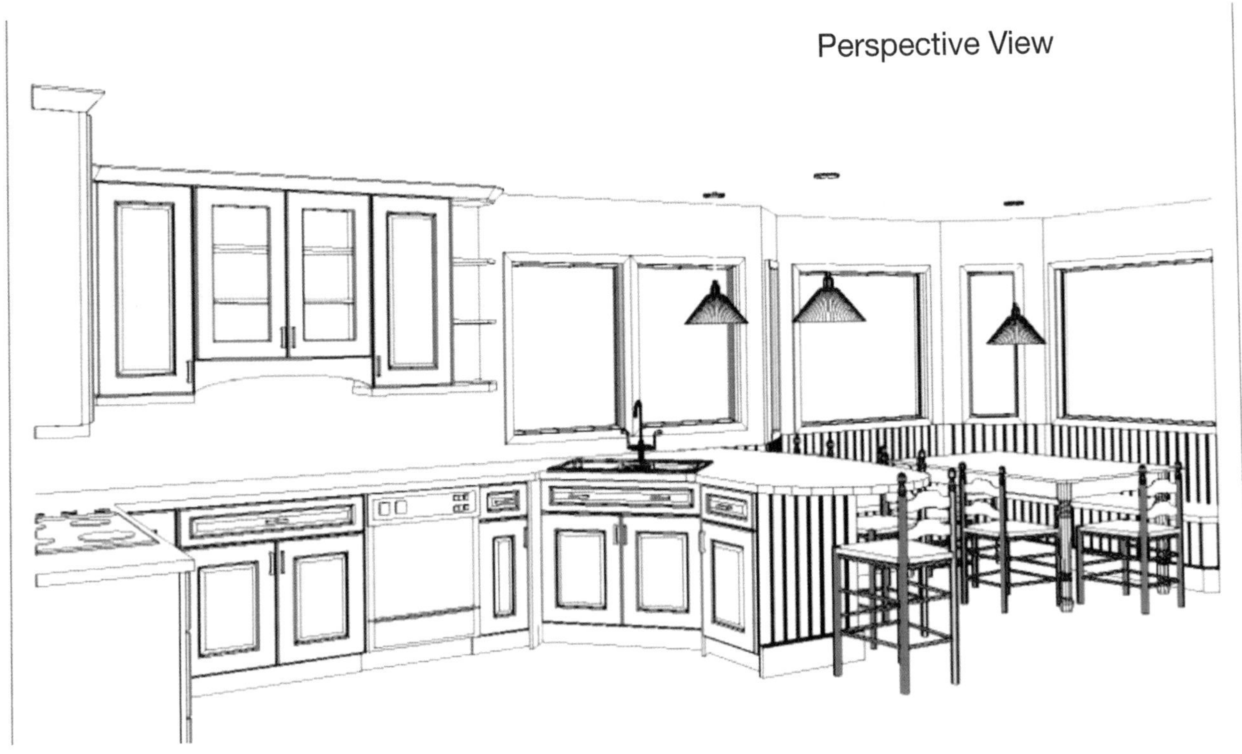

As Wendy started looking through the drawings something extraordinary occurred. Her entire body language changed and I could see that her tension had dissipated. It was clear that she could visualize the kitchen so strongly that she was mentally placing dishes, glasses, pots, pans, etc. in each of the cabinets. The clock ticked on as I waited. When she finally did speak, she said excitedly,

"I'm going to take these drawings back out to the house so that I can see how it feels."

She didn't say "*see how it LOOKS*", but "*see how it FEELS*". Not only could she visualize the kitchen, but she'd been able to mentally try it out for size in a way that I had never witnessed before. Psychologically, she'd been drawn completely into the space.

This was an early indication that what everyone wants and needs is to get a real *feel* for the outcome. This has held so constant throughout the years, that I finally decided that the

old adage, “Seeing is Believing”, was not quite apt. What really captured where all my clients wanted to be was “Feeling is Believing”.

This was crucial at the time because I knew that no matter how careful my clients were in their decision making, they never could trust their judgment enough to assuage their fear of the outcome not meeting their expectations. The fear was always present, but almost never verbalized. But when they could *feel it*; when they could judge decisions not only with their head, but with their gut; then things were different. My clients all trusted their feelings. Whenever I could help my clients make decisions that resonated with both heart and mind; we could always count on great results.

The CAD drawings had always proved valuable . In Wendy’s case, on a scale of 1-10, they rated a perfect 10. However until I worked with the client in this next story, I would never have guessed that that score could fall all the way to zero.

20

The “Cardboard “ Kitchen

Kate and her husband Gary were building a new home in the mountains west of Vail. Kate was handling most of the interior design decisions, so I found myself working exclusively with her on the plans for her new kitchen. She was a leading real estate broker in the area and her extensive experience in buying and selling homes had given her a clear picture of the items that she wanted in her new home.

Working through the selections of doors, finishes and hardware, choices were quick and easy. Then, we started working with CAD drawings. We did five iterations of the design drawings and put in a lot of effort to have the perspectives convey the look and feel of the finished room. In spite of this, things were just not clicking. Whatever picture Kate had in her head was still fuzzy and unclear. Frustrated, we both decided to wait until the framing was completed, so that we could look at the drawings while we were in the actual space.

With framing complete I arrived at the job site prior to our meeting. I needed time to mark out on the sub-floor exactly where all of the cabinets would go. I also took a marker and labeled all the appliances. With this in place, my goal was to take the take the kitchen drawings and match them up exactly with the outlines on the floor. This had always worked before.

Kate arrived, and after about thirty minutes of discussion and review, we hadn’t progressed any further. To Kate, a woman with otherwise great perspicacity, what the kitchen was going to look like was clear as mud. What to do? I grabbed some loose 2 x 4 lumber and began using it to outline the kitchen. It gave some depth to the outline, and there was some contrast between the lumber and the homogeneous grain of the wafer board

used for the subflooring. Unfortunately... same result. Another meeting was scheduled for later in the week, and it was back to the drawing board. The whole episode brought back a long forgotten memory.

A decade earlier, working for a production homebuilder, I was assisting a prospective new-home buyer who'd found visualization as difficult as Kate. The woman liked one of our model homes but needed something larger. As it was, we had just such a home with an almost identical floor plan, built and ready for sale. In a rare but fortuitous circumstance, it was also fully finished with lighting, counters, cabinets, flooring, tile, etc. It was in pristine move-in condition. I couldn't wait to show her the home. We pulled into the drive and walked inside. Only three minutes had passed before she said to me, *"Do you have one that is furnished that I can see?"* What the woman had needed was to see a model with furnishings because, even with all the finishes in place, she couldn't visualize beds, sofas, colors or accessories.

That left both of us perplexed as to what do next, and that is how I now felt with Kate. Since Kate had colors and finishes down cold, it seemed that I just had to figure out some way to bring her kitchen to life in three dimensions instead of two. We needed to get the cabinets ordered quickly because time had run out. The only thing I could come up with was to use cardboard and attempt to mock up the kitchen. Because I was also going to cut out models of the chairs and table in the dining area adjacent to the kitchen, I was going to need a lot of material.

After a making a few phone calls, I found a local, wholesale supplier of cardboard. At the supplier's warehouse I was shown 4' x 8' sheets of material, and I realized these were big enough for large islands as well as the furniture pieces. I also noticed that these sheets came in white as well as the standard brown color. Thinking that the white color would provide more contrast to the flooring at the job site, I loaded up eight sheets.

I had arrived early for my meeting with Kate. Instead of waiting around for her to show up, I got out my utility knife and start cutting out the island, appliances, and cabinet runs and laid them out on the floor. When I'd finished, I got up off the floor and found myself

with an almost subconscious urge to walk *through* the kitchen. I did just that and the white color on the cardboard seemed to jump up from the floor as though rising up to counter height. That was my impression anyway, but what would Kate think? She walked in just moments later, studied the layout silently for two minutes, then turned to me and said,

"The island is too close to the sink counter. It needs to move a few inches."

I was astounded. Before could get my brain back in gear and offer a response, she walked to the sink location and slid the island back, making the walkway two inches wider. Then she walked around the island once, and said,

"There! That's perfect."

My mouth was still hanging open when she commented,

"I don't like that refrigerator location".

She proceeded to pick up the cardboard and place it on an adjacent wall, saying,

"There that's better."

For the next twenty minutes we remodeled our *cardboard* kitchen. Now, as decisive as ever, Kate passed final judgment on our efforts by telling me,

"That's perfect!"

Elated with our breakthrough, I drew up a new set of drawings showing all the changes we'd made, but they were still of no use to her. With nothing else left to do, we rolled the dice and ordered the kitchen the way the cardboard had been laid out. This left me more than a little nervous because Kate had told me often that, for her, the kitchen was the most important room in the house.

After we installed the cabinets, Kate stopped by and remarked that she liked the finish but didn't offer any other comments. For the next two weeks I heard nothing else. I was on pins and needles wondering whether or not our design efforts had succeeded. Finally, just after the granite countertops were installed, Kate walked into the room and immediately announced,

"The kitchen is just the way I knew it would be!"

I was thrilled and relieved at the same time. I only wished that she'd been able to tell me sooner.

What had happened with Kate was astounding. The cardboard had given her the ability to visualize her new kitchen. But it had done even more because it allowed her to feel it. When she made those immediate and minute changes to the island, she was demonstrating this fact clearly. She didn't take out a tape, she didn't have to think about the distance; she could feel when it was exactly right. Her sense of how it felt was far more refined and accurate than anything she could do by calibrating distance and then consciously evaluating the result. However the process worked, it was done in an instant, was precise and gave her absolute surety in the result.

This episode with Kate allowed me a front-row seat where I could observe just how powerfully **our feelings and emotions can directly connect to the physical environment surrounding us.**

21
Radio Silence

Maria and her husband were having a vacation home built near the Vail ski resort. The builder and I had worked together on three other projects, but this was the largest yet. The home was 10,000 square feet with 7 bedrooms and 6.5 baths. It was also on a fast track because the owners wanted it finished before the upcoming Thanksgiving holiday. Maria's husband, who I never met, ran the American operations for a major German bank. He'd already invited a dozen clients and friends out for the holiday, and Maria was handling all of the decisions and coordination surrounding finishes and furnishings.

Framing was complete and the house was under roof (protected from the weather) , so it was time to start cabinet discussions. Maria and I held our first meeting at the construction site. I'd prepared design drawings and we spent the better part of an afternoon making revisions. To my astonishment Maria had already picked all of the finishes for the home, so she was able to make all her cabinet selections that same day from samples that I'd brought along.

The next day we met in Denver, and I helped her choose granite and backsplash tiles for the kitchen. I'd become accustomed to meeting the needs of clients who needed everything *yesterday*, so it was par for the course to bring along newly-revised drawings so she could give her approval before leaving for New York City the next day. That evening, she sent me all of her appliance selections and we were good to go. I'd never encountered a client that was so decisive and who could move so fast - not even close.

The last time that I saw Maria was one week later when she was back in town. She asked me to join her at the Denver Design Center to help choose between two area rugs for

the family room adjacent to the kitchen. We reviewed the pros and cons of each and made a decision that made sense to both of us. After that, nothing. I never saw or heard from her again; not after the cabinetry was installed, not when the home was finished, not at all. During the four months following completion, about every two to three weeks, I would ask the builder, *"Have you talked with Maria? Did she say whether she liked the kitchen? Did she say anything?"*

Each time I asked, the builder said the kitchen didn't come up, but he would ask in the next conversation; and then, he would forget to ask. I tried to tell myself that "*no news is good news*"; but that provided little solace. Up to this point, I had never failed to get a reaction from my clients. Finally, almost five months after completion, I received a call from the builder to tell me that Maria had called him; specifically to tell him how happy she was with the kitchen. *"Well?"* I said expectantly. *"What did she say?"* The builder paused just long enough for me to really tense up and then replied,

> *"She said they had ten guests stay for the Thanksgiving holidays, and in their two-week stay, the kitchen was so magical, no one even wanted to go out to eat."*

Considering how may fine restaurants populated the Vail Valley, that was saying a lot. It was another example of the ability of design to shape and enrich social connection.

22

Too Many Toys

Ed and his wife Betty wanted to remodel the twenty-year old kitchen of their 2200 square foot suburban home. Their home's floor plan was typical for the time it was built. As you walked into the front entry you faced the stairs leading up to the bedroom level and to your right was the living room. Adjoining the living room to form an 'L' was a small informal dining area. This area also flowed into the kitchen which was on the other side of the living room partition wall that ran length-wise along the center of the home. Unless you were entering the home from the attached garage, going through the dining area was the only way to reach the kitchen.

The kitchen was weakly lit and the only natural light came from a small window in the dinette area. The cabinetry was stained a dark brown that was almost black. Any cooking activity left you isolated from anything that might be happening in the living room (in the front of the house and on the other side of a wall). The cabinetry and the appliances had more than served their expected life spans. Several other owners in the area had already upgraded their kitchens, so by remodeling, Ed was in no danger of being a pioneer. Renovation would be a sensible investment to maintain the value of the home.

Ed's outgoing manner, great smile and natural charm gave him an instant likeability. He owned his own painting company and its success made the remodel more than financially feasible. Besides, he and Betty loved their location and the proximity to their many good friends. Ed also loved to cook. It was more than just a hobby. For him fixing great food and entertaining were woven tightly together

Knowing this, it was natural to think of joining the isolated kitchen and eating area with the living area in the front of the house. The wall that separated these areas was load-bearing, but it was not going to be difficult to open up most of it; we kept one post to carry the load. This meant that Ed could now have an island that would anchor a new great room space. There would be much more natural light and he would be able to hold court when friends and guests visited. The benefit couldn't have been made clearer than when I asked Ed where he would like to locate his cook-top. He told me enthusiastically,

"I want it on the island so that when I'm cooking things up, I can hand out samples to everyone!"

Instead of one coming before the other, cooking and socializing would be celebrated together. I could almost guess his answer when I asked how many people he would like to be able to seat at the island, *"As many as we can!"*

Growing up, Ed subscribed to the philosophy that *Anything worth doing is worth doing right,* and he certainly brought this to the table as we began design discussions. One of the first things that he wanted to do was to get out to showrooms and check out all the latest appliances. I entirely supported this because I needed his selections before I could go much further than a conceptual plan for the new space. Appliance sizes and quantities were both important aspects but Ed was about to push the envelope on both far beyond anything I could imagine.

After his showroom visits, we met to review his appliance preferences. He wanted a 48 inch Sub-Zero refrigerator, a 60 inch Wolf range with two ovens, a microwave, a dishwasher, a trash compactor, an ice maker and a warming drawer. The house was modest in size had limited wall space so his list bordered between impractical and impossible. The 60 inch range would have required a commercial ventilation system. The size would have dwarfed the available space and the cost of the ventilation system would have been almost as much as the range itself.

I got Ed to scale back to a 48 inch gas range top that would still give him six burners, a griddle option and low heat capabilities for simmering sauces. In the design, we placed it on the island and worked out how to make a 48 inch island hood work. Having chosen a range top instead of a full range, we now had to find room for two wall ovens and a microwave.

We were able to design the microwave, one oven and a warming drawer into a tall cabinet, but to preserve counter space we had to use a base cabinet for the second oven. The trash compactor and the dishwasher would flank each side of the kitchen sink, but the oversized triple sink that Ed wanted would have to be scaled back for this to work. I also talked Ed into moving down in width from a 48 inch to a 42 inch refrigerator.

With the end in sight, we found a place for the ice-maker on the island. This was pushing the limits of the available space, but it was still doable. The problem was that Ed was like the proverbial kid in a candy shop. During the next three weeks, he would call four different times to give me his latest list of *must have* appliances. His lists included a deep fryer, a pizza oven, a steam cooking unit, a wine refrigerator, and a second dishwasher. The island grew considerably and gave us enough room to include two out of the six; but I finally had to tell Ed that the only way to add anything else was to buy a bigger house.

The design changes gave the kitchen an integrated role in the daily life of the family, finishes were brightened and the new area was bathed in natural light. With the changes, Dan could work in a kitchen area where sight lines allowed him to remain in visual contact with others. Most importantly for Dan, his joy was enhanced because he could simultaneously do two things he loved- connect with others and share his love for cooking.

Three months after completion, I returned to visit and the results were fabulous. Most impressive of all was the glow on Ed's face as he described the added joy he now took in cooking and entertaining. Not all of us are as extroverted as Ed, but as I left, I thought about our universal needs for shelter, food and social connection and how important a role the kitchen can play in everyone's life.

23

The 1200 Square Foot Kitchen

I'd been doing kitchens for Richard, one of my builder clients, for about three years when he handed me a set of plans for a new spec home he was building. The drawings showed a two-story structure, with walk-out basement. The total living area was going to be about 8500 square feet. It wasn't the largest home I'd worked with, but the area on the blueprints that was identified as the kitchen (and I had to presume eating and informal entertainment) was a rectangular space 40 feet long by 35 feet wide. Even though the top left corner was notched out, it left an area of almost 1200 square feet. This was the largest such area I'd ever seen on a blueprint; and, considering the average American home in 1950 was only 950 square feet, I thought perhaps the architect was stretching things a bit too far.

Previous to this, the most challenging and interesting kitchen designs had been the smallest. Smaller spaces always came packaged with lots of parameters requiring the most creative solutions. However, this new space was so big there seemed to be no limits. The good news was that the home was already framed so I could take a look in person. The bad news was that the construction was so far along that cabinetry should have already have been ordered. I was behind even before I started.

Seeing the room in person made it seem even bigger than it had appeared on the plans. The ceiling height in the room was 10 feet except for an architecturally dramatic ceiling vault that formed a dormer and was centered above the area where we would eventually locate the kitchen sink. The fenestration (window configuration) consisted of a triple casement window with arched (eyebrow-shaped) transom above (centered in the dormer area near the start of the east wall). The room's two exterior walls (South and East) had an

exceptional number of large casement windows, which were topped with rectangular transom glass topping out at 9 feet above the finished floor. That was good because it greatly increased the amount of light penetration into the interior and kept the ceiling from feeling heavy.

The windows along the south wall offered a view looking out the 9th fairway of a championship golf course; and all of the light from both east and south found its way through the large trees surrounding the structure. This not only softened and filtered the light but actually created a dappled effect on the floor. The light pattern, visible even on the dull finish of the subfloor, seemed to dance whenever the wind would rustle the leaves in the trees. This effect would be even more dramatic on the finished flooring with its more reflective surface.

All of this left me looking for the element or elements that would be primary in determining the design. I needed some focus – a starting point. In Steve's kitchen, we had used the view connection to the foothills, in Tina's the connection with the backyard and in Robin's the harmony with the existing décor and furniture pieces. Here, I decided it was not going to be the golf course view (which could be mainly appreciated from the exterior deck), but the extraordinary tone and feel of the natural light. There were two significant obstacles that had to be overcome.

The first was the flooring. Richard was planning to put hardwood flooring not only in the kitchen area but also throughout the adjacent living room, dining room and hall (2,000 square feet in total). An expanse this large guaranteed that the selection of wood specie and its color and pattern would have a large impact on the look and feel of the home's interior. Before even considering cabinetry, I need to choose the flooring.

The selection would have to meet three criteria. First, it would have the warmth and color tone needed to augment the stone and timber materials on the home's exterior as well as those colors represented on the wooded lot. Second, it would need to enhance and amplify the natural light effect in the room. Third, it would need to draw more of an

emotional response rather than something strictly visual. In other words, it needed to support the feel that was being driven by the light rather than calling attention to itself.

The wood that best fit the bill was a select grade of walnut produced by a mill that cut the flooring from full tree stock. It would mean that the flooring planks would have a similar character (same tree) and would have a higher percentage of longer boards (fewer breaks). The variegation of the graining and the color was somewhat unique. It contained a soft cream color flowing subtly through the warm brown tones of the walnut. This kind of pattern would not only break up the mass of the area (there wouldn't be any furniture or area rugs until the house was sold and someone moved in), but it mimicked the dappling effect from the exterior light. Using random widths in the flooring planks (3, 4, and 5 inches) would also mitigate the linear effect that wood flooring often gives.

The second and more daunting challenge was deciding how to deal with the scale of the room. Whatever was done with cabinetry had to be proportionate to the space. That meant there would be a lot of cabinetry. The trick would be to find a way to avoid people entering the room and remarking, *"Wow, look at all the cabinets.*

The answer would be to use an unfitted design **(The $6.5 Million Dollar "Fixer-upper").** The cabinetry would be designed and assembled as an ensemble of furniture pieces with each piece serving specific kitchen requirements (cooking, clean-up, serving, refrigeration). Our design area was so large that even with unique furniture pieces we needed the visual focus of each piece to have a very strong center.

If we could draw attention to the centers, then those viewing would not notice the spaces between pieces. Each piece would be exert its own kind of visual and emotional gravity and create its own unique sense of place. Without this, we would just end up with a few large furniture elements floating adrift in a large sea of space. Richard did not plan to furnish or stage the home so we would be working without the benefit of area rugs, art pieces, or furniture.

This was a good design strategy but it would be best served if we could play off of architectural features already present in the room. The dominant element was an arched

arched window centered directly beneath an open dormer. If we were looking for strong centers this was the obvious place to start (See Photo Below)

This was a logical sink location and using flanking pilasters and dishwashers on either side helped us connect the cabinetry and the window into an integrated design element. This run of cabinetry was twelve feet long, so to support our vertical connection to the window, we used tall cabinetry on the left and right ends. The illusionary effect was to make the cabinetry disappear because all attention was directed toward the window and the view beyond.

There is a certain irony and truth in the fact that cabinetry can often be most powerful when it is least noticed.

With the sink area designed, our attention turned toward the refrigerator location. The two criteria were to disguise the refrigerator(s) and to develop a strong center focus. The solution was to create the impression of a large armoire flanked by taller cabinet elements on either side. The refrigerator was done with two 27 inch Sub-Zeros, set together and each hinged so that the doors would open outward from the center. They were paneled with arched cabinet fronts and given decorative handle hardware that met at the center. The arch on the doors would mimic the curve of the dormer window.

The concealment of the refrigerator and freezer would be one of the most difficult and important challenges. I didn't have long to wait before getting feedback. Shortly after finishing this part of our installation, Richard walked in with a prospective buyer. I held my breath to see what would happen. After perusing our design for about four minutes, we heard the prospect ask Richard,

"How can you have a kitchen with no refrigerator?"

(See photo below)

The island was the next design element to be addressed. It had to be large enough to anchor the space without looking overly massive. With its required physical size, there was no practical way to have it look like a furniture piece, but replicating the look of an old-fashioned bar was another matter. We used a 24 inch deep, raised counter across the back side that made the front work area completely disappear. The back was finished with decorative panels, corbels and two large turned posts at each end. The bar itself was angled into three sides with more width in the center. Angling the island back and hiding the front allowed us to minimize its perceived size, even though it appeared properly scaled and proportionate to the size of the surrounding elements. It also gave us comfortable seating area for eight adults.

The range was located on the front side of the island. We got some unexpected help from the island range hood that was selected. The hood's finish was hammered-copper and each side sloped in a gentle curve upward to the ceiling. The hood was such a strong visual element that it went a long way toward allowing the island itself to play a secondary, supporting role. (See Photo below)

The last area of cabinetry was a coffee bar that would contain a built-in espresso machine and a wine refrigerator. We wanted it resemble a sideboard. As with the other elements we drew the eye toward the center where we could highlight a tiled wall design below a wood arch. Unfortunately the effect was squandered by the pedestrian tile design that was chosen. (See Photo below).

In the end, our best-laid plans went somewhat awry. The cabinet finishes had been chosen to match up perfectly with the select walnut flooring sample I'd chosen for Richard's approval. Even though I'd emphasized the importance of the flooring and even provided him with the supplier, the pricing and lead times; Richard's regular flooring supplier sold him on a different and less expensive grade of flooring.

As soon as it arrived at the job, we could see that it had an orange cast that was wrong for the house. It also had a preponderance of smaller lengths which would make it impossible to blend in. (Look again at the previous photos and you will see the terrible color clashes). After it was installed, all you could notice about the room was the flooring. The

species was walnut, but the difference was night and day and the $6,000 Richard saved on material got eaten up in the first week-and-a-half of carrying costs as the house sat unsold month after month. The flooring selection was the foundation upon which we had built all of our other design decisions, and when that section fell apart, it greatly diminished the overall impact (i.e., it looked awful).

A friend of mine would have called this *Penny-wise and Pound Stupid*, but I considered it somewhat of a failure on my part. My efforts to help my clients get the best value for their investment had always been centered not only around helping them not spend more than necessary, but also not spending too little. The final decision was Richard's to make, but I will always wonder if I could have done a more convincing job of making the case for the flooring.

The lesson here is that each element in your room has a role to play and is inter-connected with the others. Making a decision in one area without considering the impact on adjacent elements and the room as a whole can destroy your chances for a successful outcome. **When you have a vision for your new space, you need a certain amount of courage** to keep it in the forefront of all your decisions.

24

Tic-Tac-Toe

Most people have played this kid's game at one time or another, but how many of us even know where the game originated, where the name came from, or how old it is? I haven't played it since I was a kid, but it often comes to mind on design projects. This has to do with one of the game's defensive strategies which involves putting an 'X' or 'O' in the center square. If this is done as a first move by your opponent, the best outcome you can hope for is a draw.

If you can picture winning as helping a room reach its full potential, then this move becomes analogous, because in some designs, you simply can't win (i.e. reach your goal). Metaphorically, there is an 'X' in the center square. No matter how many ways you reconfigure the space or how deftly you change perceived sizes and emotional connections; something about the structure is standing in the way.

Whenever this has occurred, I have tried to locate and find a way to pull the proverbial 'X' out of the center box. I look for that one thing, which if changed, will open the door to new possibilities. The solution can be right under your nose or it may require unconventional thinking. It was the former case when I took on the kitchen remodel of a suburban single-family home owned by Ken and Betty.

Their home was a two-story walk-out, with four bedrooms and 3 1/2 baths. Located on a ridge, the back of the house faced south and looked out over a large, protected open space that continued for miles in each direction. It was a perfect natural habitat and well-populated with a wide variety of animals and birds, including Red Fox, Coyote, Hawks, and Horned Owls. The closest homes to the south were more than a thousand yards away.

Their kitchen was awkwardly connected to an informal eating area that was adjacent but around the corner. As you approached the kitchen, your **sight lines would narrow and converge.** The room gave the appearance of being a rectangular annex to the main living area. In fact, the kitchen, living room and nook all presented themselves as loosely-connected, **disparate areas**. Together they constituted the public area of the home; but between them there was **no continuity or flow**.

The only outside light entering the kitchen came from a twin-paned, casement window on the south wall which was centered above the sink. From the sink you could see the open space beyond, and if you leaned in and craned your head to the right you could gain a partial view of the mountains to the west. The problem was that looking out, while pleasant, actually increased your awareness of being on the inside. Everything on the outside was so sunny and open, you would feel almost **claustrophobic to find yourself on the wrong side of the glass.** Compounding matters, social connections on the inside were just as strained as visual connection to the outside.

I'd pondered whether replacing the window at the sink with one that was larger would help. It would, but not enough. Another option was to add a second, smaller window just on the wall to the right. These could be placed together with only a little space in between. This would be better because it would effectively keep you from visually slamming into the corner, it would open up some of the mountain skyline, it would let light in from another direction, and it could make it desirable to place the sink on an angle so that it would be aligned with where your eyes would go if there were nothing else in the room. This was going to help, but there was something else that was wrong and I wasn't seeing it yet.

The south-facing sink wall joined the west wall of the eating nook in a manner that formed an 'L', with the sink located just right of center on the lower leg of the 'L'. As I studied this area I found myself looking at the corner where the kitchen turned into the nook. I kept thinking how great it would be if we could get rid of the corner entirely. This wasn't going to be practical because both walls were load-bearing. They were also exterior walls of the house with a second level stacked above.

Somehow this outside corner had to go. There had to be a way to make the corner disappear without impinging on the wall's structural integrity. Since it wasn't going to be possible to do this physically, we had to find a way to create a visual illusion- one that would make this corner seem to disappear..

The answer was to take out the 36 inch wide existing window at the sink as well as the upper cabinet to the left (this was the only cabinet on this wall its lack of connection to the rest of the cabinetry gave it an incongruous and somewhat orphaned appearance). With the cabinet and the old window gone we could replace them with a much wider 60 inch window. The unit consisted of a large section of picture glass, opposite our sink, and a smaller operable unit to the left. We also placed a 30 inch double casement window into the corner on the west kitchen wall.

Where the old windows had been surrounded by wood casing, both new windows were trimmed with rounded drywall. Perhaps most importantly, where the outside corner between kitchen and nook had previously had a sharp 90-degree edge, we softened its profile by changing to a rounded drywall corner with a 1 inch radius. In the transition from kitchen to eating area we now had a ***window wall*** **where the view was widened, and from the viewer's standpoint, panoramic**. The effect that this had was dramatic. Now as you approached the kitchen, the space ahead was diverging and broadening all the way out as far as the eye could see.

The old south wall with its outside corner was still there, but without the sharp edge and the lone upper cabinet, there was **nothing to stop your eye from** ***falling*** **into the view.** The south wall and the corner both seemed to disappear. When you walked into the new space, it felt as though the southern end of the kitchen was now the other side of the natural open space.

Inside the home, we had now *perceptually* eliminated the corner that had been also blocking any sense of connection between the kitchen, the eating nook and the living room. After the change the new kitchen space felt open and connected to the other living areas. (See photo below)

The corner had been the 'X' in the box, and once removed, everything could be configured to create what had now become a fabulous living area. Maria and her husband put it best,

> *"We were excited about remodeling our old kitchen but the transformation is so great, we feel like we got a new house."*

25

"You can't get there from here!"

Tony, one of my builder clients, had given me plans for a new custom home he was building. It was going to be an 8,000 square foot custom home with a rustic stone exterior and an interior decor with Portuguese and Spanish influences. The kitchen area was open and connected to a hearth area (a mini-family room) and nook. Ironically, even with 10 foot high ceilings and a large footprint, I could see that the space was going to end up feeling much smaller and even cramped.

The owner's appliance requirements also complicated the issue. They were set on having a 48 inch wide Sub-Zero refrigerator, two double ovens, two dishwashers, a microwave, a 48 inch range, and a stone hood that required 59 inches of wall space. There were several possible configurations, but by any measure, the room was going to feel smaller and more awkward once all of these items were shoehorned in. Instead of the stone hood becoming a wonderful focal point, it was going to advertise the small amount of wall space available. The items they wanted were reasonable for the style, size and cost of their home. The problem was the architect's plan.

After trying out several designs, I knew it was time to find and remove the bottleneck so our design could deliver a sense of ease, grandeur and flow. Something would have to change. Borrowing, consolidating and repurposing space is key to many remodel projects, and I could see that we would have to apply the same strategy to this new home. We needed to steal more space that would allow us to lengthen the range wall and minimize the number of wall turns (we started with four) that left the plan broken up into small sections.

The architect had designed a walk-in pantry of 70 square foot just behind our range wall. This was a good place to appropriate space because there was another area close by that could also handle pantry storage for the kitchen. However, even if the switch were made, it would not free up enough space to help. There was also no other logical place from which to grab more room.

Taking some tracing paper from a roll, I laid it over the building plans and marked out two kitchen walls. One was part of the building exterior. It would have to remain because the house was well underway and was nearly framed. The other wall was on the interior and would become part of the kitchen when the pantry was relocated. Then, I just connected the two lines. Doing this created a small triangular area that was currently part of the 3.5 car garage. I could see that it would require only a small structural beam to span this in order to support a new diagonal wall. Shrinking the garage by removing such a small triangle of space (12.25 square feet) wouldn't affect it in the least, but it would make all the difference in the kitchen.

Tony liked the idea, got the okay from the owners, and after the framing was modified, we had reduced the 90 degree wall turns from four to two. We now had a long ten foot run of wall on which to place our hood and range; and it was set at a nice 45 degree angle that visually connected it with both the eating area and the family room space. As an added bonus it was now the first thing that drew your eye upon entering the kitchen. On either side of our new range wall were two 72 inch flanking walls that angled gently away (135 degrees).

After our *new-home remodel*, suddenly we had a fabulous great room with a more inviting island that could now seat six instead of four. The builder, clients and interior designer were all thrilled with the new look; and when the home was completed the room was filled with an ambience and charm that let us know our remodel had been worth the effort. (See drawing below)

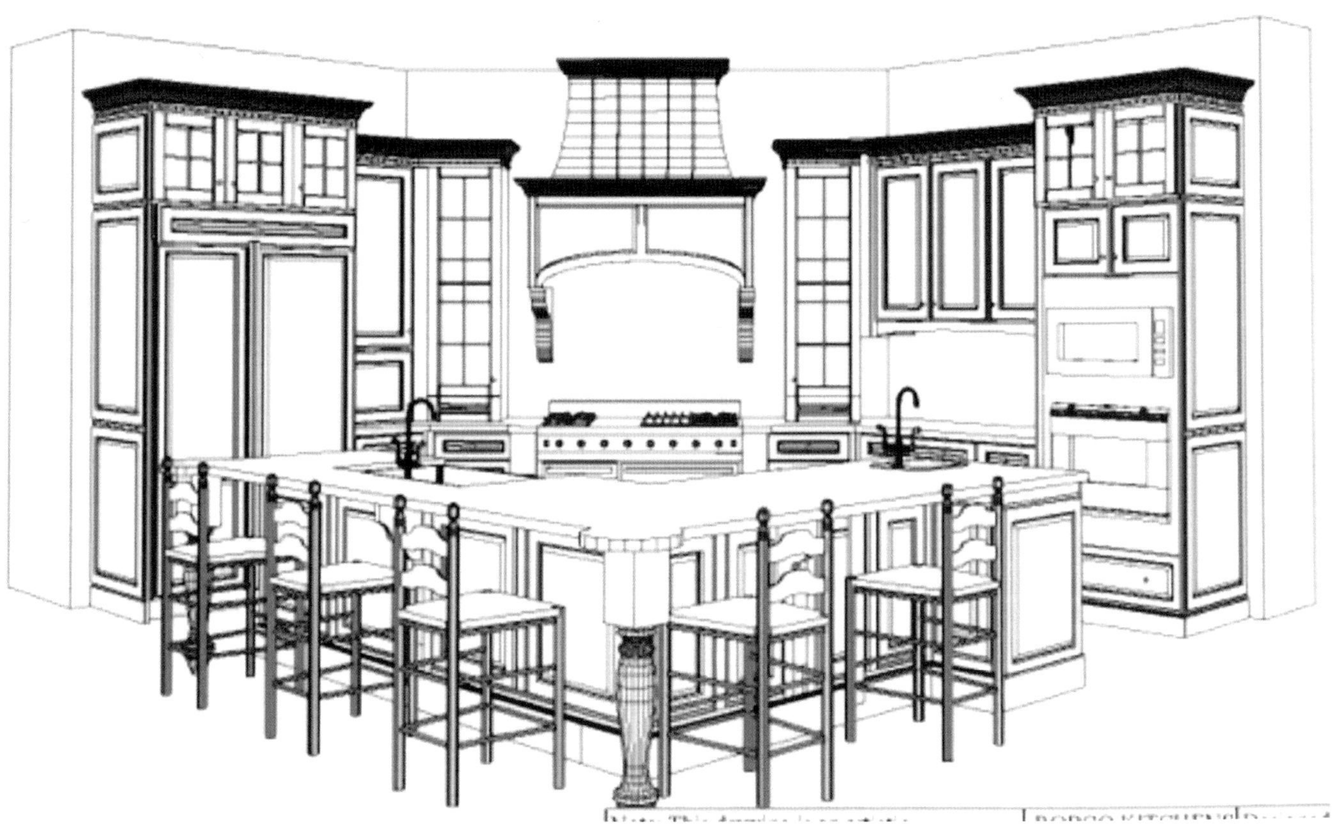

We'd gone from a problematic plan to a wonderful dream kitchen, but it could not have happened if we had not been able to find those invaluable borrowings. Being willing to consider a somewhat illogical and out-of-the-box perspective is what allowed us to move beyond the architect's creation. In more ways than one, the solution lay just outside of the plan's existing boundaries.

If you are building your own new home, this is a reminder of the benefit to be gained by **making your kitchen designer part of your home design team**. Making changes early and on paper is so much easier and less expensive than altering construction elements already in place.

26

Fiestaware

The things to which my clients found strong emotional attachment had been many; desert foothills for Steve (**The Bristlecone Pine**), a dedicated nature easement for Ken and Betty (**Tic-Tac-Toe**), and a table and furniture piece for Robin (**The Birthday Gift**). All of these disparate connections had provided inspiration for their new kitchens, but I still found myself surprised when this list expanded to include dishware and a picture frame.

Ken and Joyce were referred to me by another family member. Ken, who was the brother-in-law of a previous client, worked as a sales manager for a window company and his wife, Joyce, was an insurance company manager. Their kitchen was about twenty years old and no longer met their needs. They'd considered moving to a newer home; but like many others, they really liked the neighborhood. If the kitchen could be improved they would be happy staying where they were.

The kitchen and family room were at the rear of the home. These two adjacent areas were severely disjointed. Both areas were on the same level but had different floor materials- oak in the kitchen and carpeting in the family room. The kitchen had an 8 foot ceiling while the family room ceiling rose 17 feet into the home's second level. These two areas would both be active with friends when the couple would entertain, but they just didn't work together.

Both rooms shared the back wall of the home, but the family room had a wall full of windows and effusive lighting that left the kitchen seeming dark by comparison. Beside the change in ceiling height and floor material, a support post also visually marked the boundaries between rooms.

In the kitchen, except for a small dinette table, their was no landing area where someone might converse with a person working there. From the standpoint of social connection, flow and visual continuity the two rooms did not work together.

The kitchen work area wasn't meeting Joyce functional requirements. She complained about limited storage for dry goods (a narrow pantry cabinet with no rollouts). The countertop the left of the sink also provided little in the way of prep area once you were out of the clean-up zone. Beside the kitchen's functional deficiencies, the dark brown, oak raised-panel cabinet fronts had been passé for ten years and had no place in the owner's contemporary décor. It was time to change.

The small kitchen island opposite the sink barely larger than the old downdraft cooktop that it held and the cabinetry provided no place for pot and pan storage. There was no bar seating at the island, there was also no place to socialize unless you wanted to stand at the back side, making sure to keep your hands away from the burner areas.

Ken and Lisa described their initial thoughts and I had the opportunity to look around for items that might provide clues to unlocking a successful plan. Sitting on a square matte-black table in the corner of the family room was an attractive picture frame that had strong contemporary design elements. The wood was a honey-colored maple, it had an unusual asymmetric shape, and its accents were done in a complementary brownish-red cherry. Ken and Joyce said they had both been strongly attracted to it when they found it an art fair. I could sense their *emotional meter* hit an '8'. I began to picture shaker style cabinet fronts in the kitchen, using the same woods and color scheme as the picture frame. The color harmony between the two soft-grained woods was so remarkable that it was impossible not to envision the same scheme in maple cabinets and cherry flooring.

Walking back to the kitchen, I noticed four of the brightest dishware pieces I'd ever seen. They had a whimsical design and were done in bright, bold colors. Noticing my focus, Lisa explained that the series was called "Fiestaware". When she told me she LOVED it, I knew I her emotional connection had given me a second clue. She opened an upper cupboard and showed me similar pieces for which she had no display space.

It seemed so clear– the goal would be to create a kitchen that was the perfect home for the Fiestaware. I decided to share my thoughts with them and the immediate "Oh My God!" look in their eyes told me that they were 100% on board. There were a couple of issues to solve however. First, we would have to find more room. Our solution was to ditch the dinette table and to create a two-level island that would provide a social gathering and eating area (upper) with a great cooking area (lower). Instead of the traditional rectangular island with the cooking area on one side with the bar area along the back, our island cabinetry ran parallel to the length of the room. We made the cooking area rectangular and fronted it with built-in wine cubbies. This work area had the standard counter height of 36 inches, but as the base cabinets moved toward the patio door and space where the old dinette table had been, the countertop jumped up 6 inches to a 42" bar height. This overlapping section was asymmetrical and took off into a whimsical, curvilinear bar top with a rounded end. This relaxed the structure of the other rectilinear cabinet elements while providing seating for four. It was also a great serving counter for entertaining. The island as a whole, with its recessed and pendant lighting above, took on the look and feel of an interior art piece. It also reached out perfectly to the Fiestaware which was now showcased in open, rectangular cabinets units. (See Photo Below)

Our other task was to to tie the family room together with the kitchen so that they felt like one social gathering area. They had different ceiling heights, different flooring,

differing window treatments and there was still a structural post to deal with. Our answer was to use a new flooring material to unite them and to choose a material and color strong enough to make the ceiling irrelevant. Cherry was the perfect material, but we had to get the color just right. It was going to be one of the bigger expenses of the project, but I'd assured Ken and Lisa that it would be worth it.

When the flooring crew came out to do samples on the unfinished floor planks, the color was close but not right, even after mixing five different stain blends. I was a little worried. My flooring vendor however was one of the best in the country, so I was quick to

call for assistance. Fortunately he knew just what was required. We ended up doing something called "popping". The floor was wetted down with water so that it would open up the grain; and then when it dried, it could take on the deeper, richer color we were after. As we finished up a new test area, we could see that it was right where we wanted it. With the popping technique we now had one of the prettiest cherry floors I'd seen and we had accomplished it without losing the wood's natural grain characteristics.

Finally, there was still the issue of the post. Because it carried a large load from both the roof and second level floor it had to remain were it was. Unfortunately because of where it was located in the room, you couldn't avoid it as you followed the main traffic flow into the kitchen. We'd worked hard to have the island reach out like a social magnet to pull people in, but the post had the potential to diminish or nullify our efforts by sending the opposite signal.

Our solution was to wrap it in the same wood as the cabinetry, making sure that there were reveals (i.e. offsets at the joints) that also matched up with the cabinet details. The theory was that it would just blend into the look of the cabinetry located behind it and thus become virtually invisible. (See Photo above)

Joyce found her new kitchen was a joy to use and having just one flooring material had given her the ability to change and improve her furniture arrangement. She said entertaining was much easier. They were thrilled with the look and feel of their kitchen but thought the dynamics had changed so much that they were living in a new home.

Three months after completion they invited me to stop by for a little celebration. As I was walking into the kitchen, Ken shouted,

"Watch out for the post!"

I diverted in time, but as I did, I wondered if perhaps the quest to make the post invisible had succeeded too well.

Part Three

(Putting it all together)

"If the only tool you have is a hammer, you tend to see every problem as a nail."

...Abraham Maslow

27

Where to Start

My first solo kitchen design effort for Ellen is described in the first chapter. I began with good technical skills, experience in building custom homes, and a clear focus on helping my client, Ellen, create a great kitchen. By the end of the project however, my perspective had been turned upside down when I realized room design could be the means to helping my client find a sense of joy and personal delight.

This insight was somewhat startling because it had been hiding in plain sight. I had just been too focused on the mechanics to be able to see it. My situation reminded me of my favorite scene in the movie, "Field of Dreams"; the one in which the brother-in-law, upon seeing the ballplayers on the field for the first time, says to his sister, *"Have those players always been there?"*

So, if you are the designer, builder, architect or simply want to be the next "Ellen", where do you start? To begin, here are the four most important steps that have helped both me and my clients.

Step 1- Changing the way you think and talk about kitchens:

The word 'kitchen' and the common understanding of its meaning gives us a valuable shorthand for talking about a space dominated by objective functions of food and dish storage, clean up, preparation, and serving. The problem is the label itself can severely limit a broader understanding of the same space. This is especially the case when we step outside of the things that are easy to quantify (work triangles, walkway clearances, counter

space, and storage capacity). What happens when we want to address more subjective aspects, such as visual appeal, social connection and personal delight?

With visual attraction we move further away from an empirical realm where we can take quantitative measurements. Still, we have an array of tools at our disposal. We can refer to style books and color palettes. We can also match cabinet styling and finishes with the architectural style and interior decor of the home. We try to measure our clients attraction to muted vs saturated colors, textures and levels of reflection.

Thinking about the kitchen as a social gathering area moves us into entirely new territory because the social interactions for most families will be occurring across and within a space that extends past the traditional kitchen to include areas like family room, nook and/or sunroom. There is no measurement such as a 'Social Interaction Unit', but in terms of objective measures we can still analyze conversation triangles and sight lines that keep people connected with each other. We can gauge how to use natural and indirect lighting to enhance areas where people will congregate and how to create an easy interface between work and non-work areas. We can expand the range of landing and perching areas and help the space work across a many levels of social intimacy. With the focus turned toward social interaction, the term kitchen has become relatively useless. Because using the term actually causes us to filter input to fit the abstract concept, we are more likely than not to miss seeing new opportunities.

Finally, assessing how this larger space and all of its many characteristics can be tailored to produce personal delight takes us almost entirely in to the subjective realm. Evaluation still has to based upon how the individual client will react and that will be a function of many things. How are the desired feelings being expressed? Does the client want happy, cheerful, comfortable, relaxed, calm, uplifting? What are the main characteristics of their own sense of personal space? How open can things be before there is no sense of place or become threatening? How much visual structure will there be before things become rigid and sterile? How whimsical or playful can the design be before ambiguity starts to threaten the sense of order?

Most of us have experienced enough kitchens to know that some bring us together in ways that seem almost magical. That certainly was one of the core messages in the story of Deborah's kitchen (**Room for One More**) and it was no less true of the "neighborhood community center" that was Ellen's kitchen (**Musical Chairs**). The key is to reach the full potential of the space with the outcome measured in efficiency, beauty, interpersonal draw and in deeply personal happiness.

For these reasons, I often found it helpful to shelve the term 'kitchen' and move to another term like platform for living or social gathering space. If I need to talk about tasks I simply refer to the 'work area'. Otherwise, every time I use the word 'kitchen', I am pushing my client back into the old construct as well as directing their attention to a space that is just a part of the larger area being designed.

Step 2 – Recognize the remarkable difference there is between *physical* and *perceived* space.

The next most important term that should be broadened is the term 'space'. Instead of just addressing how you can change physical characteristics, you can also address how the space is perceived (e.g. connecting Steve's kitchen emotionally and visually to the outside scene, making posts disappear in Ken and Joyce's kitchen, etc). It is important to see that while there are limiting factors in changing physical space, perceived space is almost infinitely malleable. Recall how Linda's kitchen vault was made to seem lower and more protective with just the use of a large coved crown and how the right treatment of windows in Phil and Betty's remodel made the corner between the kitchen and eating area seem to vanish.

A broader perspective on space also makes it easy to introduce discussions of how the family or individuals interact and to address how the new area can be adapted to enhance greater social connectedness; e.g. Marla's kitchen where her family remained after dinner

Step 3 – Recognize that our physical surroundings affect both our physical and mental well-being.

Our species is unique in its ability to envision and create new realities but this skill can conceal the intimate connections that we often share with those things that surround us. We look to our homes for shelter, security, and sharing and as we personalize them they begin to reflect who we are. In House as Mirror of Self, Clare Cooper Marcus makes the point powerfully that **our homes have the ability to impact us emotionally and psychologically on both conscious and subconscious levels.** Our surroundings can affect us in positive and negative ways (e.g. the change that occurred when David found himself no longer imprisoned in the study that he had ironically called his favorite room (**The First House Call**) or the change that occurred in Amanda as she escaped from constriction and chaos into a new space that brought comfort and ease and a new sense of freedom and joy (**Comfort and Ease**).

This important connection has been recognized for at least three millennia. It is at the heart of the Chinese practice of Feng Shui; often referred to as the Art of Placement. Correct placement leads to good Chi or life energy. How I think of Chi is expressed in an insightful way often used to differentiate between introvert and extrovert. When engaged with groups of people, if you find your batteries recharged, you fall more on the extrovert side of the spectrum. If these same interactions leave you completely drained and in need of quiet and solitude, you are much more of an introvert. We pick up negative and positive charges not only from others but also our physical environment.

For most, our homes are the most personal of spaces. They represents a place where we can drop our public mask or persona and just be ourselves (like reconnecting with a good friend). When designing in an area we often consider the heart and soul of the home, this transformative impact is amplified.

Step 4 – Discover Why You Like the Things You Do.

All of us have items around us – furniture pieces, cars, jewelry, art where our connection to the objects involves strong emotional participation. For Phil and Betty (**Tic-Tac-Toe**) it was a natural open space, for Robin (**The Birthday Gift**) it was twi furniture pieces, for Steve (**The Bristlecone Pine**) it was the desert landscape, and for Joyce (**Fiestaware**) it was her collection of dishware. I explain to my clients that I will be able to tell when their emotional meter goes off the charts. In some cases, there will be clues of inflection (e.g. "I LOVE .....") or syntax (e.g. "I don't know what it is, but ....."). When people connect in a strong emotional way, the senses bypass the rational conscious mind and they find themselves without words that can adequately express this. When you feel yourself captivated by a feeling of joy and euphoria you may not fully understand it, but it is beyond the realm of doubt and you find yourself wanting to repeat it.

So, locating where your emotional attachments are is the key. But there is good and bad news. People who like the same things often like them for entirely different reasons That's the bad news. The good news is that once you find out why you like something, you will see that the underlying reasons have informed and shaped your design decisions across a broad spectrum. When it comes to the *whys*, your personal tastes that seem so disparate will suddenly exhibit amazing consistency.

At the root of the matter is that a great deal of what we know comes to us in a non-mediated way where our perceptions have not been filtered through concepts. Even though it stays mainly in our subconscious, it plays a big part in all of our lives. It also strongly influences our feelings about things - our gut reactions. You need only think about how much of our interpersonal communication is in in non-verbal form. This fact is epitomized in Brian King's lyrics from the song, *"You say it best when you say nothing at all"*.

Observing the people and the world around me, I always sense that data is flowing in faster to my subconscious than to my head; and I can never be sure when my subconscious is going to flash a message to my brain to give me a "heads-up" about what is going on.

Daniel Kahneman in his book, *Thinking Fast and Slow*, refers to this agency of our minds as System 1. Like an autopilot, it allows us to perform many functions automatically – even highway driving under routine conditions. When I find myself seeing Exit 10 on an Interstate and cannot recall any of the drive since Exit 4, I cannot help but wonder who was driving the car in the interim. In Kahneman's terms, it is System 2 that is wondering and it was System 1 that was doing the driving (my example, not his).

My point here is that giving equal credence to our feelings and instincts as well as our rational experience, leads to decisions with the highest level of certainty. When our heads tells us to act, but there is *something* that just doesn't feel right, it is often a sign that our subconscious has detected something is wrong, even though we can't say what.

The role emotion plays in our consciousness has been given new insight in the work of Antonio Damasio, a USC professor of Neurology. He has written several popular books on the subject, including The Feeling of What Happens. If you want a quick snapshot of his thinking, you can watch an interview on YouTube entitled, "When Emotions Make Better Decisions". (It was filmed on ForaTV) My essential take-away is that **in our rational decision-making, whether we are aware of it or not, there is always an emotional component that plays a strong role.**

The patterns that determine why you like the things you do may seem out of reach because they operate just below the level of our awareness. The way to find them is by identifying several of the things for which you have a powerful attachment and then studying to see the common design elements. You can also find these patterns by looking at pictures quickly (before you can think about it) and putting them into a like or dislike pile. After the exercise you will find that your subconscious has used the patterns you are looking for to do the sorting for you. When you go through the *like* pile, you can begin to sift out the connections that will identify the patterns. (This is illustrated in more detail in the next chapter)

28

What It All Means

When design results seem captivating and magical it is certainly reflective of their power to reach you at a emotional or intuitive level, but do they share common characteristics? Are there patterns hidden within the designs that can point us in a direction to achieve similar results? While I don't believe there is a one-size-fits-all formula, there are three basic elements that must be present for a design to become transformational and enhance the individual experience:

I. All the supporting elements must be in place

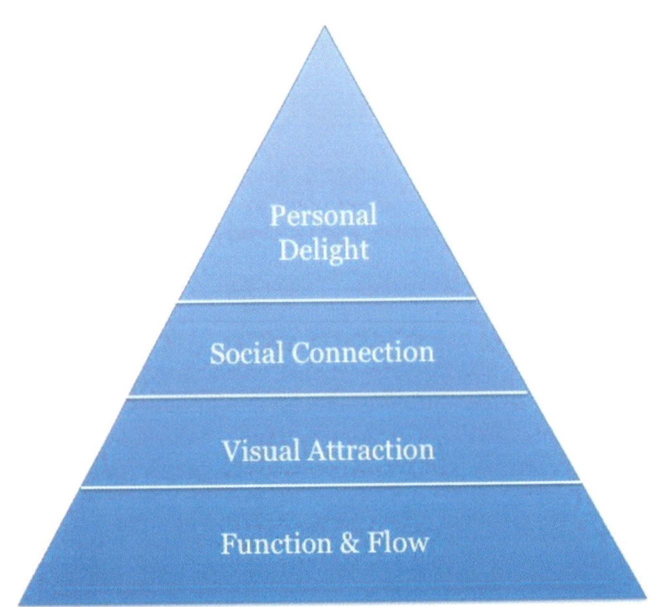

I visualize the kitchen design process as a pyramid of increasing importance. At the most basic level, it must function well – providing a cooking environment that offers organization, efficiency and good ergonomics and circulation. With these requirements fully met I can focus on the creation of visual attraction, social connection and personal delight. In the case of many of my clients, this progression took them from, "*this is a great place to cook in*" to "*this space feels so good to me that I simply don't want to leave*".

Maria and her kitchen are a perfect example (**The Dysfunctional Kitchen**). Even though she loved her new kitchen, her joy would have been greatly diminished if she was in any way dissatisfied with her new kitchen's functionality. The same would be true if she didn't find the design, colors and finishes visually pleasing. Careful planning and an almost ruthless attention to detail had delivered maximum efficiency. Reliance on the proper and artistic use of scale, proportion, form, texture, and color had helped us create a space that could provide a continuing sense of visual pleasure, surprise and discovery. Ease of use and visual attraction, the first two layers of the design pyramid, were the building blocks on which I could build the next level, which is social connection.

In Maria's heritage and that of many others, cooking is not only preparatory to eating but is an activity that provides social bonding between friends and family. It is a way of expressing love and a communion of spirit. This heritage made it even more important to help Maria's kitchen become a social gathering place for the family.

The richness of social connection will, in part, be a function of just how easily all parties can connect across different levels of social intimacy. The interface between the business and social sides of the kitchen must remain fluid and free of friction. Maria's kitchen was also a reminder of this when she said that, after dinner, no one wanted to leave. The peninsula and bar seating that we added had become a special place where the family could share meals but also simply enjoy each other's' company.

At the top of the pyramid, is customer delight. When the kitchen space becomes so intimately matched to the physical, social and aesthetic needs and desires of the client, the resulting emotional connection is palpable; it becomes their favorite place to be. Maria was

expressing this exactly when she said that she loved her kitchen so much that she didn't even want to go out to eat anymore. Reaching this point however, requires careful attention to all of the different levels on the pyramid. The resulting joy is a classic example of just how much greater the whole can be than the sum of the parts.

II. The design must be holistic in nature.

All of the design elements must work together to support the whole – none are glaring, none are discordant, none are so loud that you cannot comprehend or appreciate the beauty of the whole. While there may be a number of areas of visual focus, they must be blended to complement and complete the larger scheme. This is especially true of the cabinetry because it is a large part of the visual matrix.

This concept takes me back in time when, as a teenager, I would sometimes get a little full of myself; and to bring me back down to earth, my dad would say, *"I'll have to put a basket over your head so the sun can shine."* This admonition still resonates with me because too many cabinet designs are just a little too *bright* to allow anything else to be seen. For many years, images of kitchens were dominated by those presented by kitchen manufacturers. Because of this I've had to caution my clients about what they see because the images are designed to show off the product and not the rooms a whole. This has been greatly mitigated with the advent of internet sites like www.houzz.com.

If people's first reaction to the new kitchen is *"Wow, look at those cabinets!"*, that is usually an indication that the room has succeeded in the visual representation of the cabinets at the expense of making an emotional connection. If our focus becomes riveted on one of the parts, it is impossible to be fully drawn in and captivated by the whole. Whatever term you want to use - ambience, mood, gestalt, or feel; it's usually gone.

If you have ever stopped to admire a panoramic view in nature, you no doubt have experienced a period of time where you and the view became part of a *Oneness*. Its full power is experienced when you are *in the view* with the wind, the smell, the sky, sun,

warmth or cold, the movement of the trees, the continuity of close-in versus far-off trees, rocks, water, etc., versus being on the outside, admiring the view as a spectator. Instead of using your rational mind to make a judgment about the view, your consciousness is switched off, allowing you to get lost in the *now* of the moment.

This experience is often referred to as being unmediated because it is not filtered by the conscious, rational part of our mind. Just think of what so often happens after the fact. No matter how good our cameras are, they never can capture the totality. In recounting the experience or showing off such photos, I usually find myself apologizing that the photo doesn't do justice to what I saw; saying something like, *"I guess you needed to be there."* For most of us, trying to capture an experience in a photo (or visual representation) is a fool's errand. **What is important about a transformational design is that it is grounded in your personal experience and not in the observation.**

If the transitions between elements (texture, shape, proportion, color) allow our eyes to move easily from one part to another without getting visually stopped at the border, then we are most of the way home. Ellen's kitchen **(Musical Chairs)** is a perfect example because the strongest visual elements were woven into the fabric of the larger design. The visual and psychological connections between the family room, nook, sun room and kitchen were perfectly seamless. Visitors remembered the experience of being in the space much more than they ever did the separate design elements. And that was exactly the point.

Many years ago, I'd been interviewed to build a custom home for Barry and his wife, Jane. They were interested enough to ask if they could visit three of my previously completed homes. A few weeks after they had selected me to build their home, Barry related that they had interviewed a total of thirty builders over the previous four years. I couldn't help but ask him,

"Why did you decide to go with me?"

The answer is something I have never forgotten. Barry said,

"You had us tour three of your finished homes, and in all of them, we could sense something really special. We didn't know exactly what it was and even though none of the homes matched up with our design style, we knew we wanted our home to have that same special feeling."

My approach to building and design had always been holistic, but Barry's comment was as close as I or anyone else had come to putting it into words. I'd always designed and built based on the client experience I was hoping to create. At the time this was an entirely intuitive process, but it still required the parts not to compete with the whole.

Ten years later, I'd moved on from custom homes to custom kitchens, and had occasion to take a friend by the home I'd built for Barry and Jane. They were out of town, but Barry's mom let us come in and look around. I knew that my clients loved their home, but when I was in the kitchen with Barry's mom, she told me something amazing. She said five years after moving in, Barry had received a lucrative job offer that would have doubled his compensation, but it would have required relocation. She said that Barry turned the job down and when asked why, he said it was because he loved his home and didn't want to leave it.

The message underlying this story, as well as so many of those in this book, is that when design elements can be crafted into a whole that perfectly suits the needs and personality of the client, the result can be qualitatively many times greater than the sum of the parts.

III. The Design must be connect with the underlying patterns that drive our emotional attractions to the space and things around us.

Getting the best results involves tailoring the design of your living space to make it feel completely personal. We all know that taste is subjective and that the saying "*beauty is in the eye of the beholder*" has real currency. If you find four people who like a particular furniture piece, say a table, and then interview them about why they are attracted to the

piece, you will find that it will likely be for entirely different reasons. On the surface, one person may be especially attracted to clean lines and symmetry while the other is drawn to the color, graining and finish. Delving deeper into the *whys* of the attraction is how you find what is driving the emotional connection.

Beneath the bewildering and seemingly disconnected or inconsistent range of choices an individual makes, there is a remarkable constancy. People like the things they like for the same reasons; and the same patterns will appear in their choices of apparel and accessories, their artwork, furniture and cars. In a fortuitous circumstance I discovered an effective tool that could be used to suss out the underlying patterns.

In the months prior to starting a project, many clients would begin clipping out pictures from magazines of things they liked, organizing them into files for future use. Today, it is probably more common to see clients putting together an electronic 'Idea book' on www.houzz.com or assembling pictures at www.pinterest.com. The idea is the same. Because I found many clients starting projects without having done this work, I decided to create special **Design Boards**. At the time I had no idea just how powerful a tool they would become. They were created from hundreds of pictures cut from kitchen design magazines and books. The pictures were mounted with adhesive to fifteen different boards of foam core (16" x 20") and were grouped on each board by one of five of the following broad categories:

1. **Sleek and Serene**
2. **Clean and Purposeful**
3. **Relaxed and Earthy**
4. **Elaborate and Seductive**
5. **Gregarious and Irreverent**

In the photos below you will see that in each category there is an increasing amount of visual complexity and contrast while the amount of symmetry decreases. On each board were several color combinations chosen for their affinity for the category.

Sleek and Serene
COMBO 71-F
1. Afterglow
2. Sky Blue
3. Seafoam
4. Lilac Gray
COMBO 71-G
1. Basil
2. Blue Haze
3. Light Taupe
4. Moth
COMBO 71-H
1. Celadon
2. Aqua
3. Pussywillow Gray
4. Apricot Illusion
COMBO 71-I
1. Bone White
2. Dusk
3. Wild Dove
4. Vapor Blue
5. Twilight Blue

Sleek and Serene
COMBO 83-B
1. Deep Taupe
2. Light Taupe
3. Angora
4. Ethereal Green
5. Cinnabar
6. Deep Blue
COMBO 83-C
1. Natural
2. Shifting Sand
3. Pastel Parchment
4. Byzantium
5. Biscuit
6. Cadmium Orange
7. Rose Of Sharon
COMBO 83-D
1. Pewter
2. Storm Gray
3. Vapor
4. Golden Mist
5. Bright Red Violet
6. Imperial Blue
7. Gray Violet
COMBO 83-E
1. Walnut
2. Bark
3. Bleached Sand
4. Deep Periwinkle
5. Porcelain Rose
6. Purple Wine

Sleek and Serene
COMBO 111-B
1. Ice Flow
2. Crystal Blue
3. Vapor
4. Violet Ice
5. Lilac Hint
COMBO 111-C
1. Green Essence
2. Powder Blue
3. Norse Blue
4. Spruce
5. Loden Frost
COMBO 111-D
1. Ice
2. Evening Haze
3. Arctic Ice
4. Silver Pink
5. Mistletoe
COMBO 111-E
1. Whisper White
2. Gray Violet
3. Gull Gray
4. Frosty Spruce
5. Alpine

Clean and Purposeful
COMBO 115-F
1. White Swan
2. Almost Mauve
3. Smoke Gray
4. Burnished Lilac
5. Dawn Blue
COMBO 115-G
1. Silver Blue
2. Malachite Green
3. Tourmaline
4. Maple Sugar
COMBO 115-H
1. Gray Violet
2. Gray Dawn
3. Lavender Gray
4. Ether
5. Pink Tint
COMBO 115-I
1. Rose Smoke
2. Deauville Mauve
3. Antler
4. Rose Taupe
5. Duck Green
COMBO 115-B
1. Moonbeam
2. Shadow Gray
3. Slate Gray
4. Dawn Pink
COMBO 115-C
1. Gray Morn
2. Pinkish Gray
3. Hushed Violet
4. Abyss
5. Eucalyptus
COMBO 115-D
1. Rose Gray
2. Smoke Blue
3. Cinder
4. Atmosphere
5. Silver Fern
COMBO 115-E
1. Misty Lilac
2. Green Haze
3. Arona
4. Sparrow
5. Silver Pine

Clean and Purposeful

COMBO 99-B

1. Elm Green
2. Aspen Green
3. Spruce
4. Burnt Russet
5. Wineberry

COMBO 99-C

1. Butternut
2. Antelope
3. Misted Yellow
4. Chrysanthemum
5. Acorn

COMBO 99-D

1. Jade Gray
2. Feldspar
3. Fir
4. Rose Taupe
5. Fawn
6. Moonlight Mauve

COMBO 99-E

1. Verdant Green
2. Loden Frost
3. Shadow Green
4. Bison
5. Heather Rose

Gregarious and Irreverent
COMBO 75-B
1. English Rose
2. Smoke Gray
3. Blue Grass
4. Powder Puff
COMBO 75-C
1. Vanilla
2. Soft Pink
3. Heather
4. Lilac Gray
5. Hibiscus Violet
COMBO 75-D
1. Winter Wheat
2. Lilac Snow
3. Powder Pink
4. Garden Glade
COMBO 75-E
1. Apricot Sherbert
2. Wheat
3. Cloud Blue
4. Cameo Green
5. Italian Straw

Gregarious and Irreverent
1. Poison Green
2. Neutral Blue
3. Vivid Blue
4. Lemon Chrome
1. Bluish Lavender
2. Fandango Pink
3. Honey Gold
4. Firecracker
1. Bright White
2. Princess Blue
3. Calypso Coral
4. Super Lemon
1. Jacaranda
2. Mahogany
3. Kelly Green
4. Hot Pink

Gregarious and Irreverent
BIG BOY
COMBO 123-F
1. Garden Green
2. Hibiscus
3. Hyacinth
4. Buttercup
COMBO 123-G
1. Desert Flower
2. Azalea Pink
3. Cornflower Blue
4. Cedar Green
COMBO 123-H
1. Tigerlily
2. Dahlia
3. Golden Rod
COMBO 123-I
1. Bright White
2. Rosebud
3. Azalea
4. Dark Green

FRESH EGGS
COMBO 135-A
1. Willow Green
2. Forest Green
3. Grenadine
4. Burnt Russet
5. Harvest Pumpkin
COMBO 135-C
1. Brown Sugar
2. Red Violet
3. Autumn Glaze
4. Hedge Green
5. Old Gold
COMBO 135-B
1. Bronze Green
2. Amber Gold
3. Orange Brown
4. Bordeaux
5. Maple Sugar
COMBO 135-D
1. Sunset Gold
2. Butterum
3. Barn Red
4. Tawny Orange
5. Mustard Gold
Relaxed and Earthy

Relaxed and Earthy
COMBO 103-B
1. Rose Canyon
2. Buckskin
3. Cowhide
4. Otter
5. Dusky Green
COMBO 103-C
1. Burro
2. Faded Denim
3. Sage Green
4. Raw Sienna
5. Winter Wheat
COMBO 103-D
1. Mineral Red
2. Magenta Haze
3. Khaki
4. Golden Nugget
5. Purple Sag
COMBO 103-E
1. Sage Brush Green
2. Beaver Fur
3. Cactus Flower
4. Dusk
5. Tan

Relaxed and Earthy
COMBO 107-B
1. Bit of Blue
2. Capri Blue
3. Shell Pink
4. Mediterranean Blue
COMBO 107-C
1. Sand
2. Bleached Denim
3. Orchid Bloom
4. Oyster White
5. Papaya Punch
COMBO 107-D
1. Riviera
2. Aquamarine
3. Seashell Pink
4. Orchid Pink
5. Whitecap Gray
COMBO 107-E
1. Scallop Shell
2. Beach Sand
3. Conch Shell
4. Orchid
Dominique

Elaborate and Seductive

Elaborate and Seductive
COMBO 79-F
1. Grape Royal
2. Mallard Green
3. Stone Gray
4. Bone White
COMBO 79-G
1. Barn Red
2. Dark Denim
3. English Ivy
COMBO 79-H
1. Cardinal
2. Vanilla Ice
3. Insignia Blue
COMBO 79-I
1. Partridge
2. Plum
3. Duck Green
4. Parchment

Elaborate and Seductive
COMBO 95-F
1. Burnt Henna
2. Raw Umber
3. Velvet Morning
4. Topaz
5. Amber
COMBO 95-G
1. Mandarin Orange
2. Flame Orange
3. Cadmium Yellow
4. Turkish Sea
5. Blue Nights

The goal of these boards was to help me and my clients get quickly to the patterns that were influencing them. What made this work so remarkably was that they were shown each board and asked to quickly place it in one of two piles – *like* or *dislike*. Because this was done at a glance, there was no time for them to consider or think about their choices, and that was exactly the point of the exercise. The boards that were selected were based on a subconscious attraction.

Out of the 15 boards only three or four would end up in the *like* pile. They invariable contained strong clues. It was usually a simple matter to sort through the pictures to discover the connections that would tell us what is was that was creating the attraction. This usually took about twenty minutes and the results left the clients in awe as they understood for the first time what was driving so many of their choices. As often as not, they could immediately see connections that extended well outside the kitchen arena. Not surprisingly, these revelations gave them a new way to look at the many choices ahead (counters, cabinets, appliances, hardware, lighting, flooring, wall tiles).

Getting these results represented a milestone, but they were best applied by closely observing my client's personalities as well as their individual differences in perception.
By way of example, I mention a friend named Joyce who painted the walls and accessorized her master bedroom in intense red colors. If you just said to yourself *"Ouch!"* , I completely understand.

All the literature I have read on color theory indicates that bright red amplifies our feelings, can make us more aggressive, and can even raise our blood pressure. The fast food industry has used it for years because it can also stimulate appetite. But in terms of bedroom color choices, for most of the population, reds would come in dead last. In Joyce's case, 'stimulate' is the key word because, for her, the effect of red is the opposite of the norm. She found the color extremely calming and it helped her to get better sleep. How is that possible, and what does it have to do with understanding her personality?

I'd only met Joyce twice before I warm-heartedly assigned her the moniker *Eight Lane*. She is a high-energy individual, is extremely bright, and has a mind that operates at

lightning speed. Emotionally she might be referred to as high-strung. Trying to keep pace with her is somewhat like trying to cross an eight-lane highway where getting to the other side takes a level of focus, speed and energy – a level of peak performance, that for the average individual can be exhausting. For Joyce however, it is her normal state. It is not too surprising then that a color that would stimulate a normal mortal would actually be calming to someone operating at Joyce's speed. You can see an analogous circumstance in the fact that the stimulant Ritalin is actually prescribed to help some hyperactive patients calm down and be better able to focus.

The point is that the individual preferences may seem bewildering are actually understandable when you probe past the level of the *whats* and focus on the *whys*. In this case it was matching her color preference with her personality traits. Looking at both sides of the equation is essential. Another non-client example comes to mind and I must admit it baffled me for years. It involved my youngest daughter Louise, who was fourteen at the time. It was early evening and she was hurriedly getting dressed to go out with some of her friends. Here is what transpired. From the second floor I heard,

"Dad, what time is it?"

My response was,

"It's close to six."

From Louise,

"Dad, what TIME is it?"

My reply,

"It's about a quarter to six."

Louise then stomped halfway down the stairs to exclaim,

"Dad, I need to know WHAT TIME IT IS!"

I checked my watch and said,

"It is exactly 5:48."

In somewhat of an exasperated huff she said,

"THANK you!!!!"

She then marched back upstairs. Often when I thought about what had happened, I laughed it off as a quirk associated with teenage adolescence. Many years later however, I'd gained a better appreciation for different ways that we communicate and process information. I can see now that she has a need for exactitude and precision that plays a large role in how she navigates the world. This perspective gives her a sense of constancy and safety. The *what* that had made no sense at all to me became crystal clear as soon as I could see the *why*.

I have focused on the importance of listening carefully to pick up strong, positive emotional attachments but this always needs to be seen in the light of individual personality differences (see next chapter). The *emotional meter* can also swing into negative territory and it is every bit as important to catch these signals.

The mantra that I have repeated about clients liking things for the same reasons is just as true for those things that cause fear, discomfort or unease. When I was working with Laura (**What is a "Funk-meter?**) I was pleased with myself because I'd quickly picked up on the strong boundaries that she would need for her personal space and also that I had a ready solution to help her kitchen to feel protective. If I'd only looked a little deeper, I would have seen that she had a strong need for tradition, order and constancy and I could have addressed those needs in a more tactful manner.

Serving design clients is about finding out where they are, where they want to go and helping them get there. This involves listening *between the lines*, understanding the client's

personality, and reshaping the structure of the conversation in order to open up new and magical possibilities.

For all of us, design in any of its guises, sits atop our fundamental desire to mold and reshape our environment in ways that are not only functional but also are pleasing and affirm our sense of self. The essence of these stories is that these environments can not only be reflective of us as individuals but also offer us a sense of joy. In the next chapter I will offer you a way of looking at design patterns and personal preferences that can provide a simplified way to identify your own personal preferences without being overwhelmed by the myriad number of design styles.

29

Patterns and Preferences

My eldest daughter and her husband were just starting the process of designing a new custom home. Having had the opportunity to read early parts of this book, she told me she appreciated the concepts and perspectives but was looking for concrete tools and language that could help her identify her own design tastes and then be able to communicate them clearly to the range of professionals with whom she would be working; namely, architect, builder, kitchen designer and interior designer.

My response was to offer everyday language to outline three, distinct design polarities which you can use to assess where you fit. Each polarity represents a range of preferences, and I detail both ends of the spectrums to make it easier for you to place yourself within the range. I have chosen these parameters because they are applicable across the full range of design styles (e.g., modern, french country, southern colonial, contemporary, etc) and because they encompass the areas in which I have seen clients express both positive and negative emotional connection.

I. Open vs. Closed Design – this category is one that first presented itself whenever I worked with clients on the design of the cabinetry for a home theater or media room; and it always revolved around how the client wanted to treat the sound equipment. Clients either wanted to completely hide all of the equipment (considering it distracting) or they seemed to want to show it off. What was remarkable was that clients were always at one extreme or the other. The typical Bell Curve distribution simply didn't apply.

To allow the equipment to be visible I had to provide cabinetry that was open, but had finished interiors. If we going for concealment, we used retractable panels and doors, speaker cloth panels, motorized lifts, remote sensors – whatever was necessary to minimize the appearance of the sound and video equipment. At the time, I thought this polarity in preference revolved strictly around the issue of the equipment, but there was more involved. I found that my clients exhibited the same phenomenon when it came to cabinets with glass doors and finished interiors. They were either enthused about the glass door option or they were adamantly opposed to it. In the former instance clients often wanted to display dish ware, plates, glasses, etc. In the latter, there was an almost palpable reaction to the thought of someone looking in and seeing what was on the inside of the cabinetry.

The common thread was the emotional undercurrent. I began to get a sense of the larger issue one day when I was working in the kitchen of a Parade of Homes model home.

At the time, art glass inserts for cabinet doors, such as seeded glass or rain glass, were new to the kitchen industry and we had displayed rain glass in two doors of one of our upper cabinets. (See Photo courtesy of Pixabay.com)

Within the first five minutes of the show opening, two pairs of women came through the kitchen and both had exactly the same comment, *"Wow! Glass doors and you can't see inside of the cabinet."*

It wasn't the glass that clients objected to; it was the fact that **people seeing into the cabinets actually left them feeling psychologically exposed.** Once we started offering glass choices that offered a degree of opacity as well as decoration, it was a game changer for many. But greater selection still didn't change basic dichotomy that was driven by wanting to display items in a cabinet and hiding them from view.

The open vs. closed issue also made its appearance whenever I would ask a client if they wanted the area above the upper cabinets to be open or if they wanted to close this

area off with a soffit (dropped ceiling section). Almost always I would hear one of two things; either *"Of course, leave them open above."* or *"Definitely closed. I don't want to have to dust up there!"* Only once have I had a client tell me that they were ambivalent and okay with either option. I may not be the quickest study, but I knew that none of the clients expressing concern about dust would ever get out a step ladder and vacuum cleaner to clean the area on top.

Because their responses were so strong and so quick as to be almost automatic, I realized that the open area above the cabinets was not about dust or cleaning. It was about a design element that could impinge on their personal space. Even though I couldn't understand all of the underlying psychology, I could identify and appreciate the **boundaries that marked their comfort zones.**

This was a new idea, but I saw the pattern repeated with queries about whether or not to include open bookcases to hold cookbooks. Even if my clients wanted to have the cookbooks close by and handy, they often eschewed the idea of having them *seen*. Negative responses were often accompanied by an explanation that the cookbooks wouldn't look good because of their different sizes; but there was also enough emotional content in the answers to let me know that personal space – not personal space per se, but the need for order and symmetry and cleanliness.... was also at issue. The fact that my clients so often responded almost automatically also led me to believe that the concern was operating at a subconscious level.

When I would query clients about things that they wanted to have at counter level the open vs. closed polarity would assert itself again. Their lists of counter-level appliances usually included such things as toaster, coffee pot, mixer, and can opener. Clients were evenly divided on whether or not to include a counter-level cabinet for storing these items (commonly referred to as an *appliance garage*). If my client had a Kitchen-Aid Professional Mixer (especially if it was red in color), they were usually anxious to keep it out and on display. Indeed, some clients treated the mixer more as a decorating accessory for their kitchen and their level of accessorizing might extend to baskets above the upper cabinets, refrigerator magnets, decorative canister sets, and many other items that they felt gave

their kitchens a personal touch. In sharp contrast was a smaller client group who were adamant about wanting nothing showing on the counter; even including cabinetry. In every case where I had a client who wanted their counters completely free of any items, there was strong emotional content in their request. Such requests often came across as non-negotiable and it was easy to see that clutter on the counters was emotionally disturbing. Any sense of clutter (chaos) would register and negatively impact their sense of order and personal space.

Having seen how widespread and rooted the issue of openness could be, I became more observant. It was not just related to individual aspects of the cabinet design, but to the room as a whole. One of the most notable examples was Laura (**What's a Funk-meter?**). In her case openness would be manifest in the vaulted space above the kitchen and even the thought of it left her feeling insecure.

The **desire to protect against emotional discomfort** would also show up when working on island designs. Turning, curving, or bending the island shape to provide greater connection between the chef and others in the room also served in many cases to relieve unease as the chef's cooking area became more well-defined as well as less exposed and open to the room.

This same issue would show up in discussing walkway clearances. The industry rule of thumb is to try for a 42 inch clearance between an island and sink counter, shrinking it to 36 inches if absolutely necessary. In larger kitchen areas however, especially those that can and will accommodate two or more cooks, it is not uncommon for this clearance to range between 48 and 54 inches.

Beside issues of proportion and the establishment of enough width for *passing lanes*, personal space considerations would often enter this arena. As often as not, there was a particular distance past which the client would become uncomfortable. When Kate (**The Cardboard Kitchen**) moved the white cardboard to get two more inches of clearance between the island and the sink she said, *"There! That's perfect!"* When she said this she

was clearly relieved. That small tweak in the distance had released a significant level of psychological stress that was present before she made the change!

We all have different boundaries, but our personal space and its protection are crucially important in our ability to be at ease. When you look through the items above, you may be able to better measure your own needs and be in a position to communicate them to those assisting you.

II. Relaxed vs. Structured Design – When a client can say they have a strong preference for a particular design style, such as southwest, modern, Victorian, etc.; it is sometimes helpful because, for the designer, it will bring up specific lists of associated materials, finishes, textures and color schemes that they will likely find appealing. However, my work with Tom and Nancy **(Finding Malibu)**, proved to me beyond a doubt that latching onto a particular style without critical examination of underlying motivational factors could lead to a failed design. Tom and Nancy really liked everything they saw in a recently-finished Southwest style home, but it was this very attraction that blurred their underlying motivations. Replicating things they had seen or consulting style books would have actually guaranteed I couldn't get the information required. I had to see their existing home, artwork, and personal effects to begin to understand what had appealed to them about the southwest home.

Now, many years and many clients removed, I see that there are fundamental categories that cross style lines and are actually often more helpful when it comes to understanding why you like a particular home, kitchen or style. One of the key elements that Tom and Nancy found appealing was the soft flowing elements that had been incorporated into the home they toured. Everything in the home had been done to maximize visual flow. All interior profiles had been rounded to eliminate any hard edges, color tones were all complementary with no sharp contrasts, and many wall elements exhibited a curvilinear design that created a sense of motion, pulling one's eye along to the next element. We also had incorporated large arrays of tall glass in the exterior walls. There

was little, if anything, to impede their view as they panned from one area to the other or from the interior to the outside. For them this was not just a visual preference but a reflection of their **underlying attraction to movement, flow and change**.

For clients like Tom and Nancy, what best characterized their preference was that they liked design with a relaxed structure; very open and without rigid lines or hard edges. They were at the far end of a spectrum of preference that might find people enamored of Arts-And-Crafts style on the other end. The latter designs are characterized by rectilinear elements (square and rectangles), symmetry and order, and crisp, sharp profiles.

Whenever there was a strong design emphasis on flow and motion, clients like Tom and Nancy would usually exhibit a strong proclivity toward elements of ambiguity and motion. For clients like Laura there was little or no interest, while clients like Ken and Lisa (**Fiestaware**) were strongly attracted to designs that could combine both flowing curved elements that were in juxtaposition to more rigid, rectilinear elements. When inspecting granite slabs with a client, I found those who were tightly focused on slabs with homogeneous color and pattern were often those that were also least likely to be comfortable with designs that suggested change and motion. On the other hand, clients who found themselves going gaga about slabs with wildly flowing patterns almost invariably fell into the other side of the spectrum.

Tom and Nancy, like many with similar design preferences, were also attracted to elements of visual surprise. They liked highly reflective finishes and color accents with intense, saturated colors. In their home, most of the colors were done in blacks, pure white (often referred to as 'designer' or 'refrigerator' white) and achromatic gray (not warm or cold). The accents were done in jewel tones (ruby, sapphire, etc.) to enhance an element of whimsy or contrast. In the dining room, their black lacquer table sat on a wood floor finished with a gray wash. To set the table off, we designed a custom area rug made with black background and jewel-tone accents.

Looking to see where you fall on the spectrum between relaxed and structured design may also provide you with clues as to your desire for constancy. For many clients, these polarities represent only their dominant desire and there is room in the design for disparate elements. In (**Fiestaware**) I found Ken and Lisa had similar preferences to Tom and Nancy. If anything, they were even more open to motion in the design and the use of asymmetry (remember the picture frame that started the ball rolling). In their design, these elements were concentrated in the island elements and were actually amplified by the counterpoint provided by the rectilinear shapes (visual structure) we used with the surrounding cabinetry. A particular design element can often be strengthened by creating juxtaposition with something contrasting. (See Photo Left)

My point is that understanding your dominant preference shouldn't automatically preclude opportunities that can be gained by using contrast in form, color and finish. There are also actually some design elements that carry with them more than one effect depending on your viewing distance.

A good example is a door style that I came to recognize had some unique properties. It was a square, raised panel design and the center panel of the door was delineated with sharp, crisp lines. It offered clients a strong sense of visual structure, especially when viewed from a distance of more five feet. What made it unique, however, was the way that

the center panel transitioned to the frame that held it. The outer edge of the panel was shaped with a sinuous curve, like an ‘S’ that had been stretched. In other words, it was a profiled with a soft, undulating shape. This was significant because as my clients would get closer to the cabinetry, the crisp visual structure would fall away and the softness of the panel design would become dominant. This door allowed clients to enjoy the cabinetry from a distance in a conscious, rational way (strong crisp lines and structure) and yet connect emotionally and unconsciously (feeling the flow and softness) when in close proximity. It all depended upon the viewing distance. (See Photo Below)

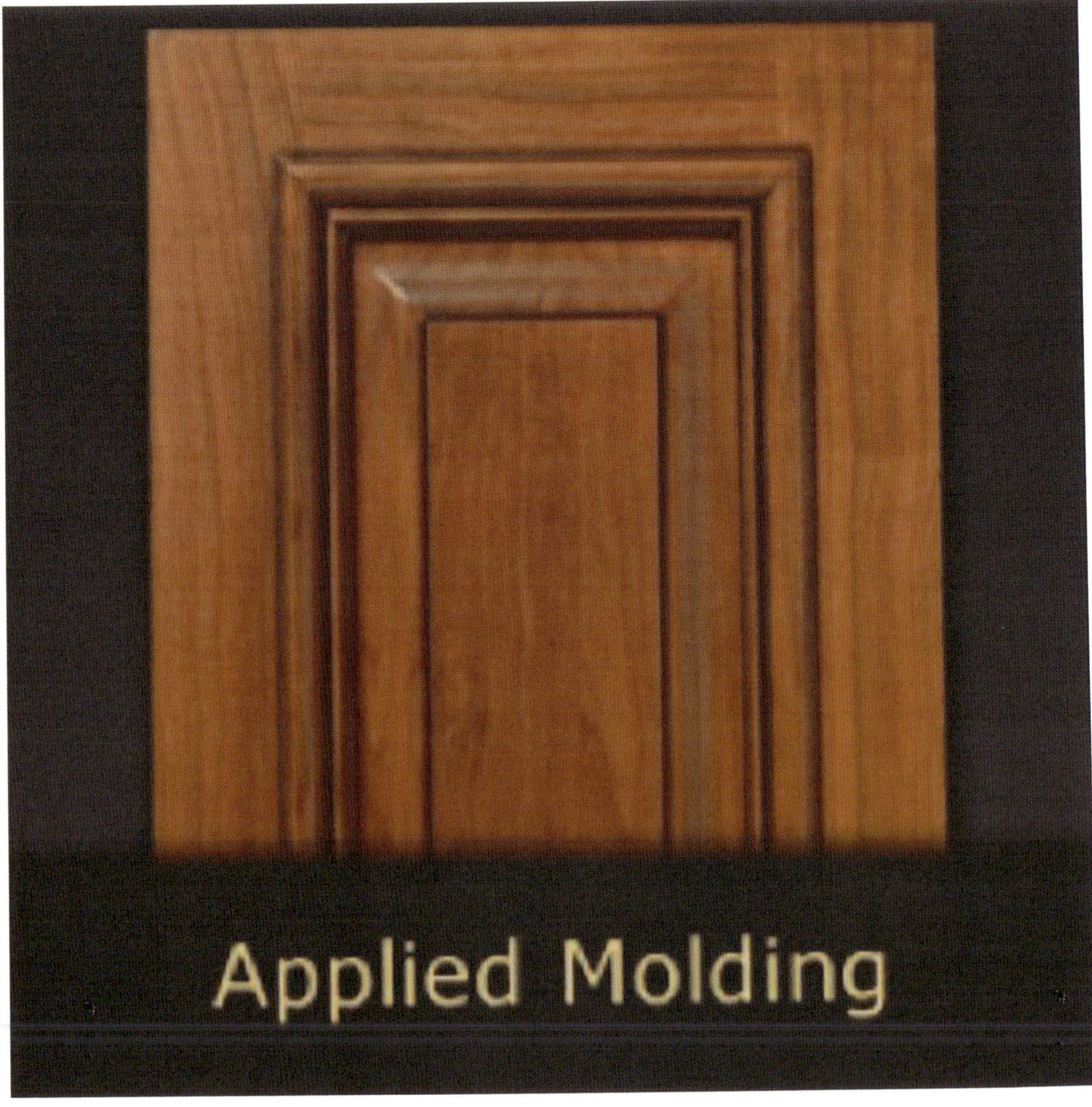

Similar non-cabinet examples abound. In 2001 the rounding and streamlining of cars may have reached its apex when the Ford Taurus came out looking like a jelly bean. It was aerodynamic but had almost NO visual structure. If you compare it to the 2010, Mercedes CL600 streamlining soft elements have not disappeared, but visual structure and connection to the road has returned. The coupe's lines are clearly soft and sleek. It is streamlined and aerodynamic. But look more closely. Along the side door panels is a crease.

The line begins just above the front wheel well and angles gently upward until it flows directly into the curved line of the trunk. Below runs a level line that is centered on the front and rear wheel hubs and runs directly into the lines of the front and rear bumpers. These two lines provide the car with a subtle, yet strong visual structure and as well as a connection to the road. The car is beautifully designed and a joy to look at; but the real sophistication for me is how effortlessly I can float back and forth across the polarities. I can appreciate the car in a rational and emotional way- almost simultaneously.

Working with polarities is useful in illustrating the spectrum across which your preferences will most likely fall. While people looking for soft, relaxed elements can still be attracted to visual structure, looking at both ends of a spectrum is simply a good way to more easily gauge which of your own leanings are dominant. You shouldn't try to average out a ranking for yourself because most of us need a little variety to best suit our needs.

Conscious and unconscious, rational and emotional aspects of our nature co-exist and operate together simultaneously. Finding your own perfect recipes will usually involve the right combination of multiple ingredients and spices.

It has been said that "*the emotional tail wags the rational dog*" (Jonathan Haidt). That is true more often that we would like to admit, but few would disagree that our decisions regarding décor and personal purchases are richly infused with both rational and emotional components. My caveat to you is that while you are looking for your own answers, as you try to grasp some of the emotional or subconscious components, think of yourself as a psychological detective who will never actually see his quarry but can pick up enough clues along the way to begin to put together a decent profile.

III. **Simple vs. Complex Design** – Early in the book I mention that a customer shared a useful perception about textured finishes, like oil-rubbed bronze. She said that they were the ones that had the power to draw you in emotionally. She was absolutely right, but years past before I could understand the underlying factors that made this so or see the broader ramifications.

There is actually a group of words that describe those items most likely to connect with us on an emotional versus rational level and they cover issues of form, material, color and finish.

- **Textured** – the dimpled cabinet knob, the nubby fabric, the wire brushed wood, the seedy glass cabinet insert and pooled drywall finishes that mimic plaster; all have a depth that we can experience both visually and tactilely.
- **Patterned** – character woods like birds-eye maple, swirl-finished stainless, pin wale fabric, herringbone brickwork, slatted window shades all exhibit visually patterning.
- **Blended** – colors that are not saturated but blended into tints or shades by adding white or black; lacquers that have been blended with color, wood inlays, tweed fabric, etc.

- **Layered** – Crown moulding assemblies with dental, rope or egg-and-dart elements; raised panel cabinet fronts, multi-layered counter edges, cabinet arrangements that exhibit changes in depth and height, carved onlay moldings (often wooden scrollwork attached to the face of other woodwork), fabric appliqués or piping, etc.

All of these elements appear to different degree in designs that move from simplicity to complexity. At each end of the spectrum are polar opposites and both extremes are represented in the book by two chapters - (**The Boardroom)** and (**The Birthday Gift**). To compare and contrast:

- **Textured** – All of the surfaces in the 'Boardroom' kitchen were sleek with no texture. This included the appliances (stainless but not brushed), walls with a smooth finish, appliances (black/black glass), hardware (none), counters (homogenous, polished granite), doors slab with a slight bevel.

In contrast, the 'Birthday' kitchen had its roots in Tuscan style, so pattern abounded almost everywhere. The floor tile had chiseled edges, the walls had a pooled texture, cabinet hardware was oil-rubbed bronze, cabinet glass inserts used a seedy glass, cabinet moldings were fluted or otherwise highly-profiled, the tile on the wall splash was all done in a tumbled marble, the tile mural above the stove was outlined in a border tile with a rope moulding.

- **Patterned** – In the 'Boardroom' kitchen there were no patterns anywhere.

In the 'Birthday' kitchen the stainless steel on the appliances was brushed (this is a pattern and a texture), the floor tiles had six different sizes and shapes that were laid in a Versailles pattern, the mural above the stove was a wine country image painted onto tumbled marble tiles, the granite counter edges had a cascading pattern (ogee over bullnose), and the hardware pulls for the cabinets had a turned-rope detail.

- **Blended** – In the 'Boardroom' kitchen there were no muted colors. The mauve on the cabinetry was saturated, the black on the kitchen granite counters was pure, and the gray in the carpeting was achromatic (neither warm nor cold). The only exception was some of the coloration in the granite top used on the custom dining table.

In the 'Birthday' kitchen there were no saturated colors. The walls were a warm, off-white (Benjamin-Moore 'mascarpone'), the cabinetry had a *wash* finish in an off-white paint color, overlaid with a light brown glaze; all of the cabinet hardware was oil-rubbed bronze, the floor tile was finished in a mottled earth tones.

- **Layered** – In the 'Boardroom' kitchen there was no layering at all. All the surfaces were flush and smooth. All of the upper and lower cabinetry had uniform height and depth.

  In the 'Birthday' kitchen layering was evident almost everywhere. The tile rope molding used for the mural was proud (in front) of the field tile, the range and flanking pilasters were pulled forward 2.5 inches, the upper cabinetry had two depth changes at the built-in microwave and at a glass door cabinet at the sink (which also had an open, plate rack element below), the crown moulding was a multiple assembly; an open, decorative upper cabinet was used above the refrigerator to minimize mass, a profiled light rail was used under all the upper cabinetry to screen the under-cabinet lighting, and furniture base (proud of the cabinet front rather than recessed) was used on the bottom of the tall pantry cabinet to give it a furniture look.

My clients for the 'Boardroom' kitchen were a good example of one end of the spectrum. They were both business organizational consultants and they were accustomed to seeing things in fixed, clearly analytical patterns. It is not so much that they viewed everything in black and white, but they were most comfortable when the reality around them could be perceived and understood in clearly defined conceptual boxes. Creating a kitchen design with such visual simplicity brought with it a kind of purity, because it could so easily be appreciated in a conscious, rational manner. There was a real order about the design. It exuded a sense of clarity; there was no ambiguity that muted elements, asymmetry or patterning might point toward. I am not suggesting that these clients were so naïve as to think that life is not full of uncertainty. I am just describing their preferred way of looking at things.

Robin, the owner of the 'birthday' kitchen ran a custom publishing business for higher-end magazines. Beside her business acumen, her work required a finely-tuned creative sensibility. It was not at all surprising that she would be most comfortable being immersed in and emotionally drawn into the various elements of her kitchen. Before we ever started work, I noticed that her drapes, rugs, art and furniture all exhibited the characteristic at the other end of the spectrum. Running her business required a keen understanding of demographics and analytics, but putting out appealing life-style magazines required a using her creativity to seek emotional connections with the readers.

The preferences of both clients are on the far sides of the spectrum and there are many clients who are looking for designs that combine both elements. More and more of my contemporary clients have asked to use natural materials as well as finishes that have considerable depth. In these cases, such elements are usually selected specifically to create a counterpoint to the dominant theme. In summary, to best understand why you like the things you do:

- **Examine your feelings about open and closed elements to gain a better sense of what is required for you to create a comfortable personal space.**

- **Look at relaxed and structured design elements to begin to gauge the role constancy, ambiguity and change may play.**

- **Look at elements of simplicity and complexity to shed light on whether you will be most comfortable with elements that require a cerebral appreciation (I like it) or a visceral reaction (Ooohh), how it looks vs. how it feels.**

The clues to your emotional connections and preferences are all around you. They hide in plain sight from you because they are rooted in your subconscious mind. When do you feel hemmed in? When are things too open for you to feel comfortable? How strongly do

you relate to soft forms and how much visual structure do you need before it is too much or too rigid? How comforting is simplicity before it becomes dull or boring and how much complexity will you find appealing before it becomes fussy or formal? You will find the answers already reflected in your furniture styles, car choices, clothing, art, watches and other accessories; almost everywhere you look.

Find the things that will meet both your rational and emotional needs and you will unlock the key to making your kitchen your favorite place to be.

Part Four - The *Remodel Roadmap*

1.

30

Remodel Stages

Hopefully you are now excited about your potential to go beyond good function and appearance to the creation of a kitchen/living platform that can offer you a sense of personal delight and improved social connectedness. Developing a clear vision of what you want to achieve in your kitchen is an essential starting point, but bringing it into reality is another matter altogether. We all love to look over *Before* and *After* pictures, but how do you actually get from one to the other. As a designer and builder, I have helped many clients to establish their vision and then implement it in a fashion that was smooth and enjoyable. Now I hope to help you do the same.

For those of you who are about to embark on a more complex kitchen remodel (one that involves cabinet replacement, permits and a contractor), there is a pressing need for guidance beyond what I have found to date in any books, articles, or TV/Cable shows. Key elements are missing in even the best material. Moreover, you will be bombarded with information from so many sides that you will quickly experience ***information overload***.

This section is designed to provide you with the knowledge, context and perspective you need to navigate your remodel process. As much as possible, the pictures and examples used in illustration will be taken from stories you have already read. The remodel process is going to require your time and commitment and there will be some surprises along the way. But be assured, with the right preparation, the process can be fun and most of the more common pitfalls and wrong turns can be avoided.

No two kitchen remodels are identical but all of them pass through the stages shown below.

Stage 1 - Planning: where preliminary and final budgets are prepared, products selected, vendors and team selected, designs finalized, funding secured, contracts signed.

Stage 2 – Pre-Construction: where preparations are made to get your kitchen ready to be remodeled, and to get you and your family ready to minimize the disruption that comes with the process.

Stage 3- Construction: the permit is posted and work commences.

1. ***Demo*** – disconnecting and removing old appliances, cabinetry, counters, flooring, etc.

2. ***Rough-in*** - modifying the plumbing, heating, and electrical systems to match the new design requirements

3. ***Finish*** activities including installing all new cabinets, flooring, appliances, finish painting, etc.

Stage 4 – Post Construction: Where you inspect the remodeled space to assure everything is just as you want it. This inevitably creates a punch list, which is a list of items needing to be done for the job to be completed to your expectations.

Careful and thorough planning is the single most important factor in managing a smooth and successful outcome. The benefit of taking the time to do your homework upfront cannot be overestimated. There will be more than enough to occupy your time once construction commences. Waiting to make basic decisions almost always leads to unnecessary expense and frustration. The adage that says, ***"Failing to plan is planning to fail."*** couldn't be more apt than in the remodel context.

In this phase there are 12 fundamental questions you and almost everyone will ask. Each of the following chapters is devoted to just one question and they are arranged in the order in which they will arise. I have inserted content that is appropriate for each question, but the material is often applicable across a broader context.

31

Should I Remodel or Move?

The first step toward achieving the kitchen you desire is to decide whether it makes sense to remodel your existing kitchen or whether you should think about a different home where the kitchen you want is already available. In the first chapter **(Musical Chairs)**, Sean and Ellen are contemplating an extensive remodel of their home. The first question they were tackling wasn't "Where do I Start?", but the more fundamental question was whether getting what they wanted (a bedroom for their older daughter and a larger kitchen) would be possible without moving to a larger and newer home. When I first met them they had already spent a considerable amount of time looking at alternatives.

This early look at the remodel versus move alternatives was something I found many of my remodel clients wrestled with. Being able to weigh the two investment options (moving or remodeling) can provide you with a broader perspective and allow you to make more informed decisions. Here is a review of the key issues.

Desirability and Feasibility – These two concepts go hand in hand and each should be given significant attention. Most clients start by enumerating their dislikes and work forward to the desired items. The dislike list includes many of the following:

1. The kitchen is dysfunctional due to a shortage of storage and counter space or poor design placements.
2. As a social gathering area, the kitchen is failing to meet the needs of family and friends.

3. Whether or not the look is dated or passé, the appearance and feel of the kitchen is no longer a fit for the owner.

4. The age of the current kitchen is such that some replacement work is going to be required soon (appliances wearing out, sinks or counters chipped, flooring worn, cabinet parts failing, finishes starting to look worn and shabby).

5. Enough kitchens in the neighborhood have upgraded that the current home can no longer be marketed and sold without incurring a lower sale price, longer selling period or both.

Items #4 and #5 above point out that a **decision to do nothing is not without some potential cost**. Eventually all things wear out and have to be replaced and buyer's evolving expectations about look, features and finish eventually make yesterday's choices seem obsolete and undesirable. Even if you can deal with the emotional issues involved with items # 1, 2, and 3, who wants to find themselves in the position of needing to remodel in order to sell to someone else? Here we move beyond what we dislike in our existing kitchen.

1. Can I find what I am looking for in another new or existing home?

2. If I can find it, what are the dollar costs associated with the new purchase, the sale of the current home, moving and decorating expense?

3. What are the intangible costs associated with a move that will entail new schools, doctors and new neighbors?

4. Can my existing kitchen be remodeled to meet my needs?

5. What will the remodeling costs be?

6. At what point will the remodel be an over-improvement for the neighborhood?

7. What percentage of my expenditures can I expect to recover upon future resale?

8. Will I encounter a cost from doing nothing if I find myself with a lower sales valuation than other neighboring homes that have already upgraded?

9. If I upgrade, how long do I expect to be in the home and will that period provide me with a good balance between enjoying the improvements and increasing valuation?

Having good data is valuable in all investment decisions, and the remodel or move decision is no exception. We would like to think we can recover all of improvement costs when and if we need to sell the house, but that is probably not a realistic expectation. It certainly depends on the amount invested in your new kitchen and home relative to those of your neighbors (or competing properties). Before you finalize your thinking about how much value your kitchen remodel can add to your home, I recommend you seek out the one or two real estate agents who concentrate their efforts and have the most listings in your neighborhood. Over the years these agents are likely to have gained the kind of in-depth knowledge that can be enormously helpful as you assess what is an appropriate amount to invest and how it will position your property in comparison with other homes. This shouldn't cost you anything because demonstrating their knowledge and expertise to you is an effective way for these agents to encourage a future listing. Your questions to these local experts might include several of the following:

1. If my home were on the market today, what would it be worth and what items would have to be taken care of immediately?

2. If my home were to be on the market in 3-5 years, what improvements might I make today that will maximize the value of my home and protect it from obsolescence?

3. What percentage of homes in my areas have already undergone remodeling in the kitchen and how extensive was the work?

4. Of the homes already remodeled, what have been the best and the worst?

5. In general, if I am going to remodel my kitchen, how can I find the best balance between spending too much and too little?

6. Will an effective remodel make my home attractive to buyers who would otherwise only look at new homes? If so, what are new home builders offering in their kitchens that might influence my own plans?

Assessing your reasons for wanting to remodel and determining how much you can spend before over-improving for the neighborhood is a good start.

32

How Much Can I Afford?

If you are planning on paying for your remodel from cash that you have on hand you can probably skip the information below. However, if you are going to consider financing either part or all of the cost you can find a *budget worksheet* to help you estimate how much you can borrow by going to www.nari.org/homeowners and then clicking 'worksheet' in the drop-down menu.

The key factors will be how much your total debt expense is in relation to your income and what percentage housing expense represent (as represented as principal, interest, taxes and insurance – PITI). This is sponsored by the National Association of the Remodeling Industry. This is not a substitute for sitting down with your own lender, but will help you quickly size up the parameters.

While going through this exercise you may find it a good time to look forward 3-5 years to identify other potential large expenditures such as car, roofing, HVAC, tuition, etc.

33

How Much Should it Cost?

You've assessed moving versus remodeling, decided remodeling makes sense, and you have an idea of what you can or want to spend; so now it is on to the planning and budgeting process. Let's presume you have pulled together a compilation of items you like. You have photos you've taken, clippings from magazines, idea books you have assembled with online sources such as www.houzz.com and www.kitchen-design-ideas.org. You will discover quickly there are just a few items that comprise the largest portion of your budget – cabinetry, appliances, flooring, and countertops.

Robin's project (**The Birthday Gift**) is a good prototype. Here is how the costs broke out for the major items. Each item includes the material and installation costs.

Cost Item	% of Total Cost
Cabinetry	36.6%
Appliances	21.0%
Granite Tops	10.8%
Floor Tile	6.9%
Backsplash Tile	7.7%
(Subtotal)	**83%**

Learning what an average cost is for the area in which you live is just a few clicks away. Every year, Realtor Magazine, in conjunction with the National Association of

Realtors, publishes a survey that presents national and regional data on the most effective remodel projects, their average costs as well as estimates of the value that can be recouped.

According to Remodeling 2012-13 Cost vs. Value Report (www.costvsvalue.com), the average investment recapture for a major kitchen remodel in a midrange home was 74.2%. This is based upon an average cost of $59,909 and an average recapture value of $40,732. But area of the country as well as level of remodel (higher-end versus mid-range) make the numbers vary significantly. For instance, the strongest overall recapture is in the Pacific area of the country where the average cost is $62,163 and the recapture is 89% at $55,020 versus a similar mid-range remodel in the West North Central area around Sioux Fall, SD, Wichita, KS and Minneapolis where a project costing $54,907 only recovers 62% at $33,805. The report can be downloaded for free at the site listed above and it is also available as a free I-Phone app (https://itunes.apple.com).

If you start looking for costs by category, just a little time online can help you estimate appliance costs. Just a short trip to a big-box store will quickly help you gauge flooring and countertop expense. The item that will require more of your time and at least a preliminary design is cabinetry. Cabinetry is not only the largest overall expense, but it is also where the available information is not cut and dried. You can't get a sense of the cost until you have a fairly good idea of what you want or need based on an initial design. It is also an area where seemingly small changes can take a modest per box cost and multiply it.

Because it is so tempting to jump right into cabinet pricing, you need to know it is quite different from any other item in your budget. In choosing cabinets you will encounter pricing variations well outside the norm of your everyday experience. For example, by the time we reach the age where we will be considering a kitchen remodel, most of us have already purchased one or two cars. Imagine then, if you had planned to by a Ford Fusion and knew the base model pricing of $21,970 (MSRP) could increase as much as 69% if you upgraded to a fully-loaded (i.e. with all available options and extras) Fusion Titanium. How might you feel if your final price actually climbed as high as $131,400 and was closer to the upper price range of a BMW 500 series?

This situation sounds contrived, but it happens every day in the cabinet business. This is because, in every cabinet line, except the very low end, the range between basic (function) and fully-loaded (complex "furniture" design, custom features and finishes) is **600% or more.** I call it the **Six 'X' factor.**

I will use a pantry cabinet to show you what can happen when it morphs into a look that is more akin to its *rich uncle*, the armoire. The picture on the left shows your basic pantry cabinet. The width is 30" and the height is 72". The depth is 12" and there are four shelves, one of which is fixed. The doors are of slab construction (no frame and center panel).

The photo below shows the center part of a custom-designed furniture element (**The $6.5 Million Dollar Fixer-upper**); the flanking bookcases have been cropped out). This actually consists of two cabinets, one stacked above the other. The two cases alone would take us to 2X, but both of these cabinets have finished wood interiors, they are a premium wood specie (cherry), and they have an increased depth of 21". The lower cabinet has raised panel rather than slab doors and the upper cabinet has custom arched, glass doors. The doors in both cabinets are on retractable hardware that allows them to be slid back out of sight once they are opened.

If you consider that most manufacturers charge premiums of 50% for finished interiors, 25% for increased depth, and 15% for cherry vs. oak; you can see that the price of these two cabinets is closer to 4X. If you add in the wood desk top in the center and the custom doors and hardware, you jump to 6X. Finally, adding in the frieze molding at the top, the crown molding above, the two pilasters on each side with fluted columns and fluted bun feet, the clear glass shelving or the interior lighting that was in the upper section and this assembly is now well

over 12X. Because this cabinet's installation cost is about seven times that of the basic cabinet, there is even more of a difference. With a custom finish with glazing and distressing the difference would go higher still.

Even with simple base cabinets the same thing can happen. When you start with a base cabinet with one drawer and then change it to a four-drawer cabinet the cost will usually go up 50%. Upgrade those drawers from melamine to wood with dovetail joints, upgrade the glides from ¾" extension on nylon rollers to full-extension on ball bearings with a soft-close feature and you move to 3X. Upgrade the drawer heads from slab to 5-piece construction (four-sided frame with a raised center panel) and then upgrade the finish and wood specie and you will be close to 5X. Add in some custom inserts in the drawers (for specialized storage) and give the base either a custom depth or width and you are at 6X or more. What is different here is the fact that the pricing jump from Chevy to Mercedes can happen within the same product line!

Because the **Six 'X' factor** is always present, please don't let anyone put into your head the idea cabinetry can be priced with any accuracy based upon the number of lineal feet. Your budget is always a constraining factor, but knowing up front the full range of price fluctuation that is inherent in the cabinetry business is an important. Measuring your price spread by the 15% premium you see when changing from oak to cherry does not begin to prepare you for what happens when you go from basic storage all the way to fine furniture. **Forewarned is forearmed.**

34

How Do I Choose a Kitchen Designer?

At this preliminary stage you need to have a design in place in order to get pricing. Unless you are using a designer who works independently, you will find yourself immersed in product consideration long before you have the information and knowledge needed to make a good decision. You will probably have spent so much time with the designer helping you that you feel guilty about talking with other suppliers. Looking at cabinetry is exciting and it is hard to see the **choice of designer and the choice of product as separate and important decisions.**

Kitchen design will typically be found as a separate service or in tandem with the offer of cabinets. Kitchen designers with extensive cabinet experience have an advantage in that they are always thinking at the total kitchen level – not just cabinets. Regardless, when you have made your final choice of designer, you are going to want someone who can create a comprehensive plan for all participants in the project to understand.

You can assess local kitchen design resources through Angie's List, asking for referrals, or looking on Google for other reviews. In any event a good deal of the decision should be based on how well you feel your potential kitchen designer understands what you are trying to achieve.

If you are going to choose a designer employed by a cabinet vendor, you choice will hinge strongly on what cabinet manufacturers they represent and you should pre-qualify the cabinet manufacturer, the supplier and the designer before making your choice. Whether or not you choose a cabinet supplier from a kitchen designer's line, a big box store, a small custom shop, or a factory outlet these same five factors still apply:

1. Supplier

a. How long have they been doing business?

b. What is the average cost of their kitchen remodels?

c. What is the full-range of services they provide? (countertops, cabinets, installation, design, or even end-to-end turnkey service)

d. What testimonials or web-based assessments can they provide to demonstrate their success in meeting client needs? Portfolio? Angie's list?

e. For the smaller cabinet dealer, can the organization carry on if the owner is incapacitated by injury or illness?

f. What supplier or other business references can they provide?

g. What percentage of their workforce are employees rather than independent contractors and what is the average length of employment?

h. Can they provide you with an insurance certificate to verify comprehensive coverage for personal liability and property damage, auto insurance (if they deliver), and workman's compensation?

i. What are their professional associations (e.g. National Kitchen & Bath Association)?

j. Will you be able to visit an on-going job before making your own decision?

2. Manufacturer

a. How long has your supplier carried this line?

b. What warranty does this manufacturer offer?

c. Has the supplier encountered situations where the manufacturer didn't stand behind their product and what was the outcome?

d. How long has the manufacturer been in business?

e. What does your supplier consider to be the manufacturer's strengths and weaknesses?

3. Designer*

a. What is the level of experience of your designer? Do they have professional certifications or awards?

b. How familiar is your designer with your cabinet line and how many jobs have they worked on?

c. Is your designer working on commission and/or a percentage of the job's profitability?

d. Will there be a fixed charge for design drawings and if you don't like the design or the costs too far exceed the budget you established up front, what are your options if there is a non-refundable fee? Will you get to keep the drawings?

e. Will your designer be responsible for taking field measurements?

f. Will your designer come out to your home to better understand your home and décor?

*If you are working with a big-box store you may likely find yourself working with a project specialist in addition to your kitchen designer. This person is the liaison with the general contractor for the job and will also be assisting you with product selections.

4. Cabinet Orderer (*not an actual job title*)

a. Who will be putting together your cabinet order and what is their track record for creating complete and correct orders?

b. Will your cabinet order be checked and verified by a manager or owner before it is released to the manufacturer?

c. After the order is sent to the plant, will an acknowledgement be required and if so, who will sign off?

d. What is drawn and what is required in the field often do not match well. Is there someone assisting that has the field experience required to ensure a smooth transition on your job?

5. Cabinet Installer(s)

a. Who will be installing your job and what is their level of experience and expertise? Are they equally skilled in the installation of framed and frameless cabinets?

b. Are they employees or independent contractors?

c. How long have they worked with or for your supplier?

d. Will they be unloading the cabinets and are they responsible for checking for completeness of the order and as well as shipping damage?

e. Do they have previous experience installing your choice of cabinetry?

Compensation for your kitchen designer will be based largely on an hourly rate of pay if you are working with a big-box store (no direct charge to you). If you are working with an independent dealer, it is much more likely your designer will be receiving mostly commission income and the percentage received will usually track the profitability of your job as well as the yearly sales volume of the designer.

With an independent dealer you may find that a non-refundable design deposit is required. You also may find that the drawings will not be turned over to you until and unless you place your cabinet order. The issue is that your designer cannot work for free. You should be expect only preliminary design and product assistance until you are ready to commit to a design deposit or a purchase.

Your other option is to start your design work with an independent designer. This has several advantages:

- By separating the design function from vendor and product selection you can narrow your focus and give yourself time to ease into the other area.
- Your designer will definitely want to come to your home to see your decor and understand how you live and what you like. They are much more

likely to be able to see the larger living area instead of just the cabinet area.

- Since you are paying them directly, you are more likely to receive a higher level of effort and you will know their compensation is tied entirely to your satisfaction with their work and not to the cabinet sale.

If you opt to start with a vendor, neither the big-box or dealer model is inherently prejudicial to your own interests. More advanced designers gravitate away from the big-box because they are seeking more challenge and because they can make much more money by working with a larger percentage of higher-end projects. They are also willing to invest in the training and effort that this requires. In either case, and regardless of how many lines are being offered, all designers know they can only be knowledgeable in three or four; and therefore they tend to focus on those cabinet lines they like best (e.g. better and more complete electronic design catalogue, better factory assistance, easier ordering, faster lead times for parts, etc.).

Whomever you choose, the better and more detailed the drawings and specifications, the more likely you will end up with what you expect and hope. The cabinet industry has software that allows for a high level of detail and specification, including flooring appliances, lighting, etc. These 2, and 3-D drawings of your new kitchen can be tremendous visual aids and they can form the basis of your contract with your supplier. On any complicated project however, these drawings are not detailed enough for installers to know how something is to be constructed or for the factory to know what parts need to be ordered. This requires what are called *shop drawings* or *install drawings.* These provide a greater level of detail. Below is a hand drawing from Robin's job illustrating the detail behind the *stacked* crown molding.

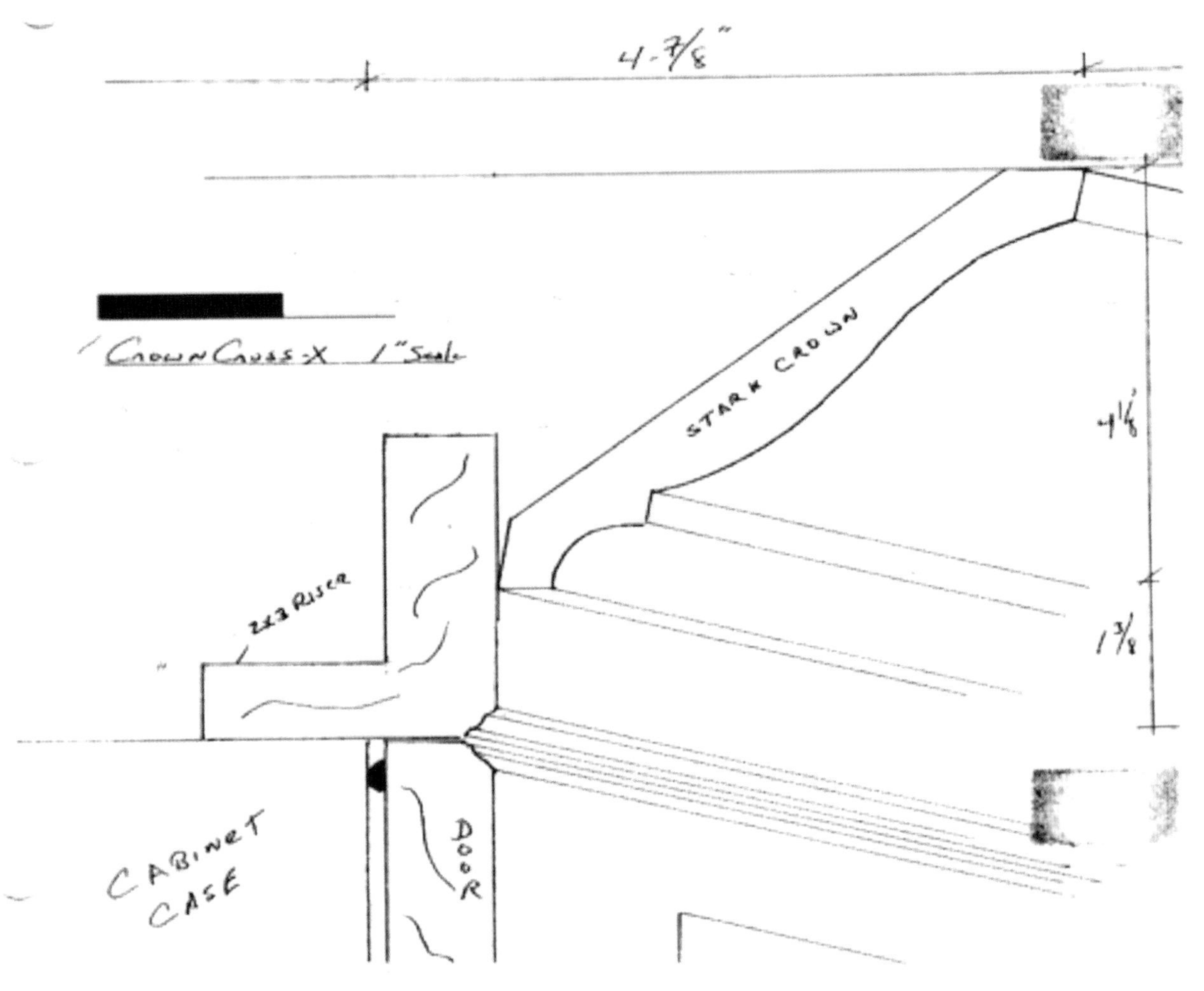

As you are selecting the designer you want to work with, ask to see examples of these drawings. What is important is that there is a certain amount of **field experience and construction knowledge required to accurately order and detail a complex job**. If this knowledge and experience is missing and your designer is thinking the order can be handled with standard drawing software, you will likely have ordering errors. **Designing and ordering are different skill sets** and for the latter you have to be able to construct the design in detail in your head. Without a fair amount of field experience to tell you what works and what does not, this is nearly impossible. This is why many dealers will have

orders double-checked by a manager before the order is released. Ordering mistakes can actually shut down the progress of a job.

Your choice of a cabinet vendor and designer will most likely determine who will be installing your cabinets. Here are some additional points to consider:

- Being able to put together the design in your head is also something every good installer of frameless cabinets can do. The tolerances are small (1/8" between doors), so the placement of cabinets and fillers (spacers) needs to be worked out before installation is begun. With framed cabinets there are usually large margins for error so it is all too common for installers to just start on one end and begin working their way down the wall. This difference is important because **if your cabinets are going to be of frameless construction you need your installers to have the requisite skill and experience.**

- If you have an opportunity to **visit an on-going job**, try to see one in the process of being installed. Even if you know nothing at all about cabinet installations, your visit should provide you with important information about the level of expertise you should expect. **Simply observing the body language of the installers as they handle the cabinetry will tell you whether they are moving boxes or handling fine furniture.** Because people treat these very differently the installer's actions will speak clearly. Shelves, doors and drawers are normally removed from the cabinet cases prior to installation. Note carefully if these items are being protected from dirt and grit.

The best installers tend to see themselves as finish carpenters rather than box installers. Being able to apply meticulous care to achieve the higher level of precision required is a large part of the psychological reward they receive from their work. A box

installer can too often be a guy with a drill and a screw gun and a blow-and-go focus on how many cabinets he can set in a day (piece rate). The finish or *trim* carpenter is more likely to be skilled with a full-range of tools and be competent in installing complex crown moldings or other such assemblies. The focus on workmanship and quality over quantity usually translates into their **work sites being very clean and their tools and materials well organized.** A casual observer will immediately see the difference.

- **Measurement of your job** to gather accurate dimensions is one of the most important aspects in the success of your project. It involves measurement of walls, doors, windows, ceiling and window heights and a trained eye to anticipate design problems in advance. There should be two measurements. The first will provide your designer with the information necessary to create a design that meets your requirements. Once a design is agreed upon, a **second measurement should be done** to ensure there were no mistakes the first time and to review the actual site conditions as they relate to the new design. With drawings in hand, the chance of the catching a potential problem early is greatly enhanced; and fixing problems at this stage can be done on paper without delays, frustration and expense. More often than not, this second measurement is done by a trained installer.

35

What Do I Need to Know about Cabinetry?

Cabinetry will represent a large portion of your entire remodel budget, it is the item most difficult to change, its life cycle will exceed most other items, and visually (in terms of wall space) it will represent a high proportion of what you see (often 50-60%). As you saw with the explanation of the Six 'X' factor, this is also an area with potential for wide price vacillations. Protecting yourself from spending too little, too much, or just too much in the wrong place is a bewildering challenge. This becomes even harder in practice because the more *experts* you talk to the more you will encounter conflicting claims.

I want to provide you an overview based on my experience with 30 different cabinet lines. This won't make you an expert. You will still need to find a pro you trust. This broader knowledge, however, should help you in several ways:

- **You'll be better able to evaluate the expertise of the designers and the quality of the product you are considering.**
- **You will present yourself as an *informed consumer* and will automatically receive a higher level of service and respect from those you are working with. You'll have a well-rounded knowledge of the range of features and options you should be considering. ***

*This is only if you use your knowledge to ask better questions and to better evaluate the information you are given. The person you are working with

will enjoy using their expertise to guide you; but if they think you are flaunting your knowledge they are likely to turn away quickly

Almost all cabinet manufacturers produce their own cabinet cases (sometimes referred to as the box or the carcass). **At the low end,** it is common to see cabinet sides and shelves made out of particle board or medium density fiberboard (MDF). The thickness ranges from 3/8 to 1/2". These are finished with vinyl-coated paper and the case is assembled using plastic fittings and either glue or staples. The doors have narrow wooden frames and the center panels are either flat or they have a raised, hollow core covered with a wood veneer or thermo-foil plastic. Specialized cabinetry is not available, size changes are not allowed, and there is usually a limited offering of moldings. Solid wood elements, when used, are going to be of a lower grade (i.e. more knots, mineral streaks, grain variations, discoloration). If the doors are of solid wood, the vertical staves that make up the center panel of the door will be greater in number to compensate for the fact that the wood has a lower level of dimensional stability. The parts that make up the drawer box will usually be held together with staples and glue and the finished drawer face will be used as front part of the drawer box. The drawer glide hardware will usually consist of a single, center track and nylon and metal rail system. Finishes applied to exposed solid wood will be of a lower quality with fewer coats.

In contrast to the cases, **few cabinet manufacturers actually make their doors and drawer fronts.** Making these parts is a separate business that is dominated by just a few players. They grade their product based upon the quality of the wood used. One of the largest suppliers uses their best grades of wood to make up their "A" doors, the next best "B" and what is left over is used to make the doors and drawer fronts you are likely to find on the lower- end cabinets just described.

You will hear a refrain that **solid wood cabinets** are much better than "cheap" particle board or fiberboard cabinetry. The fact is this is a yes and no issue. There aren't many cabinet manufacturers still using particle board in their construction, but MDF or fiberboard is found at both the low and high end of the product range. It is available in a

variety of densities and there is a large difference in quality between the two extremes. So, solid wood construction is almost always stronger and therefore better than the lower-end MDF product. At the upper end however the difference in quality is negligible. In terms of the perception of quality, the one bad apple (at the low end of MDF) has spoiled the whole bunch. The resulting confusion has afflicted cabinet dealers and designers as much as it has the consumer.

Cabinet manufacturers also do not make the internal hardware used in their products (cabinet hinges and drawer glides). These are supplied by just a few suppliers (most notably Blum), the features offered are fairly similar, and the warranties are usually "lifetime". Specialized interior cabinet fitments (Trash bins, lazy-susans, chrome rollouts, spice drawer inserts, etc.) are also outsourced to one or two vendors (e.g. Rev-a-Shelf).

At the upper end of the cabinetry range you will find all of the materials used will be of the highest grade. Shelving will always be ¾" thick, cabinet sides will be 5/8" or 3/4" in thickness, construction will focus on dovetail joinery, wood dowels or mortising of parts, rather than screws and glue and there won't be any staples used anywhere. Depth, width and height will all be easily customized, the range of offerings in terms of species and specialty finishes (crackling, washes, multiple levels of distressing, etc.) will be matched with a full complement of moldings and accessories. Lead times will be longer and the pricing will be higher. One of my manufacturers made their own doors; grading wood that was purchased from select mills. To get the quality, consistency and control they wanted, they even narrowed their purchases to select species that were grown and harvested under the same conditions.

Steering away from the low and upper ends, **most consumers find themselves in the middle**. In this range there are many good manufacturers of semi-custom lines where you have a wide range of high-value product from which to choose. Within any line, understanding the cabinetry sub-categories can help you navigate your way to the best value:

1. **Wood specie** – In stained finishes, most lines offer several species at the same price, with a few others as an upgrade. The most common upgrade is cherry and it is usually 12-15% more than a standard like oak or maple. . Most lines will offer painted as well as stained finishes. These are more expensive because of the added time and labor involved. The underlying material is usually a white wood such as poplar or maple. If you are looking for a finish done in a high-gloss polyester, the substrate will almost always be a MDF core because its smooth finish offers the least chance of telegraphing any irregularities to the finished surface.

2. **Door styles** tend to be of two types of construction. One is slab and the other is "5-piece". The latter always consists of a center panel surrounded by a picture frame of wood (2 vertical stiles and 2 horizontal rails). A raised -panel door is a 5-piece construction whose center panel is raised in the center. It is made from 4-5 pieces of solid wood that have been glued together. (look closely and you will see the grain/color variations). Your standard door is usually a flat, veneered center panel (e.g. shaker door style). Selecting a raised panel option will usually add at least 10% to your cabinet cost and if you opt to have drawer fronts with this option, the cost could easily go up another 5% (this is not true for thermo-foil cabinetry but I do not recommend this kind of cabinet for the kitchen because it does not hold up to wear and abrasion. Heat can also mar or destroy the finish).

Before you order your cabinetry, **always order a sample door from the manufacturer**. This gives you the best representation of what you will receive. Showroom displays may be dated and not accurately reflect current finishing methods. You may find exception to this rule if you are ordering cherry. The reason is any new cherry product, sample door or entire kitchen, will most assuredly NOT look like the cabinets in the showroom. **Cherry darkens as it ages and a significant difference can be seen in just a matter of weeks.** Even during the cabinet installation, if a something like another door or part or tool is sitting atop a cherry door that is exposed to the sun, that door may develop a permanent shade variation after even one day.

3. **Glass door cabinets** have a wide range of costs associated with them. If you are doing white cabinets and the interiors of your cabinets come with a standard white melamine, then you may find putting two glass inserts into one of your upper cabinet doors has a negligible impact on your costs. If however, the inserts are done in leaded, beveled glass, the inside of the cabinets are finished with a wood veneer to match the exterior, the shelving changes to glass, and the inside of the cabinet is lit with puck lighting you may find the cost of that cabinet has increased 400%.

4. **Cabinet drawers** are often offered in melamine as a standard with upgrades to wood with dove-tail construction. The cost will depend on the number and width of drawers in your design (this could apply to rollout drawers too). It wouldn't be uncommon to find this costing $75 per drawer, but my experience is that many melamine drawers are well-built. Clients also like the fact they look *clean*, are water-resistant and don't require any lining.

5. **Cabinet drawer glides** are unlike drawer box upgrades. The latter you see, but the glides are something you *feel* every time you open and close a drawer. If your glide is *full-extension* it gives you access to the entire drawer (like a file drawer), it is usually a durable, ball-bearing construction with a very smooth action; and if it also comes with a *soft-close* feature the drawer cannot be slammed shut, it usually handles more weight, it closes with the slightest push, it feels like it is moving on a cushion of air and is so quiet you almost cannot hear it. The cost of a high-end glide is about the same as the upgrade to dove-tail drawer construction. If you're trying to maximize your value and enjoyment, **I would suggest upgrading your drawer glide before your drawer box.**

6. **Cabinet hinges** have advanced a great deal from simply being self-closing. Blum and other hardware manufactures all offer a *soft-close* hinge. With this hinge, your doors close gently with only a whisper. Many lines have made this feature standard, but even as an option, the cost is negligible. One of my clients put the soft-close feature on all her drawers and doors and couldn't believe the difference. Her three teenage girls would all hit the kitchen for after-school snacks and the sound of banging doors

and drawers was startling. With the new cabinets, she said she almost couldn't tell they were there.

7. Complex, furniture-like design details requires a wide range of **ornamental moldings** and these materials and installation are the things that can most quickly catapult your costs from 3X to 6X and beyond. Some of the more elaborate and ornate moldings come from Enkeboll (www.enkebolldesigns.com) ; and it is not at all uncommon for the cost of one moulding to be as much as an entire cabinet. Multiple crown moldings, rope moldings, egg-and-dart moulding, fluted and spiral-turned pilasters, bun feet, corbels, bead board, furniture toe are but a few of the offerings you will find. They are expensive to install and more often than not they are most effective when you are also modifying cabinet depths and heights. These modifications alone usually add 25-50% to a cabinet cost. The following photos will help illustrate a wide variety of ornamental molding:

Glass
Cabinet
over
Applianc
e
Garage
with
Joint
Covered
by Door
Plant
Corbel on
Beadboard
Backing

This piece shown above has a custom raised panel valence just above the arched refrigerator panels, crown and rope moulding above, and fluted pilasters flanking the center refrigerator. The moldings were essential to the refrigerator location take on the appearance of an armoire.

Enkeboll Carving
on Arched Valence
Bun Feet

The office installation shown below uses wood carvings on the center valence as well as the upper sections of the fluted pilasters that flank the center base cabinet.

8. Roll-out shelves in a base cabinet may add 25% to the cost, but they usually add the same amount of increased, usable storage. When you consider the ease and convenience, **these are going to be some of your best value-added items.**

9. Cabinet fitments (often referred to as inserts) comprise those items that are designed to provide **specialized capabilities for organization** and storage; such as drawer organizers, tray dividers that let you stack

cookie sheets and trays vertically, cutlery dividers, lifts for mixers, etc. Most semi-custom cabinet lines offer a wealth of options and you should study them carefully to maximize organization, ease and convenience. (https://www.rev-a-shelf.com).

10. **Cabinet hardware** (pulls and/or knobs) is a choice most customers will often make while choosing their cabinetry. Hardware is best seen as an accessory to your doors and drawers. It should have the right color, texture, detailing, finish and sheen so that it is the perfect complement for the door or drawer. **You don't want your hardware to call attention to itself.** Cabinetry and hardware need to be seen as matched pairs.

    The decision to use pulls versus knobs or some combination is largely a matter of personal taste. You should make sure the size of your hardware is proportionate to the doors and drawers it will be attached to. If you are putting hardware on a dishwasher for instance, you may need a pull with more substance than that required for an easy open drawer. On small base cabinets with 5-piece drawer fronts your hardware pulls may not fit on the raised center panel (knobs will probably be required). **Check to see that your selection for your top drawers will not catch and snag your clothing.** In all cases take note of the *feel* of the hardware as well as how well it fits your hand. You will be using the hardware many thousands of times over the life of your cabinets so it's smart to take the time up front to make sure you have the right selection. (See www.amerock.com, www.hafele.com/us)

36

How Do I Create a Preliminary Estimate?

At this stage you will have put together estimates of the major cost items (tops, flooring, backsplash, cabinetry, lighting and appliances). In order to go much further, you need a preliminary budget. You want to know early on if what you will have to spend is going to match up with what you can afford and with how much the value of your home will warrant. Here is a tool I use. It is an Excel spreadsheet that lists in an itemized fashion most cost categories you will need to consider to have an inclusive estimate.

The cost categories are divided into hard and soft costs. The latter describes costs that cannot be associated with a particular product or trade. The most difficult items to estimate will be the hard costs of electrical, plumbing, ventilation, framing, and drywall. The hourly rate for these trades will probably range from $90/hour (electrical) to $40/hour (drywall). I have outlined some sample costs that reflect work you are most likely to require; e.g. a plumber to hook up the ice maker line, the dishwasher, the sink and the waste disposer.

One of the budget categories listed below is **'Contingencies'**. You don't have to do much reading or talk long with friends who have remodeled before encountering the advice to work with a budget that has at least a 15-20% surplus. **This area is one of the least understood and least explored parts of the remodel.** You may wonder why you need to set aside such a large percentage; especially if you are carefully detailing your requirements and intend to get a firm, guaranteed price from your builder.

(Your name) Kitchen Remodel - preliminary budget				
Hard Costs	**Vendor Name**	**Quote / Estimate**	**% of total**	**Notes**
Cabinetry	Cabinet Dealer	12,533	25.3%	Includes install and delivery
Cabinet Knobs	Same or Big Box	425	0.9%	Amerock, oil-rubbed bronze
Countertops	Big Box	6,700	13.5%	5/4 granite, bull-nose edge, no splash
Flooring	Big Box	1,917	3.9%	12" porcelain tile.
Backsplash	Big Box	1,455	2.9%	4" tumbled marble with Deco inserts
Appliances	Big Box	6,850	13.8%	Range, Hood, Ref, D/W, M/W
Light Fixtures	Big Box	565	1.1%	Island pendants, U/C lites
Plumbing Fixtures	Big Box	750	1.5%	Sink, Disposer, Faucet
Painting		600	1.2%	3 Walls and trim touch-up only
Electrical		850	1.7%	Wire hood, dishwasher, install lites
Plumbing		650	1.3%	Cap off old lines, install new fixtures
HVAC		285	0.6%	Install new hood
	Sub-total	**33,580**	**67.7%**	
Soft Costs				
Demo Labor		672	1.4%	2.0% of hard costs
Trash Removal		336	0.7%	1.0% of hard costs
Job Preparation		450	0.9%	Safety, dust mitigation, floor protection
Bldg. Permit		336	0.7%	1.0% of hard costs
Supervision		2,351	4.7%	7% of hard costs, on-site supervision
Contingencies		5,037	10.2%	15% of hard costs
	Sub-total	**9,181**	**18.5%**	
Contractor Fee		6,842	13.8%	16% of hard and soft costs
	Total	**49,603**	**100%**	

There are actually three factors that underlie and necessitate this cost category:

A. Ancillary Expenses – these indirect costs are too often omitted in the budget and they include the following:

1. Moving and temporary storage of furniture.

2. Additional cost of eating meals out.

3. Appraisal and bank financing fees.

4. Decorating expense for new blinds, window coverings, area rugs or accessories. (Robin added a chandelier above the dinette table).

5. Attorney fees for contract review.

6. Interior design fees.

7. Fees for permits or architectural drawings.

B. Unknowables – these are costs associated with remedial work that can't be seen until you're well into demo (demolition) and mechanical work. When you reach the *Remodel Roadmap* later in this section, you will see in detail actual items that fell into this category **(The Birthday Kitchen)**.

1. **Electrical** – when the drywall was torn out and we could see how the previous wiring had been done we realized the main electrical panel would require some re-wiring. We also found one circuit where the wiring had been done in aluminum instead of copper; which necessitated it being replaced for safety reasons.

2. **Plumbing** – we were relocating the sink in the new plan. When we went into the crawl space to run the new piping we found PVC drains had been improperly run into cast iron fittings and had to be changed.

3. **Insulation** – rewiring the electrical panel required us getting into the attic where we found that wind gusts had blown away 40% of the insulation. This led us to take a closer look on

the main floor where we found four areas where frost had damaged the ceiling joints and remedial work was required.

4. **Framing** – our visit into the attic also revealed a wood beam in the kitchen ceiling had been improperly framed when the home was originally built and it required us to provide added support.

5. **Flooring** – when the old flooring was removed there were dozens of areas where the plywood subfloor was not screwed down tightly and where some leveling was required. There was also a second layer old flooring that had to be removed.

6. **Roofing** – when we were in the attic we could see stains that indicated roof leaks. Further inspection revealed dry rot on the fascia boards of the garage. The boards had to be replaced and the roof itself was so old and faulty it also had to be replaced.

C. **Owner Changes** – these are changes that are requested for things the owner didn't anticipate. These tend to fall into two categories.

1. **Convenience** – this is work you have thought about but deferred doing in the past. It will come to the forefront when you realize you will already have certain trades on the job to do the kitchen work. In the case study, when it became apparent the painter would need to paint the new fascia trim on the garage, Robin decided to repaint the entire outside. It would have been required in a couple of years anyway and this seemed like the right time to do it. She knew the electrician would be working on the job and she had wanted for a long time to change out her old wall switches and plugs with a more modern design, so she added this to the scope of the work. Robin also realized having the dumpster at the house could allow her to toss out belongings she wanted to get rid of. Her *clean-out/clean-up* effort resulted in four additional dumpster loads.

2. **Consistency** – these are changes you decid to make when you become aware that the fresh, new look in the kitchen may have a negative impact on other areas. Once we had created the arched entrance between the kitchen and family room, Robin felt the enhanced visual flow between the rooms necessitated painting the family room to match. In

> other areas of the house, she felt that the interior slab doors on closets and bedrooms were too dated and needed to be changed out to six-panel doors. She knew of course that we would have trim carpenters working in the kitchen as well as the painter .... they now had even more work.

Of the three categories above little can be done about the "Unknowables". The other two however can be dealt with up front. The reason I cover them in such detail is that you can become so focused on developing a solid budget for your direct costs, these other items never seem to come into view until theproject is well under way.

Your preliminary budget will be a work in progress and will evolve as you attempt to fill in each category with either a quote, and estimate or a guesstimate. This is not a substitute for a budget that has been constructed on firm bids based upon comprehensive descriptions of what you want. That will come when you are working with a construction professional and have moved further along in the process. Using the sample above will provide you with a good grounding in the process that will make later efforts easier and more fruitful.

37

How Do I Choose a Building Professional?

Choosing the building professional for your project will be one of your most important decisions because this is the person/organization that will be managing the schedule, selecting the subcontractors, overseeing the work, ensuring quality, watching the budget; all while bringing to reality your vision for your new kitchen. Excellent material such as that prepared by the NAHB (National Association of Homebuilders), "Checklist for Finding and Hiring a Builder or Remodeler" (www.nahb.org/generic.aspx?sectionID=716&genericContentID=125965) is readily available. Another excellent resource is the information provided by NARI (National Association for the Remodeling Industry). The link to their guidelines is www.nari.org/homeowners/protypes (I encourage you to check out their full offering). I also like the recommendations from http://www.houselogic.com/home-advice/contracting/five-essential-questions-ask-before-hiring-contractor/

While builders come in all sizes, shapes and colors; it is important to understand there are two quite different business models out there. Neither model is right or wrong, but knowing the differences and weighing them against your own needs is extremely important. This knowledge will also impact how soon you decided start your builder search. Here are the two models and their salient characteristics:

A. Contractor – this model is characterized by the bid process. The builder will submit a price to do the work based upon plans and specifications that have been submitted by you. The contractor's goal is to price your job low enough to get the job, but high enough to make money.

1. Main focus is structuring bids in a manner that maximizes their chance securing the owner's job and then executing against the contract. **The contractor is responsible for cost overruns** and will be the one to benefit from cost savings. This fact often puts the contractor and the client in opposition about who is going to be responsible when grey areas present themselves.

2. Subcontractor selection is driven by performance and the ability to price work in a way that maximizes a successful bid.

3. Most common contract model is a **bid price with guarantee**. This represents somewhat of a zero-sum model where shaving costs and charging for all extras are actions directly aligned with maintaining and maximizing profitability.

B. **Construction Management** – this model characterizes a person or organization that is set up to provide an owner with a menu of professional services to help them complete their project.

1. Focus is on management of the entire *customer experience* as opposed to that of the job. **Assisting the client through the process is on a parity with managing construction.**

2. The construction management process carries a fiduciary responsibility because the **manager is the agent of the owner client** and is therefore always charged with looking after the client's best interests.

3. There is a strong emphasis on educating the owner and exploring the pros and cons of various options and alternatives.

4. **Involvement usually starts early in the process** so the firm can provide their expertise at the earliest stages, helping with design, estimates and specifications, team selection, and value engineering (see below).

5. The **most common contract model is cost plus** where the firm works for a percentage of the cost. Sometimes firms will offer an "upset price" which is a guarantee total cost will not exceed a specified amount. **Clients are always looking at actual costs and are always aware of what their construction manager is earning.**

Both of the contractor models are equally legitimate, but my own opinion is the Contractor model may not be as well suited to the newbie owner as it is to those who have the benefit of previous experience as well as a strong architect on their team. (If you went to the NARI sight, you might see that they add a category of "Design-Builder". This has to do largely with whether or not the contracting firm brings design "in-house" and therefore references a service that can be provided by either of the models I mention.)

All source material seems to omit something I consider most important- enthusiasm. In the past when I would speak to groups on how to choose a builder, I would save this item for the very last. I would tell the audience the most important thing of all I wanted them to take away was this - ***"If your (prospective) builder is not as enthused about your project as you are, get another builder!"*** Here is why. Beside referrals from previous clients, strong enthusiasm is often your best insurance that three things will happen:

a. Your project will receive focused effort with responsive attentiveness.

b. Your builder will be unflagging in giving your project his best effort.

c. The psychological ownership felt by the builder will ensure yours is a project he wants to put his name on. **He (or she) will have a personal stake in the outcome.**

At this point you will have reached a fork in the road. If you want to solicit bids from a number of builders, you are going to be choosing the contractor model and you will need to move your drawings and specifications (see below) much further along to ensure you have everyone bidding the same thing and representing exactly what you have chosen.

On the other hand, if you think you can better improve your efforts by bringing a construction professional into the process early, then the construction management model is better aligned. Professional assistance at this earlier stage can help you more quickly match up the design and your product selections with your budget requirements. Making significant changes later can be quite difficult and cause many people to either become disillusioned and drop their plans or plod ahead with a plan that is more expensive than it had to be. A real benefit to help at this stage can lie in the area of **Value Engineering**.

Value Engineering is another service that either model can provide. It is at the core of any company that describes their services as "design-build". It is the model I implemented and it is important you understand what it means. For any project, there's always any number of ways to design and build it, but some are more costly than others. There are **some designs that end up being too expensive to build**, when in fact they didn't have to end up that way. Here is an example:

> In 1987 a new client came to me with blueprints for his new home. He was extremely frustrated because, even after cutting back on many of the features and finishes he and his wife most wanted, two different builders had given him quotes of $530,000 and $460,000. Not only were the bids widely divergent, but the lowest of the two was still far beyond his maximum of $400,000. When I first saw the plans and flipped through the various sheets it was already clear the excessive costs were being driven largely by the design itself.
>
> In the week following our meeting I studied various changes and modifications that might be made to help make the house more affordable. When we met next, I had to tell the owner he needed to scrap the plans (for which he had paid $20,000). I summarized the basic problems and assured him we could design a new plan for $5,000 and that the construction cost would fall comfortably within

> his budget. In less than a month we had a new plan that was functional and great looking; and when we cost it out with all of the goodies he had wanted, the total cost was $362,000.

There are definite benefits to be gained from early involvement by a company with a strong understanding of value engineering. Early guidance and cost feedback during the design progresses is often the key to success. I have used a "new home" example, but the concept applies equally to remodeling. If you hire someone who knows how to effectively balance design and cost requirements, there are many benefits (such as less time and frustration lost to re-design efforts, more opportunity to balance goals and costs together in real time).

38

How Do I Finalize My Plans and Objectives?

The ability to arrive at accurate and meaningful cost estimates correlates to just how clearly you can describe the work and materials required. **'Specifications'** is a general term used to denote both the **scope of work** to be performed (labor) as well as the **material specifications** that enumerate those materials to be used. On commercial projects these and the architectural drawings always form the core of the **Contract Documents**. A simple way to think about this language is to consider one area of work, such as painting. The material specifications will denote Brand (Benjamin Moore, Sherwin-Williams, etc.), type of paint (latex vs oil-based), the line of paint, the sheen (flat, satin, eggshell, semi-gloss, gloss) and the color and color number. The scope of work will describe what work is expected (putty nail holes and pops, repair stress cracks, priming, number of coats of paint, etc.).

Residential projects will have drawings of one kind or another, but in 25 years I have never seen a set of detailed specifications. For commercial projects, specifications can often run into the hundreds of pages, but this would be overkill in the residential realm. To match up your own expectations, with what is called for in the contract with your builder or supplier, **everything must be spelled out in clearly and in detail.** Descriptions of every item must include manufacturer, model number, color, color number, finish, etc. For most kitchen remodels this can usually be done in less than a dozen pages.

If you are remodeling your kitchen, you should already have detailed drawings. Because these 2- and 3-Dimensional drawings tend to be visually engaging they provide an effective canvas for annotating the details that describe your exact choices. This is an easy

thing for your kitchen designer to do and signing and dating your final set of these drawings can reference and be appended to the contracts with your kitchen supplier and even that of your builder. Here are the items that should be included:

a. Kitchen layout, including wall and window dimensions
b. Wood specie (Cherry, Oak, etc).
c. Door and drawer style.
d. Cabinet hardware, count and location notes.
e. Fitments (rollouts, spice inserts, etc.)
f. Drawer construction (wood dovetail, melamine, etc.)
g. Drawer glide type (full extension, soft-close, etc.)
h. Cabinet finish
i. Cabinet moldings
j. Appliance specifications and opening sizes (ovens, refrigerators, hoods, cooktops)

On the drawings shown below, the notes added to floor plan and the elevation illustrate what my customers and builders were routinely provided:

Notes indicate door style, specie, finish, drawer and glide specifications as well as cabinet inserts and moulding selections.

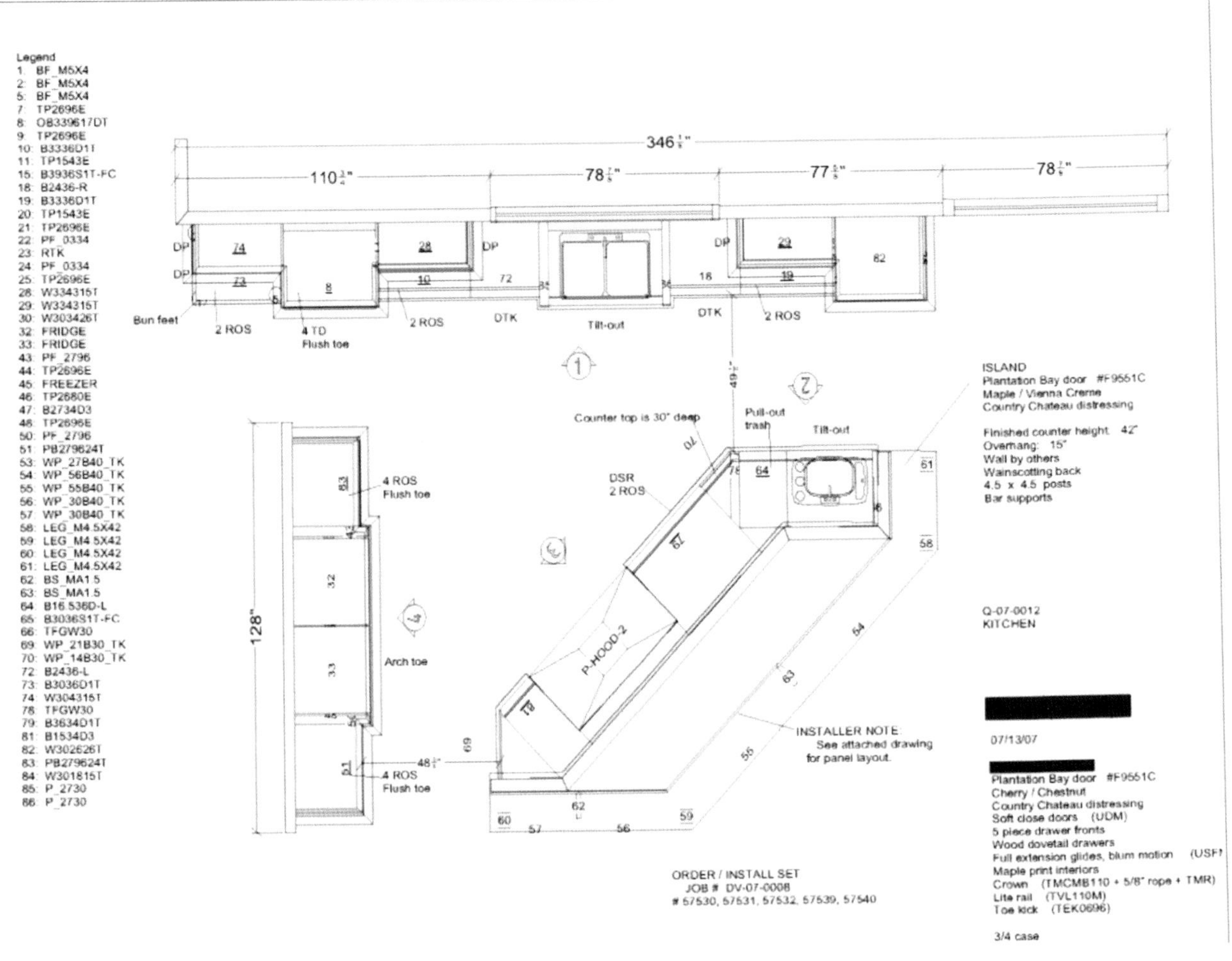

Appliance information is of such critical importance that it was always shown on the drawings. This ensured that the specialized cabinets were built to the correct sizes and with the correct openings (and cut-outs) to match up with the recommendations of the appliance manufacturer. If door panels were used on the refrigerator or warming drawer they would be the correct size. The information also provided a way for the installers to make sure they were aware of the sizes and tolerances required. Finally, it offered everyone some protection when the manufacturer changed model specifications without posting new size requirements.

The front-facing, 2D view (*elevation*) was the best place we found to place the notes. (See Drawing below)

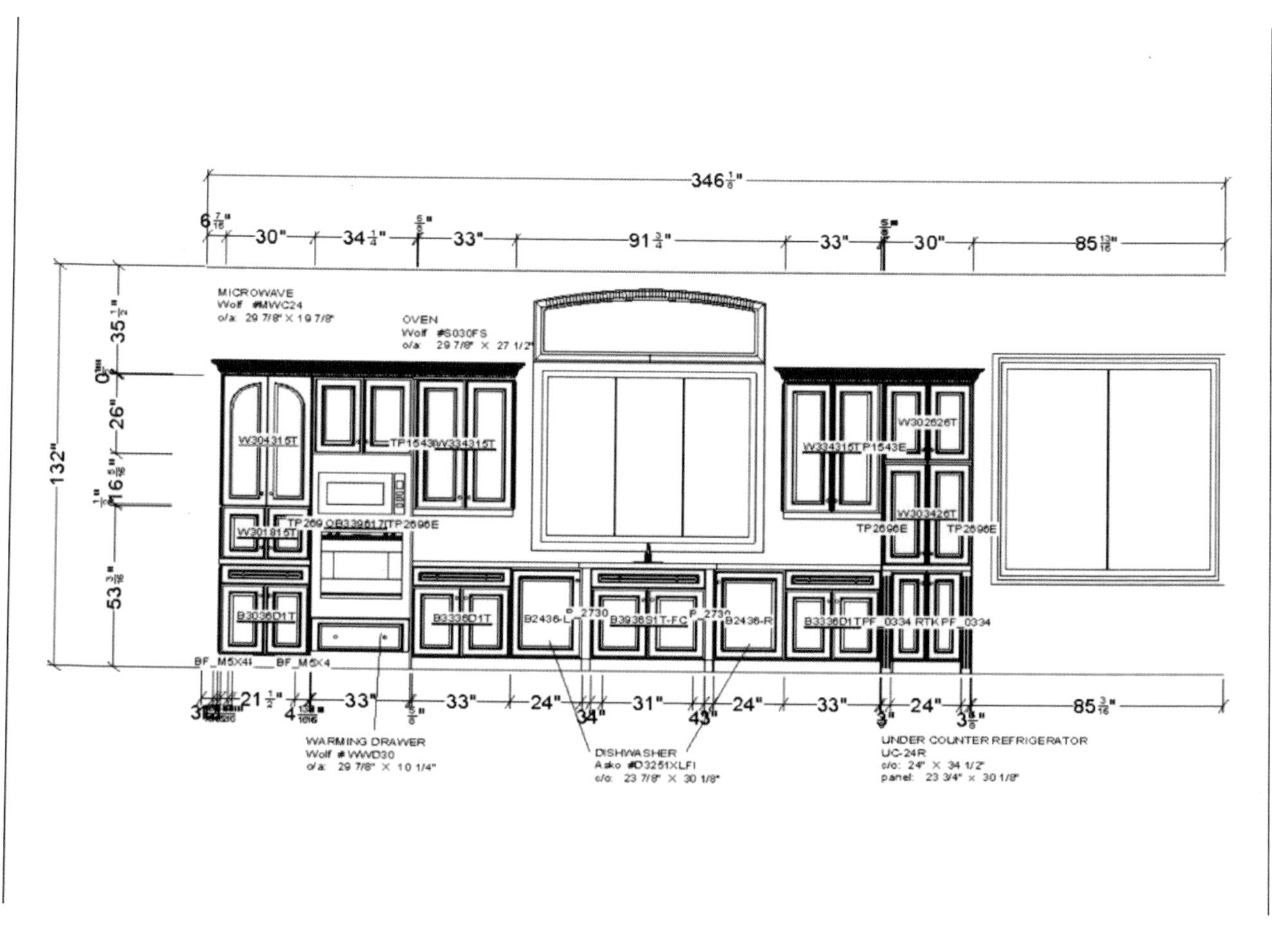

Items not associated with your kitchen vendor can also be added. These might include lighting, flooring, backsplash and countertop notes as well as specifications for wall finish and color. Getting as much specificity and clarity so that all parties are on the same pages is essential in **avoiding surprises, delays, and unexpected added costs.**

With one final set of **signed contract drawings** each of my subcontractors could always reference these whenever there was a question. Using this method also eliminates the many problems that can result from someone working with an earlier revision rather than the final design. **Everyone knew that if they were working with a set of drawings not signed by the owner it was not final and therefore not to be used in the field!**

I will use just one item, the refrigerator, to illustrate just how many people can be affected when key details are missing:

1. **Plumber** – if a water shut-off box or gas line need to be run to a specific location (e.g. Wolf, Sub-Zero)
2. **Electrician** – if the manufacturer requires the outlet to be in a predetermined location (e.g. Sub-Zero)
3. **Cabinet Supplier and Installers** – if panels for the appliances are to be ordered. These items usually require matching exactly the manufacturer's size and profile specifications.
4. **Appliance vendor** – cabinet panels often require ordering a special kit and depending on the look that is desired it **may even require a specific model of refrigerator**.
5. **Hardware supplier** – cabinet panels on the refrigerator often require special hardware and placement to function properly. This hardware often requires a special order with longer lead times and it also has to be installed prior to the installation of the panels.
6. **Framer, Drywaller and Painter** – if the added height of a custom refrigerator (84" vs. 69.5") requires reframing to raise the height of a dropped soffit. These trades can also be involved if a return wall needs to be shortened in order to allow the refrigerator door to open fully (this can occur where the refrigerator abuts and sits back from the front of the return wall).
7. **Flooring vendor** – built-in refrigerators are usually 24" deep vs. a more typical depth of 28.5". On some projects the change in the footprint can impact whether or not additional flooring work is required.

The non-inclusion of what might seem like a small detail can have **outsized impacts on schedule and costs.** In whatever way you outline (in written form) the scope of work and material specifications, understand they are there not only for your protection but also for everyone's benefit. Nothing is quite so difficult to handle as when you find what you

wanted and were expecting, was not what the contractor had in mind. Even with the best of intentions and highest integrity on the part of owner and contractor, starting forth without having taken the time necessary to fully define and spell out the details is the surest recipe for trouble and hard feelings.

39

Who Else Do I Want on My Team?

When doing a comprehensive remodel of a kitchen, a detailed plan is essential. It communicates to the different suppliers and contractors and construction personnel exactly what is to be where. You can get plans developed by architects, kitchen designers, and the cabinet sales personnel or service people in a kitchen shop or big box store. A note on each option:

Architects play a pivotal role in many remodels, but this occurs more commonly when the work requires to an addition to a home rather than a reconfiguration of your kitchen. With additions there are typically structural and engineering components of the design work as well as architectural approvals. The greater the changes to the existing structure, the more likely it is you will need stamped design drawings prior to seeking approvals (from building departments and architectural control committees) and contract drawings prior to seeking contractor bids.

If you are hiring an architect, try to end up with both **a contractor and an architect on your team that already have a good working relationship**. This can help you avoid a large number of potential problems where design execution and budget constraints are in conflict.

Beside your contractor and cabinet supplier there are other professionals whose services may be of assistance and that certainly includes an **interior designer**. The recurrent theme of this book is that kitchen design and interior design should be melded seamlessly together to achieve the best results. Many interior designers love working with kitchens and have acquired significant experience; their work with furniture usually gives

them a great sense of how to use moldings and ornamentation to augment the desired look. After years of working with floor plan arrangements, they will have valuable input into how to develop good circulation as well as visual flow. They also have the background to match the look of your cabinetry with your home's décor as well as its architectural style. When it comes to helping you match up wall colors, flooring selections, cabinetry finishes, hardware, lighting, window coverings, countertops and back splashes, an interior designer's experience with color, pattern, texture, and proportion can help you achieve your goals with much less effort.

One caveat is to understand exactly how your interior designer is to be compensated. There are many designers who will work for a fixed fee, a cost-plus arrangement, or some combination. Receiving additional compensation through referral fees is also quite common. However there are designers who refer you to a cabinet vendor because they have a pre-existing fee arrangement. It is important to know whether this is being treated by the vendor as a normal marketing expense or whether your cabinet price has been inflated to cover the fee. **Ensuring your designer's incentives are fully aligned with you as the client is a matter of insisting on full disclosure.** No good interior design professional will find such disclosure offensive or unreasonable.

If you choose an interior designer ,it is probably not going to be the same person who does your cabinet design. The difference in the two disciplines is significant. A good kitchen designer not only has to be creative but also needs to employ the mechanical thought process of an engineer. Matching each job's physical characteristics to the correct cabinet configuration leaves hundreds of opportunities for errors to occur. This is magnified even more because of the unique nomenclature and product design variations between manufacturers. **It takes most cabinet designers years of experience to become knowledgeable enough to safely navigate these challenges.**

40

What Should I Know About the Product Selection Process?

The product selection process for cabinetry as well as other items requires you to make judgments based upon multiple factors such as these:

- **Cost and value over time.** Where are the points where I can be hurt by spending too much or too little? Will one product have a significantly higher residual value upon resale? (e.g. wood flooring vs. carpeting).
- **Durability**. Will my selection hold up well over time given the expected usage?
- **Suitability.** Am I choosing a product that is well suited for my intended use? (e.g. indoor grilling and Indian cuisine typically require greater hood ventilation to handle smoke and odors)
- **Features.** Does the product have all of the features and benefits that will match up with my wants and needs? (e.g. if you entertain formally you might look for a dishwasher that has a setting for fine china)
- **Look and Feel.** Do I like the touch and feel of the product and will it harmonize with my décor and my other selections? When I make my decision am I carefully considering color, finish, texture, pattern, depth, motion and scale?
- **Warranties.** What recourse do I have if the product is defective?
- **Maintenance.** What are the costs of operating or maintaining the product?

As I run through a selection of materials other than cabinetry, I will point out the most important things you should know in order to avoid common pitfalls. You can easily find comprehensive information for these and others; but for the ones I have chosen, I want to offer you context and perspective that comes with having worked with these materials over many years.

Granite Countertops - If you are viewing granite countertop samples at a big-box store, you are looking at a tiny representation of what is actually available. **Granite comes in the widest range of looks of any product you will consider**. Some look like windswept sands of the desert and others can look like an underwater picture taken in the Caribbean. The granites chosen for the store sample kits have been selected because they are the ones that tend to be readily available, consistent in appearance (each slab looks the same as the next), and relatively homogenous in their appearance (each section of a slab looks the same as the other). To discover what this material is about **find a local granite distributor**. They will usually have hundreds of slabs in inventory available and set up for you to view. (See http://www.igmcorp.com/products/granite/).

Looking at granite early is one of the best ways to start your product selection process.

There are two reasons for this. First, the selections are so diverse that viewing them can provide one of the fastest ways for you to judge how you value color, texture, pattern, motion, scale and depth. Second, when most people find the perfect granite they have also discovered there is an emotional connection to the product. I find it most akin to falling in love with a painting. If you find this kind of connection early, you can take a sample of the slab and use it as a kind of touchstone when looking at other products and materials. It has a way of letting you know if your other selections have the same *feel*. (If this is a new experience you can expect to be overwhelmed with visual overload. It will usually take a second or third visit before you can begin to connect on more than a visual level. It is however, a quick and easily acquired skill.)

Early in your granite search it is important to find and begin working with a fabricator (they make the tops from the slabs of stone). These are the people who can tell you the cost of the materials you are looking at and they also can let you know (based on your kitchen design), how many slabs you will need and approximately what size slabs will work best to minimize seams. Most fabricators will also let you visit their facility before fabrication to indicate to them where in your design you might wish to highlight special markings or colorations on the slab. Most distributors can provide you with a list of fabricators.

Slabs with the same name may bear a family resemblance, but they can have quite different looks and markings. If you find the slabs you want, buy them and have them delivered to your fabricator. Do not assume you can come back and find the same thing (think original art).

I find granite to be one of my favorite countertop choices for several reasons. First, its natural beauty is extraordinary and it is something where you can choose something unique. Second, it has great resale value. Third, because it is a solid surface material, it can be fabricated into any number of curved designs. Covering the tops of cabinets does not begin to show off what you can do with this material. (See photos left and below)

Finally, it has great durability and offers minimal upkeep. The only dissatisfaction I ever heard was from a woman who said the particular pattern of her granite made it difficult to see if she had left either salt or pepper on the surface.

With granite or any other solid surface material, play special attention to the **edge design.** There are many profiles from which to choose, a few of which you can see on www.houzz.com. You will find a wider selection at www.marble.com. I recommend choosing from a group of profiles that mirror other design elements such as cabinetry edges and moldings. Edge profiles will usually fall into one of two categories based on pricing. Standard edges are the easiest to fabricate and their cost will all be built into the cost of your top. Premium edges are usually priced separately and they consist of more complex laminations, created by bonding two or more layers of granite together to achieve a greater

thickness and more dramatic look. Edges have such a large impact because the edge is where your eye is naturally drawn. (See photo below showing a laminated edge detail).

Wood Flooring - To be inclusive, I want to cover wood floors that are pre-finished, site-finished and those that are designed to offer the look of wood (laminate floors). A common pitfall in determining what you like is to not looking closely enough at what you are seeing. This is especially true with wood flooring choices.

You need to see the coloration, the level of sheen, texture, grain characteristics and board width (or random widths). All of these factors will determine how formal or relaxed your room will feel as well as how it looks. Maple and cherry have a soft, flowing grain pattern that is in marked contrast to the jagged and aggressive pattern found in red oak. Deep colors, like espresso, with a high gloss finish tend to create a more formal appearance. Wider or random plank widths in a satin tone with blended color tones and hand-scraped

textures will usually create a relaxed, rustic feel. Whatever your ultimate choice you need to remember the following points:

- **Inside a store is not the place to make a final decision**. The lighting is almost always a fluorescent with bulbs that are not color corrected. More often than not, these bulbs add a green cast to the light. (I have a brown jacket that turns noticeably green whenever I walk into fluorescent lighting). Get samples you can take to your home so you can see them in your home's light conditions.

- Using **small sample blocks to make your selection decisions is very risky**. Products vary greatly in the amount of their color and grain variation, so seeing a larger sample will give you a much more realistic perception of what to expect.

- Whenever possible, **look over two or three samples instead of one**. For most people, being able to compare and contrast will allow the color undertones to be recognized. If your selection is too (yellow, orange, red, gray, etc.) you will be better able to detect this.

- When you have a sample material to view at your home you can get a good look, but many clients have found **if the material is simply around the house for a few days**, without even noticing it they pick up a sense of how the material feels. The **result is often a strong sense of certainty**. You might think of your visual inspection as analogous to interviewing a job candidate and checking out all their salient characteristics on the resume. After a matter of days on the job however, most employers will have picked up a strong sense about how well this new employee is going to fit in with the rest of the team.

Solid wood flooring can be site-finished or pre-finished. The latter is usually sold in boxes with the maximum length being less than 48". The edges have small beveling that creates a micro-groove. Just like site-finished material, planks are joined with tongue-and-groove edges and the material is nailed down. (See Drawing Below)

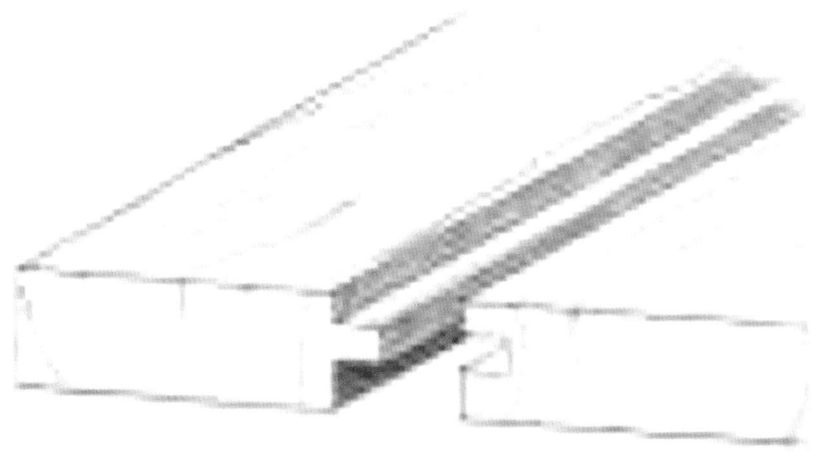

Site-finished material is sanded and finished with stain, sealed, sanded and then top-coated with two or more layers of protective finish. From a design perspective the biggest difference is when using site-finished material you will have more choice and more control over what you are buying. Wood graded *Select and Better* will usually mean you will get more longer lengths, fewer short pieces and no micro-beveled edges common with pre-finished material. You can also choose unique grain patterns (e.g. "rift" cut boards can provide uniformly straight grain patterns). All of this means less patterning with more of an opportunity for the natural look of the wood to come through. You also have the benefit of having the stain color sampled on your new wood floor before the finishing process begins. The tight fit between the boards is a benefit because there is greater protection from water spills penetrating into the wood.

In terms of durability, different wood species have different levels of hardness. You can easily evaluate the wood's hardness by looking up its ***Janka rating*** (see www.hardwood-info.com). There is no perfect wood floor but a big plus with all solid wood floors (site- and pre-finished) is they can be sanded and refinished (bamboo is a unique exception because of its grain characteristics).

Planked wood flooring that is not solid is referred to as **Engineered Wood**. The top layer is a veneer of real wood and in some cases it is thick enough it can be refinished at least once. In many cases the top veneer is too thin to allow this. Beneath the upper veneer is the core, and it is usually comprised of layered wood (like plywood) or pressed fiberboard. The thickness is usually .375" to .5" as opposed to solid wood which is .75". Most of this product is designed with a tongue-and-groove joint that locks into place. No nailing is required and usually the packaging and displays refer to **Lock and Fold.** This material floats above the subfloor (it is not attached to the subfloor below it) and is therefore a good choice for concrete, where nailing is not possible. It also is offered with a non-locking joint where the preferred installation is usually a glue-down method. The glue-down application has the advantage that it is going to feel and sound more like a solid wood floor than one that floats. **Many clients find they are very uncomfortable with the feel and sound of these floating floors. Do not purchase without finding your own reaction.** You should know that most floating floors offer glue-down as a secondary installation method and it usually only adds about .50 per square foot to the install cost. These products usually have some rating of their relative hardness, but with a veneered product Janka hardness ratings do not apply. Bruce, a division of Armstrong, is one company that offers a product that specifically promotes dent and abrasion resistance. It is sold under different names but what gives it special characteristics is that the top wood layer has been infused with an acrylic resin. (it cannot be sanded and refinished).

Another option for a wood look is the laminate floor. This will always a floating floor. The construction is usually a core of pressed fiberboard overlain with a "deco" (photographic) layer. The top layer is the wear layer. This type of flooring is rated for wear by its (AC) abrasion classification. The scale runs from 1-5 and most of the product you will find at the retail level has a rating of AC3 or AC4. AC4 is rated for light- commercial traffic. The thickness of the product ranges between 7 and 12mm. I would not recommend ever using a product less than 8mm in thickness. You will also find that many of the offerings look much more realistic than others. That is usually because they have been made with a different manufacturing process referred to embossed-in-register.

When you are choosing a kitchen floor that will have a wood appearance you should avoid the common misconception that you need to match the look of your cabinetry. In almost all cases you will get a more satisfying result by either complementing or contrasting the look of your cabinetry.

Countertop Backsplash - This refers primarily to the area between the top of the counter and the underside of the cabinetry. This height is usually about 18". In areas where there is a range or cook-top, the splash area is usually higher and in some cases goes all the way to the ceiling. The materials used are most commonly ceramic, glass, granite or marble tiles although stainless steel is not uncommon.

The splash in the photo below was done with 4" glass tiles of multiple colors. The bright colors were chosen to augment visual excitement. The lighted glass upper cabinets, the backsplash and the pendant lights provide a balance to the cherry used in the cabinetry. The splash area is so visually striking it almost makes the window invisible. This was actually the intention because the window is off-center from the taller appliance elements to the left and right. Stainless cover plates were used to allow the outlets to blend in.

Looking toward the arched opening over the cook-top (left) you can see that slab granite was used as a full-height splash material. (See Photo below)

In Robin's kitchen (**The Birthday Gift**) we used a tumbled marble that extended to the ceiling to create a relaxed look and feel. The mural design, bordered in a tile rope moulding, helps give the cooking area a sense of place by reinforcing the vertical relationship between the range, the mural and the hood. The symmetrical flanking elements to the left and right also enhance the look and feel of the center. (See above)

The photo below shows the range wall and island of a new home where our goal was to integrate a contemporary flair with the charm and feel of the arts-and-crafts design so prevalent in the neighborhood. The juxtaposition of the brick and stainless provided the perfect counterpoint for that effect. The look of the brick is greatly enhanced by the under-cabinet lighting and by the countertop color which is paired to the color of the mortar joints.

The four photos above illustrate what an important impact the design and material chosen for your splash can have on the overall effect. Look back over these photos one more time and see that the one thing in common is that the splash areas help impart visual balance to each kitchen. They all change the essential composition of the picture and they keep the look from being dominated by the cabinetry. The room as a whole needs to be the star and it is the emotional connection that is your ultimate goal. Too many customers

make all of their other decisions and then say to themselves, *"I guess we need to pick out something we like as a backsplash."* You and your design team should be using this area as a key driver in reaching your goals.

Wood Countertops - Seldom do you see a kitchen with all wood countertops. More common is to see butcher block used to give a special look and feel to an island or other area of the kitchen. (See below)

The butcher block top on the island and the hand-crafted, wooden pot rack and painted tin ceiling above were important in helping my client establish an area in the kitchen that gave her a sense of ease and of connection to the larger themes of the home. From the island she could fully appreciate the sun-filled space that had been augmented by using more windows and less upper cabinetry. The home design replicated a home in southern France.

Here is a view from the other side of the island. (See Photo Below)

Wood tops in combination with other materials offer an extraordinary opportunity to enhance the look and feel of your kitchen. With different wood species and construction from both edge and end grain there are a multitude of terrific options from which to choose (see www.Johnboos.com).

Ceramic Tile - This material offers potential advantages you may want to consider:

- Greater resistance to leaks and spills. (by one estimate, 95% of all wood floor claims are water or moisture related)

- Easy care and clean up. No topical finishes are required to keep it looking good and with today's grout additives, grout can remain looking good for many years without added cleaning or sealing.
- Your ability to match up your expectations of quality and performance is greatly aided by the fact the same tile rating systems are used by almost all manufacturers and the information is readily available to you.

You can be well on your way to making smart product choices in this category by visiting these three websites; click the "tile" tab at www.nationalfloorcoveringalliance.com, www.nkba.org/Learn/Homeowners/Tips/Tile/ChoosingTheRightTile.aspx , and look for "Your Floor: How to Shop for Tile" at www.houzz.com/ideabooks .

If your kitchen layout has a degree of visual rigidity your tile layout can often provide a solution. Many kitchen layouts are similar to shape below (as seen from above).

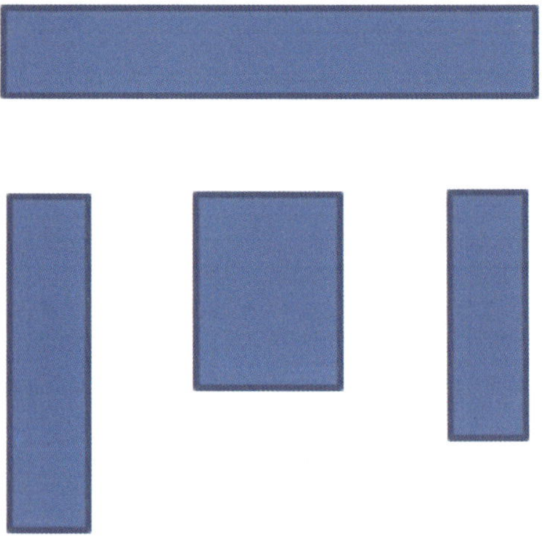

By running your tile in a diagonal pattern you can make it much less likely your view of the kitchen will be influenced by the parallel lines of the cabinetry.

Appliances - From Aga to Zephyr, there is almost an entire alphabet of manufacturers bringing their products to this category. Over the years many name brands have changed their specifications and manufacturing processes in order broaden their market by offering lower pricing. Some at the upper end have deemed it necessary to provide product offerings aimed at the entry level (often calling this their "OPP" product – Original Price Point). So you now have a more bewildering array of options facing you.

After you have looked at pricing, design, features, ratings from "Consumer Reports" and energy-ratings; how do you assure yourself your selection will meet your expectations when it is installed in your home? My suggestion is to read consumer reviews from as many sources as possible. Users like you are on the receiving end where promise and performance inevitably meet. If there are serious problems that have escaped the manufacturer's product testing, you can be assured the users will be commenting on both the problem as well as their success and failure in rectifying the problem.

My wife and I recently were considering a dual-fuel (gas burners, electric oven) range from a top brand. A large part of the attraction was the stellar reputation of the manufacturer as well as the fact the price was at least 40% lower than their other offerings in the same category. As soon as we checked for online reviews we found that purchasers had been plagued with poor quality in the control knobs. Months after being notified, the manufacturer was still looking for a solution. Keep in mind that we were shopping in a higher-end showroom and the showroom manager was helping us. She had no knowledge of this quality problem!

The simplest (one step) action you can take is to go to www.google.com and type the following in the search bar: "(model # of your appliance) review". You will instantly have review links from Consumer Reports, Amazon, and others. I especially like the reviews from Amazon because they often have the largest number of reviews and because they are diligent about keeping out reviews that are not from actual product users.

Lighting - Throughout this book the text and the pictures will attest to the one thing I regard as the **most important of all design tools; and that is the effective use of natural and artificial lighting.** My best advice to you is to make your lighting a top priority and when you budget for this category, don't skimp. In the design palette of your new kitchen; lighting is the finishing touch!

There has never been a wider selection of affordable options from which to choose as you consider direct and indirect light sources for work, mood or accent. One of your best places to start looking is at http://www.houzz.com/ideabooks/Kitchen-Lighting.

Your final product selections and detailed drawings form the basis for your contractor to quote you price. Your contractor should be able to help you with this process by referring you to vendors that have proven to be reliable, knowledgeable, and value-oriented.

41

What is the Timetable for My Project?

Make sure you have received and reviewed a written schedule with your contractor. You will want to ask the following questions:

- *What is your level of confidence with the schedule?*
- *Do you have everything from us that you need to start?*
- *What kinds of things might alter your schedule and do you have suggestions as to how to be proactive in preventing this?*
- *As you proceed, what are the key actions and decisions you will need from me to keep things rolling smoothly and when will you need them?*

Here is the schedule that was used in Robin's kitchen (**The Birthday Gift**). As you can see, this was a simple Excel spreadsheet that identified each stage. The schedule is split into the basic project sections (Prep, Demo,Rough-in, and Finish), and each day's activities are listed along with pertinent notes. Because of its simplicity and clarity, Robin found the schedule provided her an ongoing picture of the work that would be taking place each week. Having this knowledge and gaining trust in its accuracy went a long way toward removing uncertainty and anxiety from the process.

Job Progress Schedule

STAGE	DAY	DATE	DAY	VENDOR	SCOPE OF WORK	NOTES
Prep	1	1/28/06	Saturday		Remove all items from kit, back hall and powder room	Set up temp cooking area in lower level
	2	1/29/06	Sunday		Make space in garage alcove for double oven and cabinet	We will wire circuit during rough stage
	3	1/30/06	Monday		Set up 20 roll-off at W. end of drive	
	3	1/30/06	Monday		Install lock box, fire extinguisher, first aid kit, post permit	Post drawings, schedule and emergency numbers
	3	1/30/06	Monday		Install floor protection, vinyl barriers, zip doors	Zip doors at hall and F.Rm, poly at DR and FR
Demo	4	1/31/06	Tuesday		Template kid's bath, remove granite and pull bath slabs	This will be early am
	5	1/31/06	Tuesday		Disconnect Sink and cap off drain and supplies	Install new shut-off at icemaker if required
	6	1/31/06	Tuesday		Disconnect appliances, shut off appliance circuits	Rough in 220 in garage for oven?
	7	1/31/06	Tuesday		Remove oven, micro,dw, cooktop and cabinetry	Oven goes to garage, rest to dumpster
	8	2/1/06	Wednesday		Remove soffit, vinyl, underlayment, chair rail, din rm door	Check walls and floor for level, square and straight
	9	2/2/06	Thursday		Make framing corrections, layout cabinet for rough trades	Screw off floor to eliminate squeaks, block for hood
Rough-in	10	2/2/06	Thursday		Rough in new sink location, start rough-in of gas pipe	
	11	2/2/06	Thursday		Rough in for micro, uc lites, new cans, etc	
	12	2/3/06	Friday		Rough in for micro, uc lites, new cans, etc	Start smoke detectors on 2/06/06
	13	2/6/08	Monday		Finish Rough in work	
	14	2/7/06	Tuesday		Finish Rough in work	
	15	2/8/06	Wednesday		Rough Inspections	
	16	2/9/06	Thursday		Patch ceiling and holes in kitchen and garage	Radius Corners at skylight and chase
	17	2/10/06	Friday		Drywall Inspection	
	18	2/13/06	Monday		Blend texture at patch areas	
Finish	19	2/14/06	Tuesday		Level Floor, Start underlayment	
	20	2/15/06	Wednesday		Install Floor tile	
	21	2/16/06	Thursday		Install Floor tile	
	22	2/17/06	Friday		Install Floor tile	Grout Floor
	16	2/20/06	Monday		Start Cabinet Installation	
	17	2/21/06	Tuesday		Cabinet Installation	Pull Doors for Glazing
	18	2/21/06	Tuesday		Template for Granite tops	Template in afternoon
	19	2/22/06	Wednesday		Cabinet Installation	
	20	2/23/06	Thursday		Cabinet Installation	
	21	2/24/06	Friday		Install Cabinetry	Install Cabinet Hardware, crown in room
Finish	22	3/2/06	Thursday		Install Granite tops	
	22	3/3/06	Friday		Install Granite tops	
	23	3/6/06	Monday		Install Splash areas	
	24	3/7/06	Tuesday		Install Splash areas	
	25	3/8/06	Wednesday		Install Splash areas	
	31	3/9/06	Thursday		Install Splash areas	Grout and Seal Splash
	32	3/10/06	Friday		Trim outlets, lites, install microwave and hood	
	33	3/13/06	Monday		Trim outlets, lites, install microwave and hood	
	34	3/14/06	Tuesday		Install venting for hood, change rusted vent flashing	
	35	3/14/06	Tuesday		Patch roof at penetrations	Tie in with roof replacement schedule
	36	3/14/06	Tuesday		Install range and refrigerator	
	37	3/14/06	Tuesday		Hook up sink, faucet, disposer, and range	
	38	3/15/06	Wednesday		Paint walls and trim	
	39	3/16/06	Thursday		Painting of ceiling, walls, trim	
	40	3/17/06	Friday		Painting of ceiling, walls, trim	
	41	3/20/06	Monday		Final Inspection	
	42	3/21/06	Tuesday		Punch Work	Pull out protection materials
	43	3/22/06	Wednesday		Punch Work	

42

What Should I Look for in the Construction Agreement?

This single document is of ultimate importance. A good introduction to the items you should have in this document can be found at http://www.angieslist.com/articles/10-things-every-remodeling-contract-should-contain.htm. To augment this list, make certain that, whatever form your drawings and specifications take, they are attached to and become part of your contract documents.

It is common to think of the contract as a way to protect yourself if things go sideways, but I want to suggest that thoroughly working through all aspects of the agreement with your builder is your best preventive measure. So **tamp down your enthusiasm to *get going* with construction long enough so you don't skip or shortchange this important step.**

It is impossible for me to not to tell you to have your contract reviewed by an attorney, but this step can be greatly expedited by the use of one of the numerous contract documents that have been developed by the AIA (American Institute of Architects). Their contract documents cover just about every type of situation and payment arrangement, they have well-establish protections built-in, and they are usually well known to contract attorneys. I always used one for my work. I knew the document would leave my client's well protected and would provide reasonable solutions to resolve disagreements. I also found my client's attorneys could approve them in short order. This kept legal review cost down and got us under way with construction more quickly. (See http://www.aia.org/contractdocs/ownersdevelopers/)

43

Pre-construction

Your contract is signed, your team is in place, funding is arranged, insurance coverages for you and your contractor are verified and the building permit has been issued. You are ready to move from planning to pre-construction.

Your cabinetry and any materials with long lead times have been ordered so that they will be received and verified before demo work begins. Now is the time for you and your contractor to work out the logistics of two different activities.

A. Home Preparation

1. Set in motion plans for a temporary kitchen that can allow simple meals and snacks to be prepared. You may move your refrigerator to a new location as well as your microwave. Dish ware may be washed in a laundry sink or be made from a disposable material.

2. Make plans for the storage of all kitchen items, furniture and personal items that need to be removed. You may need to look into POD (container) storage.

3. Secure a separate access and/or access code (or key) for construction personnel.

4. Determine if tradespeople will use a bathroom inside the house or a portable facility outside.

5. Determine what floor areas will need temporary protection.

6. Let the contractor know in advance what areas of the house are off limits.

7. Determine how to deal with household pets to keep them from getting lost or injured.

B. Job Preparation

1. Determine placement for a dumpster and placement of the building permit.
2. Secure storage for materials that need to be kept on-site.
3. Establish a plan for dust mitigation.
4. Address any safety issues and post all contact and emergency numbers (bilingually, if required). There should be a first-aid kit and fire extinguisher close at hand.
5. Post information on the location of all utility shut-off valves.
6. Have an approved set of plans and specifications available for easy reference.
7. Notify adjacent neighbors of the work and give them contact information to use if they have any concerns or problems.
8. Finalize any schedule changes and review days of the week and hours of the day that work is to be performed.
9. Determine who will be doing the supervision, how often it is to be done, its typical duration and how the results will be reported back to you.

All of these items will seem like common sense and almost too obvious to be mentioned. In actual practice, the majority of these items are missed or never mentioned at all.

44

Construction: Your *Remodel Roadmap*

I had put my builder hat back on for the remodel of Robin's kitchen (**The Birthday Gift**); but, before that, I had been frustrated because clients were not being given a clear and effective introduction to the remodel process. Beyond this, the language and terminology used by architects, builders, designers and others is unknown to most clients, thus increasing the possibility of misunderstandings. At the time, of course, this was the builder's responsibility; but this deficit still impacted the overall satisfaction of my kitchen clients.

After searching extensively I realized that the problem did not lie entirely with the builders. There simply wasn't any good material available. Before I began work on Robin's kitchen remodel, I decided that I would use the work on her project to create a tool that could fill the gap. I photographed each stage of Robin's job to create an illustrated explanation of the kitchen remodel process. It is presented the following pages. As you step through the various stages, I will describe the activity, provide pictures for additional clarity as well as notes to help you better understand what was taking place as we moved from ***Before*** to ***After*** (see below).

Robin's kitchen was lacking in many areas. Her biggest frustration was that when she fixed dinners for herself and her two teenagers it was hard to stay connected with them. Working at the sink left her turned away from the kids and also staring at a blank wall. You will have a chance to see all of the individual changes, but most notable in the *after* picture is the greater connection Robin experienced with the new sink location, which is more oriented toward the table where her teenagers did homework after school.

"Before"

"After"

The photos below shows action designed to protect areas and surfaces of the home from the inevitable dust and construction traffic that will occur during construction .

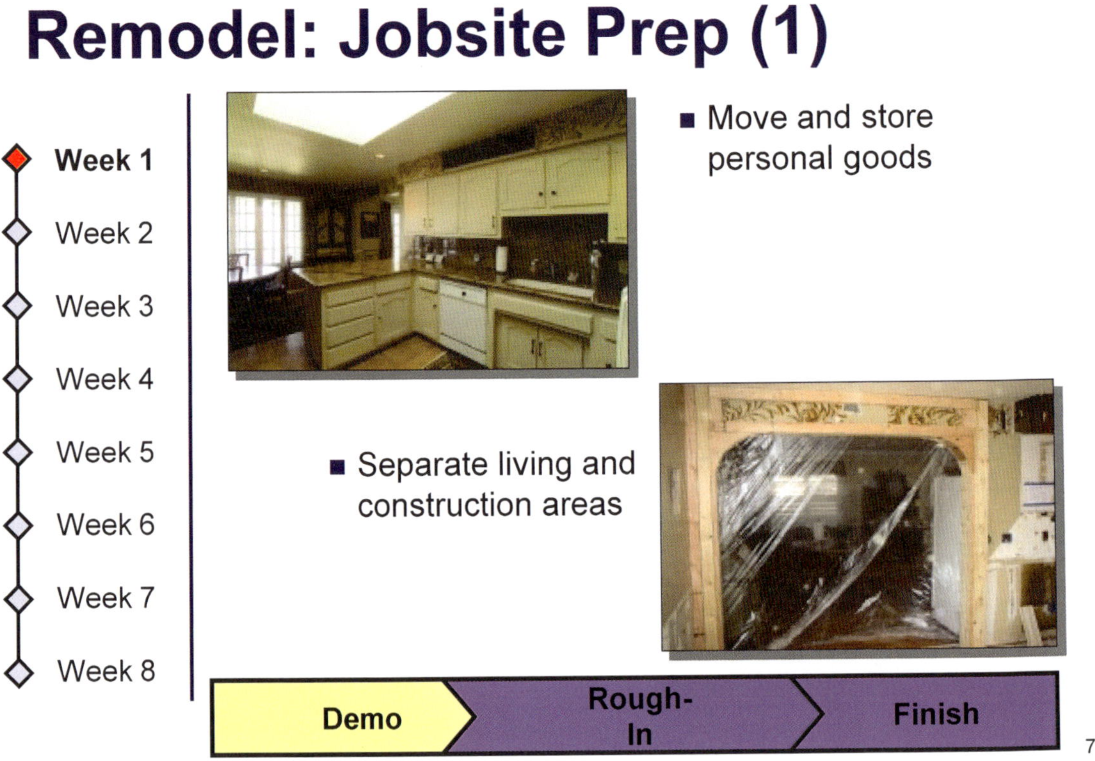

Between the garage entry and the kitchen was a hallway with wood parquet flooring. For protection, it was covered with 1/4" Masonite panels. As shown in the picture above, the joints were taped to prevent penetration of dust or foreign objects. Speaking of dust, we knew demolition work and construction would create a great deal, so we closed off the work area with barriers of plastic sheeting. Where access was required, we installed zippered access panels. (See Photo Below)

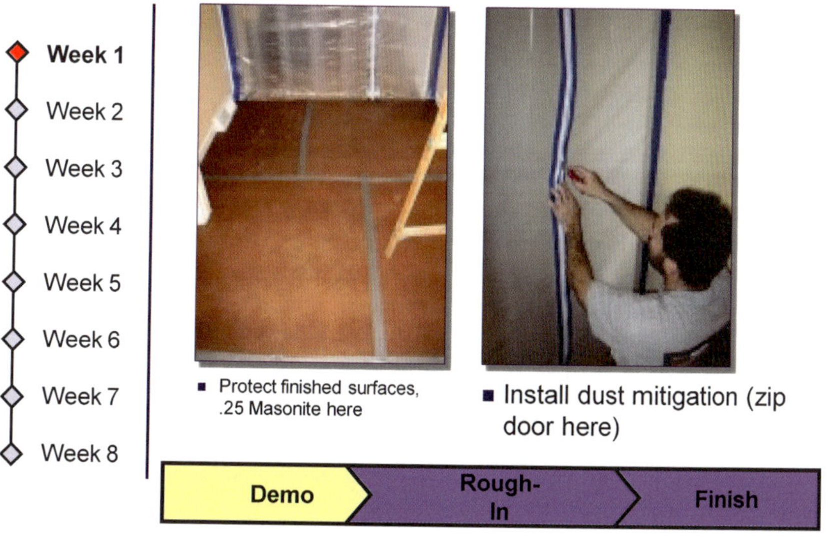

The photo below shows the posted building permit, the dumpster and the temporary lock sets we installed for the construction entrance.

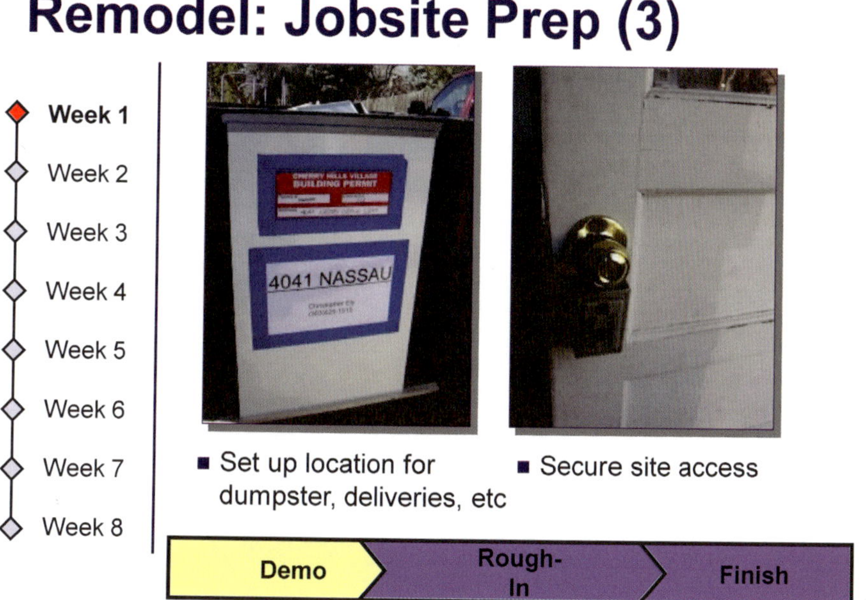

On Robin's job we arranged for storage space in her garage for special order items where we could physically verify the order and condition of the products. This included the tiles that would be on the custom mural above the range, the appliances, and the new light fixture we hung over the dinette table. Because of their longer lead times and their critical importance to the schedule, all of these items were ordered before construction commenced. That is also true of the cabinetry, which was delivered and held in a local warehouse where it could be inspected. The cabinets are so critical to ensuring on-time completion that I have always advised every client to **order the cabinetry and have it delivered to a local warehouse or to the job site before starting construction**.

The garage contents were rearranged so Robin could park in a space one bay removed from where we would be bringing in other materials. It is also where we installed a new outlet and put the old refrigerator so it could be used during the construction process. Just off the back hall where we would be entering, there was a powder room. Robin determined we could use that bathroom for the crews, so we removed all personal items and brought in soap, towels, toilet paper and cleaning supplies.

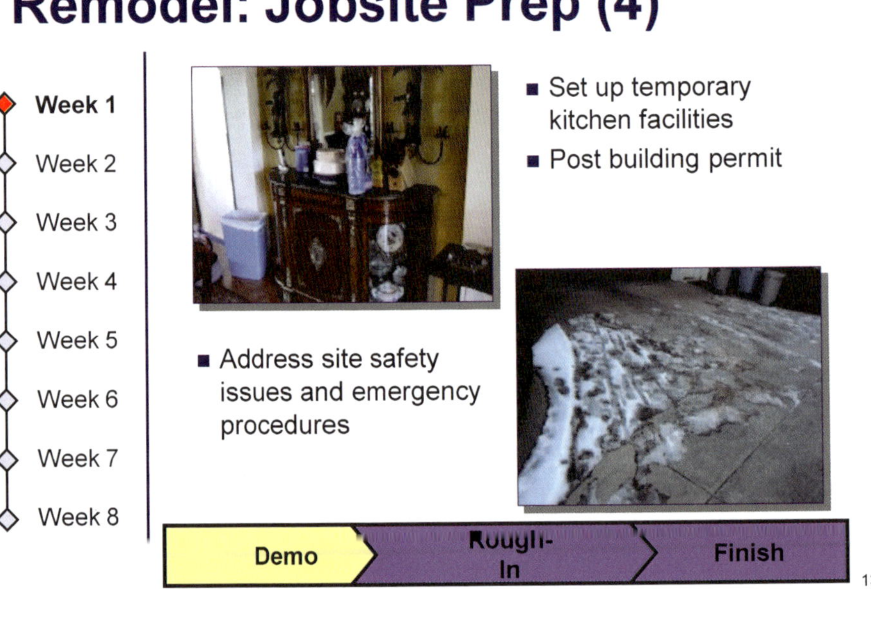

The photo (left) shows part of the temporary kitchen Robin set up. This was created in the dining area next to the kitchen. The old microwave was relocated to this area and with the old refrigerator plugged into our new outlet in the garage, Robin and

her kids had the means to fix simple meals without having to go out to a restaurant. Glasses and plates were washed by hand in the laundry room. **Setting up your own temporary kitchen is one of the most important things you can do to minimized disruption to your daily routine.**

Also shown is an icy walkway that was one of the safety concerns we needed to address. We were starting construction during winter; and snow, just outside the garage doors, had already been compacted into ice. This was a fall hazard for anyone, but especially for tradesmen carrying in tools and materials that could obscure their view of the ground below. We got rid of the ice and kept a shovel, scraper and Ice-Melt in the garage to help us keep this area ice and snow-free.

To be prepared for any accidents we also kept a fully-stocked first-aid kit in the garage along with a fire extinguisher. Next to the first-aid kit we posted a list of emergency numbers. All proper safety procedures were followed on the job (eye protection, no taped electrical cords, guards on all saws, etc.) and **at the end of every day the materials were organized neatly, the floors vacuumed and tools removed.**

We knew Robin, her kids, and friends and neighbors would be stopping by when we were not there so our work area had to be as safe as we could make it. In spite of the best efforts, accidents do occur on construction projects and it happened on Robin's. One of my cabinet installers was pulling a little too hard as he worked to take out the old oven cabinet and a board snapped and bloodied his forehead. I drove him to the nearest ER and by the next day he was back at work with only a bruise.

After preparation comes **demolition** (demo). In Robin's kitchen everything was being torn out, and by the end of the second day it was all gone. This stage is always one of the most dramatic and surprising. You walk in Monday and your kitchen of many years is there; by Wednesday, everything has been stripped down to the walls and any trace of finish materials is gone! **If you're keeping a photo journal of the progress, this may be your first photo op.**

Remodel: Demolition (1)

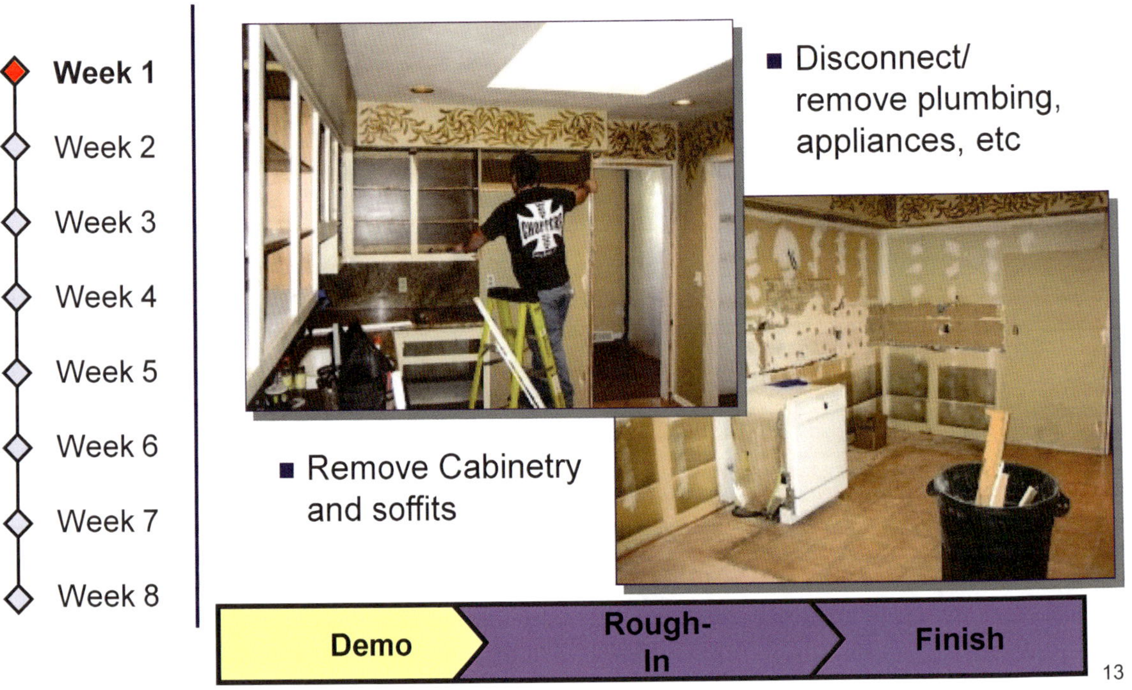

In the photo above we are removing the old cabinetry which did not consist of individual modular boxes as are virtually all cabinets are today. The cabinetry had been originally been built in place. Refuse was always put into the trash bin or carted off to the dumpster which we had located in the driveway.

The photo (above in the lower right) shows the cabinetry now gone, but the soffit (a dropped ceiling detail) hadn't yet been removed. This was a detail we were eliminating so we could install taller upper cabinets with more storage and also help the room feel more open and expansive.

We wanted someone to be able to reuse the granite tops so we had the granite fabricator send out his crews to remove them. Because they had the tools and experience for this work, we also had assurance that no one would get injured during the process. It also eliminate any chance that the tops or the house would be damaged during the process. (See Photo below).

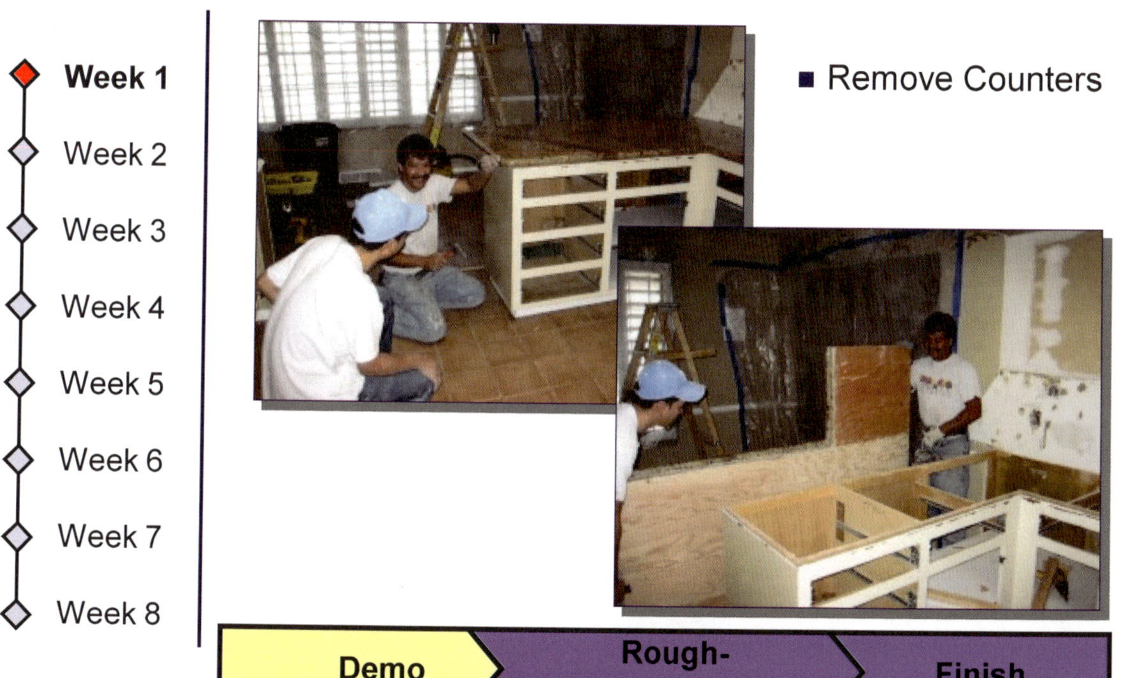

The old sheet vinyl flooring had been glued down. Scraping it loose from the sub-floor below required a lot of care, especially as we got close to the adjacent wood parquet flooring. We also found one of our first surprise discoveries. Just below the vinyl was a second, older floor that had to be removed. (See Photo below)

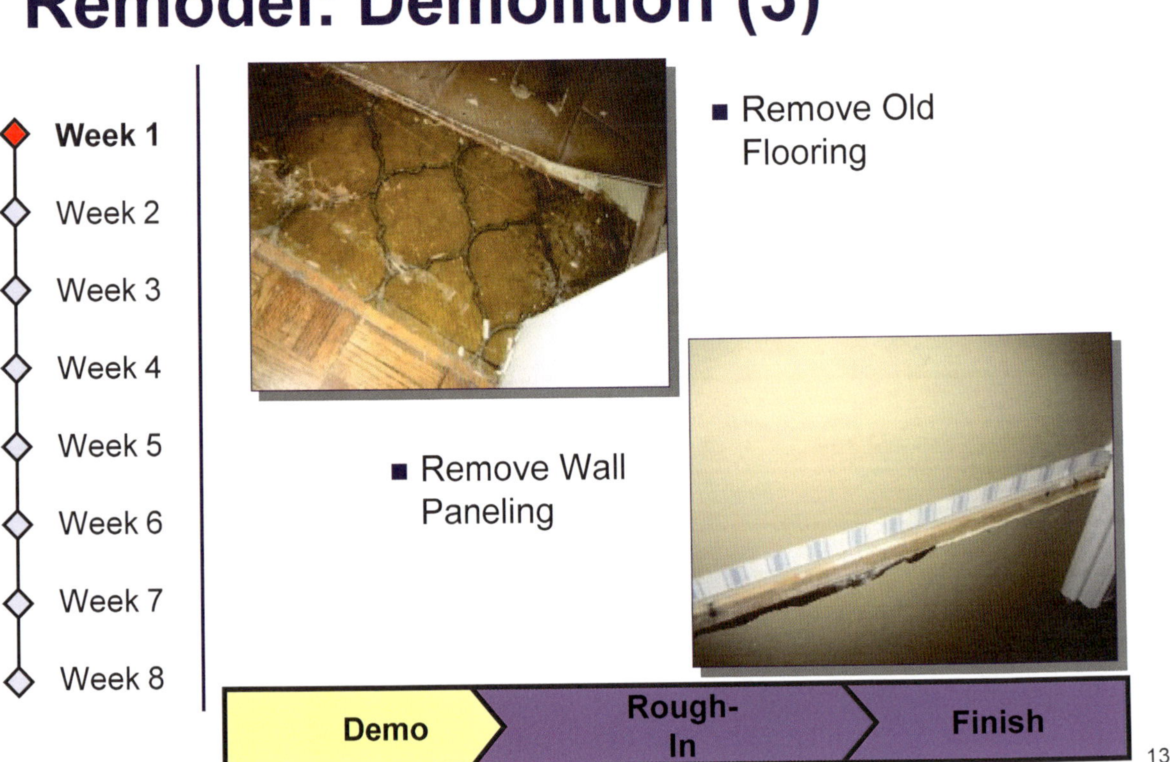

When you open up walls or delve into attics and crawl spaces it is common to find items that need correction or modification. Robin's project was no different. Frequently, wiring or plumbing may need to be brought up to code. At this point, you can see things previously hidden. This gives you a good idea what additional things you will need to do versus your original specifications. **This is a good time to reassess your budget and the changed requirements.**

In the photo below we are reframing the opening to the family room to give it a soft arch. By also increasing the wall depth from 4.5 inches to 10 inches we had an inviting entrance that created a new visual flow between the two rooms.

Remodel: Framing (2)

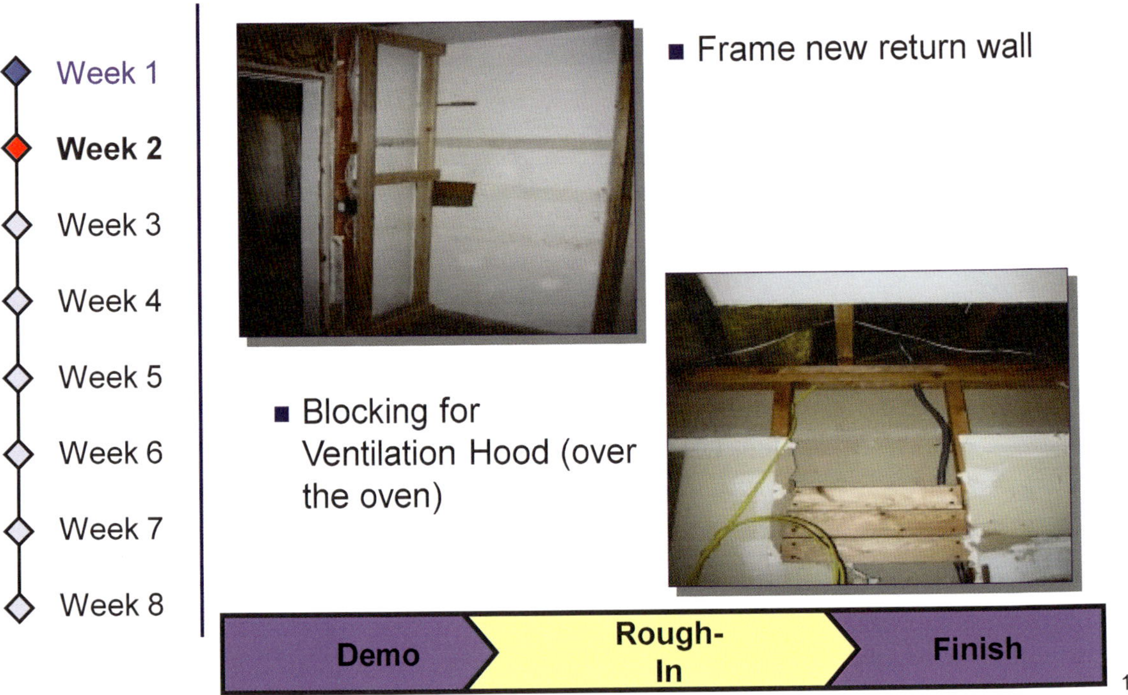

The first photo (above left) shows the framing that is going to define the left and right side of the new range area. The *return walls* are those that turn back 90 degrees from the face of the longer run of wall. Maybe they should be called turn walls, but they aren't. Typically they are much shorter in length, often extending out just past the depth of a standard countertop (25.5 inches) or a refrigerator (28.5-30 inches). The second photo shows the wood blocking we needed to support the new hood going in over the range.

'Mechanicals' is a termed used to refer to plumbing, electrical and heating and air-conditioning (HVAC). The term 'Rough-in' refers to the installation of fittings inside the walls. The photo below and left shows my electrician rewiring the electrical service panel for the new circuits required. On the right he is shown moving one of many electrical outlet locations.

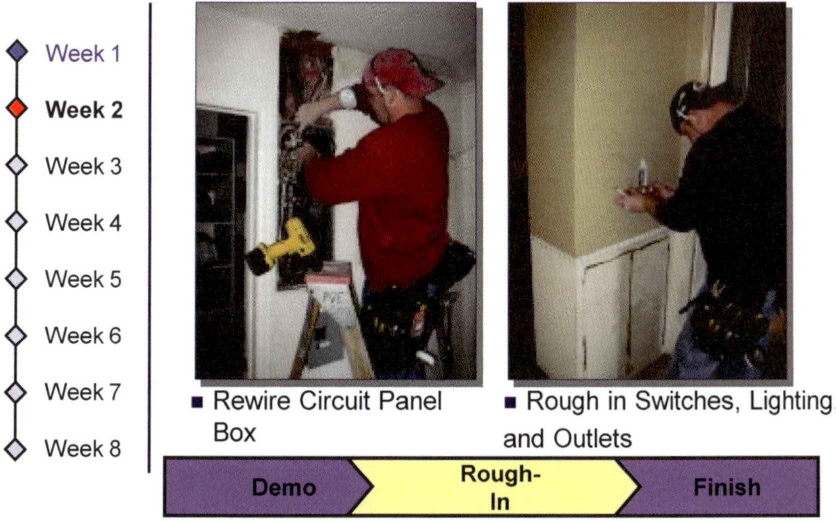

The photo below bringing drain and water pipe to the new sink location. We were able to access the piping from the crawl space below.

Remodel: Pre-wires

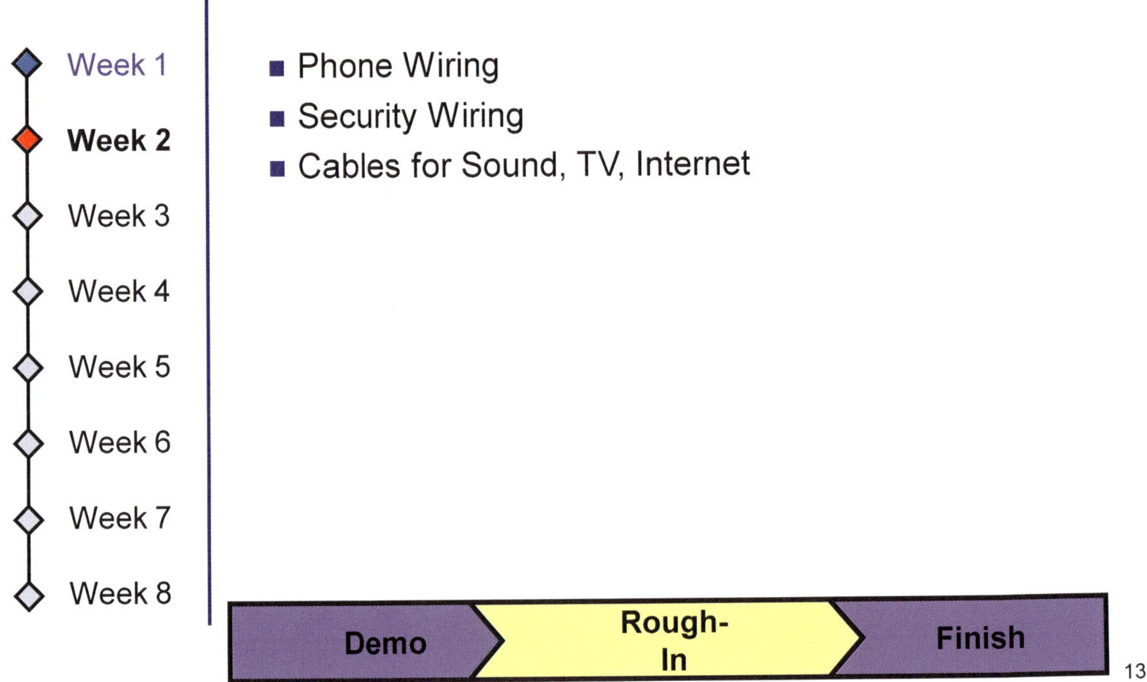

With wireless connections becoming the norm for phones, computers, and printers; this pre-wire category is somewhat diminished in importance. In this project it was necessary for us to move only two wall connections, one for TV and one for phone.

Getting the building permit at the beginning of the project is what necessitated inspection and approval by the city (see chart below).

Remodel: Inspections

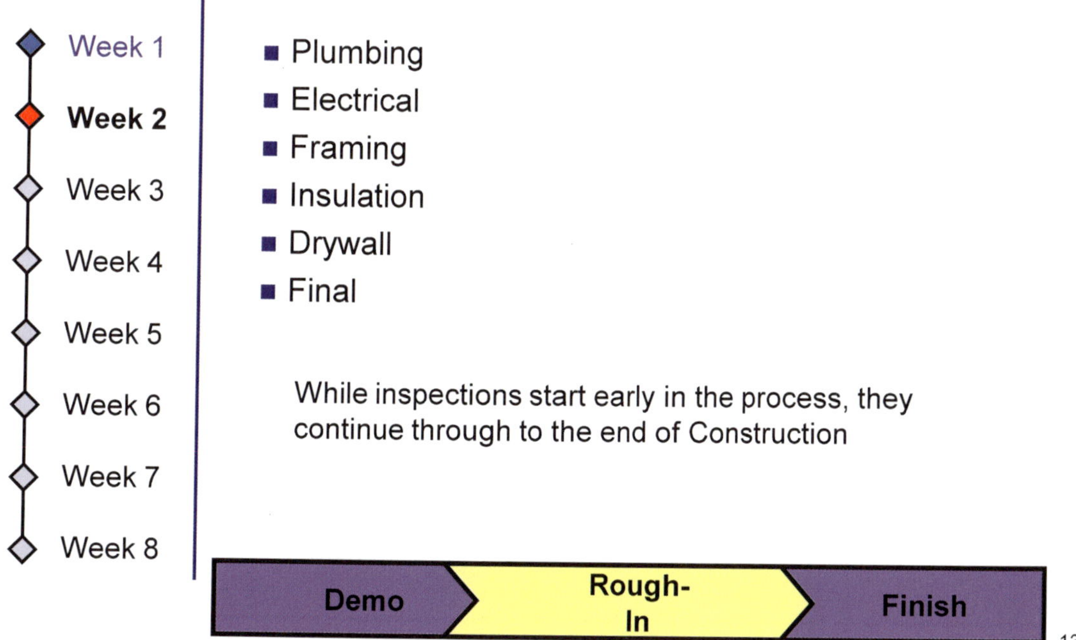

I have been asked so many times whether a building permit is needed, that I want to offer some guidelines.

- If your project will require structural or mechanical work your municipality will undoubtedly require you or your contractor to pull a permit. The permit will require the use of licensed tradespeople for all of the mechanical work.

- If your project involves replacement and/or refurbishment, with appliances, lighting, outlets, switches and fans remaining in their present locations, then a permit is probably not going to be required.

- **You are likely to be told by neighbors, friends, and even contractors you do not need a permit, when in fact, you do.**

- Starting work without a permit when one is required can cost you a lot in fines and lost time if you get caught and you are ***red-tagged*** with a stop-work order.

- Permit costs are a small part of the total budget (0.8% in Robin's case) and are an inexpensive way to have independent trained inspectors looking at the quality of the work performed.

- Having a permit for your work can be an asset upon future resale because prospective owners will have greater assurance about what they are buying.

- Inspections should add only a modest amount to your schedule (3 days in Robin's case)

- Insisting on a permit for the work may help weed out less qualified contractors when you are doing your builder selection.

The fastest and surest way to educate yourself is to place a call to your local building inspection official. In all of my experience, these officials have always bent over backwards to be helpful when speaking with the homeowner. It is also a quick way to assure yourself that your contractor or prospective contractor is licensed in your municipality as well as determine their job history in your municipality.

Remodel: Wallboard/Texture

This work done in the photo above is shown as occurring in week two, but that is because we were running a few days ahead of schedule. In the top photo the workman is taping a drywall joint where the ceiling and wall were patched after the old soffits were removed. To the right, you can see we had to pull our plastic dust barrier further into the family room so we would have room to do the drywall and finish work on the back side of the arch. You can also see the difference in room colors that Robin later decided to eliminate. The edges of the arched opening are radiused (rounded). This was done throughout the room to soften the look of the room and to make it look larger than it would have if we had kept the original hard edges.

When we pulled and scraped off the old vinyl flooring we were left with the original ½” plywood sub-flooring. We needed another layer (underlayment) that would give us added rigidity as well as the proper surface on which to apply the mortar that would hold the tile. In this case we used the ½” backer board which you see in the photo below.

Remodel: Flooring (1)

- Week 1
- Week 2
- **Week 3**
- Week 4
- Week 5
- Week 6
- Week 7
- Week 8

- Remove Floor Squeaks
- Install Underlayment

Demo → Rough-In → **Finish**

13

Remodel: Flooring (2)

The photo above shows the chalk lines we snapped out on the underlayment to act as guides. Our tile pattern involved the repetition of six different tile shapes to achieve a random pattern. The visual flow of the pattern allowed the room to look larger and gave us a great deal of color depth and texture with which to work. After the mortar had set up, the tile joints were grouted and then sealed the next day. The floor work took a total of 4 days.

Remodel: Cabinetry / Millwork (1)

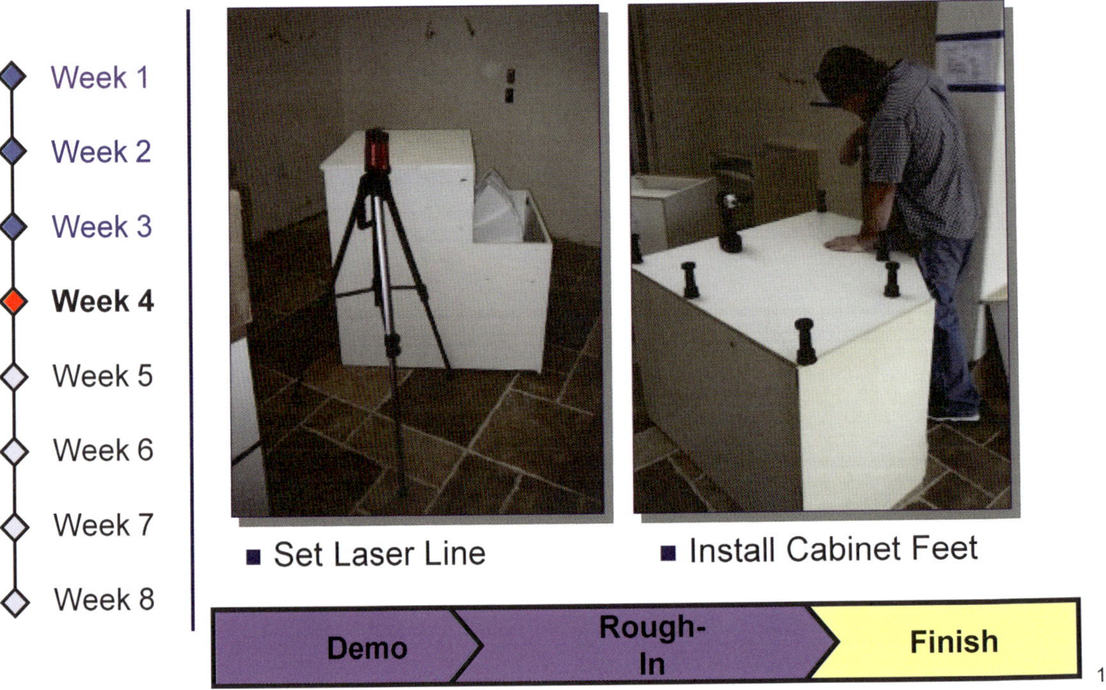

The cabinets used were frameless (meaning the cases were held together without using a wooden face frame that circumscribed the cabinet openings). The photos above illustrate how we used a combination of laser (to set our level lines) and adjustable cabinet legs to make our cabinets perfectly level from left to right and front to back.

As you will see in the pictures to follow, the frameless cabinetry allowed us to create a smooth transition between the cabinet doors and drawers because the gap was only 1/8". This was another area where we were augmenting visual flow to make the room seem more spacious. ('Millwork' is the term used to describe doors and trim moldings such as base, casing, crown moulding, etc.)

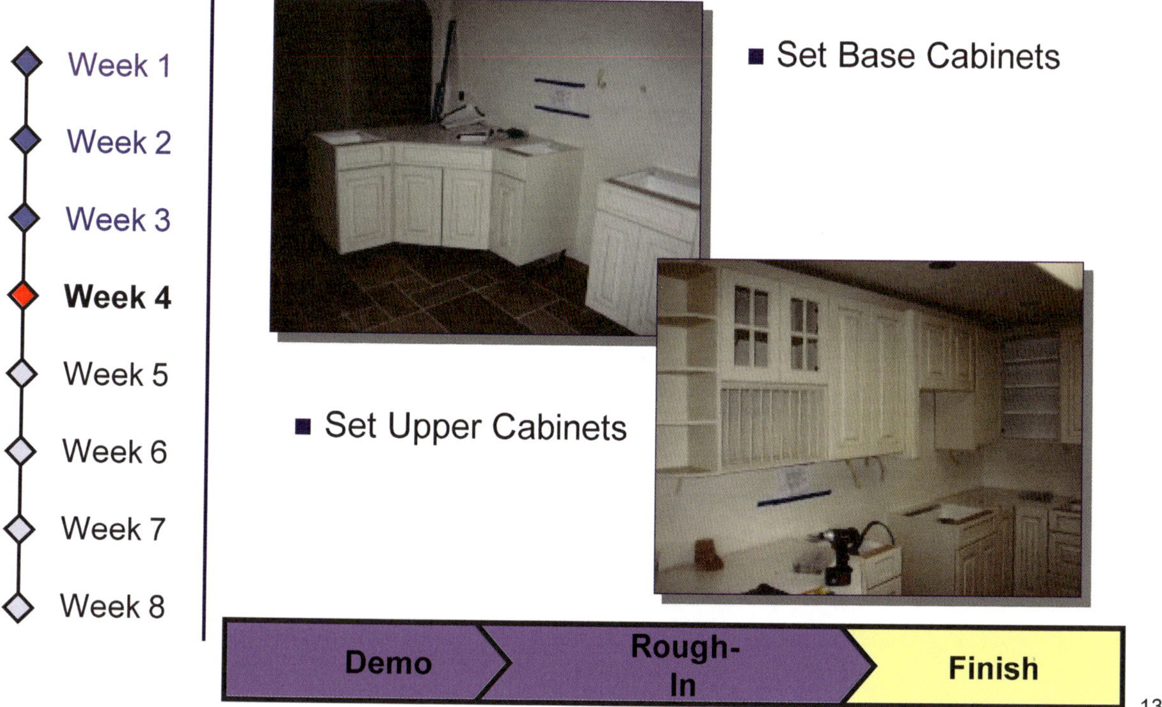

Remodel: Cabinetry / Millwork (3)

- Week 1
- Week 2
- Week 3
- **Week 4**
- Week 5
- Week 6
- Week 7
- Week 8

- Install Crown Moulding

Demo | **Rough-In** | **Finish**

13

Crown moulding ran along the top of the cabinetry and throughout the room. The old space had been visually divided into cooking and eating area, but the new space would deliver the sense of one large gathering area. The close-up of the crown moulding shows how we wrapped it around the radiused edge of the drywall.

Remodel: Cabinetry / Millwork (4)

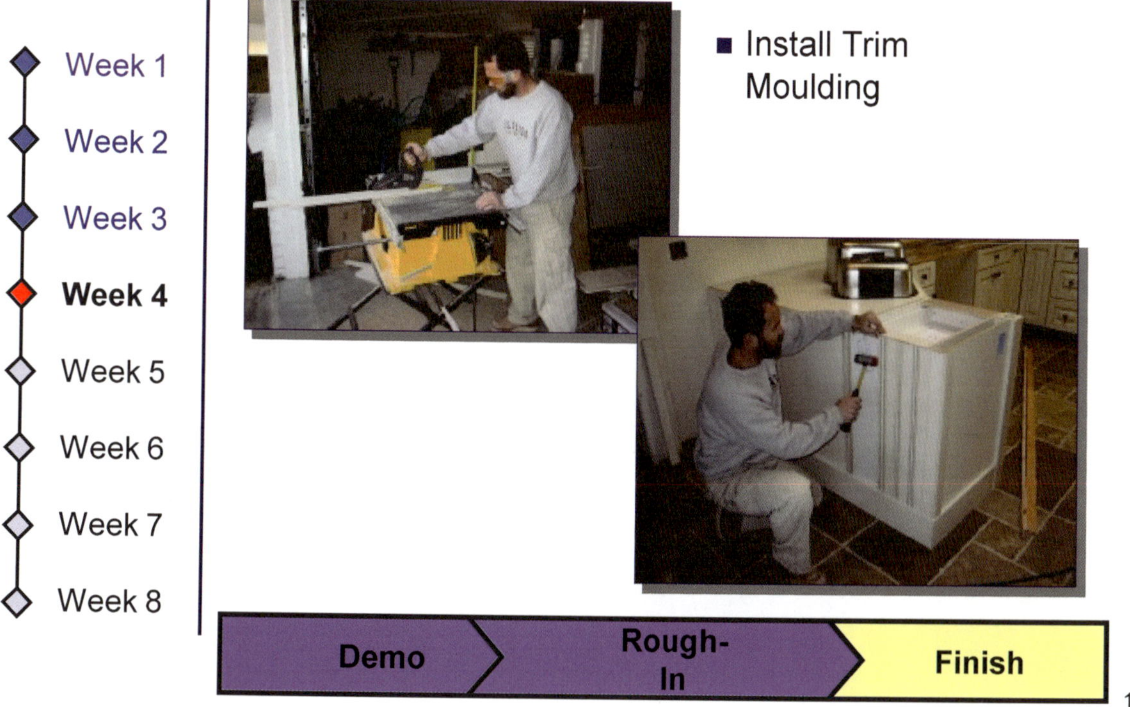

The photo (upper left) shows one of my installers cutting and installing beaded, vertical battens along the back side and edge of the new peninsula. The new design pulled this cabinetry further back and shortened its length six inches to eliminate the cramped condition with the dinette table. The beading as well as the more defined counter and edge design we used at this location were an attempt to open up the space and to better reach out to the finely detailed artistry of the table. With comparable levels of ornamentation, we were better able to make the transition between the cooking area and the eating area seamless and invisible to the eye.

The photo (right) shows the pattern provided to my granite fabricator so they could produce the exact shape we wanted to see at the end of the peninsula.

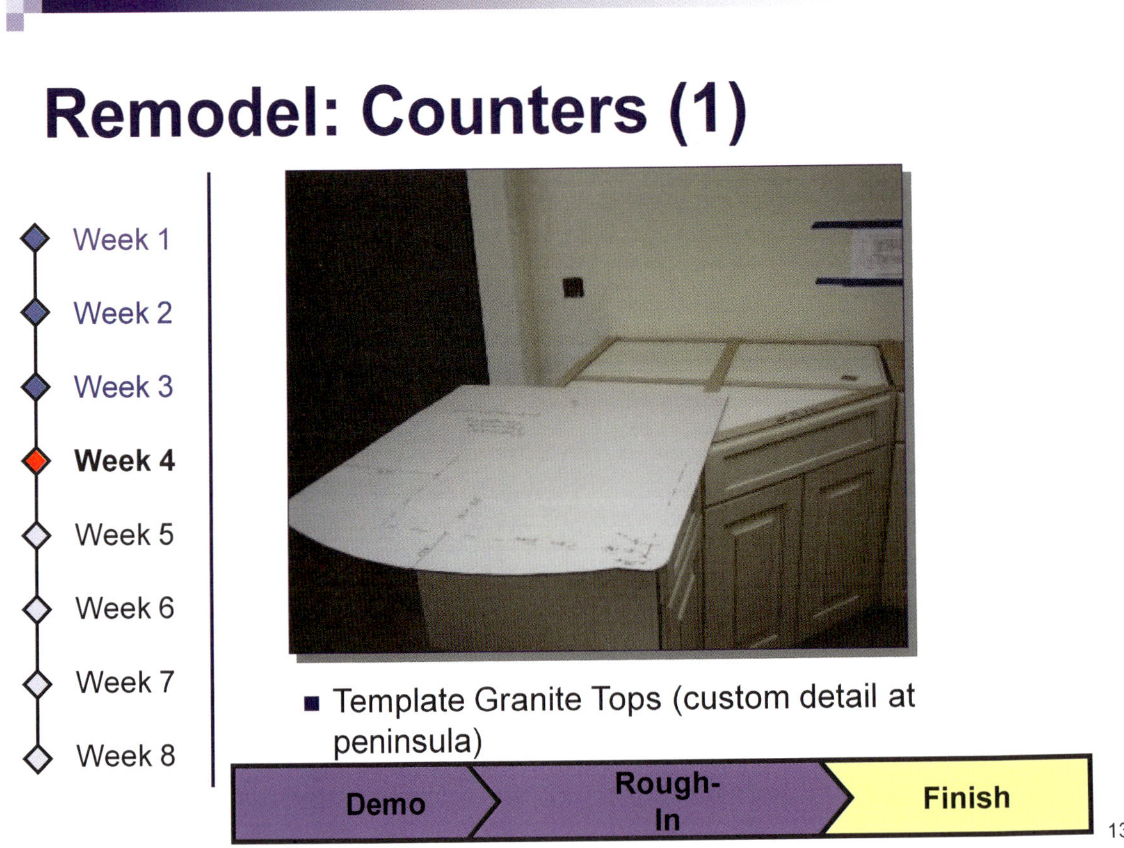

With a solid-surface top like granite, clients usually opt for the more streamlined look of an under-mount sink. With the sink mounted to the underside of the top, it offers a cleaner look as well as easier clean-up. Typically, it is the countertop fabricator who attaches the sink to the top. The plumber then just hooks up the piping. This also means that the new sink needs to be provided to or by your fabricator because it is mounted before the finished tops are installed. (See Photo below)

Remodel: Counters (2)

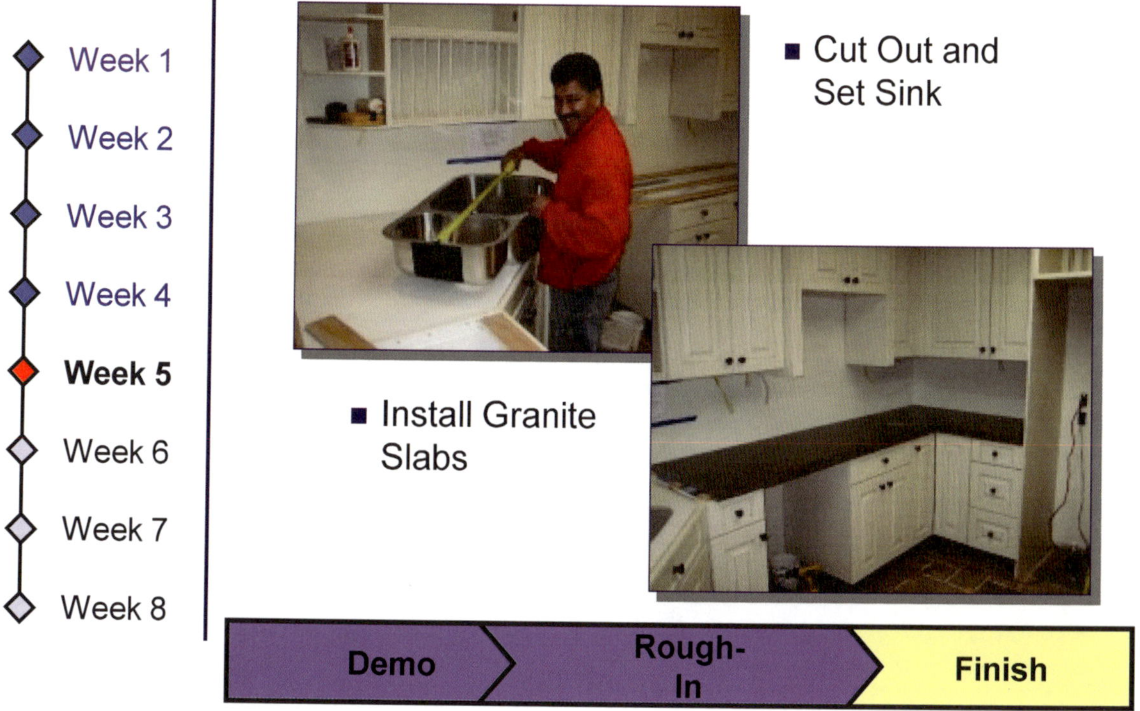

What is unusual about the photo (above right) is that cabinet hardware (knobs and/or pulls) wouldn't normally be installed at this stage of construction. It is usually one of the last items installed. As I mentioned in "The Birthday Gift", we were always on the lookout for opportunities to provide Robin with things that would delight her. We knew as soon as the cabinets were set, she would want to open and close the doors and drawers and look inside the cabinets. With that in mind, we put on all of the hardware, adjusted all the doors and drawer fronts, and cleaned the dust out of all the interiors. When she was opening her cabinetry for the first time or showing it off to a friend (or Paul), we wanted everything to look its best. **First impressions still count.**

The backsplash area lies between the top of counter and underside of upper cabinetry. The tiles selected as well as the layout design played an important role. In the photo below you can see that our field tiles were placed diagonally to create more visual flow. With the tile playing such important roles, we didn't want to have the normal placement of outlets and switches compromise our effort. Where there would normally have been wall outlets, we installed continuous strips of plug-moulding at the back underside of the cabinetry where it would be hidden from site. The strips were mounted at a 60 degree angle to make it easier to access. The yellow wires dangling from the underside of the upper cabinetry were connected to the under-cabinet lighting.

The strips of plug moulding as well as the under-counter halogen lighting would both be concealed with the help of a moulding detail at the bottom of the upper cabinets (referred to as *light rail* and shown in the photo below). The switch for the garbage disposal was a round push-button mechanism that was mounted in the granite counter. Other switches for ceiling lighting and for the under-counter lighting were relocated to areas away from the tiled area.

Remodel: Lighting/Hood/Appl's

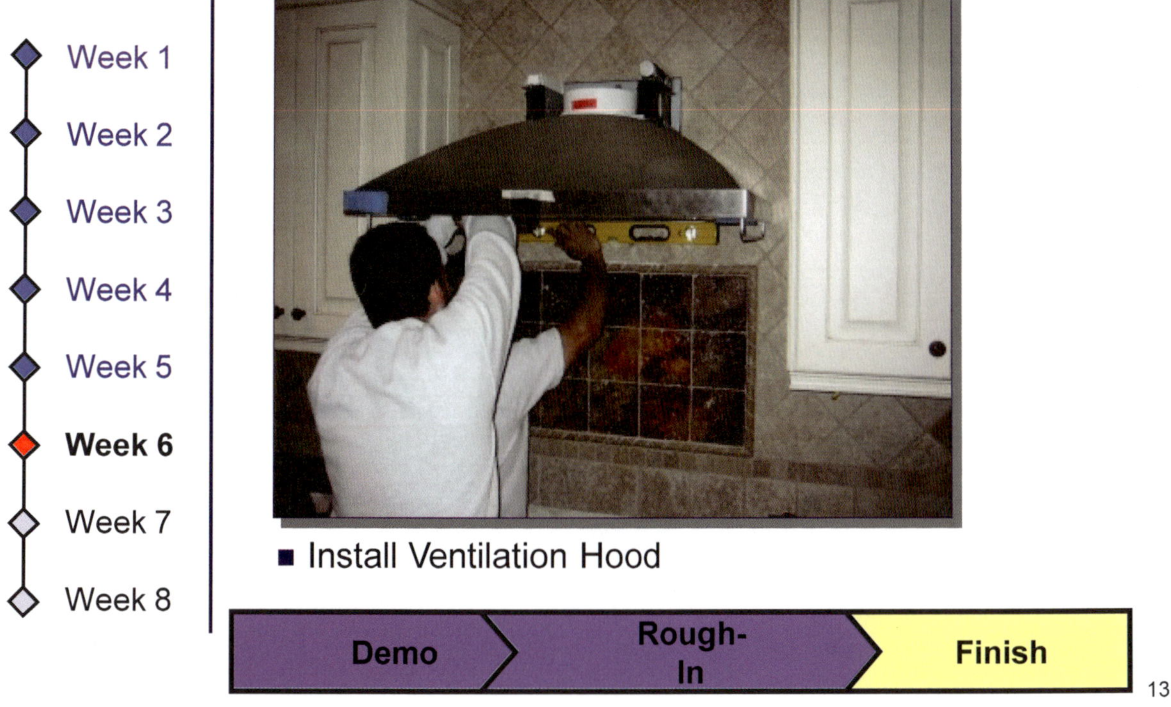

In the photo above you can see that the narrow profile of the hood allowed the tile to maintain its visual dominance. The hood was there to strengthen the mural design and not to compete. That is also the reason we took the tile all the way to the ceiling.

Remodel: Lighting/Hood/Appl's

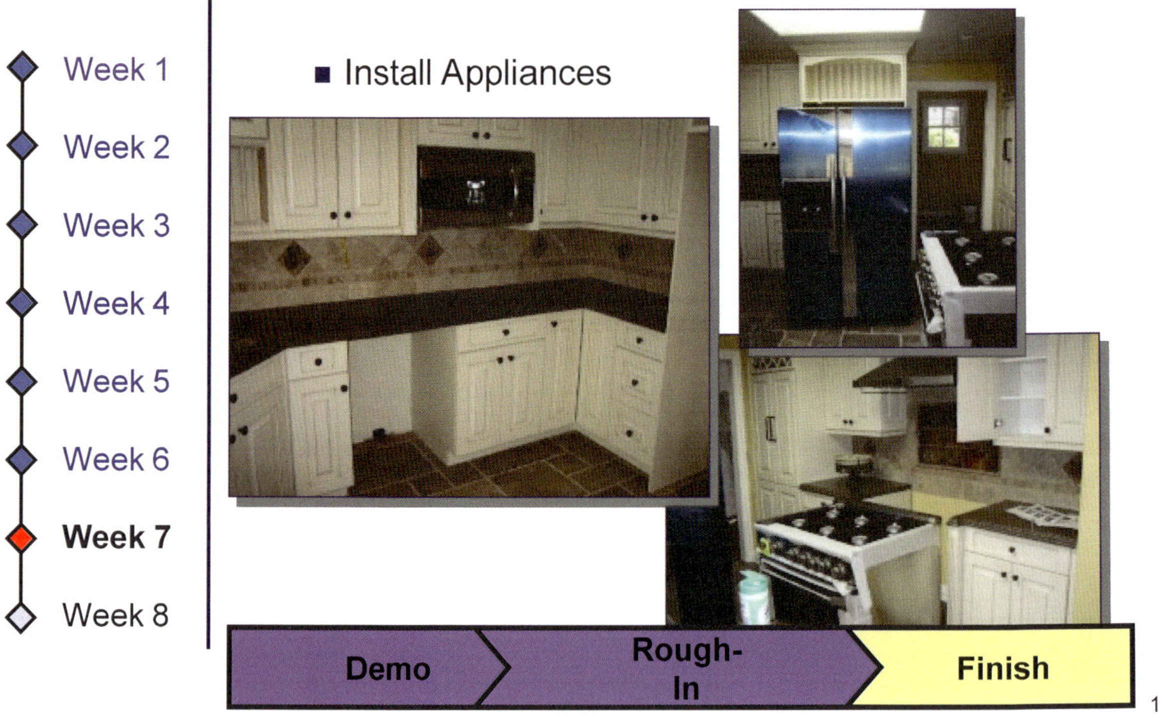

In the photo above you can see we used an open cabinet with a beaded back to pull the eye past the face of the refrigerator, thus minimizing the mass of this appliance as well as making the room seem larger. When it came to the microwave we gave it a more ornate and customized look by pulling it forward 2.5 inches from the face of the upper cabinetry and by flanking it with 3 inches wide, fluted pilasters (vertical pillars).

Most paint contractors prefer to complete their work after the cabinetry and other finish items are in place. It requires a great deal of masking, but minimizes repair and touch-up that might otherwise be required. (See photo below)

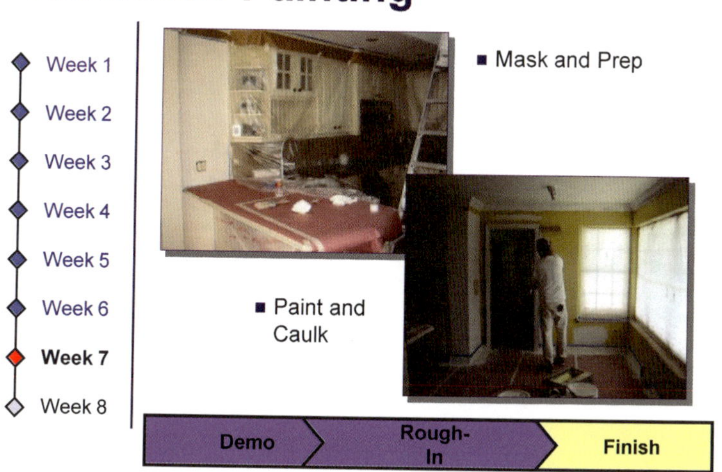

The last item of construction is referred to as *Punch Work*. It involves final touch ups and adjustments . (See Photo below).

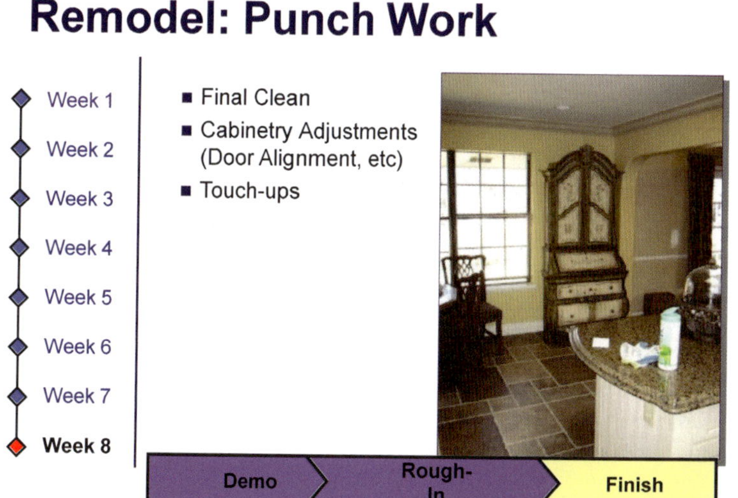

Before and After Photos (1)

13

Before and After Photos (2)

13

After Photos (1)

After Photos (2)

7

There is probably no typical remodel but this project was large enough in scope to present a wide perspective. With work occurring every day (except weekends), we went from start to finish in just over seven weeks. Materials were always kept in an organized fashion and the job was swept and vacuumed at the end of each work day. At the end of each week we made sure the owner would be able to see significant visual change. As often as not, this allowed the owner to show off the progress to friends and neighbors. It also left the positive impression that the job was always progressing ahead of schedule.

If you have read this far you may be thinking that tackling your remodel is going to take more effort than you thought. It will. The good news is you're now equipped to enjoy the process just as much as my clients have in the past. My fervent hope is that when your project is complete, you can say,

"It came out just the way I hoped!"

45

Post-Construction

This is the stage where everything looks fresh, new and ready for use – except it's not. You can't wait to have your contractor gone, your home and privacy back, as well as the use of your new kitchen. This is where **your patience at the end will pay big dividends.** Your contractor needs time at the end to double check every detail and make any final adjustments. This effort involves many trades returning and can easily take a week to complete. Rushing this stage will usually be self-defeating because you are likely to endure months where you have to call about small things you keep discovering and where the contractor has a much harder time getting his crews back (they are paid in full by this time and busy on other jobs with their own schedule requirements).

One of the most effective ways to catch the majority of items for your list is to clean everything by hand and test all the appliances. This may seem like unnecessary additional work on your part, but it works.

After you have done a thorough walk-through with your builder and he has finished any final items, it is time to pack up your temporary kitchen, put your stored items away and beginning enjoying the fruits of your efforts!

46

Takeaways

As an author I have tried to entertain and inform you at the same time. In the end, however, if you are asking yourself, *"What did I get out of the book?"*, I hope your answer may include many of the following:

- A *Completely Personal Kitchen* is a living space tailored to your personality to feel so comfortable and inviting it brings forth an experience of joy and delight. Please don't settle for less.

- Knowing what you like is important, but not understanding *why* can lead you into a world of frustration and disappointment. Make your decisions on function, look and feel.

- Kitchen and family rooms merged decades ago; design your larger social gathering area and not just your kitchen. Keep your transitions seamless and never let food preparation preclude social connection.

- Your most important design tool is light because it plays such a critical role in how your new space will look and feel. Keep it in the forefront.

- You can pick '10's on all of your individual selections, but if you aren't looking at the whole, they may average only a '6' or '7'. Keep your samples together as you move through the selection process.

- Even when you cannot change your physical space, you can *always* change the way it is perceived as well as its efficiency and capacity.

47

Essential Ideas

"There are so many key ideas I want to revisit, but I don't remember where they were addressed". This early response from two of my clients who read the manuscript has encouraged me to offer and index of ideas instead of terms.

Transformation rather than Renovation

About the Author

The author's 35 years of experience has been enriched by working across the disciplines of interior, architectural and kitchen design. His kitchens and custom homes have been featured in national magazines.

He currently lives in South Carolina where he is providing design consulting to remodel and new home clients, as well as architects and designers.

Case studies, additional resource material and comments on current design topics can be found on his web site. For more information or to contact Chris, go to www.completelypersonalkitchens.com.

Made in the USA
Columbia, SC
15 November 2017

Made in the USA
Las Vegas, NV
25 April 2022

THANK YOU FOR READING MY BOOK! I HOPE YOU ENJOYED IT! DON'T FORGET TO CHECK OUT MY TIKTOK @CUPCAYLA FOR A BEHIND THE SCENES LOOK AT HOW THE PAGES CAME TO LIFE AND HOW TO DRAW ME!!!

“RRRREEEEEEEEEEEEE!!!!!!!!”

THERE'S FROSTING LEFT OVER AND IT'S FORMING A MONSTER!!!!!!

IT APPEARS THAT THE STUDENTS DIDN'T CLEAN UP ALL OF THE MESS!!!!

WAIT!!! WAIT!!!!

CUPCAYLA TOLD HER CLASS ABOUT EVERYTHING!!! BUT THAT IS A STORY FOR ANOTHER TIME.... THE END!

CUPCAYLA TOOK A SEAT AT HER DESK. "OH THERE'S SO MUCH TO TELL!" SHE EXCLAIMED. "MY CAT SCUDDY! AND PETUNIA THE PUP CAKE! THE STRAWBERRY LEMONADE MERMAIDS! AND THE DRAGOCORN!!! AND.. AND..."

"WELL THAT WAS SOMETHING!" SAID MS. LAURIE SMILING. "GREAT JOB WORKING TOGETHER! MAYBE NOW YOU CAN TELL US A LITTLE MORE ABOUT YOURSELF, CUPCAYLA!"

BY THE TIME THAT RECESS WAS OVER, SCOTT ELEMENTARY WAS GOOD AS NEW AND SPARKLY CLEAN!

THEY SCRUBBED AND BRUSHED AND MOPPED!

NOW EVERYONE WAS DOING THEIR PART IN CLEANING UP THE BIG FROSTING MESS.

DAVID, SEAN AND CUPCAYLA HELPED LOGAN TAME THE WILD HOSE!!!!!

"WOOAHHHH!' YELLED LOGAN. HE LAUNCHED INTO THE AIR MAKING CUPCAYLA LAUGH! "HEHEHEH!" SHE GIGGLED.

THE WATER CAME RUSHING THROUGH THE HOSE!!! BLURB BLURB BLURB!!!!!

"WE'LL TURN ON THE WATER!!!!" YELLED DAVID AND SEAN.

"I'VE GOT THE HOSE!!!!!" SAID LOGAN

THE CHILDREN GRABBED MOPS, BRUSHES AND RAGS. "IT'S OKAY CUPCAYLA!" SAID TEMPY. "YOU ARE ONE OF US! AND WE ALWAYS HELP EACH OTHER!!"

"LOOK WHAT I FOUND!" YELLED ZAY. ZAY HAD GATHERED SOME CLEANING SUPPLIES! "IF WE ALL WORK TOGETHER, WE CAN HAVE THIS CLEANED UP IN NO TIME!"

UH OH! MS. LAURIE WAS DRENCHED IN FROSTING TOO! BUT SHE DIDN'T SEEM TO MIND. SHE WAS STILL SMILING LIKE SHE ALWAYS DID. "I LOOK LIKE A LAVA LAMP!" SAID MS. LAURIE.

CUPCAYLA SAT UP AGAINST THE WALL AND BEGAN TO CRY. "SURELY I'LL BE IN TROUBLE FOR THIS."SHE SOBBED. CUPCAYLA WISHED THAT HER CAT, SCUDDY WERE HERE. SCUDDY ALWAYS CLEANED UP HER FROSTING DRIPS.

...THE ENTIRE PLAYGROUND AND SCHOOL WERE COVERED IN FROSTING.

IT WAS THE BIGGEST MESS SHE HAD EVER SEEN! CHILDREN COVERED FROM HEAD TO TOE! FLINGING AND SPLATTING FROSTING EVERYWHERE! ON EVERYTHING!!!!

AND BEFORE SHE KNEW IT....

"OH NO!!!!" SHE THOUGHT. THERE WAS NOTHING SHE COULD DO.

BUT IT WAS TOO LATE. OTHER STUDENTS HAD ALREADY BEEN DOWN THE SLIDE AFTER HER AND THEY KEPT COMING. CHILDREN WERE COVERED IN TEAL, PINK AND YELLOW FROSTING! TRACKING IT ALL OVER THE PLAYGROUND!!!

BY THE TIME CUPCAYLA GOT TO HER FEET AND TURNED AROUND TO LOOK AT THE SLIDE SHE HAD JUST HAD SO MUCH FUN GOING DOWN SHE REALIZED WHAT HAPPENED. SHE LEFT FROSTING ALL DOWN THE SLIDE!!

CUPCAYLA ZIPPED DOWN THE SLIDE LEAVING BEHIND HER, A STREAK OF TEAL, PINK AND YELLOW FROSTING.

SPLAT!!! SPLAT!!! LANDING ON THE OTHER STUDENT'S HEADS!!!! CUPCAYLA HAD NO IDEA!!!!

BITS OF FROSTING WERE FALLING DOWN SPLATTERING BENEATH HER!! PLOP!!! **PLAP!!! ALL** OVER THE LADDER!!!!

CUPCAYLA DIDN'T REALIZE BUT HER FROSTING STARTED TO DRIP!!! OH NO!!!!!

CUPCAYLA DECIDED TO FACE HER FEAR. SHE WAITED HER TURN AND STARTED UP THE LADDER. "THIS WILL BE SO MUCH FUN!" SHE THOUGHT. CUPCAYLA WAS VERY PROUD OF HERSELF!

CUPCAYLA LOOKED UP AND SAW BRAY CHASING DANIEL. CASH, JOHN AND SEAN WERE PLAYING ON THE SLIDE. CUPCAYLA REALLY WANTED TO GO DOWN THE SLIDE TOO EVEN THOUGH SHE WAS JUST A LITTLE SCARED OF HEIGHTS!

MS. LAURIE NOTICED WHAT WAS GOING ON. "NOW THAT'S NOT RESPECTING OTHER'S PERSONAL SPACE. AND WE DON'T EAT OUR FRIEND'S HAIR!" SHE SAID.

CUPCAYLA WAS TOO BUSY TALKING TO ZAY TO NOTICE! "ARE YOU A CUPCAKE?" ASKED ZAY. "NO" REPLIED CUPCAYLA "I'M A GIRL! I JUST HAVE FROSTING FOR HAIR! IT'S COMPLETELY NORMAL WHERE I'M FROM!"

THEY EACH TOOK A FINGER AND SWIPED RIGHT THROUGH CUPCAYLA'S FROSTING JUST LIKE YOU WOULD A CUPCAKE!

WHILE ON RECESS, DAVID AND TEMPY SAW THEIR CHANCE TO TRY SOME FROSTING!

RING RING RING!!!!! THE RECESS BELL WENT OFF VERY LOUDLY! "TIME FOR RECESS CLASS!" EXCLAIMED MS. LAURIE.

THERE WERE NINE OTHER CHILDREN IN HER CLASS! TEMPY, JOHN, BRAY, DAVID, SEAN, ZAY, CASH, LOGAN AND DANIEL! "SHE HAS ICING FOR HAIR!" SAID BRAY. "I WONDER WHAT KIND OF CONDITIONER SHE USES!" SAID TEMPY. "HER CHEEKS HAVE SPRINKLES ON THEM!" WHISPERED SEAN

CUPCAYLA WAS VERY NERVOUS. SHE WAS WORRIED THAT SHE WOULDN'T MAKE FRIENDS. WHAT IF NOBODY LIKED HER? WOULD SHE FIND A BEST FRIEND?

MS. LAURIE WAS GOING TO BE CUPCAYLA'S TEACHER. SHE WAS THE NICEST TEACHER AND WAS ALWAYS SMILING! "CLASS! CLASS LISTEN UP! WE HAVE A NEW STUDENT JOINING US TODAY. HER NAME IS CUPCAYLA! LET'S GIVE HER A NICE WARM WELCOME!" SAID MS. LAURIE GENTLY

"WHAT A BEAUTIFUL SCHOOL!" SHE THOUGHT TO HERSELF. CUPCAYLA COULDN'T WAIT TO MEET HER TEACHER AND MAKE FRIENDS!

CUPCAYLA WAS A VERY SPECIAL GIRL! SHE HAD FROSTING FOR HAIR, SPRINKLE CHEEKS AND A CHERRY ON TOP! SHE CAME FROM A LAND FAR AWAY BUT THAT'S A STORY FOR ANOTHER TIME! TODAY WAS HER FIRST DAY AT A NEW SCHOOL! SCOTT ELEMENTARY. SHE WAS VERY EXCITED!!